VMware vSphere Design

VMware vSphere Design

Forbes Guthrie

Scott Lowe

Maish Saidel-Keesing

WILEY

Wiley Publishing, Inc.

Acquisitions Editor: Agatha Kim
Development Editor: Alexa Murphy
Technical Editor: Jason Boche
Editorial Consultant: Scott Lowe
Production Editor: Liz Britten
Copy Editor: Tiffany Taylor
Editorial Manager: Pete Gaughan
Production Manager: Tim Tate
Vice President and Executive Group Publisher: Richard Swadley
Vice President and Publisher: Neil Edde
Book Designer: Maureen Forys, Happenstance Type-O-Rama; Judy Fung
Proofreader: WordOne, New York
Indexer: Ted Laux
Project Coordinator, Cover: Katie Crocker
Cover Designer: Ryan Sneed

Dear Reader,

Thank you for choosing *VMware vSphere Design*. This book is part of a family of premium-quality Sybex books, all of which are written by outstanding authors who combine practical experience with a gift for teaching.

Sybex was founded in 1976. More than 30 years later, we're still committed to producing consistently exceptional books. With each of our titles, we're working hard to set a new standard for the industry. From the paper we print on, to the authors we work with, our goal is to bring you the best books available.

I hope you see all that reflected in these pages. I'd be very interested to hear your comments and get your feedback on how we're doing. Feel free to let me know what you think about this or any other Sybex book by sending me an email at nedde@wiley.com. If you think you've found a technical error in this book, please visit http://sybex.custhelp.com. Customer feedback is critical to our efforts at Sybex.

Best regards,

Neil Edde
Vice President and Publisher
Sybex, an Imprint of Wiley

This book is dedicated to my beautiful wife Tarn. I grow and find inspiration from those around me; no one is closer. Ever yours.

— Forbes Guthrie

I'd like to dedicate this book to my Lord, who is the source of all knowledge (Proverbs 2:6). Thank you, Lord, for always giving me the knowledge I need, and help me give this knowledge to others. This book is also dedicated to my wife Crystal and our kids, especially Sean and Cameron. Guys, thanks for hanging in there!

— Scott Lowe

For my Njoesh: you are and will always be my biggest fan. Thank you.

— Maish Saidel-Keesing

Acknowledgments

This book has been a considerable part of my life for the last six months. It was only possible to devote so much time to it with the help and support of my wife, Tarn. Without her encouragement, this book would never have had my contribution. I can't overstate the part she played; without her considerable *mateship*, I would never have gotten through it. Thank you.

I would like to acknowledge the book's coauthors, Scott and Maish. Their expertise and knowledge shine through in their chapters and enhance the depth of entire book. Scott created the outline for the book back at the beginning of 2010, with input from Duncan Epping of Yellow-Bricks' fame. Maish jumped on board, and finally myself. For a while, Maish and I forged ahead with the writing, until Scott agreed to join as an author.

This being my first published book, I was amazed at the number of publishing house staff involved in a single project. First and foremost I would like to thank Agatha Kim, the acquisitions editor, for her project steerage and the encouragement she gave to all the authors. We were all incredibly blessed to have Jason Boche (the Virtualization Evangelist) as our technical editor to check the subject matter and make suggestions so that every area was covered appropriately and was technically correct.

I grew up and was educated in Scotland, and I've lived and worked across the UK and in several English speaking nations including New Zealand, Australia, and subsequently Canada. My interpretation of country-specific English lexicon, mixed with unique colloquialisms, makes for a frankly weird concoction of vernacular English. The Sybex editors' ability to decipher and translate this into something representing a sane American English dialect was undoubtedly no easy task. (However, I still maintain that the Queen's English is the only true authority, and virtualization should really be spelt with an *s*.) Alexa Murphy as the development editor probably bore the brunt of this and was always central to the smooth passage of the editing process. The Sybex team of Pete Gaughan, Connor O'Brien, and Jenni Housh kept a close guard on standards and made sure things were ticking along. The production team, headed up by Christine O'Connor and Liz Britten, did a tremendous job, with Tiffany Taylor as the copy editor tidying the grammar into something my Mother might be proud of. Proofreader Jen Larsen's rapier-like eye for detail helped spot all the little mistakes that the rest of us managed to miss along the way, and Ted Laux had the unenviable but crucial task of indexing the text — thanks, guys.

From a technical perspective, the vast collection of resources from the VMware community, the bloggers, the book writers, the podcasters, the VMworld presenters, the instructors, and the forum members, all helped immensely. My knowledge and understanding of the vSphere product line is directly attributable to all of you. There are unfortunately too many people who deserve rich thanks, but for fear of this turning into an Oscar speech, I can only say a huge *thank you*. You all know who you are. Here is a big virtual pat on the back from me.

Finally, I'd like to thank the wonderful baristas of Caffè Artigiano and Waves Coffee House on West Broadway, Vancouver, for their delicious highly caffeinated beverages and working refuge.

— *Forbes Guthrie*

As with any book, many people deserve credit for the book you're now reading. First and foremost, I'd like to thank coauthors Forbes and Maish for their outstanding work and unwavering dedication to getting this book completed, and for allowing me to be part of it. It's been a blast.

I'd also like to thank the team at Sybex: Agatha Kim, Alexa Murphy, Neil Edde, and the rest of the Sybex/Wiley team that worked so hard to bring this book to print. As with the previous books I've done with Sybex, it's been a pleasure, and I'm looking forward to more books in the future.

My thanks go to our technical editor, Jason Boche, for his efforts on this book. Jason, thank you for your honest feedback; I do believe this book is better as a result of your input.

Finally, I'd like to thank my family for putting up with me as I raced to meet deadlines while trying to balance work and home life. You guys are the greatest!

— *Scott Lowe*

First and foremost, I would like to thank Hashem for giving me guidance and direction in the writing of this book.

I would to thank my wife Danja and my daughters Noa, Michal, and Avital for bearing with me throughout this adventure. Without your support and encouragement, I would not have gone on this journey and I would never have been able to complete this book.

To my Mom and my Dad: I hope this gives you great Naches.

I would also like to thank Agatha and the whole Sybex team for the opportunity to participate in this project. I appreciate your patience and understanding.

To my coauthors, Forbes and Scott, and to Jason, our technical editor, thank you for all the ideas and for your help with the late-night questions.

And last but not least, a huge *thank you* to all of you in the virtualization community. Without you, we would not have so much to talk about and would not be able to bounce ideas off each other. Together, we improve each other's knowledge; and by sharing that knowledge with others, we make the world a better place.

— *Maish Saidel-Keesing*

About the Authors

Forbes Guthrie is a systems engineer and infrastructure architect who specializes in virtualization and storage. He has worked in variety of technical roles for over 12 years and achieved several industry certifications including VMware's VCP2, VCP3, and VCP4. His experience spans many different industries, and he has worked in Europe, Asia-Pacific, and North America. He holds a bachelor's degree in mathematics and business analysis and is a former Captain in the British Army.

Forbes' blog, `www.vReference.com`, is well regarded in the virtualization field and is aggregated on VMware's Planet V12n web site. He is probably best known for his collection of free reference cards, long revered by those studying for their VMware qualifications. Forbes was awarded the luminary designation of vExpert by VMware for his contribution to the virtualization community. His passion and knowledge have also been rewarded with the peer-reviewed top virtualization bloggers listing for the last two years running.

Scott Lowe is an author, blogger, and consultant focusing on virtualization, networking, storage, and other enterprise technologies. Scott is currently the team CTO for the vSpecialist team at EMC Corporation. In this role, Scott provides support, technical leadership, and training to the vSpecialist team worldwide.

Scott's technical expertise extends into several areas. He holds industry certifications from Cisco, EMC, Microsoft, NetApp, and others. He's also one of the few people who have achieved the status of VMware Certified Design Expert (VCDX); Scott is VCDX #39. For his leadership and contributions in support of the VMware community, Scott was awarded the VMware vExpert award in both 2009 and 2010.

Scott has published numerous articles on virtualization and VMware with a number of different online magazines, and has been a featured speaker at VMworld as well as other virtualization conferences. He has two other published books, *Mastering VMware vSphere 4* and *VMware vSphere 4 Administration Instant Reference* (with Jase McCarty and Matthew Johnson), both by Sybex.

Scott is perhaps best known for his acclaimed blog at `http://blog.scottlowe.org`, where he regularly posts technical articles on a wide variety of topics. Scott's weblog is one of the oldest virtualization-centric weblogs that is still active; he's been blogging since early 2005.

Scott lives in the Raleigh-Durham, NC, area with his wife Crystal, the two youngest of their seven children, and their two dogs, Bo and Zach.

Maish Saidel-Keesing is a virtualization and systems architect working in Israel. He first started playing with computers when the Commodore 64 and ZX Spectrum were around, and he's been at it ever since. He has been working in IT for 12 years with Microsoft infrastructures and specifically with VMware environments for the last 5 years.

Maish was awarded the VMware vExpert award for 2010, for his contribution to the virtualization community, the only Israeli to receive this award in that year.

Maish currently holds certifications from several international vendors, including VMware, Microsoft, IBM, Red Hat, and Novell. He is a member of the Server Virtualization Advisory

Board of `http://searchservervirtualization.techtarget.com`, where he provides regular insight into and contributions to the virtualization industry.

On his popular blog Technodrone at `http://technodrone.blogspot.com`, Maish regularly writes about virtualization, Windows, PowerShell, PowerCLI scripting, and how to go virtual in the physical world.

When he has free time, he likes to listen to music and spend time with his family. In general, he spends too much of his time on the computer.

Contents at a Glance

Contents

Introduction

When we were first approached about contributing to this book it stood out as a particularly interesting project. A multitude of vSphere textbooks are available, explaining every facet of configuring ESX, ESXi, and vCenter. If you want to know how to do something in vSphere, you're literally spoiled for choice. However, in our minds, there are few resources properly encompassing the design process. They exist for very specific features, and some older pre-vSphere works are still available; but little cover the entire design of a vSphere implementation in sufficient depth.

vSphere is the leading industry standard for hypervisors. It's simply the best enterprise solution available today. It has become this popular largely because of its wide range of features, efficiency, and flexibility. But for it to perform effectively in your datacenter, you must have a suitable architecture in place. This book is written to help you achieve that.

Above all, this is a technical book about a very complex subject. But it's not concerned with the minutiae of every command-line tool, but rather the underlying concepts. As vSphere has evolved from the early ESX days, it has grown in size to the point that every detail can't be covered in a single tome. But we sincerely believe this book covers its intended purpose better than anything else available. We'll dive into some areas not traditionally covered in such depth.

To that end, this book isn't a how-to manual with endless bullet-point instructions, but one that aims to make you think a little. It's for those of us who plan, design, implement, and optimize vSphere solutions. We hope it will challenge some of your preconceptions regarding the norm or what you consider best practice. Just because you designed a particular configuration one way in the past, doesn't mean it's a best fit for the next rollout. Here we try to question that prescriptive bias. Usually, that choice exists because different situations call for different answers. If there was one best solution for every case, then frankly no one would consider it a design choice at all.

This book isn't just for consultants who week by week deliver architectural solutions (although I hope you guys are here for the ride, too); it's for anyone who runs vSphere in their environment. It should make you question why things are set up the way are, and encourage you to examine how to improve your environment even further.

There are constant advances in hardware, and vSphere is an ever-evolving tool, so it's always worth considering your existing deployments. Even if the hardware and software remain static in your environment, you can bet that new VMs will continue to appear. Nothing stands still for long, so your design should also be constantly growing to embrace those changes.

Each design decision has its own impact, and often these have knock-on effects on many other elements. vSphere involves many disparate skills, such as guest OSs, server hardware, storage, and networking, and that's before you begin to consider the actual hypervisor. One of the hardest parts of a creating a viable design is that normally, no individual choice can be made in isolation. Although this book is naturally split into chapters, sections, and subsections, it's only when the design is considered as a complete solution that it can truly succeed.

The book employs several techniques to understand how you can approach design. The critical requirements and constraints; the impacts, benefits, and drawbacks of each choice; and how to decipher what will be best for you.

Who Should Read This Book

This book focuses on the design aspects of vSphere. It isn't primarily intended to teach you how to complete certain vSphere tasks, but rather to make you think about the *why* behind your different architectural decisions. We expect this book will be most useful for the following readers:

◆ Infrastructure architects designing new vSphere environments

◆ Engineers and architects charged with maintaining existing vSphere deployments, who wish to further optimize their setup

◆ Anyone who appreciates the basics of vSphere but wants to learn more by understanding in depth why things are the way they are

◆ Long-time experts who are always searching for that extra nugget of hidden information

Ways to Read the Book

There are several ways to approach this book. Clearly, you can read it from cover to cover, and we certainly encourage anyone wanting the fullest understanding of vSphere design to do so. Alternatively, if you need to brush up your knowledge on one key area, you can read each chapter in isolation. Or, if you need a specific answer to a key design decision, you should be able to jump in and use this as a reference book. *VMware vSphere Design* has been written so each section stands on its own, if that is all you need from it, but it should also be a jolly good read if you want to sit down and immerse yourself.

Other Resources Available

We're often asked for good sources of vSphere information, for those seeking *absolute knowledge*. Fortunately, there is a plethora of good places to look. The first stop for anyone (beyond this book, obviously) is VMware's own library of technical product documentation, which you can find at www.vmware.com/support/pubs. Along with the standard PDFs, the site also offers a wide variety of whitepapers, best practices, case studies, and knowledge-based articles.

Sybex has a number of excellent vSphere-focused books, such as *Mastering VMware vSphere 4*, a VCP Study Guide and a Review Guide, and *Instant Reference for Administration*, among others.

A strong community of VMware users share knowledge through a number of different channels. The VMware forums at http://communities.vmware.com/community/vmtn are an excellent source of information and support for specific queries. There are a good number of vSphere-oriented blogs, the best of which tend to be aggregated on the popular Planet V12n site at www.vmware.com/vmtn/planet/v12n. Finally, if you want something a little closer to home, user groups are available in many places (see http://vmware.com/vmug), where you have the chance to meet other VMware users face to face to discuss and learn more about vSphere.

What You Need

To get started with *VMware vSphere Design*, you should have a basic understanding of virtualization, vSphere itself, and the associated VMware products. Both networking and storage concepts are discussed, because they're integral to any vSphere architecture, so a basic knowledge of them is assumed. The more hands-on experience you have with vSphere, the more you're likely to get out of this book. However, you don't need to be an expert beforehand.

No specific hardware or software is required while following this book, as long as you've seen the product before. But a lab is always useful to test some of many concepts we discuss. A simple nested VM lab run on a single platform should be sufficient to practice and explore most of the book's content.

What's Inside

Here is a glance at each chapter:

Chapter 1: An Introduction to Designing vSphere Environments   We begin by introducing you to the design process for vSphere delivery. This chapter explains how to understand the basic requirements, and how to assess and then design a successful, valid implementation.

Chapter 2: ESX vs. ESXi   We explain the fundamental differences between VMware's two enterprise hypervisors: how to design around ESX and how to design around ESXi. This chapter compares the merits of each and provides advice for those wishing to migrate an existing ESX deployment across to ESXi.

Chapter 3: Designing the Management Layer   In this chapter, we look at many of the software management pieces and how best to use them in different design configurations.

Chapter 4: Server Hardware   This chapter provides an in-depth examination of the components that make up a server, and how each one affects the performance of vSphere. You need to consider many factors when selecting server hardware, and we look at them, including scaling up versus scaling out approaches. We also debate the merits of blade and rack servers.

Chapter 5: Designing Your Network   This chapter covers the complex decisions you need to make to ensure that network traffic provides sufficient throughput, redundancy, and security. We look how different vSphere components can affect those designs and provide some example configurations.

Chapter 6: Storage   In this chapter, we analyze the different factors that influence a complete virtualization storage strategy, comparing availability, performance, and capacity. We contrast different storage protocols and, finally, explain how to configure multipathing in different setups.

Chapter 7: Virtual Machines   In this chapter, we describe each VM component in turn, to help you understand how VMs should be designed to make the most efficient solution for you. We look at how to optimize the OS and the applications within VMs, and then explain different methods of efficiently replicating the VM design though the use of clones and templates. Additionally, we look at some of the techniques to protect those VMs with clustering solutions.

Chapter 8: Datacenter Design   This chapter examines in detail each element of a vSphere inventory's hierarchy. It looks at the importance of clusters in the design and how to successfully implement the resource-management and redundancy features of a cluster. We discuss resource pools, DRS, DPM, HA, and FT, and what interdependencies exist when they're used in combination.

Chapter 9: Designing with Security in Mind   Chapter 9 highlights some of the areas that security-conscious environments can use to ensure that vSphere is suitably strengthened. It explains the different security measures included in the hypervisor and the management tools, and how best to tighten that security as required.

Chapter 10: Monitoring and Capacity Planning   This chapter explains the concepts of monitoring and capacity planning. Monitoring relates to the present or recent past, whereas capacity planning looks to the future. The chapter also examines some of the common tools used for both and how to involve them in your design.

Chapter 11: Bringing It All Together   In this chapter, we return to the overall design strategy by looking at a specific example through a design for a fictitious company. We look at several of the decisions made during the design, examine the justifications behind those decisions, and consider alternative choices that could have been made.

How to Get in Touch with the Authors

We welcome feedback from you about this book or about books you'd like to see from us in the future. You can reach Forbes Guthrie by writing to forbesguthrie@vReference.com or by visiting his blog at www.vReference.com. You can reach Scott Lowe at scott.lowe@scottlowe.org or visit his blog at http://blog.scottlowe.org. You can reach Maish Saidel-Keesing at maishsk@gmail.com or on Twitter at @maishsk. Or, visit his web site: http://technodrone.blogspot.com.

Sybex strives to keep you supplied with the latest tools and information you need for your work. Please check their web site at www.sybex.com, where we'll post additional content and updates that supplement this book should the need arise. Enter **vSphere** in the Search box (or type the book's ISBN — **978-0470922026**), and click Go to get to the book's update page.

Chapter 1

An Introduction to Designing VMware Environments

Designing VMware vSphere environments can be a complex topic, one that means many different things to many different people. In this chapter, we'll provide an introduction to designing VMware vSphere implementations. This introduction will give a preview of some of the more detailed discussions that take place in later chapters, and will provide a framework for how all the other chapters fit into the overall process.

This chapter will cover the following topics:

◆ The importance of functional requirements in VMware vSphere design

◆ The what, who, and how questions involved in VMware vSphere design and why they're important

◆ An overview of the VMware vSphere design process

What Is Design?

When we talk about "designing your VMware vSphere environment," what exactly does that mean? In the context of VMware vSphere, what is design? What does design entail? These are excellent questions — questions that we intend to answer in this chapter and the coming chapters throughout this book.

In our definition, *design* is the process of determining the way in which the different elements that make up a VMware vSphere environment should be assembled and configured to create a virtual infrastructure that is strong yet flexible. Design also includes the process of determining how this virtual infrastructure will integrate with existing infrastructure as well as how the virtual infrastructure will be operated after the implementation is complete.

That's a reasonable definition; but for someone who is new to VMware vSphere design, does this really describe what design is? Does it help understand the nature of design, or what makes up a design?

In looking at a VMware vSphere design, you can say that VMware vSphere design has three key facets: the technical or structural facet, the organizational facet, and the operational facet. Figure 1.1 shows how these three facets are all part of the larger entity that we refer to as *design*.

FIGURE 1.1
The different parts of VMware vSphere design are merely facets of a larger entity.

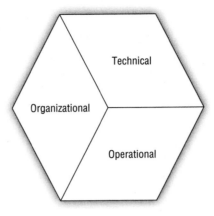

These three facets serve to organize the design in a way that is logical to us, grouping together information, decisions, criteria, constraints, and standards. We'll explore these facets in more detail later in this chapter in the section titled "The Facets of vSphere Design."

When defined or described in this way, VMware vSphere design seems simple. As you'll see in this book — or perhaps as you've already seen, depending on your experience — it can be complex. Even in the most complex of designs, however, there is a single unifying element that brings the different facets together. What is this single unifying element that ties everything together, as illustrated in Figure 1.2? This element is the functional requirements of the design.

FIGURE 1.2
The functional requirements unify the different facets of the design.

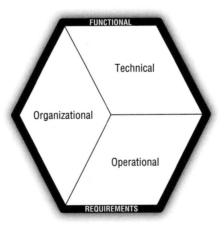

Functional requirements are incredibly important. In fact, we can't stress enough the key role that functional requirements play in VMware vSphere design (or any IT design task, for that matter). Functional requirements are important because they answer the question "What *things* should this design *do*?"

It's important to remember that companies implement VMware vSphere for a reason, not just for the sake of having vSphere installed. As much as VMware would love for that to be the case, it's not. In every instance, there's a driving factor, a force, a purpose behind the implementation.

There's a reason the company or organization is implementing VMware vSphere. That reason, naturally, varies from customer to customer and organization to organization.

Here are some example reasons taken from our own experience in the virtualization industry:

Consolidation   The company or organization has too many physical servers and needs to reduce the number of physical servers. The need to reduce the number of physical servers can be driven by any number of reasons, including a need to reduce data-center space usage, a need to cut power and cooling costs, or an attempt to reduce hardware refresh costs.

New Application Rollout   The company or organization is deploying a new application or a new service in its data center, and it has chosen to use virtualization as the vehicle to accomplish that deployment. This may be a deployment of a new version of an application; for example, a company currently using Exchange 2007 may decide to roll out Exchange 2010 in a virtualized environment on VMware vSphere. As another example, a company deploying SAP may choose to do on VMware vSphere. The reasons for choosing to deploy on a virtualized environment are too numerous to list here, but they can include increased utilization, simplified deployment, and better support for a disaster recovery/business continuity (DR/BC) solution.

Disaster Recovery/Business Continuity (DR/BC)   The company or organization is in the midst of developing or enhancing its DR/BC solution and has chosen to use virtualization as a key component of that solution. Perhaps the company is using array-based replication and wishes to use VMware vSphere and VMware Site Recovery Manager (SRM) to provide a more automated DR/BC solution. The choice to use virtualization as a component of a DR/BC solution is almost always a financial one; the company or organization wishes to reduce the amount of downtime (thus minimizing losses due to downtime) or reduce the cost of implementing the solution.

Virtual Desktop Infrastructure   The company or organization wishes to deploy a virtual desktop infrastructure (VDI) in order to gain desktop mobility, a better remote-access solution, increased security, or reduced desktop-management costs. Whatever the motivation, the reason for the VMware vSphere environment is to support that VDI deployment.

As you can see, the reasons for adopting virtualization are as varied as the companies and organizations. There is no one reason a company will adopt virtualization, but there will be a reason. There will often be multiple reasons. These reasons become the basis for the functional requirements of the design. The reasons are the *things* the design must *do*. Functional requirements formalize the reasons why the company or organization is adopting VMware vSphere and turn them into actionable items that you'll use to drive all the other decisions in the design.

Think about some of the examples we just provided. Does the organization plan to virtualize a new rollout of Microsoft Exchange Server 2010? If so, then the VMware vSphere design had better accommodate that functional requirement. The design must specifically accommodate Microsoft Exchange Server 2010 and its configuration needs, supportability requirements, and resource constraints. If you fail to properly account for the fact that Microsoft Exchange Server 2010 will run in this virtualized environment, then you've failed to consider one of the design's functional requirements — and, in all likelihood, the implementation will be a failure. The design will fail to *do* the *thing* the company needs it to do: run Microsoft Exchange Server 2010.

With this in mind, you can look back at Figure 1.2 and better understand how the functional requirements both surround and unify the facets of VMware vSphere design. Continuing in our example of an organization that is deploying Exchange Server 2010 in a virtualized environment, the functional requirements that derive from that reason will affect a number of different areas:

- The server hardware selected needs to be capable of running the virtual machines configured with enough resources to run Microsoft Exchange Server 2010.

- The virtual machines that will run Exchange will, most likely, need to be configured with more RAM, more virtual CPUs (vCPUs), and more available disk space.

- The configuration of Exchange Server 2010 will affect cluster configurations like the use of VMware High Availability (HA), VMwareDistributed Resource Scheduler (DRS), and VMwareFault Tolerance (FT).

- The cluster configuration, such as the ability (or inability) to use VMware FT, will in turn affect the networking configuration of the VMware ESX/ESXi hosts in the environment.

- Operational procedures need to be included in the design as a result of the use (or lack of use) of features like VMwareHA, VMwareDRS, and VMwareFT.

This list can go on and on, but at this point you should get the idea. The functional requirements affect almost every decision point in every facet of the design; as a result, they lie at the core of creating a VMware vSphere design. Any design that doesn't directly address the organization's functional requirements is a poor design, and the implementation won't be a success. Any consultant or VMware vSphere architect who attempts to design a vSphere environment without knowledge of the functional requirements will fail. After all, the functional requirements are the targets the design is aiming to hit; how can the design hit those targets if the targets aren't known and understood?

Interestingly, although the functional requirements directly affect the decision points — things like what servers to use, the form factor of the servers, the number and type of network interface cards (NICs), and so on — these decision points also affect the functional requirements. An inherent interdependency exists between the functional requirements and the decisions, as shown in Figure 1.3.

FIGURE 1.3
Functional require-
ments and design
decision points are
interdependent.

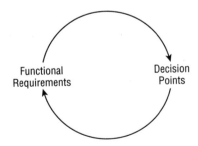

NOTE You'll likely see the term *design constraints* used in formal VMware design documentation. A design constraint is a decision point—such as the type of server you'll use, the type of storage you'll use, or the way in which you'll connect to an existing network—that has already been made and can't be changed. Because this decision point can't be changed, it constrains your design.

As a result of this interdependency, you'll find that creating a design is often an iterative process. Based on the functional requirements, you make a decision. Then, based on that decision, you ensure that the decision is capable of supporting the functional requirements. If so, you proceed with other decision points. If not, you revise the decision point based on the functional requirements. This iterative process again underscores the importance of the functional requirements in the creation of the design.

At the beginning of this section, we told you that design is the process of determining the way in which the different elements that make up a VMware vSphere environment should be assembled and configured to create a virtual infrastructure that is strong yet flexible. When we factor in the key role that functional requirements play in unifying the technical, organizational, and operational facets of a design, perhaps a better definition is that design is the process of determining the way in which the different elements that make up a VMware vSphere environment should be assembled and configured in order to satisfy the functional requirements. Or, in simpler terms, design is making the VMware vSphere environment *do* the *things* it needs to do.

Now that you have a better understanding of what VMware vSphere design is and why it's important, in the next section we'll take a closer look at the facets of design.

The Facets of vSphere Design

As we described in the previous section and illustrated in Figure 1.1, your design must address three facets, or the design will be incomplete. These three facets — technical, organizational, and operational — are unified by the functional requirements; but within each facet, a wide variety of decision points must be specified in the design.

The best way to understand how these facets differ from each other is to look at the types of decisions that fall in each facet. This is graphically depicted in Figure 1.4.

FIGURE 1.4
Each facet of the design primarily addresses a different type of decision, such as who, what, or how.

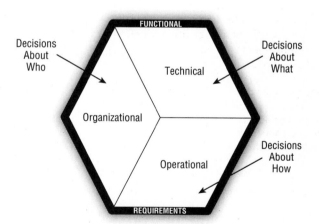

In each facet of the design, you'll make decisions based on the functional requirements, followed by an iterative review (as illustrated in Figure 1.3) to ensure that the functional requirements are still met based on the decision. In this section of this chapter, we'll take a deeper and more detailed look at these facets, examining some of the decision points that are involved.

We'll start with the technical facet.

The Technical Facet

The *technical facet* is the facet that IT people most closely identify with design. It involves the pieces and parts of technology that make up the final environment: things like what servers to use, what quantity of random access memory (RAM) the servers will have, what configuration the storage array will use for its datastores, and what the networking configuration will look like. You might also see the technical facet referred to as the *physical design*, although it incorporates certain logical aspects as well. These are all decisions about what will or won't be included in the design, and all these decisions fall into the technical facet, as illustrated in Figure 1.5.

FIGURE 1.5
The technical facet includes the "what" decisions that are familiar to many IT professionals.

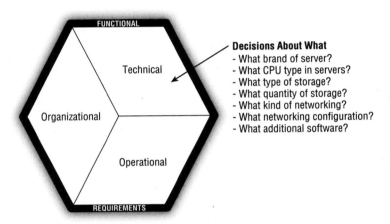

It's important to be sure the technical facet is as complete as possible, so the design should include — at the very least — decisions in the following technical areas:

◆ The number and type of servers in the environment

◆ The number, type, and speed of the CPUs in the servers

◆ The amount of RAM in the servers

◆ The type of connectivity to the shared storage

◆ The type or configuration of the shared storage

◆ The number of physical NIC ports available

◆ The manufacturer and model of the NICs in the servers

◆ The exact configuration of the virtual switches (vSwitches) and distributed vSwitches in the environment

◆ The amount of power required by the equipment

◆ The amount of cooling required by the equipment

◆ The amount of rack space or floor space required by the equipment

This is, of course, just a small list to get you started thinking about the detail you should provide when crafting a design for a VMware vSphere environment. Subsequent chapters examine each of these areas in much more detail. For example, VMware vSphere networking is covered in detail in Chapter 5, "Designing Your Network"; Chapter 6, "Shared Storage," discusses shared storage in more depth.

A complete and thorough design addresses more than just the technical facet, though. Your design should also address the organizational facet.

The Organizational Facet

Although the technical facet is important, equally as important is the *organizational facet*. It's concerned with questions centered on "who," as you can see in Figure 1.6.

FIGURE 1.6
The "who"-focused decisions of a VMware vSphere design fall into the organizational facet.

Decisions About Who
- Who manages the environment?
- Who provisions storage?
- Who configures the network?
- Who's responsible for backups?
- Who will handle troubleshooting?
- Who will patch VMs?
- Who is responsible for security?

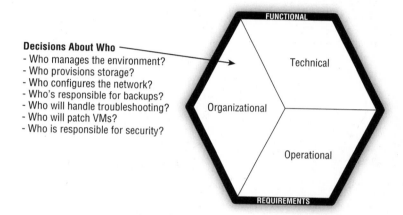

You might initially think that these "who"-focused questions aren't important or aren't your responsibility. Aren't these the sort of decisions that should be made by the customer? In a certain respect, yes — these decisions are driven by the functional requirements every bit as much as the "what" questions in the technical facet. As you'll see later in this chapter, in the section "The Process of Design," gathering the functional requirements from the customer or organization (if it's your own organization) means gathering information about who is responsible for the various tasks within a virtualized infrastructure.

The other thing to consider regarding these "who"-focused questions, though, is the fact that the customer or company might not know or understand who will be responsible for certain aspects of the design. For organizations that are new to virtualization, the convergence of server administrators, network administrators, storage administrators, and security administrators often means they're confused and don't understand who can or should be responsible for the different areas of the new VMware vSphere environment. By embedding the answers to these questions in your design, you can help the customer (or your own organization) better understand how these responsibilities should be divided and who should be responsible for each area.

The final facet of VMware vSphere design addresses an equally important but often overlooked type of question: how should the environment be operated? This is the operational facet, and we discuss it in the next section.

The Operational Facet

The *operational facet* of a VMware vSphere design answers questions focused on "how," such as those illustrated in Figure 1.7.

FIGURE 1.7
Decisions about how you'll operate a VMware vSphere environment fall into the operational facet.

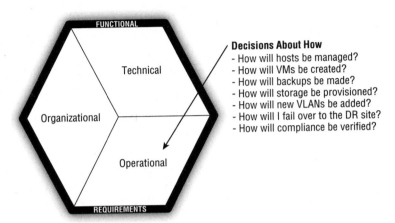

Decisions About How
- How will hosts be managed?
- How will VMs be created?
- How will backups be made?
- How will storage be provisioned?
- How will new VLANs be added?
- How will I fail over to the DR site?
- How will compliance be verified?

As with the organizational facet, you might ask, "Why would I need to define operational procedures in a VMware vSphere design? Should these sorts of operations be tasks the organization already knows how to do?"

In the event of an organization that is new to virtualization, the answer to that question is no. Virtualization changes the way the data center operates — and the customer or company implementing virtualization for the first time must have these operational decisions spelled out in the design.

Even for organizations that are familiar with virtualization, the operational facet is still a critical part of a complete and comprehensive VMware vSphere design. It's possible, even likely, that the "what" decisions made in the technical facet of this design will be different than the "what" decisions made in the technical facet of earlier designs. Server models change. Storage vendors introduce new products with new functionality — and new operational requirements. Networking vendors change the way their products work over time. All of these factors add up to a need to include operational information in every design to ensure that the organization implementing the design has the information it needs to operate the environment.

As an example, consider an organization that adopted virtualization a couple of years ago. It deployed VMware Infrastructure 3 (VI3) on HP ProLiant rack-mounted servers attached to a NetApp storage array via Fibre Channel (FC). Now, the company is implementing VMware vSphere 4.1 on Cisco UCS attached to an EMC storage array via FC over Ethernet (FCoE). Do you think the operational procedures from the last implementation will be the same as the operational procedures from this new implementation? No, of course not. Just as technology changes over time, operations change over time as well. This is why the operational aspect is important not only for new VMware vSphere users but for existing users as well.

Before we wrap up this chapter and start a more detailed look at the decision of whether to use VMware ESX or VMware ESXi in Chapter 2, we want to discuss one more area. That's the process of VMware vSphere design, and it's the focus of the next section.

The Process of Design

Now that we've discussed the facets of design, it's time to discuss the *process* of design. In this section, we'll cover how you go about creating a VMware vSphere design, some of the tasks involved, and some of the tools you can use to complete those tasks.

We'll start with what is, as we've said before, one of the most important areas: functional requirements.

Gathering and Defining Functional Requirements

Functional requirements form the basis, the driver, for almost everything in the design. Most other decisions in the design are based on or affected by the functional requirements, so it's incredibly important to be as thorough and complete as possible during the process of gathering and defining the functional requirements.

In many situations, some of the functional requirements are provided to you. For example, if an organization is adopting VMware vSphere in order to support a consolidation initiative, the business might clearly specify a functional requirement in a statement like this: "The virtualization environment must support the consolidation of 250 physical server workloads." No additional effort is required on your part to define this requirement. (But additional effort is clearly required to implement that functional requirement in the design.)

It's uncommon, in our experience, to have situations where all the functional requirements are provided to you. In these cases, you'll have to gather information to define the functional requirement. There are two primary ways to gather the information necessary to define the design's functional requirements:

◆ Reviewing documentation

◆ Performing interviews

Reviewing Documentation

In some cases, the customer or organization implementing VMware vSphere has documentation that outlines the functional requirements. Remembering that virtualization is implemented in order to accomplish a goal (to "do something"), documentation is often created that outlines what the organization is attempting to achieve. For example, perhaps the organization is implementing virtualization as part of a desktop virtualization initiative. In that case, some of the functional requirements of the VMware vSphere environment can be derived directly from the documentation prepared for the desktop virtualization project. If the desktop virtualization documentation specifies that the VMware vSphere environment will automatically restart desktop VMs in the event of a host failure, that should immediately sound a mental alarm — your vSphere environment will need to use VMware HA in order to meet that functional requirement. And because you'll use VMware HA, you'll also need to use clusters, which means you'll require redundant management connections, which affects the networking design ... and so on.

In another example, suppose the organization is migrating into a new data center and has compiled a list of all the applications that will be migrated. You can use that documentation to understand the applications' needs and determine the functional requirements necessary to support those needs. Perhaps the application documentation indicates that the I/O profile is primarily writes instead of reads and that the application needs to sustain a specific number of transactions per second (TPS). That information translates into storage requirements that will dictate the RAID level, array type, storage protocol, and capacity in I/O operations per second (IOPS).

Although reviewing documentation can be helpful, it's unlikely that you'll find all the information you need in a company's documentation. If the organization is like a lot of others, documentation is sparse and incomplete. In these instances, you'll need to gather information by going straight to the source: the people in the organization.

PERFORMING INTERVIEWS

Interviewing individuals in the organization or company that is implementing VMware vSphere is the second major way to gather the information necessary to understand the functional requirements.

Generally speaking, unless you've already gotten the information you need from somewhere else (and even then, you might want to conduct interviews to ensure that you haven't missed something), you'll want to interview the following people in the organization:

- Desktop support staff
- Server administrators
- Network administrators
- Storage administrators
- Security managers
- Compliance/legal staff
- Application owners
- Business leaders
- Project managers or project sponsors/owners
- Executive/managerial sponsors
- Architects

Not all designs or situations require you to speak with all these individuals, so be selective but thorough.

These individuals can provide you with information about the applications currently supported in the environment, the requirements of the applications, service level agreements (SLAs) that are in place, dependencies between different applications or services in the data center, plans for future trends or projects, compliance or regulatory requirements, business-level requirements, financial objectives, and other facts that can be used to derive the functional requirements for the design.

Assessing the Environment

After you've gathered the information necessary to determine the design's functional requirements, it's then necessary to assess the current environment. Assessing the environment fills a couple of purposes:

◆ The results of the assessment can, in some instances, verify or clarify the information provided during the information-gathering process of defining the functional requirements. People are just people and are known to make mistakes or accidentally omit information. By performing an assessment of the environment, you can verify that the applications you were told were present are, in fact, present.

◆ The assessment provides useful information necessary to complete the technical facet of the design. An assessment reveals the current types and configurations of the servers in the environment, the current network configurations, and the current storage configurations. All this information is crucial to putting together a new structure that will properly interoperate with the existing structure. If the organization is currently using iSCSI, then you know that implementing FC might create interoperability issues. Having this knowledge through an assessment of the current environment helps you tailor the technical facet of the design appropriately.

You can use a number of different tools or methods to assess the environment. If the organization already has a robust management system in place, this management system might have the inventory, configuration, and performance information you need. If not, you'll have to start digging through the environment, gathering information from such sources as:

◆ Active Directory

◆ LDAP directories

◆ Network-management tools

◆ Enterprise-wide logging solutions

◆ IP addressing documentation

◆ Network equipment configurations

◆ Server performance data

◆ Server configuration data

You can imagine that in anything larger than most small environments, assessing the existing environment manually like this can be time-consuming and potentially error-prone. Fortunately, VMware and other vendors have released assessment tools that help gather this information in an automated fashion, to save you time and help you avoid missing critical data. Even the virtualization community has stepped up, providing scripts and other tools that gather information about existing physical and/or virtual environments.

Examples of some these tools that have been created by vendors and community members include:

◆ VMware Capacity Planner

◆ Various community-supplied health check scripts

◆ Novell PlateSpin Power Recon

◆ CiRBA

We'll discuss some of these tools in Chapter 10, "Monitoring and Capacity Planning." Because part of capacity planning involves previrtualization assessment, these tools are also useful in assessing an organization's existing environment in preparation for completing a design.

At this point, you're armed with some functional requirements, the information necessary to define other functional requirements, and knowledge of the existing environment. You're ready to assemble the design.

Assembling the Design

Assembling the design is the iterative process we described earlier and depicted in Figure 1.3. While assembling the design, you'll make decisions within each of the three facets. Those decisions, focused on the what/who/how theme, will be based on the functional requirements that you've been given or have defined. Each decision has a cascading effect, forcing a series of what we call *downstream* decisions, as shown in Figure 1.8.

FIGURE 1.8
Each decision forces other decisions in a complex decision tree. The results of each decision must be compared against the functional requirements.

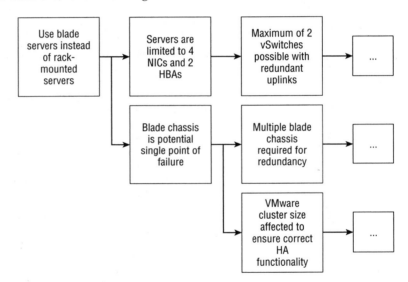

When you make a decision in the design, you then need to compare the result of that decision — and all the downstream decisions resulting from that decision — to ensure that you're still meeting all the functional requirements. If so, you continue; if not, you need to change that decision or violate one or more of the functional requirements.

VIOLATING FUNCTIONAL REQUIREMENTS MIGHT BE NECESSARY

Sometimes, organizations have an unrealistic view of the functional requirements. In situations like this, it may be necessary to violate a functional requirement. As long as you can show why the functional requirement is violated and can provide a potential remediation for the violation, it's up to the organization to determine whether that functional requirement really is a requirement or if the design can be accepted and implemented as described.

It's here, while assembling the design, that you'll define standards and best practices for the VMware vSphere environment:

Standards A good design defines standards for host names, networking configuration, storage layouts, resource allocation, virtual machine configurations, and so on. Standards are important because standardization reduces complexity. When complexity is reduced, operations are simplified, and costs are generally reduced. Without standards, environments become too complex to operate efficiently — and inefficiency is the bane of a VMware vSphere environment.

Best Practices A good design both defines and enforces best practices where those best practices align with the organization's needs and functional requirements. The term *best practices* doesn't just mean the recommendations made by vendors for configuring their products; it also means the operational processes that the organization should follow. For example, a best practice states that all Windows-based VMs should have their file systems properly aligned in the virtual disk. Yes, that's a recommendation made by VMware, but it's also an operational recommendation made by a good design to ensure the efficient and stable operation of the environment. A good design includes other best practices that are specific to this particular implementation, such as the structure of new VMs, or the configuration for new datastores.

DON'T ACCEPT BEST PRACTICES BLINDLY

When it comes to vendor best practices, don't accept them blindly. Examine those best practices and try to understand the reasons behind them. If the storage vendor says it's a best practice to use a particular multipathing policy, take a deeper look to understand why that multipathing policy is recommended. If a server vendor provides certain BIOS settings as best practices, try to figure out why those settings are defined as best practices. Doing so will give you a deeper, more complete understanding of the environment and make you better prepared to provide implementation-specific best practices.

Assembling the design is a time-consuming and detailed process. Most, if not all, of the remaining chapters in this book focus on specific technical areas and the decisions you must make when building your VMware vSphere design.

Documenting the Design

When the design has been assembled — that is, after you've made all the decisions that need to be made in each facet of the design, and you've compared the results of those decisions (and all the downstream decisions) against the functional requirements to ensure that the requirements are still being met — then you're ready to document the design.

This portion of the design process might happen concurrently with the assembly of the design and is, for the most part, straightforward. You should ensure that your documentation addresses each of the three facets of the design. In many instances, IT professionals tend to forget about the organizational and operational facets, but these are just as important as the technical facet and deserve equal treatment in your final design documentation.

In particular, be sure the design documentation includes at least the following documents:

◆ A description of the functional requirements that were provided to you or defined by you

◆ A comprehensive description of the technical facet decisions (the "what" decisions) made in the design

◆ A complete review of the organizational facet decisions (the "who" decisions) made in the design

◆ A thorough review of the operational facet decisions (the "how" decisions) found in the design

◆ Build documents — sometimes referred to as *blueprints* — that describe the specifics involved in building or constructing the design specified in your documentation

◆ Test plans describing how you can verify that the design satisfies the functional requirements

◆ A high-level architectural design document that ties all these facets together and tells the story of the design

Performing the Implementation

After the design is complete and has been accepted by the organization, you might also have the opportunity to perform the implementation. Doing so will afford you the opportunity to use your own documentation to build the environment.

If you aren't performing the implementation, then someone else will have to build your design. This is why it's important to be thorough and complete with the design documentation — when someone else comes along to build your design, that person won't have access to the thought processes inside your head. Be sure to provide as much information as possible in the design documentation so the build process is simple and straightforward.

Summary

Throughout this book, we'll draw on our experience and knowledge to help you understand the complexities of VMware vSphere design. In this chapter, we've discussed the three key facets of design — the technical facet, the organizational facet, and the operational facet — and the importance of each. We've also discussed the process of design and some of the tasks involved in creating a design. In coming chapters, we'll take a more detailed look at the different areas of VMware vSphere design, starting in Chapter 2 with an examination of VMware ESX versus VMware ESXi.

Chapter 2

ESX vs. ESXi

Underpinning any design based on vSphere technologies is the hypervisor. ESX and ESXi host software drives vSphere deployments and makes guest virtualization possible. VMware's hypervisors have evolved rapidly over the years, and the basis of the enterprise offering is again going through a transition phase.

The current push is the migration of users from the old ESX-style architecture to the newer, slimmer ESXi option. VMware has made its position clear regarding the future of the vSphere product, but two choices are still available to customers; both are supported and viable. The marketing machine at VMware is nudging everyone toward its chosen path, but that doesn't mean it's currently the best option for everyone.

This chapter will look more closely at both hypervisors — what makes them tick and what differentiates them. In particular, it will examine how to design an environment around the newer and generally less-understood ESXi hypervisor. We'll compare both options, looking at the advantages of each and which may be more appropriate in different circumstances. Finally, we'll discuss how to migrate an existing ESX deployment to ESXi, what implications this may have on how the environment is managed, and how this affects design planning going forward.

The chapter is split into the following sections:

◆ The vSphere hypervisors

◆ ESX classic design options

◆ ESXi design options

◆ Comparing ESX and ESXi

◆ Migration considerations when moving from ESX to ESXi

Two vSphere Hypervisors

vSphere 4 hosts run one of two available hypervisor operating systems. The *hypervisor* is the software that virtualizes the host's hardware and makes it available to multiple guest OSs. vSphere hosts are what is known as *type 1* hypervisors, or *bare-metal* hypervisors. Unlike a *type 2* (or *hosted*) hypervisor, which runs atop a standard OS such as Windows or Linux, a type 1 hypervisor runs natively on the physical hardware, without the need for an intermediary OS. This gives the hypervisor direct access to the hardware, reducing the performance overhead of running on an intermediary OS, and without the security and stability issues that adding another layer to the stack brings.

VMware released its GSX (type 2) and ESX (type 1) products in 2001. VMware GSX was renamed VMware Server in 2006; it follows a lineage close to that of VMware's other hosted products such as Workstation, Player, and Fusion. The ESX enterprise hypervisor has steadily evolved over the years; the latest versions, 4.0 and 4.1, were released in 2009 and 2010, respectively.

When ESX 3.5 was released in December 2007, VMware also made the first public release of ESXi 3.5. This marked the first significant fork in the ESX model, and since then VMware has released both ESX and ESXi alongside each other. Ever since the initial release of ESXi, VMware has made no secret of the fact that it planned to replace ESX with the newer ESXi product. However, with the announcement of version 4.1, the company proclaimed that this would be the last of the ESX line, and all subsequent vSphere hypervisors would be ESXi based.

Since the introduction of a competing vSphere host with a remarkably similar moniker, ESX has often been referred to as *ESX classic* to help distinguish it from its ESXi brethren. This chapter closely examines their differing architectural designs, but it's worth pointing out at this stage ESX and ESXi have far more in common than they have differences. Their hypervisors are based on the same underlying code, and their capabilities are practically at parity these days.

ESXi was often regarded as the lesser of the two, because it initially couldn't match ESX classic's features. In what turned out to be a somewhat counterproductive move, in an effort to promote ESXi over ESX and to let it compete with other hypervisor products on the market, VMware made the base ESXi host software available free via download. This gave many people the impression that ESXi was less valuable than the well-regarded ESX classic software. With vSphere 4.1, the list of feature deficiencies was reduced, making both products effectively equivalent in capabilities.

Both products, with the exception of the free standalone ESXi version, are priced and licensed identically. ESX classic and ESXi hosts can even coexist in the same cluster at the same time and share resources among VMs. Unless you work hands-on with the hosts themselves, you may not notice the difference in the client when connecting to vCenter. VM administrators, storage or network teams, and IT managers may understandably be oblivious to the difference. However, if you design or manage vSphere hosts, then you'll be interested in the choice.

It's clear that VMware is keen to move forward with the unification of the host software as soon as possible. It makes economic sense for the company to curtail the ESX classic line and concentrate on ESXi, and customers will need to follow if they want to take advantage of new features in the future. VMware wants its host servers and software to become commodity items, with which customers fill their datacenters. New greenfield deployments are an obvious place to consider a switch to a different contemporary design paradigm. But the decision whether to design around ESX classic or ESXi (or migrate from ESX classic to ESXi) isn't as clear-cut as some salesmen may make out. There are distinct advantages to each platform, and you must carefully consider the existing environment.

ESX Design

ESX classic consists of three main elements that run on the physical hardware, providing the virtualized environment for the guest OSs (see Figure 2.1):

VMkernel The VMkernel is VMware's 64 bit microkernel OS, which manages the hardware of the physical server. It coordinates all of the CPU's resource scheduling and the memory allocation. It controls the disk and network I/O stacks and handles the device drivers for all the approved hardware compatibility list (HCL) compliant hardware.

FIGURE 2.1
Basic ESX
architecture

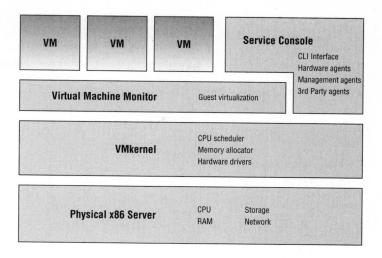

Virtual Machine Monitor   The Virtual Machine Monitor (VMM) is the abstraction that allows each guest OS to see its own x86 virtualized hardware. It presents the hardware including the BIOS to each VM, allocating the necessary vCPUs, RAM, disks, vNICs, and so on. It also determines the monitor mode for each VM, depending on the physical CPUs in the server and the guest OS selected, choosing between Full Virtualization (binary translation), Paravirtualization (VMI), or Hardware Assisted Virtualization.

Service Console   The Service Console, also known as the Console Operating System (COS) or VMnix, is the command-line interface and management console. It's a modified Red Hat Enterprise Linux build and allows user-privileged access to the VMkernel. It doesn't have any direct access to the physical server and its hardware components, although additional hardware drivers can be installed within it. It also enables scripts to be run; and infrastructure, hardware, and third-party agents to run.

Some of the more noteworthy daemons running within the Service Console are as follows:

vmware-hostd   hostd (which is stewarded by the service `mgmt-vmware`) is the primary management daemon. It's used to interface with the VMkernel and is the connection for direct vSphere Clients and remote API calls.

vmware-vpxa   vpxa is the agent that allows a vCenter instance to connect to the Service Console. When you first connect a host ESX server to vCenter, it initiates the vpxa service, which acts as the intermediary to the Service Console's functions under the vpxuser account.

syslog   The syslog daemon can forward logs to a remote syslog server.

vmware-webAccess   Web Access provides a web-based interface for basic VM manipulation. It's disabled by default.

iptables   The Service Console's iptables are the firewall protection that is configured via the `esxcfg-firewall` command.

snmp   An snmp service is available, although disabled by default, to send monitor messages about the host and its VMs.

ntpd   ntpd provides the time service to keep the Service Console synchronized to remote time servers. This is important, because several inter-server services such as high availability (HA) and directory-based authentication rely on accurate timekeeping. You can also set the VMs to synchronize their guest OS to the local host.

ESX hosts have a number of initial design options available to them. These are split into two distinct groups: those configured during OS installation and those set up after the installation is complete.

Installation Design Options

To install ESX classic, you need to consider several factors. First, the hardware should match the required specifications, and you should verify that all the components are supported on the HCL. Chapter 4, "Server Hardware," looks in detail at hardware requirements. However, as a basic starting point, the server should have 64-bit x86 CPUs with a minimum of 2 GB of RAM. 10 GB of disk space is required to complete the installation.

Ordinarily, you start the installation from a DVD image that you downloaded from the VMware website. But you can also use a USB flash drive if the server's BIOS is capable of booting from USB devices. Finally, you can start the installer via a Preboot Execution Environment (PXE) boot from one of the server's network cards. PXE booting is invoked when the server starts and is going through its Power On Self Test (POST). Usually a particular keystroke is required; or, often, if a server doesn't find a suitable bootable image on one of its storage devices, it will automatically try to find a PXE server. The network card broadcasts, looking for a response from a suitable PXE server. If discoverable, the PXE server replies to requests and can be configured to offer up the ESX installation media as a bootable device. PXE servers offer a convenient solution to centrally storing installation media in a LAN environment. If you have several servers in one location, you can use PXE-based ESX media depots to speed up installations, because each server doesn't need to be physically touched as it's built (or rebuilt). However, if you have several sites with WAN interconnects, you need a PXE server at each location. Installing an OS of several hundred megabytes over a WAN link is impractical. Such an installation would be slow, would saturate the WAN link, and would probably fail before it finished.

In addition to initiating the installer from several possible sources, you can store the files to be installed in a remote central location. This *media depot* can be accessed via FTP, HTTP, HTTPS, or NFS. This allows you to use a single image for all installations. You can update the install files to the latest version, add new drivers/tools/scripts, and perform extra customizations just once, in a single place.

Whether you start the installation from DVD, USB flash drive, or PXE boot, and regardless of where the files for the install reside, the installation can be either interactive or scripted.

INTERACTIVE INSTALL

In an *interactive install,* you select the answers to different options at the server's console (or via a remote hardware console such as iLO, RSA, or a DRAC card) while the software is being set up. By default, when the installer starts, it launches into a GUI setup routine, which is based on Red Hat's anaconda installer common to Red Hat Enterprise Linux (RHEL), Community Enterprise Operating System (CentOS), and Fedora installs. Figure 2.2 shows the GUI installer. It's a wizard-based installation routine, which prompts you for answers on each page.

If the server has issues displaying the interactive GUI install routine, you can opt for a text-based installer. During the installer startup, a screen opens in which you can choose various boot options. At this stage, if you enter **TEXT**, the installer runs in text mode as opposed to the GUI version. The installation options from that point on are the same as in the GUI installer. Figure 2.3 shows the format of the text-based installer.

```
volume:   datastore1
   type     size      mountpoint
   swap     600 MB    (no mount point)
   ext3     2.00 GB   /var/log
   ext3     5.00 GB   /

Do you want to change the partition layout?

1) Keep
2) Change
<) Back
?) Help
!) Exit

> 2
Service Console Virtual Disk Image--------------------------------
Type of partition change:
1) Create a new partition
2) Edit an existing partition
3) Delete an existing partition
4) Reset (discard modifications)
<) Back
?) Help

>
```

Normally, the GUI installer is the best option, because it's easiest and quickest. But the text-based mode is useful in some circumstances. Occasionally, the anaconda installer can't detect the video card correctly or doesn't have the required drivers. Also, if the installation is being done via a remote console card, and the WAN connection is particularly constraining (for example, a satellite link), then it may be easier to use the text installer, which doesn't need complex screen refreshes. The text installer is also useful if the KVM connected to the server doesn't have access to a working mouse. You can navigate the GUI installer with keystrokes such as the Tab key and the spacebar, but this technique isn't intuitive to some users; often, they prefer to reboot and restart the installation in text mode.

SCRIPTED INSTALL

A scripted install can produce the same result as an interactive install. The difference is that you provide the answers for the installation options in a text file and feed that to the installer at the start. This is similar to an answer file that Windows installations can use. The scripted install process is based on the Red Hat kickstart format, although there are differences that are particular to ESX.

Kickstart file-scripted installations provide several benefits:

◆ Provides a perfectly repeatable process, should you need to rebuild the server

◆ Makes it faster to build and rebuild a server

◆ Creates a standardized build that can be applied to multiple servers

◆ Provides additional installation options

The last point is worth highlighting. Most vSphere architects and engineers will recognize the upsides of creating scripted OS installs; but with the ESX scripted install, you can create a more customized partitioning scheme than is available with the regular interactive install.

When you combine a kickstart script with a PXE boot-installer startup and a centralized media depot, then a practically hands-free install is possible. Obviously, some effort is required to set up, test, and suitably customize each part to make this work, so these types of build environments are best suited to larger enterprises that will be provisioning tens or hundreds of servers. As usual, you must weigh the benefits of a scripted build against the development time required to create one.

A couple of community-driven projects aim to simplify the PXE server, media depot, and kickstart scripts. Both projects are very similar but offer a slightly different experience. They're freely downloadable virtual appliances that provide web-based consoles to create customized scripted builds:

◆ ESX Deployment Appliance (EDA): http://www.virtualappliances.eu/

◆ Ultimate Deployment Appliance (UDA): http://www.ultimatedeployment.org/

INSTALLATION CHOICES

Whether you're installing interactively or via a kickstart script, the options are largely the same. You have several choices, such as keyboard type and time zone, which should be fairly obvious. But from a design perspective, three options in particular need further discussion.

IP Address

During the install, you can allow DHCP to configure the network settings for you, or you can specify a static IP address. It's always advisable to use static IP addresses for ESX hosts with the corresponding hostname registered in DNS, because so many functions rely on name resolution and dependable IP connectivity. However, you may prefer to use DHCP reservations to assign the same DHCP leased address to the server via its MAC address. Using purely dynamically leased DHCP addresses, which have the potential to change regularly, isn't advisable for ESX servers.

Installation Location

Ordinarily, the ESX OS is installed on the first local disk volume. The installation needs a minimum of 10 GB, although you can allocate more space to the OS. The remaining disk space can be used for a local Virtual Machine File System (VMFS) datastore, which can house VMs, templates, ISOs, and so on.

A second option for ESX is to install the OS to boot from SAN. This configuration allows for diskless servers, which are particularly popular in blade environments, and eliminates the maintenance associated with local server disks. Each server needs to have its own logical unit number (LUN), which should be zoned off to that single host. ESX supports booting from a supported Fibre Channel (FC) host bus adapter (HBA), Fibre Channel over Ethernet (FCoE) Converged Network Adapter (CNA), or an iSCSI SAN via a hardware iSCSI HBA. You can't boot from an NFS device.

Booting from SAN provides some advantages such as making the servers cheaper to purchase; using SAN disks, which have greater consolidation and greater failure protection; and making the servers practically stateless so a failed server can be replaced and re-pointed to the SAN LUN. But a number of issues remain, which you should consider before choosing this approach:

- Boot-from-SAN configurations are more complicated to configure, requiring individual fabric zoning for each server and potentially complex HBA/CNA configuration.

- SAN storage is more usually more expensive than server disks, so any saving on server storage is lost on the extra SAN disks.

- A SAN LUN needs to be provisioned and managed for every server, which can create significant additional work for a storage team.

- Periods of heavy Service Console disk I/O can affect the VM's disk performance, because they share the same disk I/O channels.

- VMs configured with Microsoft Clustering (MSCS or Failover Clustering) aren't supported on boot-from-SAN configurations.

Partitioning

ESX partitioning changed significantly with vSphere 4. Only three physical partitions are created: a boot partition, a vmkcore partition, and a logical VMFS partition that holds a special Virtual Machine Disk Format (VMDK) file. This VMDK file, `esxconsole.vmdk`, holds all the additional partitions associated with the Service Console. Table 2.1 shows the default partitioning scheme used. The rest of the space on the VMFS volume is available for use like any other datastore.

TABLE 2.1:   Default ESX partitioning

MOUNT POINT	FORMAT	DEFAULT SIZE & VMWARE RECOMMENDATIONS	LOCATION
/boot	ext3	1100 MB	Primary partition
	vmkcore	110 MB	Primary partition
/vmfs	vmfs3	Fills remaining first disk	Logical partition
/(root)	ext3	5 GB (default minimum, may be larger)	In esxconsole.vmdk file
	Swap	Varies according to server's RAM (recommended minimum 600 MB, maximum 1600 MB)	In esxconsole.vmdk file
/home	ext3	Optional; recommended 512 MB	In esxconsole.vmdk file
/tmp	ext3	Optional; recommended 1024 MB	In esxconsole.vmdk file
/usr	ext3	Optional; no size recommended	In esxconsole.vmdk file
/var/log	ext3	Optional; recommended 2000 MB	In esxconsole.vmdk file

It's possible to change the partitions in the esxconsole.vmdk via the GUI or text-based install, but the physical partitions can only be changed via a scripted install. One customization you can incorporate in an installation's design using a scripted install is to cut the default VMFS partition short. By creating this partition so it's just large enough to accommodate the esxconsole.vmdk file, and creating a second VMFS partition for use with VMs, you protect the Service Console's VMDK file by isolating it. This way, no thin-provisioned VMs or wayward snapshots can inadvertently fill the datastore housing the Service Console. This in itself is one of the justifications for using a scripted install.

In addition to the default partitioning, you can apply the following changes. They use extra disk capacity, but local disk space is normally abundant, and a few extra gigabytes to protect the Service Console's partitions is usually justified:

/home   Consider increasing this, particularly if a number of administrators are likely to log on to the Service Console regularly.

/opt   Additional software packages often install themselves here and use this partition for logging, so it's advisable to segregate this onto its own partition.

/tmp   This partition has lots of uses and is often a dumping ground for files. vCenter Update Manager (VUM) is configured by default to stage its patches here and can use up several gigabytes. It's recommended that you make this at least 5 GB.

/var   Despite the default partition split of /var/log in table 2.1, it's sensible to use /var as a mount point instead. Several other things can accumulate in /var beyond the /var/log directory, that can cause the root partition to fill to capacity.

Swap   The maximum swap partition allowed is 1600 MB, and it's common practice to increase it to its maximum size. Any additional Service Console agents use extra memory, and VMware recommends having this swap partition set to twice the size of the allocated Service Console memory. It's easier to create this as large as possible from the outset, even if you don't initially increase the memory allocation, because growing the partition later is much more complicated and may require a rebuild of the OS.

Post-Installation Design Options

From a design perspective, a number of configurations are important for your deployed hosts. You can include many of these in the post-install section of a kickstart script, use a separate shell or PowerShell script, push them out through host profiles, or configure them manually. But you should set these — as your host design isn't complete without them.

Here is a list of common post-install tasks that you may consider for an ESX server deployment:

User Permissions   There are several options here. You allocate permissions to most users via vCenter Server, but you can also create local user accounts. Local user accounts are obviously important if the design won't have access to a vCenter, but their management doesn't scale well past a handful of users and servers. With vSphere 4.1, VMware introduced a more robust Active Directory (AD)-integrated authentication solution for local access, which is discussed in much more depth in Chapter 9, "Designing with Security in Mind." Local host access is important if users will connect directly to the host's Service Console via the vSphere Client or Web Access.

Service Console Memory   As mentioned previously, a common post-install configuration change across ESX hosts is to increase the Service Console memory allocation to the maximum value of 800 MB. This can prevent issues caused by third-party agents using excessive memory and impacting the Service Console's normal operations. The extra memory is worth it for additional protection, if the server has a suitably large amount of RAM.

Networking   Post install, you should configure the host's networking for vMotion, fault tolerance (FT) logging, NFS or software iSCSI connections, VM port groups, and so on. Chapter 5, "Designing Your Network," looks carefully at host networking design.

Storage   Post install, you also need to configure the host's storage and the connections. Chapter 6, "Storage," examines host storage design.

NTP   You should configure the ESX server to point to an external time source or Network Time Protocol (NTP) server. Various aspects of the Service Console rely on accurate time, such as logging, HA, AD authentication; and VMs can use the Service Console's time to synchronize their time via the VMware tools applet.

Patching   After you deploy an ESX server it is an opportune time to make sure all the latest patches are applied, before you launch the server into production.

Connecting to vCenter   If licensed for vCenter, you need to add the host to the datacenter, folder, or cluster of your choice. Connecting the ESX host to vCenter automatically creates the local vpxuser account and installs the vmware-vpxa daemon. Depending on the location and settings in vCenter, additional software such as HA's aam daemon may be configured at this stage as well.

Licensing   Each ESX host needs a valid license key. The server will run in evaluation mode for the first 60 days, after which a license is required. Ordinarily, vCenter is used to centrally manage the license keys; when the host is added to vCenter, you can apply the license. But if no vCenter is available, you can apply license keys directly through the vSphere Client. ESX hosts are licensed by the number of physical sockets used in the server.

Enable Web Access   Beginning with vSphere 4.0, VMware decided to disable the ESX host's Web Access by default, citing security reasons. The tool isn't used much anymore, and any web-based access increases potential vulnerabilities that can lead to a host being compromised. It isn't recommended that you enable it, but some administrators like to be able to access it. If the vCenter server is virtualized, you may want Web Access to fall back on as a GUI tool to restart the VM. A better practice is to leave it disabled and only enable it when it's required.

Firewall Ports   Finally, you may need to open a number of ports if your hosts and other infrastructure pieces are divided with firewalls. Don't confuse this with the Service Console's local security settings (iptables). The primary ports required are listed in Table 2.2. Other ports that may be required are: 21 FTP, 88/389/464 AD and LDAP, 161/162 SNMP, 445 SMB, 514 syslog, 5988 CIM, 111/2049 NFS, 3260 iSCSI, 2050-2250/8042-8045 HA, and 8100/8200 FT. You can find an excellent firewall ports diagram showing the relationship between the vSphere items at `www.vreference.com/firewall-diagram`.

TABLE 2.2:   ESX host firewall requirements

PORT	SOURCE	DESTINATION	DIRECTION RELATIVE TO HOST	PROTOCOL	ESX PORT	DESCRIPTION OF ESX SERVICE
22	SSH client	ESX server	Inbound	TCP	Service Console	SSH access to server
53	ESX server	DNS servers	Outbound	UDP	Service Console	Name resolution
80	vSphere Client	ESX server	Inbound	TCP	Service Console	HTTP access
123	ESX server	NTP	Outbound	UDP	Service Console	NTP (time)
427	Other hosts and vSphere Clients	ESX server	Inbound	UDP	Service Console	Service location (SLPv2)
427	ESX server	Other hosts and vSphere Clients	Outbound	UDP	Service Console	Service location (SLPv2)

TABLE 2.2: ESX host firewall requirements (continued)

PORT	SOURCE	DESTINATION	DIRECTION RELATIVE TO HOST	PROTOCOL	ESX PORT	DESCRIPTION OF ESX SERVICE
443	Other hosts, vSphere Clients, and vCenter	ESX server	Inbound	TCP	Service Console	HTTPS access
902	Other hosts, vSphere Clients, and vCenter	ESX server	Inbound	TCP	Service Console	Authentication, provisioning, and migration
902	ESX server	Other hosts and vCenter	Outbound	UDP	Service Console	Authentication, provisioning, and migration
903	vSphere Clients	ESX server	Inbound	TCP	Service Console	VM console
5900-5964	vCenter	ESX server	Inbound	TCP	Service Console	Management tools (VNC)
5900-5964	ESX server	vCenter	Outbound	TCP	Service Console	Management tools (VNC)
5988, 5989	vCenter	ESX server	Inbound	TCP	Service Console	CIM updates
5988, 5989	ESX server	vCenter	Outbound	TCP	Service Console	CIM updates
8000	Other hosts	ESX server	Inbound	TCP	VMkernel	VMotion requests
8000	ESX server	Other hosts	Outbound	TCP	VMkernel	VMotion requests

ESXi Design

The ESXi hypervisor shares many common elements with its older big brother ESX classic, but the main differentiator is that the Linux-based Service Console has been stripped out. ESXi retains VMkernel and VMM components similar to ESX, but it has additional features built into the VMkernel; a new, much smaller management console; and other user-mode processes to replace the old Service Console OS functionality.

ESXi was redesigned this way to allow VMware users to scale out through a hypervisor that was more akin to a hardware appliance. The vision was a base OS that is capable of autoconfiguring itself, receiving its settings remotely, and running from memory without disks. But it's also an OS that's flexible enough to be installed on hard disks, along with a locally saved state and user-defined settings, for smaller, ready-to-use installations that don't require additional infrastructure.

Removing the Service Console obviously had an impact. A number of services and agents that were normally installed had to be rethought. The familiar command-line interface with its access to management, troubleshooting, and configuration tools is gone in ESXi. The Linux-styled third-party agents for backups, hardware monitoring, and the like must be provisioned in different ways.

ESXi Components

The ESXi OS is built on three layers. It achieves the same VM environment as ESX classic, but it has some significant architectural differences:

VMkernel Just as with ESX classic, the VMkernel sits at the foundation of ESXi. It shares the same code base as ESX, but it's built specifically for ESXi. It's a 64-bit microkernel POSIX-styled OS, designed by VMware to be not a general-purpose OS but one specifically tuned to operate as a hypervisor.

VMkernel Extensions In additional to the VMkernel itself, there are a number of special kernel modules and drivers. These extensions let the OS interact with the hardware via device drivers, support different file systems, and allow additional system calls. Whereas in ESX classic you can install arbitrary third-party agents and drivers, ESXi allows only authorized code, and these modules have to be digitally signed by VMware. This restriction on VMkernel extensions helps to secure the environment, preserve system resources, and maintain a tight codebase.

Worlds VMware calls its schedulable user spaces *worlds*. These worlds allow for memory protection and sharing as well as CPU scheduling, and define the basis of privilege separation. There are three types of worlds:

System Worlds System worlds are special kernel-mode worlds that can run processes with system privileges. For example, processes such as idle and helper run as system worlds.

VMM Worlds VMM worlds are user-space abstractions that let each guest OS see its own x86 virtualized hardware. Each VM runs in its own scheduled VMM world.

User Worlds User worlds are any processes that don't need to make calls with the privileges afforded to the system worlds. They can make system calls to the VMkernel to interact with VMs or the system itself.

Importantly — and something that differentiates ESXi from many common OSs — is the fact that because the entire OS is loaded into memory when it boots up, these user-space worlds are never swapped to disk. However, you can control these worlds via resource pools much the same as VMs. They have CPU and memory reservations, shares, and limits. This presents one advantage over ESX classic, where the Service Console runs as one world and a single Service Console agent using excessive memory can affect other processes. This is why Service

Console memory is often increased to the maximum amount, to try to prevent the hostd process from being swamped. With ESXi, these processes are better protected.

ESXi Agents

Many of the agents and daemons that run in the Service Console in ESX classic have been converted to run directly on the VMkernel in ESXi. There are replacement VMkernel processes for some of the Service Console's daemons, such as hostd, vpxa, snmp, syslog, and ntpd. In addition, three new processes have been introduced in ESXi that are particularly relevant to comparative discussions:

DCUI   The Direct Console User Interface (DCUI) is the BIOS-style yellow interface that opens on the server's console screen. It lets you set basic configuration, permit access, and restart management agents.

CIM Broker   The Common Information Model (CIM) broker provides agentless access to hardware monitoring via an externally accessible API. This reduces reliance on third-party hardware agents and SNMP.

TSM   Technical Support Mode (TSM) was introduced in ESXi 4.0 but was hidden, and its use was unsupported. In ESXi 4.1, it was made more accessible, and it's now a supported management tool. It provides a very slim-line replacement for some of the command-line tools available on the Service Console.

These three processes will be examined in more depth later in the chapter, to show the effect the new tools can have on a design based around the ESXi hypervisor.

ESXi System Image

Before we explain the installation and deployment options of an ESXi design, it's important for you to understand the structure of the ESXi image. The *system image* is a bootable image that is loaded into memory and runs the hypervisor. The installer uses this same system image to copy the files onto a bootable device for future boots. On its first boot, the image auto-discovers the hardware and runs an autoconfiguration based on the type of installation used. The system image can boot from CD, PXE, USB storage, local disk, FC, or iSCSI SAN.

Because the system image is loaded into memory, it doesn't rely on its boot device when it's running. This means the boot device can fail or become disconnected, and the OS will continue to run. Changes that are made to the file system but that don't modify the system image are lost after a reboot. All added components and configuration changes must update the image in order to be persistent, or must be reloaded each time.

In addition to a handful of files used to bootstrap ESXi, an ESXi image includes two main sets of files:

VMkernel Executives   The VMkernel executives are the compressed files that make up the VMkernel. You can recognize them by their .gz file extension. These files don't show up in the file system after ESXi is loaded.

Archive Files   The archives are the files that make up the visible file system. They're VMware Installation Bundle (VIB) files with a .vgz or .tgz file extension. As each archive is extracted, it's overlaid onto the file system. As archives are consecutively laid down, only the latest changes are visible. If an archive is removed, then the previous branch is visible in the file system.

Server vendors and OEM hardware manufacturers can supply their own archive files to extend special support for their hardware, including drivers and CIM plug-ins.

The last archive to be overlaid is called the *state archive* (state.tgz). This archive contains all the configuration settings, such as the /etc files. To save excessive wear on the boot disk, which may be flash based, the state archive file is updated only every 10 minutes. This means some recent changes may not survive a reboot. This state archive tardisk forms the basis of the backup and restore routines.

The system image can also contain additional files such as copies of the vSphere Client and VMware tools for different guest OSs.

ESXi Flavors: Installable and Embedded

ESXi comes in two flavors, which dictates how it can be deployed. ESXi Installable is currently the most common and allows you to install this hypervisor on your own server hardware. ESXi Embedded is an OEM option that you can purchase preinstalled on new servers.

The following section discusses ESXi Installable and ESXi Embedded and focuses on the primary differences from ESX classic. These elements affect the design of a host deployment and your selection of hypervisor. This section won't try to cover aspects that are common to both ESXi and ESX classic.

ESXi INSTALLABLE

ESXi Installable is the version of ESXi that you install yourself to run on a server. It doesn't come pre-embedded on the hardware. Various options exist for the installation; and despite the name, you can boot and run it without installing it to a local drive.

Hardware Requirements

As with ESX classic, the hardware should match the required specifications, and all the components should be verified as supported on the HCL. The server should have 64-bit x86 CPUs with a minimum of 2 GB of RAM.

Installation

When you install ESXi, several factors determine how the image is deployed, and these are similar to ESX classic. The one significant difference is that the system image is copied to the install location, and no installation per se is required. This makes the process significantly faster than a regular ESX classic install. The following explains the design factors in an ESXi Installable deployment:

Booting the Installer   You can start the ESXi installer from several locations. The most common method is to download the installer, create a bootable CD, and start booting the server from the CD. But the server can also boot from USB (as long as the server's BIOS supports this) or PXE boot from a network card.

Image Location   When the installation process begins, normally it copies the system image from which the installer booted. But you can use the installer to deploy an image from a different location by changing the boot flag options. Supported repositories for the image location are CD, USB flash drive, FTP, HTTP, HTTPS, and NFS export.

Installation Instructions   Since vSphere 4.1, you can run the installation in interactive mode or script it via a kickstart file (vSphere 4.0 didn't have a scripted install option). Interactive mode, which is the default installation method, is a simple text-based routine. Alternatively, you can specify a kickstart file that answers the installation options automatically. The kickstart syntax for ESXi is similar to that for ESX classic but excludes some options that aren't appropriate. The kickstart script file can be located on a CD, USB flash drive, FTP, HTTP, HTTPS, or NFS export.

Destination   The system image can be deployed to several locations. Ordinarily, you deploy it to a local hard drive or USB flash drive.

With the introduction of vSphere 4.1, you can also install the system image on a SAN LUN. The SAN LUN can be FC, FCoE, or iSCSI. But as opposed to ESX classic, which can only boot from an iSCSI LUN if you're using an independent hardware initiator, ESXi can only boot from an iSCSI LUN if you use a software initiator and the network card supports an iSCSI Boot Firmware Table (iBFT). The iBFT format allows the iSCSI parameter to be saved in the network card's onboard memory.

Another possible destination is to boot the server from a PXE location. Because the image is relatively small, you can boot from the network every time. This is different from a boot-from-SAN scenario, where the image is installed in a dedicated storage LUN. Booting from PXE means the server is truly diskless, because it has no access to a writable boot disk after it has started. At the time of writing, this feature is still classed as experimental, and as such support from VMware is on a best-effort basis. But this is a significant enough feature to discuss in this section, because it provides insight into the direction that VMware envisages future large-scale vSphere deployments following.

Stateless Installation

In a *stateless installation*, the system's state isn't persisted on the ESXi server. The state archive file that's resaved every 10 minutes is saved to a volatile ramdisk. If an ESXi server is configured as diskless (remember, boot-from-USB flash drive or boot-from-SAN doesn't qualify as diskless), then it will also be stateless by default. If the server has a writeable boot disk, then by default it will be stateful and save the state archive. However, these defaults are configurable: by using boot options, you can force a diskless server to be stateful by using remote storage, or a diskful server to be stateless.

Why would you want a server that forgets all its settings every time it reboots? Stateless servers normally receive their state from a central authority, which makes hardware much more interchangeable and allows for easy redeployment. In the same way that you can consider hosts to be compute resources that you give to the cluster to be distributed to VMs, you can imagine the ability to automatically *rebuild* hosts in minutes en masse to suit new cluster configurations with new network and storage settings. The likely method to provision this environment uses servers configured for PXE boot, with an IP address set via a DHCP reservation, and the vCenter set via a small prebuilt custom state tardisk on the image depot. After boot, you could push down the server's configuration via vCenter's host profiles.

ESXi Persistence

ESXi is loaded into memory when it boots up, and runs from RAM. In memory, it uses tardisk archives that are static files, and ramdisks that grow and shrink as they're used. In addition to the tardisks and ramdisks, you can configure a number of disk partitions.

A *scratch partition* is a 4 GB virtual FAT (VFAT) partition that's created by default if a local disk is found on the first boot. The scratch partition persists the state archive and captures running state files such as logs, core dumps if the server unexpectedly crashes (on ESX classic servers, this is stored in the vmkcore partition), and diagnostic bundles that you can create if you're troubleshooting an issue. You can make the scratch partition sit on a VMFS or NFS volume if the server is diskless. If the scratch partition doesn't exist, the scratch directory is redirected to /tmp on a ramdisk. This means the contents of the scratch partition won't survive a reboot. It also means that up to 4 GB of RAM can be committed just with these files.

The bootbank partition is the system image on the file system. If there is a writable boot device, it stores up to two bootbank copies. Only one of the two is mounted in the file system in the /bootbank directory; the second is used during upgrades to keep a second backup image in case of problems.

The /locker directory stores the vSphere Client and VMware tools if there is a disk to store them.

Table 2.3 shows where the scratch, locker, and bootbank directories are stored, depending on whether the server is diskful/diskless and stateful/stateless.

TABLE 2.3: ESXi persistent storage options

	DISKFUL (WRITEABLE BOOT DEVICE)	DISKLESS (NO WRITEABLE BOOT DEVICE)
STATEFUL (SCRATCH CONFIGURED)	/scratch ➤ 4 GB scratch partition /locker ➤ boot disk /bootbank ➤ boot disk	/scratch ➤ 4 GB scratch partition /locker ➤ 4 GB scratch partition (but no tools or client saved) /bootbank ➤ /tmp (ramdisk)
STATELESS (SCRATCH NOT CONFIGURED)	/scratch ➤ /tmp (ramdisk) /locker ➤ boot disk /bootbank ➤ boot disk	/scratch ➤ /tmp (ramdisk) /locker ➤ /tmp (ramdisk) (but no tools or client saved) /bootbank ➤ /tmp (ramdisk)

Vendor-Specific Images

The main server vendors produce their own customized images. These images are enhanced versions of the regular VMware images, with hardware-specific additions. They can include new or improved hardware drivers, extra CIM plug-ins to provide better hardware monitoring, and added support information.

Scaling Deployments

From the myriad of options, you can choose many different ways to deploy ESXi Installable. A small company with only a handful of host servers is likely to opt to manually install each server using a bootable CD and the interactive install routine. As the company grows and the level of automation increases, the company is likely to look at kickstart files to script the installs.

In companies with most servers in one location, or locations with good WAN links, then PXE boot servers are a convenient way to centralize the image. This approach combined with kick-start scripts allows for a scalable option, providing quick and centrally managed install points. The largest companies, with vSphere Enterprise Plus licensing, usually consider automated post-install methods to make initial configurations and maintain these environments through policies. As stateless deployments become more common and better supported, this is the way such companies will be able to scale up to very large implementations.

ESXi Embedded

ESXi Embedded is a version of ESXi that server vendors can sell onboard their equipment at the time of purchase. The ESXi image is preinstalled as firmware in the factory or burned to a USB flash drive and installed in an internal USB socket on the main system board. Usually, the ESXi image includes the hardware drivers and CIM plug-ins that vendors provide in their custom-ized versions of ESXi Installable. The software is installed out of the box and is only awaiting setup details after it's first powered on.

The important point is that everything else about the image is the same. The hardware may vary, the manufacturer's warranty and support details may be different, but the software image of ESXi Embedded is the same image used in ESXi Installable.

But ESXi Embedded is only an option on new hardware. You can't retroactively add it to an existing server. That said, because the image is the same, by installing ESXi Installable to a USB flash drive, you're effectively getting the same thing.

Comparing Installable and Embedded

If you're procuring new server hardware and have decided on ESXi, then what is the difference between ESXi Installable and Embedded?

Advantages of ESXi Installable

◆ You can use Installable across all your existing servers, so you have a unified installation method and can continue to purchase the same hardware as before.

◆ Installable's HCL is much more extensive, meaning you have more choices to customize the hardware to your exact requirements.

◆ Servers bought for Installable can be repurposed in other server roles, because you know they're off-the-shelf servers.

◆ Servers that were purchased for Installable are likely to have local disks, meaning they can be diskful and stateful if required.

Advantages of ESXi Embedded

◆ No installation is required.

◆ Servers are potentially cheaper, because manufacturers don't need to configure them with RAID cards and local disks.

◆ Servers have an appliance-style nature, so you know all hardware will work out of the box and be fully supported.

ESXi Management

ESXi differs from ESX classic in the way that it's managed. With the removal of the Service Console, many of the methods and tools used previously aren't applicable or no longer exist. These differences fundamentally affect your design of a vSphere environment, how it will be maintained, and therefore your hypervisor choice.

COMMON MANAGEMENT TOOLS

Before we describe any alternate management techniques, note that many familiar ESX tools are available and compatible with ESXi:

vSphere Client The vSphere Client connects to an ESXi host directly in the same way it would to an ESX classic host. When directly connected, it uses the local ESXi accounts. All the same functionality is available, but small differences exist in the configuration section to account for the underlying difference in hypervisors.

vCenter ESXi hosts can join vCenter servers alongside ESX hosts. vCenter treats the hosts the same and allows them to mix in the same clusters, use the same licensing, apply the same permissions, create the same alarms, and provide the same monitoring capabilities. In vCenter, it isn't obvious what hypervisor a host is running unless you first select it and look carefully at its object description and details. Just as with a directly connected client, vCenter shows the appropriate configuration sections applicable to ESXi.

vCLI and vMA The vSphere command-line interface (vCLI) is a Perl-based set of scripts that mimics most of the commands available at the ESX Service Console. The first and most apparent difference is that instead of the normal `esxcfg-` prefix, the commands have a `vicfg-` prefix (although aliases exist for the `esxcfg-` counterparts to improve compatibility with preexisting scripts). The other major difference between vCLI commands and Service Console commands is that in the command syntax, you need to specify which host or vCenter you wish to direct the command to and with what credentials. The vCLI is packaged for both Linux and Windows.

The vSphere Management Assistant (vMA) is a small Just enough OS (JeOS) prepackaged Linux virtual appliance that comes with the vCLI already installed, ready to use. It's a convenient way to get the vCLI toolkit up and running quickly. You can also use the vMA as a syslog server for your ESXi hosts. And you can use it to run scripts, create scheduled tasks with cron, and centrally run commands to several hosts at once.

Both the vCLI and the vMA can be used against ESX and ESXi hosts and vCenter.

PowerCLI The PowerCLI is similar to the vCLI, except that instead of Perl and Unix style syntax, it's Microsoft PowerShell based. It's a toolkit that you can install on Windows PCs with PowerShell installed. You can use it to run remote commands and scripts against ESX and ESXi hosts and vCenter. Like the vCLI, it has a vibrant community around it with many sample code snippets and scripts openly available.

VUM and `vihostupdate` The two most commonly used patching tools for vSphere hosts are available for both ESX and ESXi servers. VUM is a vCenter plug-in that can scan hosts for missing updates, upgrades, and third-party driver and CIM modules, and centrally push out those patches and coordinate their installation. It's very useful for large environments where patching hosts regularly can otherwise prove to be an onerous task.

The second cross-host patching utility is `vihostupdate`, a vCLI command that you can use to update and upgrade both ESX and ESXi hosts. This is particularly useful for patching single hosts, sites with poor WAN connectivity to vCenter, and companies with no vCenter.

DCUI

The DCUI is the BIOS-styled yellow menu tool that appears on an ESXi server's console screen. Figure 2.4 shows a typical DCUI screen.

FIGURE 2.4
DCUI interface

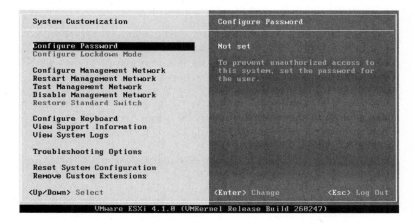

You can use the DCUI to initially configure the management network's details, set the administrative password, monitor and restart management agents, view logs locally, enable access to the TSM and turn on lockdown mode. It allows onsite first-line staff to set basic configuration options and perform rudimentary troubleshooting actions. This allows more complex configuration and management tasks to be performed remotely. The DCUI is focused on all the tasks that can prevent successful remote connections, such as network-configuration errors and failed management agents.

TSM

The TSM is a simple shell that provides a local console on which you can perform advanced troubleshooting and technical support. It isn't designed to be a full replacement for the Service Console and isn't an environment suitable for scripting or for everyday administration tasks. Regular maintenance tasks are still best executed with tools such as the vSphere Client and the vMA. In addition to local access, the tool offers remote TSM mode, which allows remote connections through SSH. Figure 2.5 shows an active logged-in local TSM session.

The TSM shell is based on a small executable called BusyBox (`www.busybox.net`). BusyBox is commonly used in embedded devices that benefit from a small POSIX-type shell with no dependencies that can run on a base Linux kernel. As opposed to a regular Linux shell made up of hundreds of binary command-line files, BusyBox is a single binary that can be called with different arguments. These arguments have hard or symbolic links that mask the executable and appear to the user to be separate programs.

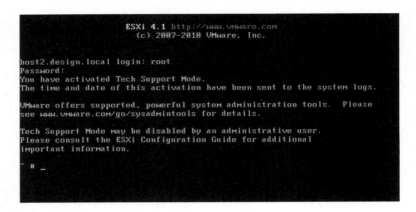

In the TSM, VMware lies on top of the BusyBox shell, the equivalent of the vCLI commands to provide all the regular ESX-style commands. The TSM isn't a regular Linux shell and doesn't give you the same environment that the Service Console does. It uses the ash shell, instead of the more common bash shell, and it doesn't include all the normal Linux commands. For example, the current ESXi TSM mode doesn't include man (manual) pages for commands. Those commands that are present may not offer the same arguments and options and so may be limited and may not operate as you expect. The TSM a very useful tool for quick break-fix situations; but due to its small size (customized for ESXi), it doesn't always work like the Service Console.

The TSM was available with ESXi 4.0 but was hidden and considered unsupported; it was reserved for VMware's technical support staff. With vSphere 4.1, it has been promoted to a fully supported option. It's disabled by default and must be turned on via the DCUI or vSphere Client before use. All commands are logged by the syslog service, so a full audit trail remains; and a timeout is available for both local TSM and remote TSM modes to ensure that no sessions stay logged in.

The TSM can be very useful if management agents are unresponsive, because at that point the vSphere Client, vCenter, vMA, or PowerCLI tools won't help. You can log in to the DCUI and try to restart the agents; if there are further problems, the TSM gives you console access to troubleshoot the issue. The TSM is usually quicker to use than some of the remote tools, so it's ideal when you need a fix as soon as possible. However, the file system presented in the TSM is formed from relatively small ramdisks; you must be careful not to copy large files to it as you may have done on a Service Console, because filling up any of the partitions is likely to make the entire server unstable. Also remember that the system's files are laid out as it boots from the system image, so files that you change or add may not survive a reboot. The TSM is a user world on ESXi and so is limited by the resource constraints that the VMkernel sets. This means the console can run out of memory if too many commands are run at once.

Local TSM and remote TSM access are both available to local users who are granted the Administrator role. The modes must be enabled for use, and access can be affected by the lockdown mode discussed later in the chapter.

BROWSER-BASED TOOLS

A notable deficiency of ESXi in comparison to ESX classic is the lack of Web Access. Web Access is a web-based console used to interact with a host's VMs. It doesn't allow any host configuration and is a fairly basic tool. In vSphere 4.0, VMware disabled it by default on ESX hosts because the company considered it somewhat superfluous and classed it as an additional security risk that didn't merit enabling. It's primarily used as a get-out-of-jail-free card if vCenter is virtualized and its residing host crashes. Some users also like to have it available because the vSphere Client is a Windows-only tool, and the Web Access console allows them to log in to a GUI tool that is available on any platform or device with a web browser. However, Web Access is very limited, so the fact that it's missing isn't considered a deal-breaker for most users of ESXi. As long as the ESXi host is attached to vCenter, then you can control VMs through vCenter's Web Access.

A nice web-based feature that is available on all vSphere hosts is a listing of the configuration files and log files. Although very simplistic, it gives a quick one-stop view of a host's settings. Figure 2.6 shows an example of the file listing, which is available through http://<hostname>/host.

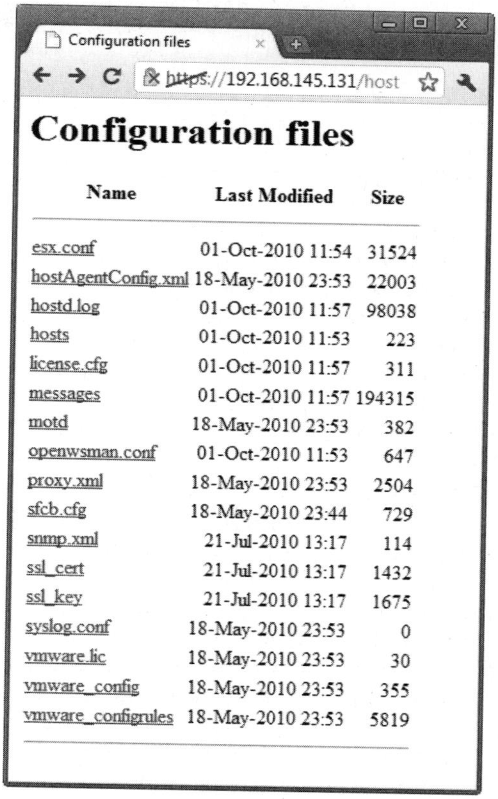

FIGURE 2.6
Web browser access to configuration and log files

Configuration files

Name	Last Modified	Size
esx.conf	01-Oct-2010 11:54	31524
hostAgentConfig.xml	18-May-2010 23:53	22003
hostd.log	01-Oct-2010 11:57	98038
hosts	01-Oct-2010 11:53	223
license.cfg	01-Oct-2010 11:57	311
messages	01-Oct-2010 11:57	194315
motd	18-May-2010 23:53	382
openwsman.conf	01-Oct-2010 11:53	647
proxy.xml	18-May-2010 23:53	2504
sfcb.cfg	18-May-2010 23:44	729
snmp.xml	21-Jul-2010 13:17	114
ssl_cert	21-Jul-2010 13:17	1432
ssl_key	21-Jul-2010 13:17	1675
syslog.conf	18-May-2010 23:53	0
vmware.lic	18-May-2010 23:53	30
vmware_config	18-May-2010 23:53	355
vmware_configrules	18-May-2010 23:53	5819

There is also a similar web-based access to view a host's datastores on http://<hostname>/folder.

Host Profiles

Host profiles are a vCenter feature that can check for and apply consistency across ESX and ESXi hosts. This feature allows you to set a standard configuration to a single host or a cluster of hosts and also automatically check for compliance to that standard. It reduces the management overhead associated with maintaining host configurations, helps to prevent misconfigurations, and alleviates some of the repetitive burden of setting up each host. Hosts must have Enterprise Plus licensing to use host profiles.

Although host profiles are just as applicable to ESX hosts as they are to ESXi hosts, they have a growing relevance to ESXi hosts moving forward. As organizations look to automatic host deployments and more stateless hosts, host profiles provide an especially useful tool to automate the post-install configuration.

Host profiles are also valuable to companies with very large numbers of hosts, to keep their settings consistent. You can create scheduled tasks in vCenter to check on host compliance. By default, a check for compliance is set to run once every 24 hours when a host profile is applied. Alarms triggers can also be applied, to alert you that profiles are being applied or non-compliance exists. You can only schedule tasks around compliance, not tasks to apply profiles.

Host profiles are particularly suited to new server installations, because this is when most of the work involving configuration-setting takes place, and host profiles work best on clusters of identical hardware. Slight differences between hardware can be tolerated, but it's advisable to start with the oldest server with the fewest hardware options (such as additional PCI cards). The profile won't work properly if the reference host has more settings configured than a recipient host can apply.

Each profile is captured from a reference host when the settings of one host that has been configured properly are recorded. You can export each profile to a file with the extension .vpf; it's a simple XML-formatted file. To modify and update a profile, you can either change the settings on the reference host and recapture the profile or use the Profile Editor in vCenter, which lets you apply more advanced options. When you use the Profile Editor to change an existing profile, it's advisable to export the original first, rename it, and import it back in. Then, you can work on a duplicate profile, test it before it's applied to an entire cluster, and still have the base profile to roll-back to.

Profiles are flexible enough to allow per-host settings, so even though most of the configuration options will be exactly same for every host, each host can vary. The options available for each setting are as follows:

Fixed Configuration   Every host will be identical.

Allow the User to Specify   Before applying a profile, the user is asked for the value. This is useful for per-server settings like hostname and IP address.

Let vCenter Pick   The best value is chosen by vCenter. This option is often used for network settings and selecting which adapters to use.

Disregard Setting   The setting will be ignored by the profile.

Although you can apply host profiles just to hosts, doing so limits its use to compliancy. To make the most of this feature, you should try to apply profiles to entire clusters. You can apply only one profile per cluster, and every host in that cluster receives it. You can't apply a profile to a host and a different one to the cluster in which it resides. If you have multiple vCenters in linked mode, then the host profiles aren't available across them. You can export a profile from one vCenter to use in another, but it won't remain synchronized.

Try to minimize the number of different configurations where possible, and group like hosts together. You can apply a profile to a mixed cluster containing VMware Infrastructure 3 (VI3) hosts. In this case, the profiles are applied to the vSphere 4 hosts, but the VI3 hosts don't have the settings applied and will fail compliance checks. To apply a profile to a host, that host must first be in maintenance mode. For that reason, you must maintain sufficient redundant capacity with the servers to apply profiles without causing VM outages. Clusters have inherent compliance checks for special features such as DRS, distributed power management (DPM), HA, and FT. You don't need host profiles to keep these settings consistent.

You can apply ESX classic profiles to ESXi hosts but not vice versa. The host profiles feature can translate the Service Console and VMkernel traffic settings to ESXi management networks, but not the other way around. Therefore, if you have clusters with mixtures of ESX and ESXi hosts, you should use one of the ESX hosts as the reference host to avoid issues.

SECURITY

vSphere security is a topic that is covered in much more depth in Chapter 9, but a couple of topics are worth mentioning as we discuss the differentiators between ESX and ESXi.

Remote Services

On ESXi servers, you can enable and disable access to certain remote access services, as you can see in Figure 2.7. This is analogous to the iptables-based `esxcfg-firewall` control in the Service Console. But you're merely specifying that listed daemons can start or stop, and the setting of their runlevels. You can't specify extra ports or alter the default listed services.

FIGURE 2.7
ESXi remote access
to services

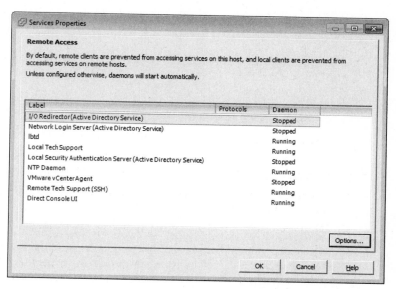

External Firewalls

The external firewall requirements of hosts are basically the same between ESX and ESXi, and Table 2.2 still applies. The one noticeable difference is that on ESXi servers, all traffic is destined for the management network, because there is no separate Service Console IP address.

Local Authentication

ESXi local authentication is very similar to that of ESX hosts. Local users are configured on a per-host basis and provided user roles akin to vCenter roles, to graduate levels of access and control. You can also join vSphere hosts to an AD domain, so authenticated users can be granted local ESXi access and use roles granted via directory-based user and group accounts.

Lockdown Mode

Lockdown mode is a vCenter feature that can increase the security of ESXi hosts by forcing all interactions through vCenter. It disables remote access, except for vCenter's vpxuser account. This means it can take advantage of the centralized nature of vCenter's roles and permissions and makes vCenter audit all remote access. The root user can still access the ESXi host locally on the DCUI interface.

Lockdown mode doesn't disable local TSM or remote TSM services, but it does prevent any user including root from accessing them because the authentication permissions are locked.

You can only enable lockdown mode on vCenter-connected hosts. It's disabled by default but can be enabled via the vSphere Client or the DCUI. Figure 2.8 shows the lockdown mode interface on the vSphere Client.

FIGURE 2.8
Lockdown mode

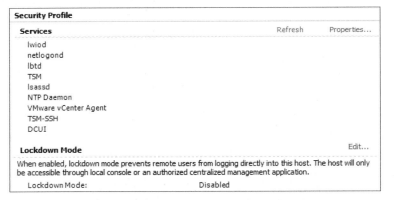

Lockdown mode on ESXi 4.0 hosts differed in that it only disabled root permissions, leaving non-root accounts unaffected. Also, 4.0 lockdown mode didn't alter TSM access. This has been strengthened in ESXi 4.1, and now all remote access for all accounts must be via vCenter. Be aware of this if you intend to upgrade ESXi 4.0 to 4.1, because lockdown behavior on the upgraded hosts won't be changed to the new model. To ensure that all your ESXi 4.1 hosts respect the tighter lockdown mode, either reinstall each host or follow one of the techniques in VMware's KB article 1017628. Table 2.4 shows how lockdown mode affects each remote-access method for 4.1 hosts.

TABLE 2.4:   Lockdown mode impact

ACCESS	DEFAULT MODE	LOCKDOWN MODE
DCUI	Root and users with admin privileges	Root only
Local TSM	Root and users with admin privileges	No access
Remote TSM (SSH)	Root and users with admin privileges	No access

TABLE 2.4:   Lockdown mode impact   *(CONTINUED)*

ACCESS	DEFAULT MODE	LOCKDOWN MODE
vSphere Client direct to host	Root and users with admin privileges	No access
vSphere Client via vCenter	Users with admin privileges	Users with admin privileges
vCLI/vMA script to host	Root and users with admin privileges	No access
PowerCLI script to host	Root and users with admin privileges	No access

Third-party monitoring software that uses the CIM broker on each host is also affected by lockdown mode. A CIM customer must connect directly to hosts to get the hardware information, but in lockdown mode it must get an authentication ticket from vCenter. This allows it to use the vpxuser credentials to gather the details from the host's CIM interface.

Lockdown mode is reversible and can be disabled on a host-by-host basis. Despite lockdown mode being disabled by default, it's worth considering enabling it across an environment during your design. If you need remote access to the host, you can temporarily disable lockdown while you perform administrative local tasks, and then re-enable it afterward. However, enabling lockdown mode via the DCUI causes the local user and group permissions to be lost. To retain these local permissions, be sure you enable lockdown mode via vCenter.

For very security-conscious settings, you can take an additional step known as *total lockdown mode*. This is a combination of enabling lockdown mode and disabling the DCUI. Access can only be granted via vCenter, preventing anyone with the root password from disabling lockdown mode locally via the DCUI. But if the DCUI is disabled, and vCenter isn't available and can't be restored, then your only recourse to gain administrative access to the host is to reinstall ESXi.

HARDWARE MONITORING

Whereas ESX relies on SNMP and third-party agents to monitor a server's hardware, ESXi's primary hardware monitoring is based on CIM. CIM is an open standard that allows information to be exchanged and can allow control of managed items. For example, Windows Management Instrumentation (WMI) is a CIM implementation, and storage vendors have a version of CIM known as Storage Management Initiative - Specification (SMI-S).

ESXi's CIM usage provides an agentless service to monitor hardware resources. It consists of two pieces: the CIM providers that allow access to particular device drivers and hardware, and the CIM broker that collects the information from all the providers and makes it available via a common API. In addition to the default VMware CIM providers for common hardware on the HCL, you can install supplementary server-vendor– and OEM manufacturer–specific CIM providers to extend the hardware-monitoring capabilities.

Because CIM is a common standard, most server-monitoring software can collect information from ESXi servers. vCenter can use the CIM information from the ESXi brokers. You can view this from connected vSphere Clients, and you can set vCenter alarms to warn of failures.

Originally, ESXi had no SNMP support, but the slow uptake of CIM-based monitoring has meant that SNMP is being added. With ESXi 4.1, SNMP traps are available. You must manually enable this feature in the TSM; currently it doesn't support "get" polling. ESXi support is for SNMP version 2, and it can optionally send information to a syslog server.

LOGGING

ESXi hosts use a slightly different structure for logging. They combine many of the logs into these three files:

◆ VMkernel: `/var/log/messages` (also includes hostd logs)

◆ Management daemon: `/var/log/vmware/hostd.log`

◆ vCenter agent: `/var/log/vmware/vpxa.log`

The collation and retention of logs is not only vital for troubleshooting host issues but also usually necessary for legal compliance reasons. It's important that you configure the hosts correctly for time synchronization with a suitable NTP time source, to ensure that the logs are accurate.

The biggest change in the way ESXi deals with its logs is related to its storage and persistence. By default, ESXi hosts store their logs in the scratch partition if one is available. If not, logs are stored in a ramdisk and therefore don't persist across reboots or crashes. In addition, via a syslog process, ESXi can store a copy either on any accessible datastore or to an external syslog server. Thus it's important in stateless configurations to redirect the logs.

You can review the ESXi logs in a number of ways:

◆ DCUI: select View System Logs

◆ TSM console (local or remote): tail each log file

◆ vMA/vCLI/PowerCLI: programmatically retrieve files

◆ vSphere Client (connected to host or vCenter): export diagnostic data

◆ Web browser: `http://<hostname>/host`

◆ Syslog server: use vMA as a syslog server

ESX vs. ESXi

The last couple of sections have discussed both the ESX classic and ESXi hypervisors in depth: their underlying architecture, methods of deployment, and basic strategies for configuring and administering them. This leaves the obvious question of which hypervisor to use and why. Both are exceptionally efficient products, very capable for their purpose, and fully supported by VMware.

This section will compare the advantages and use cases for each. It's easy to apply personal preferences and unfair presumptions to a platform. This objective analysis should help define which option to choose in differing circumstances.

Similarities

It's important to understand from the outset that ESX and ESXi have much more in common than they have differences. The underlying VMkernel and VMM software for both are based on the same code base and are extremely similar in what they provide.

When ESXi was initially released, several of the functions that everyone had grown accustomed to were missing. This left a first impression that ESXi was deficient and a lesser product. However, with each new release, VMware has folded more functionality (which would normally reside in the Service Console) into the ESXi product. With the release of vSphere 4.1, ESXi has reached a point of near feature parity. There is little left that ESXi can't accomplish compared to ESX.

The installations are obviously different, but the overarching deployment methods are very similar, with interactive and scripted installs possible. Both can be PXE booted; and the installation routines, files to install, and scripts can be loaded from similar sources. Even the kickstart-based installation scripts are relatively similar. After they're installed, the storage and networking requirements and configuration are largely the same.

Although some of the tools to monitor and troubleshoot the hypervisors are different, they both use the same terms, the same techniques, and the same skill sets. Both types of hosts connect to vCenter and are managed almost identically from there. Many of the management tools work similarly across hosts, such as the vSphere Client, vMA/vCLI, and PowerShell scripts. The APIs provided by VMware to allow third-party applications to interact, work across hosts, so many of these additional products will happily connect to either ESX or ESXi.

Existing VMs will function across either host, with the same virtual hardware being presented to the guest OS. This makes migrations between products relatively straightforward. Mixing hosts in the same vCenter cluster is also supported, so VMs can coexist across hosts and even vMotion between them; no downtime to move VMs occurs. Advanced vSphere functionality such as resource allocation, HA, and DRS is available across both ESX and ESXi.

Finally, the vSphere licensing is same across hosts, meaning you can move easily between platforms without incurring additional costs. No new budget planning is needed to transition from one to the other. You can compare each product on its own merits and not concern yourself with financial analysis. You can make the decision to use one or the other, or to migrate an existing solution from one to the other, purely on technical suitability.

When to Use ESX

VMware ESX was first released in 2001 and since then has grown to become the market leader and de facto choice of virtualization software for a company's datacenter. It's a tried and tested solution that is respected for its solid and dependable operation. When you compare ESX to any other bare-metal hypervisor (even ESXi), it's worth remembering why it became so popular. It's software that enterprise customers have come to rely upon for its uptime and stability. It hosts many tier 1 solutions in the most critical and demanding operations worldwide.

Together with the relative longevity of ESX, this means there is now a large pool of trained and experienced engineers with hands-on experience. The tools and skills to install, configure, maintain, and troubleshoot are becoming more and more commonplace. This makes it easier for companies to support ESX and also makes it more affordable to hire staff while requiring less immediate training. ESX is an accepted part of many datacenters and IT departments, and associated groups like storage and network teams are suitably versed in providing the required services.

Much of this experience is transferable and even applicable to ESXi. However, there is a perception that ESXi is a very different beast, which requires significant retraining and retooling. This is mostly unfounded these days, so this is hardly a valid reason not to choose ESXi. Nevertheless, pushing an option other than ESX is likely to face stiff opposition from some quarters, and additional justification and bargaining are a reality for a technical architect producing a vSphere design around anything other than ESX classic.

As much as VMware itself is keen to get rid of the Service Console, it's a well-loved environment for many who work with vSphere regularly. It's familiar and also very useful. ESXi does have tools that provide a certain level of equivalency, but truth be told, some are clumsy in their implementation, require additional syntax, and are deficient in certain elements. Because the

ESX Service Console is based on a fairly standard Red Hat build, many Unix and Linux engineers feel comfortable with its shell. Also, a surprising number of engineers with Windows-based experience enjoy the opportunity to use a Linux-style offering at work. With such a standard Linux base, a huge amount of documentation, training, scripts, and tools are available. This makes the platform accessible and inviting to those new to ESX.

One of the great advantages of ESX is the large collection of third-party tools available. VMware has long created a compelling set of APIs and rich developer tools to encourage a vibrant ecosphere around the product. Many developers choose to implement their solution via the Service Console. Most application vendors are migrating their tools across to newer techniques that don't rely on the Service Console, but it's still true that more tools are currently available for ESX than for ESXi.

Corporate standards often dictate software selection, and ESX is the virtualization platform of choice for most midsize to large companies. The process of introducing a replacement to the trusted status quo can require a significant amount of work. This in itself isn't a good reason not to continue to investigate other options and plump for ESX. But in the corporate world, no one will change such a fundamental piece of software overnight or without substantial justification. ESX is here to stay for a while, and it will continue to be the most commonly used hypervisor for a few years yet.

This is possibly the greatest reason for using ESX now. It has a massive user base; and although that may seem like a lame technical reason to use it, it would be foolish to underestimate the importance of its following. Despite VMware referring to the move to ESXi as a migration or transition, make no mistake: the hosts require a complete rebuild. ESXi may be just as good or even slightly better than ESX, but does that justify the effort and expense of rebuilding an entire existing environment? Not only must you rebuild the hosts, but you may also have to upgrade third-party tools prior to the move. In-house maintenance scripts and deployment methods will need to be redesigned. Until VMware gets to a point that ESXi is the only option and offers a compelling set of reasons to migrate, then most companies will be more than happy to stay with ESX.

This inertia is compounded by the fact that some pundits are waiting for better migration tools to appear. ESX 4 changed its partitioning scheme to accommodate a much larger /boot partition than was previously seen and a separate VMDK-based Service Console. Some speculate that with a future version of ESXi, this extra space on ESX 4 hosts will be used to allow a true in-place upgrade, where the Service Console settings will be combined into an ESXi install on the existing /boot space. Undoubtedly the ESXi management tools will improve, so many argue that they should hold off on any changes now and wait for an easier rollout in the future.

When to Use ESXi

VMware has openly stated for some time that ESXi is the destiny of the company's bare-metal virtualization line. With the release of vSphere 4.1, VMware made it clear that this would be the last to include ESX, and major updates will not include the Service Console. VMware even goes so far as to describe ESXi as an *upgrade* over the established ESX. The company is keen for customers to move as quickly as possible and is likely to release "4.1 plus 1" as soon as possible. The company doesn't want to have to support two platforms any longer than necessary, and the number of support calls it fields that relate to purely Service Console issues is a burden it wishes to see the back of.

ESXi Installable almost matches the HCL list of ESX, so hardware compatibility is now very similar. It isn't unreasonable to expect that as time goes on, hardware vendors and VMware will press for new equipment to be certified for ESXi first (and perhaps only ESXi). The reality is that there is no future in ESX; the sooner a business moves to ESXi, the less it will waste on developing processes around and supporting an end-of-life product.

Until vSphere 4.1, ESXi had significant feature omissions. But 4.1 brought ESXi to a more comparable level, and few things remain that can justifiably prevent it from being described as an adequate replacement for ESX. In fact, there are now several distinct technical advantages to deploying ESXi.

Although some unfairly regard ESXi as less powerful than the heavy-hitting ESX, ESXi's performance can surpass ESX. Fundamentally, ESXi has a smaller and less demanding footprint, which means the hypervisor consumes less host resources to perform essentially the same functions. ESXi also uses significantly less disk space, whether local disk or boot-from-SAN space. The Service Console of ESX hosts effectively runs as a single vCPU guest, which means all of its processes run serially. With ESXi, those functions have been moved to the VMkernel, which means there is greater scope for those processes to run in parallel using much more sophisticated scheduling.

One unequivocal advantage of ESXi's reduced code base is the greater level of security it brings. An ESX install comes in at around 2 GB of installed files, whereas ESXi currently is near 70 MB — less than 5% of ESX. It's easy to see that so much less code means less to keep secure with a smaller attack vector. During the same time frame, ESXi 3.5 required only around one-tenth the number of patches that ESX classic 3.5 needed. The Service Console provides additional software that must be secured, which ESXi avoids.

With fewer patches to apply, ESXi can reduce the frequency of host server reboots and lessen the administrative burden of regular patching. Any large enterprise with a sizable collection of ESX hosts will be only too familiar with the seemingly never-ending cycle of host patching. ESXi patches come as a single relatively small file, as opposed to ESX patches, which can be very large. Patching is also easier to manage if hosts are spread across several remote sites, particularly where slow WAN links cause issues with VUM's ability to push out these large packages. Another advantage with ESXi's patches is that they come as a single firmware-like image, which updates everything. Compare this to ESX patches, which come in multiple updates, potentially with dependencies on previous patches, and requiring multiple reboots.

An ESXi host is also arguably likely to be more reliable than an ESX classic host. It effectively has less code to go wrong and fewer processes running over and above the VMs. The ability of the Service Console to run third-party agents was a double-edged sword, because although it allowed you to add extra functionality, some of the available agents caused stability issues on hosts. The inability of ESXi hosts to run unmanaged code means this is no longer a concern. Additionally, the dual-image nature of ESXi means there is always a standby bootable copy of the OS to roll back to, should you have any problems with an update.

ESXi brings with it the possibility of running hosts in a practically stateless mode, meaning host servers become more comparable to hardware appliances. Various options exist, such as boot-from-SAN, booting from a PXE image, and applying configurations via host profiles. You can more easily switch failed hardware in and out, because replacing each individual server requires less work.

The deployment techniques available for ESXi are similar to those for ESX, but the install itself is easier. You're prompted for very little information, and the install time is incredibly short. You don't need to understand the nuances of a POSIX file system and how best to carve up an ESX's partitions. Even rebooting an ESXi server takes considerably less time than rebooting an equivalent ESX classic host.

The simplification of host management, with no need to understand a Service Console when configuring and troubleshooting, means a lower entry bar for staff to install and maintain new vSphere environments. Although a Service Console–like tool exists in the TSM, it's considerably less noticeable. The simple DCUI screen is more comparable to a BIOS setup screen and far less intimidating to staff unfamiliar with Linux. If a problem exists in a remote office, and there are no remote access cards or a KVM switch, then it's more feasible that an onsite employee may be able to assist in restarting a management daemon.

Some of the advantages of ESXi are clear and tangible, but the tipping point for any business isn't so obvious. One clear choice for ESXi deployments are so-called *greenfields*. Greenfield data-centers are typically startup companies that need brand-new IT infrastructure deployments. They have no legacy hardware or software, no dependency on older tools, and no previous processes or affiliations around ESX. This makes it easy to suggest ESXi from the outset.

But brownfields — existing companies with regular ties — can choose their moment to deploy ESXi. A good time to move forward is when an existing company wants a new vSphere deployment. Although it has existing IT infrastructure, the company may be new to virtualization. There is little point in deploying ESX from the outset. Another opportunity for brownfields occurs during hardware replacements: when a company buys new ESX servers, they can be purchased with ESXi Embedded or be set up with ESXi Installable. Many companies are still running VI3 hosts but are contemplating the upgrade to vSphere 4. Why not upgrade to ESXi in the process?

Migrating to ESXi

Designing a new vSphere deployment from scratch gives you the opportunity to decide which of the available hypervisors to use. Each has its advantages, but you're likely to use only one in a fresh setup. This makes the design task relatively straightforward.

A common project at the moment among businesses with existing vSphere environments is migrating from ESX to ESXi. These conversions undoubtedly require testing and planning, but it's important to go back to the fundamental design of your vSphere hosts to ensure that the principle objectives are still met and to determine whether any additional improvements can and should be made. Although ESX and ESXi have more commonalities than differences, it's beneficial to understand how you can transition an existing ESX design to ESXi.

The overriding difference between the two is the removal of the Service Console from ESXi. Many daemons and tools have been migrated or replaced with something similar, but differences remain. Moving to these new techniques early on can be beneficial; many of them have been backported to ESX classic to help users get used to the changes so they can begin to use them as soon as the migration process begins.

Testing

Prior to any redeployment of ESX hosts to ESXi, you should run a testing phase that looks at the existing disposition and examines whether each element is suitable for ESXi. Obviously, a pilot is a good way to test the sociability of ESXi in your existing configuration. However, it's difficult to test every possible scenario via a small pilot, because usually large enterprises have many different types of hardware, versions of hardware, connections to different network and storage devices, backup tools, monitoring tools, and so on.

It may be prudent to provide a contingency plan in case ESXi doesn't fit in a particular situation; the plan may provide financing to replace equipment, or it may specify that you keep ESX classic in that circumstance and migrate later when the equipment is due for replacement. It's feasible to mix ESX and ESXi hosts during a migration, even within the same cluster. If you are thinking of making some ESX hosts a more permanent fixture, then you may consider some of the side effects of supporting mixed hosts, such as maintaining two patching cycles, troubleshooting two types of hosts, and collecting hardware-monitoring data in different ways.

You need to look at your server hardware carefully to be sure it's compatible with and fully supported for ESXi. The HCL listing for ESXi Installable is now very close to ESX's, but it still lacks some of the older servers. At the time of writing, ESXi Installable has about 80% of the coverage of ESX. As time goes on, ESXi will undoubtedly surpass ESX; but when you're considering migrating older servers, you should check that the servers and their add-on components are listed on the HCL.

If there are hosts that you can't migrate for whatever reason, consider treating them like ESXi hosts as much as possible with regard to how you manage them. Most of the VMware and third-party tools can now connect to either type of host. You can use tools that replace some Service Console functionality, such as the vMA and PowerShell commands, to manage ESX classic hosts. You can also use ESXi tools in a mixed environment and no longer have to rely on the Service Console.

Deployment

VMware markets redeploying ESXi across a fleet of existing ESX hosts as an "upgrade." However, the transition process requires a full rebuild of each host. All settings and data are normally lost during the process, and the newly rebuilt servers must be reconfigured.

Larger companies with dedicated server staff are probably familiar with rebuilding OSs instead of upgrading them. But smaller companies that may have used external consultants to initially deploy ESX may be less prepared to run full installs across all their hosts.

If you completely rebuild the hosts, you should move all the data off any local VMFS volumes — VMs, templates, ISO files, and so on. Check the file system for files in the /home directories, /tmp, and anywhere else a local user may have saved files. Finally, you may wish to back up the files, particularly those in the /etc directory for configuration settings and the /opt directory for third-party installed agent software.

If you wish to avoid VM downtime, you must have access to shared storage and at least the equivalent spare capacity of your most powerful server in each cluster. That way, you should be able to migrate the VMs around the hosts as you remove one at a time from the cluster to rebuild it.

Fortunately, many of the deployment methods you may have used for your ESX classic hosts are re-useable. ESXi can use PXE servers you've already set up — you just need to copy the new images to the server. You need to modify ESX kickstart scripts for ESXi, but they can use largely the same syntax for the configuration; and usually you need to remove unneeded lines rather than add new lines.

Management

One of the more obvious techniques to smooth a transition is to begin using the newer cross-host management tools as early as possible. Most of the utilities currently available for ESX classic hosts work with ESXi hosts. vSphere Client, vCenter Server, vCenter Web Access, vCLI, and PowerCLI are host-agnostic and will make any transition less disruptive. There is no reason not to start working with these tools from the outset; even if you decide not to migrate at that stage, you'll be better prepared when ESXi hosts begin to appear in your environment.

The primary management loss when you replace ESX is the Service Console. This is the one tool that, if you use it regularly, it must be replaced with an equivalent. There are two main contenders: the vCLI and the TSM. The vCLI provides the same Linux-style commands as the Service Console. The easiest way to get it is to download the vMA virtual appliance. This includes a Linux shell and all the associated environmental tools you'd expect. Generally, anything you can do at a Service Console prompt, you can do in the vMA. Most scripts can be converted over to vMA command syntax relatively easily.

The second option, which became fully supported in ESXi 4.1, is the TSM. Although it's a stripped-down, bare-bones environment, it provides the majority of vSphere-specific commands that you'd otherwise find in the Service Console. Some of the more Linux-centric commands may not be available; but it provides a more familiar feel than the vMA, because it's host-specific and therefore the syntax is closer to that of the Service Console.

In addition to rewriting scripts, you'll need to replace other services that ESX includes in the Service Console. For ESXi hosts without persistent storage for a scratch partition, it's important to either redirect the logs to a remote datastore or configure the host to point to a remote syslog server. ESXi hosts don't have their own Web Access as ESX hosts do. It's unlikely that this is a regularly used feature, but if you've relied on it in certain circumstances, then you need to choose an alternative. If Web Access is a critical feature, consider using vCenter's version of it. Finally, if you've used the Service Console for host monitoring via SNMP or a server vendor's hardware agent, then you'll need to use a substitute method. ESXi has built-in CIM agents for hardware on the HCL, and many vendors can supply enhanced modules for their particular hardware. With these CIM modules, you can set up alerts in vCenter, and some third-party hardware-monitoring software can use the information. ESXi also provides some SNMP support, which you can use to replace any lost functionality of Service Console agents.

If your hosts are licensed for Enterprise Plus, host profiles can provide a convenient method of migrating host settings from ESX to ESXi. You can capture an existing ESX classic host in a cluster as a reference host, rebuild one of the servers to ESXi, and apply that profile to receive a common set of configuration settings. The new ESXi host with the cluster's profiles applied can then be the basis of a new profile that you can apply to all the other hosts as they're rebuilt. If you're migrating existing servers whose design doesn't need to change, host profiles can be an excellent time saver.

You also need to replace any third-party applications that used the Service Console. Most add-ons are now available in ESXi-friendly versions, so you should be able to continue to use the applications you rely on, although you may need to upgrade them to the latest version. Most of these tools use a common set of APIs that works equally with either host. Check with your vendors to be sure they're ESXi host compatible; if they don't offer this, consider migrating to an equivalent tool from another vendor that does.

Summary

Host design is an important foundation for any vSphere deployment. Whether you opt for the tried-and-tested ESX classic or the newer, leaner ESXi hypervisor, many design questions remain. The most important thing is the reasoning behind your host design and not the hypervisor choice. Any well-planned, modern host design should survive either hypervisor. There are far more similarities than difference between the two, and a sound architectural blueprint should fit either model with few changes.

We've discussed two key elements of host design. The first is the deployment method: how to install and configure the hosts post-install. You can use several approaches, depending on whether this is an existing vSphere or VI installation, or a fresh landscape; and depending on the scale and arrangement of the hosts. Second, the host design relies heavily on how you'll manage the hosts going forward: how to manage the hardware and the host hypervisor, how to monitor and troubleshoot, and how to secure the host.

Whether your design centers on ESX or ESXi, the deployment and management are likely to be similar. Basing your design around a single hypervisor will obviously reduce complexity and overhead and is the preferred option, but that approach may not be possible in all cases. Be flexible enough to accommodate a mixture, at least for a time. Try to ensure that regardless of which hypervisor your design uses, the deployment and management use common tools.

Chapter 3

Designing the Management Layer

In this chapter, we'll discuss the points you should take into account when you're designing your management layer. We'll examine the components of this layer and how you incorporate them into your design.

The management layer comprises several components. In this chapter, we'll address what you should consider for your design regarding these items, among others:

◆ Operating system and resources to use for your vCenter

◆ Deciding whether your vCenter should be physical or virtual

◆ Providing redundancy for the vCenter Server

◆ Planning for the security of the management layer

Components of the Management Layer

What is the management layer? It's definitely not the board of directors of your company. We're talking about the components you use to manage your entire virtual infrastructure on a day-to-day basis. Let's start with the first and main component, vCenter Server.

VMware vCenter Server

vCenter Server (which was once known as Virtual Center Server) is a Windows application that you can install on number of Windows operating systems and is one of the most centrally critical elements of your virtual infrastructure. It's the management application you'll likely use to manage your virtual datacenter. You'll create datacenters, clusters, resource pools, networks, and datastores; assign permissions; configure alerts; and monitor performance. All of this functionality is centrally configured in the vCenter Server. You should therefore dedicate part of your design to building a robust and scalable vCenter Server.

COMPATIBILITY MATRIX

Always check the current VMware compatibility matrix before deciding which platform you'll install vCenter Server on. VMware will provide support only if your Infrastructure is installed on supported software. This includes your ESX/ESXi hardware, vCenter Server, underlying database, vSphere client, update manager, and so on.

You can download the most up-to-date version of vCenter from the VMware site. It comes in two forms: an ISO image or a ZIP file. It's a relatively large package (about 1.5GB).

Choosing the Operating System for your vCenter

vCenter is a server and should be installed on a server OS. As of the time of this writing, there is no supported vCenter Server on a Linux platform. A community preview version was released because of the noise created by the community demanding such a product, but it has never taken off, and there seems to be no reason for it to do so in the future.

As of vSphere 4.1, the requirements for vCenter are a Windows 64-bit OS only, so the best design choice is Windows 2008 Server R2 64-bit. VMware has gone down this road for multiple reasons. Microsoft has declared that Windows 2008 R2 and all consequent server OSs will be 64-bit only. Gone are the days when you could install a server OS on a 32-bit OS for vCenter. However, some products are still supported on 32-bit OSs only (such as Lab Manager and View Composer). In addition, the memory barrier is too low for the 32-bit OS.

vCenter Components

A vCenter installation requires two components in order for you to get started:

- Windows OS (a domain member server — it can't be a domain controller).

- Access to a database. This can be a remote database (Oracle or Microsoft SQL/SQL Express), or it can be installed locally on the vCenter Server.

Database

One of the questions that always comes up during the design phase is, "Do I use a central database server or install the database locally on the vCenter Server?"

The perfect IT answer is, "It depends." Does a central corporate server host all your databases? Will you be installing additional databases in your organization in the future? Do you need to provide redundancy for this database server, and how will you do so?

After you've considered your options and come to the proper conclusions, you can plan the hardware resources needed for your vCenter Server.

We'll get into the specifics of these considerations later in this chapter when we deal with the ways you can provide redundancy for your vCenter Server.

Hardware Resources

It's best to consult the ESX and vCenter Server Installation Guide to size your hardware accordingly. The minimum resources required for vCenter are as follows:

- 2 CPUs (physical/virtual cores). A *processor* is defined as a 2.0GHz or faster Intel or AMD processor. The requirements may be higher if the database runs on the same machine.

- 3GB RAM. This requirement may be higher if the database runs on the same machine. VMware VirtualCenter Management Webservices requires from 128MB to 1.5GB of additional memory. The VirtualCenter Management Webservices process allocates the required memory at startup. The engine that drives these web services is Tomcat JVM.

◆ 2GB hard disk space. The requirements may be higher if the database runs on the same machine and/or if you host the Update Manager database and store the updates on that machine. While installing vCenter, you'll need up to 2GB in which to decompress the Microsoft SQL Server 2005 Express installation archive. Approximately 1.5GB of these files are deleted after the installation is complete.

◆ A gigabit network connection is recommended.

These minimum requirements are fine for a test environment and for kicking the tires. But if you already know that you'll be deploying a large number of hosts and virtual machines, you'll need more than the minimums. You shouldn't plan for the immediate need, but rather for the expected or required expansion.

The guidelines provided by VMware are listed in Table 3.1.

TABLE 3.1: Optimal recommendations for vCenter Server

	NUMBER OF CPUS	GB RAM
50 hosts and 250 powered-on VMs	2	4
200 hosts and 2,000 powered-on VMs	4	4
300 hosts and 3,000 powered-on VMs	4	8

vSphere Client

This is the interface you'll use to manage your infrastructure. It can be installed on almost any Windows OS:

◆ Windows XP Pro, SP3

◆ Windows XP Pro 64-bit, SP2

◆ Windows Server 2003, SP1

◆ Windows Server 2003, SP2

◆ Windows Server 2003 Standard, SP2

◆ Windows Server 2003 Enterprise, SP2

◆ Windows Server 2003 R2, SP2

◆ Windows Vista Business, SP2

◆ Windows Vista Enterprise, SP2

◆ Windows Vista Business 64-bit, SP2

◆ Windows Vista Enterprise 64-bit, SP2

◆ Windows 7 Client (32-bit and 64-bit)

◆ Windows Server 2008 Enterprise, SP2

◆ Windows Server 2008 Standard, SP2

◆ Windows Server 2008 Datacenter, SP2

◆ Windows Server 2008 Enterprise 64-bit, SP2

◆ Windows Server 2008 Standard 64-bit, SP2

◆ Windows 2008 R2 64-bit

The minimum resources required for the client are as follows:

◆ 266MHz or faster Intel or AMD processor (500MHz recommended)

◆ 1GB RAM

◆ 1GB free disk space for a complete installation, which includes the following components:

    ◆ Microsoft .NET 2.0

    ◆ Microsoft .NET 3.0 SP1

    ◆ Microsoft Visual J#

You'll also need 400MB free on the drive that has the `%temp%` directory during installation.

If all of the prerequisites are already installed, 300MB of free space is required on the drive that has the `%temp` directory, and 450MB is required for vSphere.

◆ A gigabit network connection is recommended.

VMware Update Manager

Update Manager (VUM) is an add-on that VMware provides in order to update your ESX hosts and VMs. VUM (`www.vmware.com/products/update-manager`) is VMware's patch-management solution for your virtual environment. It's included with most tiers of vSphere.

VUM allows you to provide a patch-management solution not only for your ESX hosts but also for all the supported VMs. VMware has declared that it will discontinue the patch-management component for the VMs in future versions, because most enterprise environments already have a patch-management solution in place and usually continue to patch their VMs the same way they patch their physical machines.

Update Manager Components

A VUM installation requires a few components in order to get started:

◆ Windows OS (a domain member server, which can be the on the same server as the vCenter Server).

◆ Access to a database. This can be a remote database (Oracle or Microsoft SQL/SQL Express), or it can be installed locally on the VUM server.

DATABASE

VUM can reside side by side with the vCenter database on the same SQL server, but it can't be the same database as the vCenter Server.

When you install vCenter Server, you create a system data source name (DSN) entry for the database. You need to create an additional DSN entry for the VUM database as well, as you can see in Figure 3.1.

FIGURE 3.1
Adding an addition ODBC connection for VMware VUM

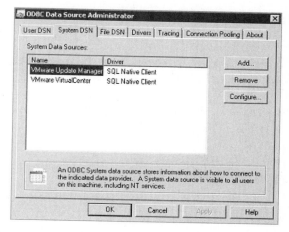

After you've installed VUM, you have to go through the stages of setting up the updates you want to download. Updates for hosts are downloaded from a repository at VMware, and updates for VMs (Microsoft and Linux) are downloaded from Shavlik (www.shavlik.com) — a security company that provides patch-management solutions of its own. You can schedule the automatic download of the patches, set up notifications, scan your ESX hosts and VMs, and update them all.

Management Applications

Logging in to each host to perform a management task — such as configuring a network vSwitch or setting the maximum number of NFS mounts you can connect on an ESX host — can be a tiresome and repetitive task. It may become a nightmare if (and when) your infrastructure grows.

Let's start with the basics. ESX has a management console. In the full ESX, it's a customized Linux kernel; and with ESXi, it's a BusyBox environment. To connect these consoles remotely, you need an SSH client. Most administrators prefer using PuTTY (www.chiark.greenend.org .uk/~sgtatham/putty). Several other tools provide the same functionality, and every administrator has a preference.

ESX and vCenter have an extensive API you can use to perform remote management. VMware provide several tools to manage vCenter and your ESX hosts remotely:

◆ vSphere command-line interface (vCLI)

◆ PowerCLI

◆ vSphere Management Assistant (vMA)

The good thing about the different tools is that you don't have to choose between them: you can use them all. Both the Perl and PowerShell platforms have dedicated followers who constantly expand the ways you can use these tools in your environment.

vCLI

The vCLI command set allows you to run common system-administration commands against ESX/ESXi systems from any machine with network access to those systems. You can run most vCLI commands against a vCenter Server system and target any ESX/ESXi system that the vCenter Server system manages. vCLI commands are especially useful for ESXi hosts because ESXi doesn't include a service console.

vCLI commands run on top of the vSphere SDK for Perl. vCLI and the vSphere SDK for Perl are included in the same installation package.

The supported platforms are as follows:

◆ Windows XP SP2 32-bit

◆ Windows XP SP2 64-bit

◆ Windows Vista Enterprise SP1 32-bit

◆ Windows Vista Enterprise SP1 64-bit

◆ Red Hat Enterprise Linux (RHEL) 5.2 (64-bit)

◆ Red Hat Enterprise Linux (RHEL) 5.2 (32-bit)

◆ SUSE Enterprise Server 10 SP1 32-bit

The commands you run on vCLI for management aren't exactly the same as the commands you can run on the ESX console, so you may have to adjust to the difference. Table 3.2 shows a couple of examples.

TABLE 3.2:   vCLI syntax as compared to console syntax

vCLI	ESX Console
`vicfg-vmknic`	`esxcfg-vmknic`
`vicfg-nics`	`esxcfg-nics`

VMware KB Article 1008194 (`http://kb.vmware.com/kb/1008194`) gives the full list of differences/similarities between vCLI commands and ESX service-console commands.

When you're connecting to a remote host, you must — at minimum — specify the following parameters: server, username, password, and command to perform. Authentication precedence is in the order described in Table 3.3.

TABLE 3.3:   vCLI authentication precedence

AUTHENTICATION METHOD	DESCRIPTION
Command line.	Password (--password), session file (--sessionfile), or configuration file (--config) specified on the command line.
Configuration file.	Password specified in a .visdkrc configuration file.
Environment variable.	Password specified in an environment variable.
Credential store.	Password retrieved from the credential store.
Current account (Active Directory).	Current account information used to establish an SSPI connection. Available only on Windows.
Prompt the user for a password.	Password isn't echoed to the screen.

Let's consider an example to see how these work. The environment is built as detailed in Table 3.4.

TABLE 3.4:   Example for vSphere environment

vCenter Server	vcenter.design.local
Username	Viadmin
Password	a:123456

You need to create a configuration file to define these settings. The file must be accessible while running your vCLI session. A session file for the configuration in Table 3.4 looks like Figure 3.2.

FIGURE 3.2
Configuration file
for vCLI

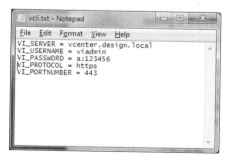

WARNING This file isn't encrypted in any way, so all passwords in the file are stored in plain text. Access to this file should be limited!

You can run your commands against the hosts defined in the configuration file without having to input the credentials each time you connect to a server. Here's an example:

```
vicfg-nas --config /home/admin/.vcli.txt -a -o storage1.design.local -s /shared
NFS_datastore1
```

`vicfg-nas` — The command to configure NFS storage (the equivalent on the Service Console is `esxcfg-nas`).

`--config` — The path to the configuration file containing your stored credentials.

`-a` — Adds a new datastore

`-o storage1.design.local` — The FQDN (you can also enter an IP) of the storage device you're connecting to.

`/shared` — The mount point you're connecting to.

`NFS_datastore1` — The name you give to the datastore.

PowerCLI

PowerShell is becoming the default scripting language for all Windows applications. Many articles explain why it's easier, better, and simpler to use PowerShell to manage your environment. The good thing is that VMware has made a strategic decision to follow suit and provide a PowerShell management environment for vCenter and ESX: PowerCLI.

PowerCLI currently has 229 cmdlets (as of Build 208462) that deal with practically all the elements of your infrastructure. You can configure and manage ESX hosts, VMs, the OSs of the VMs — more or less anything. A vibrant community is constantly developing ways you can use PowerCLI to allow administrators to perform their jobs more easily.

For a list of all the cmdlets, see the online cmdlet reference:

```
www.vmware.com/support/developer/windowstoolkit/wintk40u1/html/index.html
```

What can you do with PowerCLI? In addition to making your toast in the morning, pretty much anything. Seriously, though, anything that is exposed in the vSphere SDK, you can access (and therefore manipulate).

Just as you create in vCLI a configuration file to store your credentials so you don't have to enter them each time you connect to your vCenter/ESX host, you can do the same in PowerCLI. This isn't a unique feature of PowerCLI — it's more a PowerShell feature — but because you're using PowerShell, you can use it. Let's see how. First, let's look at the code for saving the credentials:

```
$vicredential = get-credential
$vicredential.Password | ConvertFrom-SecureString | Out-File c:\temp\viadmin.txt
$VIcred = New-Object System.Management.Automation.PsCredential "viadmin@design
.local", (Get-Content c:\temp\viadmin.txt | ConvertTo-SecureString)

Connect-VIServer -Server vcenter.design.local -Credential $VIcred
```

`Get-Credential` is a PowerShell cmdlet that lets you store credentials in an object for use without having to expose the contents of the password. Here, you store it in a variable named `$vicredential`. Next, you export the password from the variable into a text file. Don't worry, unlike in vCLI, the password isn't in plain text; rather, it looks something like this:

```
01000000d08c9ddf0115d1118c7a00c04fc297eb01000000c39f99b56e206a40a56c6e8e4ebc6ec0
000000000200000000003660000c000000010000000395d0ba992b59f39e42e30a30e9c972b0000
000004800000a0000000100000008deee87fd1ebd9d74990d6ed44d984d018000000494b8c989a3f
55018cd9b7a743450f1d09a214843fda25b4140000005226217e4587317d235557ad8e5177541859
094b
```

That is pretty hard to decipher. You export the password because you'll use this credential more than once — instead of having to insert the password each time, you can create a variable to store it. This is done in line 3: a variable named `$VIcred` is created with an already-known username, but the password is imported from the file you saved. This is what the variable holds:

```
UserName                                    Password
--------                                    --------
viadmin@design.local                        System.Security.SecureString
```

Last but not least, you connect to your vCenter Server with the credentials supplied in the variable.

After you've connected, let's use the same example as before with vCLI:

```
New-Datastore -Nfs -VMHost (get-vmhost) -Name NFS_datastore1 -Path "/shared"
-NfsHost $storage1.design.local
```

`New-datastore` — The command to configure storage (the equivalent on the Service Console is `esxcfg-nas`).

`-NFS` — Parameter for the kind of datastore (VMFS/NFS)

`-VMHost` — The host on which this will be created (in this case, all hosts registered under vCenter).

`-Name NFS_datastore1` — The name you give to the datastore.

`-Path "/shared"` — The mount point you're connecting to.

`-NfsHost storage1.design.local` — The FQDN (you can also enter an IP) of the storage device you're connecting to.

vMA

vMA is a VM appliance provided by VMware that includes prepackaged software. Administrators and developers can use vMA to run scripts and agents to manage both ESX/ESXi and vCenter Server 4.0 systems. vMA includes the vSphere SDK for Perl and vCLI). It also includes an authentication component (`vi-fastpass`) that allows a centralized direct connection to established target servers; and a logging component (`vi-logger`) that lets you collect logs from ESX/ESXi and vCenter Server systems and store the logs on vMA for analysis.

vMA is becoming much more relevant now that VMware has said that ESXi will be the only platform starting with the next version — the company is moving away from the full Service Console. The reasons (among others) are less code, a smaller attack surface, and less frequent security patches. Without the Service Console, you can't run third-party applications (which you should do only if necessary).

Sizing Your vCenter Server

You need to take the following elements into account while sizing your vCenter Server:

◆ OS

◆ Database placement

◆ Number of objects managed

◆ VUM

Operating System

vCenter can be installed on a number of OSs:

◆ Windows XP

◆ Windows Server 2003 (Standard, Enterprise, Datacenter)

◆ Windows Server 2008

◆ Windows Server 2008 R2

Starting from vSphere 4.1, these must all be 64-bit. So, if you need to implement a new vCenter Server, the recommendation is Windows Server 2008 R2 Standard.

Why not choose one of the other editions (Enterprise or Datacenter)? One limitation of a Windows 32-bit OS is that it can only support (natively) 4GB RAM. When we look at the requirements shortly, you'll see that in some cases, that isn't sufficient. Many vCenters were installed in the past with Enterprise Edition OSs to overcome that boundary. With a Standard license of Windows Server 2008 R2, you're limited to 32GB RAM, which should be more than sufficient for 95% of vCenter deployments. In addition, licensing for the higher versions of both the Windows OS and SQL Server is substantially more expensive than a standard license.

Using a Remote or Local Server

Here's a topic for endless discussion: "Where do I install the database: on the vCenter Server or on a remote server?" Let's go into the rationale behind both options.

LOCAL

Having your database *local* means you've installed it on the same OS as your vCenter. Here are some of the benefits of having all the components on one server:

Microsoft SQL Express   This is bundled with the vCenter installation. The software doesn't cost anything, but it isn't suitable for large-scale enterprise environments. vCenter is by default installed with SQL Express, so this can be suitable for test or small environments.

Full Database Installation   You can install a full database server on your vCenter Server — be it Oracle or Microsoft SQL. This provides enterprise-level functions that are suitable for a production environment.

Faster Access to the Database   Having the data local on the same box is in most cases quicker than accessing the data over the network. You don't have to go over the wire, and you're not dependent on factors such as network congestion.

An All-in-One Box   You know where your weaknesses lie. You won't be affected by other applications abusing resources on the network on the shared SQL Server.

Backup and Restore   A sound and solid backup infrastructure doesn't come cheap. Having all the components on one server saves you from having to back up multiple servers and track which part of the infrastructure is located in which part of your enterprise.

REMOTE

As opposed to local, here we're talking about installing vCenter software on one server and connecting to a database that doesn't reside on the same machine. The reasons to choose this option are as follows:

Central Database Server   You already have a central location for the databases in your organization. If this is the case, you shouldn't start spreading around additional database servers for each and every application. Your DBA won't like you.

Separation of Duties Between Databases and Applications   This is perceived as best practice. Servers have dedicated roles, and these roles should be on separate boxes. vCenter software and VUM software should be installed on one server, and the database on which these applications rely should be on a different machine. This ensures that loss of data on one of the servers doesn't cause lengthy downtime.

Corporate Policies (Separate DBA Team)   Your organization has an established database administrator. In most cases, they will probably be more knowledgeable about performance, optimization, and troubleshooting of any issues that arise in the future. So, a database installed on the central server is usually maintained in a better fashion that you could administer it on your own. The Virtual(ization) Infrastructure Admin (VIAdmin) usually gets busy very quickly and doesn't have the time or the resources to acquire the knowledge needed to manage and maintain your database server in addition to all the new duties you inherited with the system.

Fewer Resources Needed for vCenter Server   If you're going to join the roles of application and database on the same box, you need larger resources for the vCenter Server. (See the next section, "Resources.")

Providing Clustered Services (Redundancy) for the Database   SQL and Oracle can be clustered. Doing so provides resilience in case of a database server failure. You can't do this if the database resides on the same server as vCenter.

RESOURCES

Microsoft recommends 1GB minimum and 4GB for optimal performance for a SQL database server. In addition, take into account the resources needed for the vCenter service, web services, and plug-ins — you're looking at another 2–4GB RAM for the vCenter host. It's most likely that in an enterprise environment, you have a properly sized database server that can accommodate the vCenter database without any major issues.

The following article provides more information about the recommended resources for SQL:

http://msdn.microsoft.com/en-us/library/ms143506.aspx

This article explains that you need at least 1GB RAM with at least one 1.4GHz CPU. But more realistically, the recommended resources are as follows:

◆ 1 CPU, 2.0GHz and up

◆ 4GB RAM

Taking this into account, if you install both the vCenter and the database server on the same box, you need approximately 8GB RAM and at least a quad core machine.

REDUNDANCY

We'll get into this topic a bit later in the chapter. But in short, there's no point in providing a clustered solution only for one database. If you're setting up a cluster to protect the database, you may as well protect more databases at the same time. Thus it's useless to install the database locally.

Number of Objects Managed

VMware's documentation for installing and setting up vCenter provides the numbers in Table 3.5 as recommendations for optimal performance.

TABLE 3.5: Recommendations for optimal performance

	NUMBER OF CPUs	RAM (GB)	DISK (GB)
Up to 50 hosts and 250 powered-on VMs	2	4	3
Up to 200 hosts and 2,000 powered-on VMs	4	4	3
Up to 300 hosts and 3,000 powered-on VMs	4	8	3

http://pubs.vmware.com/vsp40/install/wwhelp/wwhimpl/common/html/wwhelp.htm#href=c_vc_hw.html&single=true

You can clearly see that at most, you need four CPUs and 8GB RAM. The sizing of your vCenter will depend on how big a deployment you're planning.

Update Manager

Will you be using your vCenter Server as a VUM server as well? Why does this make a difference?

In terms of CPU or RAM resources, you won't need additional resources if you don't have the SQL Server running on the vCenter Server. What you'll need is disk space. VMware provides a tool that assists in sizing your installation: VMware vCenter Update Manager Sizing Estimator:

`www.vmware.com/support/vsphere4/doc/vsp_vum_40_sizing_estimator.xls`

This is an Excel spreadsheet that requests information about your environment:

- Version of hosts you'll be patching (3.0x/3.5x/4.x)
- ESX and/or ESXi
- Number of concurrent upgrades
- Number of hosts
- Number of VMs
- OS locale
- Service pack levels
- Frequency of scans for hosts, VMs, and VMware tools

The results you get from the spreadsheet will look like Table 3.6.

TABLE 3.6:   Results from Update Manager Sizing Estimator

RESOURCE	INITIAL UTILIZATION MB	ESTIMATED MONTHLY UTILIZATION MB		
		Median	20%	-20%
Database space usage	150	133	160	107
Disk utilization — Patch Content	50	13,100	15,720	10,480

The biggest resource you need for VUM is disk space. Due to all the patches you'll download, the required disk space will increase depending on how many versions of the software you're downloading for (either version of ESX, and the different OS service packs).

It's recommended that you not install the patch repository in the default location provided during the installation (`C:\Documents and Settings\All Users\Application Data\VMware\VMware Update Manager\Data\`). Most administrators don't notice this question during the installation; then, somewhere along the way, they begin to run out of space on the C: drive of their vCenter Server, and they wonder why. It's better to allocate a separate partition and folder for the downloaded updates, for these reasons:

Backup   You don't always want to back up patches that are downloaded. The content hardly changes, and it can easily be downloaded again if needed.

Not Enough Space on the System Drive   If you aren't careful, your system drive will fill up.

DATABASE SIZING FOR VCENTER AND UPDATE MANAGER

When you follow the previous recommendations and decide to use a database server that isn't the same as the vCenter Server, you next have to plan the size of the database. Before we get into sizing, let's review the purpose of the database in a vCenter installation.

The database is the central repository of the logic and structure of your virtual infrastructure: resource pools, permissions on each item in vCenter, alarms, thresholds, the cluster structure, distributed resource scheduling (DRS), and, of course, the biggest consumer — statistics. All the statistics for every object and counter in your environment are stored in the database, including CPU, RAM, disk, network, and uptime. And each category has multiple counters associated with it.

VMware also provides the vCenter Server 4.x Database Sizing Calculator for Microsoft SQL Server:

```
www.vmware.com/support/vsphere4/doc/vsp_4x_db_calculator.xls
```

It's very similar to the calculator mentioned earlier for VUM. But in this case, a larger number of parameters are required in addition to those we've already covered:

- Number of NICS per host

- Number of NICs per VM

- Number of datastores per host

- Number of VMDKs per VM

- Number of pCPUs

- Number of vCPUs

And most important, how long will you keep each level of statistics? The configuration for this setting is set in vCenter as shown in Figure 3.3.

The higher the level of statistics collected for each interval, the larger your database will become. VMware's report "VMware vCenter 4.0 Database Performance for Microsoft SQL Server 2008" includes the recommendations in Table 3.7.

TABLE 3.7: VMware recommendations for database performance with Microsoft SQL Server 2008

STATISTICS INTERVAL	STATISTICS LEVEL
Past day	Level 2
Past week	Level 2
Past month	Level 1
Past year	Level 1

FIGURE 3.3
vCenter statistics
intervals

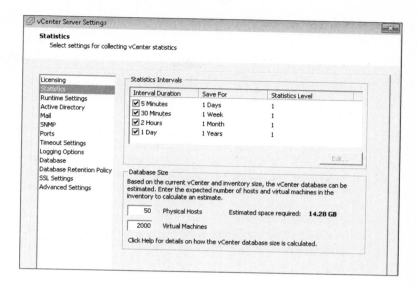

The document also provides a few additional recommendations. You need to allocate enough RAM for your database server. A good rule of thumb for all relational databases is to allocate the server as much memory as necessary to allow for the caching of all the needed data in memory. You should refer to the documentation for the amount of memory to give to the OS and any other applications that run on the server you use for your database. You should go with a 64-bit server for the same reason we mentioned earlier regarding the 4GB RAM memory limitation on Windows 32-bit OSs.

Plug-ins

Plug-ins are great. They allow you to perform all the tasks you need in one management console without having to use a multitude of tools to manage your environment.

Unfortunately, with the advantages come some disadvantages that you didn't plan for — especially the additional resources needed to run the plug-ins. You need to take into account the following resources:

♦ Disk space

♦ Memory

Let's look at two examples of when you have to consider these resources.

Guided Consolidation

Guided Consolidation is a mini version of VMware's Capacity Planner. Once upon a time, even the application code base was the same.

Guided Consolidation lets you "analyze" a physical server in your environment. It collects the CPU, RAM, disk, and network usage from the server and "predicts" whether the machine is a good candidate for conversion into your virtual infrastructure. Notice that we use a number of quotation marks, because this isn't a robust product. You can't analyze the data. You can't define when the data should be collected and for how long. Other products allow you to perform proper capacity planning for a project — this one doesn't. But all the data is stored in files on your vCenter Server. And unless you actively delete the data, it will stay there.

Storage Vendor Plug-in

Most of the major vendors (NetApp, EMC, Dell, HP, and IBM) already have (or are actively working on) plug-ins that let you configure the virtualization part of the storage array. You can create new LUNS/datastores, view statistics of your VMs in correlation to the storage back-end, optimize the ESX hosts according to the vendor's best practices, and much more.

What isn't well known is that each of these plug-ins usually needs a web server in order to function. What better web server to use than an Apache Tomcat instance? But these instances aren't always recycled, so you're likely to end up with three to five different instances of Tomcat running on your vCenter Server — and each one uses RAM. Take, for example, two storage plug-ins that use 512MB RAM each; you need an additional 1GB RAM for your vCenter Server.

Linked Mode

In this section, we'll go into detail about vCenter Linked Mode. VMware added this feature in the release of vCenter 4. It solves the issue of very large environments that need multiple vCenters to manage the infrastructure due to the sheer size and number of hosts and VMs.

The limit on the number of ESX hosts that one vCenter can manage is 1,000; the limit for VMs is 10,000 per vCenter. For many organizations, this suffices — they can only dream of reaching that number of VMs. But for others, this limit is too small.

In comes Linked Mode. By joining your vCenter instances together, you can expand your infrastructure to 10 vCenter Servers, 3,000 hosts, and 30,000 VMs.

LICENSING CAVEAT

Linked Mode can only be used with the Standard Edition of vCenter Server. If you've purchased an Essentials or Foundation Bundle (which doesn't have a Standard vCenter license), you can't join the vCenter instances together in Linked Mode.

Prerequisites

The following requirements apply to each vCenter Server system that is a member of a Linked Mode group:

◆ DNS infrastructure must be operational for Linked Mode replication to work.

◆ The vCenter Server instances in a Linked Mode group can be in different domains as long as the domains have a two-way trust relationship.

◆ When adding a vCenter Server instance to a Linked Mode group, the installer must be run by a domain user who has administrator credentials on both the machine where vCenter Server is installed and the target machine of the Linked Mode group.

◆ All vCenter Server instances must have network time synchronization. The vCenter Server installer validates that the machine clocks aren't more than 5 minutes apart.

Considerations

You should take into account several considerations before you configure a Linked Mode group:

◆ Each vCenter Server user sees the vCenter Server instances on which they have valid permissions. If you wish to block certain parts of your environment from other users, you need to specifically deny permissions on that section.

◆ When you're first setting up a vCenter Server Linked Mode group, the first vCenter Server must be installed as a stand-alone instance because you don't yet have a remote vCenter Server machine to join. Any vCenter Server instances thereafter can join the first vCenter Server or other vCenter Server instances that have joined the Linked Mode group.

◆ If you're joining a vCenter Server to a stand-alone instance that isn't part of a domain, you must add the stand-alone instance to a domain and add a domain user as an administrator. Linked Mode isn't supported in Workgroup environments — but then again, why would you use linked mode in a workgroup?

◆ The vCenter Server instances in a Linked Mode group don't need to have the same domain user login.

◆ The vCenter service can run under different accounts. By default, it runs as the machine's LocalSystem account.

◆ You can't join a Linked Mode group during the upgrade procedure when you're upgrading from VirtualCenter 2.5 to vCenter Server 4.1. Only after you've completed the upgrade can you join a Linked Mode.

Under the Covers

How does Linked Mode work? VMware uses Active Directory Lightweight Directory Services (AD LDS, previously known as Active Directory Application Mode [ADAM]).

Instead of using your organization's Active Directory database to store the directory-enabled application data, you can use AD LDS to store the data. AD LDS can be used in conjunction with AD DS so that you can have a central location for security accounts (AD DS) and another location to support the application configuration and directory data (AD LDS). By using AD LDS, you can reduce the overhead associated with Active Directory replication, you don't have to extend the Active Directory schema to support the application, and you can partition the directory structure so that the AD LDS service is deployed only to the servers that need to support the directory-enabled application.

Linked Mode behaves like an Active Directory application. Let's connect to it and see what information is inside. Figure 3.4 shows an example of using `ldp.exe` (`http://support`

.microsoft.com/kb/224543) to connect to a vCenter Server on port 389 (unless you've changed the default port).

FIGURE 3.4
LDP tool connecting to a vCenter LDS instance

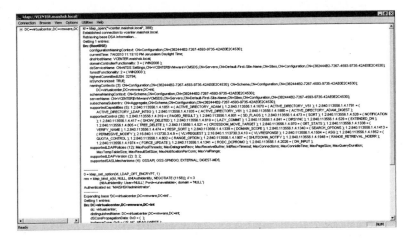

It's easier to use ADSI Edit to see all the properties. Connect to your vCenter Server with the correct credentials, using the naming context DC=virtualcenter,DC=vmware,DC=int as shown in Figure 3.5 and Figure 3.6.

FIGURE 3.5
Connecting to vCenter LDS with ADSI Edit

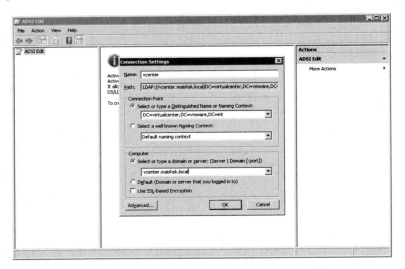

You can connect to three naming contexts:

◆ DC=virtualcenter,DC=vmware,DC=int'

◆ CN=Schema,CN=Configuration,CN={382444B2-7267-4593-9735-42AE0E2C4530} (the GUID is unique to each vCenter installation)

◆ CN=Configuration,CN={382444B2-7267-4593-9735-42AE0E2C4530}

FIGURE 3.6
vCenter LDS structure in ADSI Edit

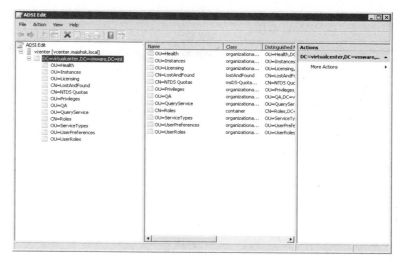

It's a good idea to get acquainted with the structure of the schema and the configuration of the LDS instance. They aren't documented well, and the information may come in handy one day.

Roles

You need to know several things about roles when joining two or more servers in Linked Mode:

♦ The roles defined on each vCenter Server system are replicated to all the other vCenter Servers connected in the Linked Mode group.

♦ If the roles defined on each vCenter Server system are different, the role lists of the systems are combined into a single common list. For example, if vCenter Server 1 has a role named ESX_Admins and vCenter Server 2 has a role named Admins_ESX, then both servers will have both ESX_Admins and Admins_ESX after they're joined in a Linked Mode group.

♦ If two vCenter Server systems have roles with the same name, the roles are combined into a single role if they contain the same privileges on each vCenter Server system. If the role exists on two vCenter Servers but they're assigned different privileges on the two servers, this conflict must be resolved by renaming at least one of the roles. You can choose to resolve the conflicting roles either automatically or manually.

If you choose to reconcile the roles automatically, the role on the joining system is renamed to <vcenter_name> <role_name>, where <vcenter_name> is the name of the vCenter Server system that is joining the Linked Mode group and <role_name> is the name of the original role.

If you choose to reconcile the roles manually, you have to connect to one of the vCenter Server systems with the vSphere Client and rename one instance of the role before proceeding to join the vCenter Server system to the Linked Mode group.

♦ If you remove a vCenter Server system from a Linked Mode group, the vCenter Server system retains all the roles it had as part of the group.

vCenter: Virtual or Physical

There is a long-standing discussion in the VMware world about whether you should install vCenter Server as a VM or a physical server. In the following section, we'll cover the reasons for both sides of the argument.

Physical Server

This book is about designing a virtual infrastructure environment, so why are we talking about physical hardware? Well, a certain amount of hardware has to be involved: your ESX hosts. But why would you consider installing vCenter on a physical server?

THE CHICKEN AND THE EGG

We're sure you're familiar with the chicken-and-egg dilemma. Some people use this analogy for vCenter as a VM.

Let's say you have a large environment — 100 ESX hosts. For some reason, you have a serious outage. For example, you lose the LUN on which the vCenter VM is stored. For all sorts of reasons, you won't have the VM backup for another 4–6 hours. You may say, "OK no problem" — until something goes seriously wrong with your environment. Some VMs start to not behave due to high CPU RAM usage, so you go and find them in the mass of VMs among your 100 ESX hosts and 2,000 VMs. Are you thinking "nightmare"? You find the VM. Lucky you — it was on the third ESX host you checked. And you want to vMotion the VM, but hey, you have no vCenter to perform the migration.

This is one example of what can happen if your vCenter is a VM. Another could be in a VMware View or Lab Manager environment — you can't deploy any new VMs because your vCenter is down. You can't perform certain actions to restore your environment because you have no vCenter, and you have no vCenter because your environment isn't functioning correctly. As you can see, serious issues may arise if your virtual vCenter Server isn't available.

SEPARATION OF DUTIES

Certain organizations will insist that because of issues like those just discussed, thou shall not have the management application of your environment running as part the environment itself. This doesn't mean you can't run vCenter as a VM — it can be run on a stand-alone host — but you'll losing a certain number of features as you'll see shortly.

AMOUNT OF RESOURCES

You've seen that the size of your vCenter Server can easily reach 4 vCPUs, 8GB, and even much higher. Do you want to use that amount of resources in your infrastructure on a single VM?

Virtual

We've discussed why it could be necessary, or better, for your environment to have vCenter on physical hardware. Now, let's look at the other side of the coin: why you could choose to go for vCenter as a VM.

THE CHICKEN AND THE EGG

With proper planning and some preparation, you can mitigate all the problems that may arise from the earlier scenario. It's all about how to find the issues that may occur and provide a solution to address those issues if or when they happen. Let's take the issue of the LUN going down.

vCenter is just an application (well, not "just," but it's an application). The guts of the environment is the database on which the vCenter relies. So in the earlier case, there is no way you should be down for 6 hours. If you separate the vCenter database from the vCenter Server, they're on separate servers. If they're VMs, they should be kept on separate ESX hosts.

Table 3.8 shows how you can address some of these issues.

TABLE 3.8: Risk mitigation for a virtual vCenter Server

POTENTIAL RISK	MITIGATION ACTION
vCenter is lost when the database fails.	Separate the SQL instance on a different server.
Both vCenter and SQL are VMs on the virtual infrastructure.	Place them on separate hosts with Affinity rules.
Both vCenter and SQL are on the same storage.	Place the VMs on different LUNS or different storage devices.
SQL data corruption occurs on the LUN.	Plan for database snapshots at regular intervals.
vCenter/SQL suffers a performance hit due to other VMs.	Ensure that your vCenter/SQL have guaranteed resources with reservations.
vCenter completely crashes.	Install a new VM to replace the failed VM, attach to the database, and you're back in business.

SERVER CONSOLIDATION

The whole idea of using a virtual infrastructure is to consolidate your physical servers into VMs running on ESX hosts. And here you're doing exactly the opposite. With the proper planning, there is no reason not to virtualize any workload. It's also officially a VMware best practice.

SNAPSHOTS

Suppose you're about to patch your vCenter Server, add a plug-in, or make a configuration change to one of the `.cfg` files. One of the greatest advantages you have with vCenter as a VM is the built-in ability to snapshot the VM before making any changes. If something goes drastically wrong, you can always revert back to the snapshot you took before the change.

PORTABILITY

A VM can be replicated to your disaster recovery (DR) site if need be. You can duplicate the vCenter Server easily if you want to create a test environment. You can even keep a cold backup of the vCenter Server in the event of a vCenter crash — you can bring the machine back up running on anything from VMware Player to Server to Workstation to a stand-alone ESXi server.

REDUNDANCY

As soon as you install vCenter on an HA cluster, you're automatically making the vCenter resilient to hardware failure. In order to get the same level of redundancy with physical hardware, you'd need a Microsoft cluster — and that would only be for the SQL database. vCenter isn't a cluster-aware application. Several third-party tools can provide this level of redundancy, but they aren't cheap.

And today, with fault tolerance (FT), you can provide a higher level of redundancy for your vCenter. At the present time, FT doesn't support more than one vCPU; therefore you can't protect the vCenter this way. Support for multiple vCPUs will be available in the future.

EATING YOUR OWN DOG FOOD

How can you as the virtualization administrator say to all your clients and customers that you have faith in the platform, its capabilities, and its features, when you aren't willing to put one of your critical servers on the infrastructure? We all know that, with the correct planning, the product will perform just as well as a physical server, and you'll get the huge additional benefit of running the server as a VM. If you believe in the product, then you should use it.

Redundancy

There are a couple of ways you can provide a level of redundancy for your vCenter Server:

◆   VMware HA

◆   vCenter Server Heartbeat

Before we talk about how to provide redundancy, you need to understand the implications of not having your vCenter available. Table 3.9 lists the functions that will/won't be affected.

TABLE 3.9:   Functions not available when vCenter fails

ENTITY	FUNCTION		REMARK
HA	Restart VM	**Yes**	Full functionality.
	Admission control	No	vCenter is required as the source of the load information.
	Add new host to cluster	No	vCenter is required to resolve IP addresses of cluster members.

TABLE 3.9:   Functions not available when vCenter fails   *(CONTINUED)*

ENTITY	FUNCTION			REMARK
	Host rejoins the Cluster	Yes		Resolved host information is stored in /etc/FT_HOST.
DRS	Manual	No		Impossible without the vCenter.
	Automatic	No		Impossible without the vCenter.
	Affinity rules	No		Impossible without the vCenter.
Resource pools	Create	No		Meaningless without the vCenter.
	Add VM	No		Meaningless without the vCenter.
	Remove VM	No		Meaningless without the vCenter.
VMotion		**No**		No Motion.
ESX host	Shutdown	Degraded		Through the direct connection to the ESX host server only.
	Startup	Yes	E	
	Maintenance	Degraded		Meaningless without the vCenter.
	Deregister	No		Meaningless without the vCenter.
	Register	No		Meaningless without the vCenter.
Virtual machine	Power on	**Degraded**	E	Through the direct connection to the ESX host server only.
	Power off	Degraded		Through the direct connection to the ESX host server only.
	Register	No		Meaningless without the vCenter.
	Deregister	No		Meaningless without the vCenter.
	Hot migration	No		No VMotion.
	Cold migration	Degraded		Within one ESX host only.
Template	Convert from VM	Degraded		Direct connection to host only / meaningless without vCenter.
	Convert to VM	Degraded		Direct connection to host only / meaningless without vCenter.

Continues

TABLE 3.9: Functions not available when vCenter fails *(CONTINUED)*

ENTITY	FUNCTION		REMARK
	Deploy VM	No	No VM deployment.
Guest	All functions	Yes	No impact.
Alarms	All functions	**No**	Unless you have direct agents on the ESX hosts.
Statistics	All functions	No	Not collected during the outage.
Yes	*Same functionality as without the VCenter*		
Degraded	*Functionality degradation without the vCenter*		
No	*Functionality lost without the vCenter*		
E	*Functionality will expire after the 14-day grace period*		

VMware

As you can see from the table, most of the management tasks related to vCenter won't work or will only partially function. The good news is that redundancy is still there, and not all VMs are affected.

Redundancy should be divided into two parts: your vCenter application and your database. Let's examine how you can provide redundancy to vCenter — first, the easiest way.

vCenter

The first component you'll be protecting is vCenter. You should consider several options; it all depends on what level of redundancy is necessary for your environment and how critical it is to have your vCenter available the entire time.

VMWARE HA

By running vCenter as a VM on an HA cluster, you automatically provide a certain amount of redundancy against hardware failure. If your ESX host fails, then vCenter will automatically restart on another host within a short period of time and reconnect to the database. This is a very acceptable solution in the case of host hardware failure; you shouldn't have any major downtime.

vCENTER SERVER HEARTBEAT

vCenter Server Heartbeat is a relatively new product from VMware that's specifically targeted at organizations that can't afford even the slightest downtime or failure of their vCenter Server. The product provides automatic failover and failback of VMware vCenter Server using failure detection and the failover process, making manual recovery and failover process definitions unnecessary. It enables administrators to schedule maintenance windows and maintain availability by initiating a manual switchover to the standby server. You can find vCenter Server Heartbeat at:

www.vmware.com/products/vcenter-server-heartbeat/

The product also provides protection for the vCenter database, *even if the database is installed on a separate server*. The technology is based on a product from Neverfail (www.neverfailgroup .com). Figure 3.7 shows the product design.

FIGURE 3.7
vCenter Heartbeat
design overview

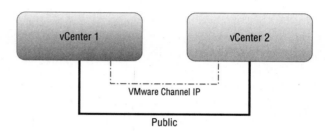

The great thing about vCenter Server Heartbeat is that it can be placed across the WAN. If you have two datacenters (US and Europe), you can place each node in a different location to provide full redundancy.

You'll need to address certain prerequisites and limitations:

- vCenter Server Heartbeat can't be installed on a domain controller, global catalog, or DNS.

- It only protects Microsoft SQL Server applications.

- No other critical business applications should be installed on the SQL Server besides the vCenter database.

- Both primary and secondary servers must have identical system date, time, and *time zone* settings.

- Latency on the link between the two locations must not fall below the standard defined for a T1 connection.

You can install the configuration in three ways:

- Virtual to virtual (V2V)

- Physical to virtual (P2V):

    - Similar CPU.

    - Identical memory.

    - The secondary VM must have sufficient priority in resource-management settings to assure the performance of the VM.

    - Each virtual NIC must use a separate virtual switch.

- Physical to physical (P2P):

  - The primary server must meet certain hardware and software requirements.

  - The secondary should be equivalent to the primary server to ensure adequate performance.

  - Advanced Configuration and Power Interface (ACPI) compliance must match the primary server.

We won't go into the details of how to install, because this isn't a step-by-step book (if you haven't noticed by now).

I need to point out a few things. First, the product is relatively new. I haven't met anyone who has implemented it in their environment, because it's targeted at the highest percentile of customers who can't — at any cost — have their vCenter down. It also isn't a cheap solution: it starts at approximately $12,000 per license.

Also, judging from the community activity (or lack thereof), vCenter Server Heartbeat hasn't been implemented widely. Or perhaps it works like a charm, so no one has any issues with it. See:

`http://communities.vmware.com/community/vmtn/mgmt/heartbeat`

Now, on to the second component: the database.

SQL/Oracle Database

There are several ways to protect the database for your vCenter Server. Database protection is important because the database is the heart and soul of your virtual environment. All the settings (DRS, HA, permissions — basically, everything) are stored in the database.

VMware HA

The vCenter Server is protected with HA, and the same goes for your database server. But the chance of data corruption is much higher with a database server. If the server crashes during a write operation, the data can become corrupt, and your database may be rendered unusable. In this case, a single database on an HA cluster can cause you problems.

Microsoft Cluster/Oracle Cluster

Both Microsoft and Oracle provide their own solution for active-active and active-passive clusters for databases. The great thing is that you can combine these two options: HA and Microsoft/Oracle Cluster.

You can create a highly available database on vSphere. VMware has best practices for both platforms:

- Oracle Databases on VMware vSphere 4: `www.vmware.com/"les/pdf/Oracle_Databases_on_vSphere_Deployment_Tips.pdf`

- Setup for Failover Clustering and Microsoft Cluster Service: `www.vmware.com/pdf/vsphere4/r41/vsp_41_mscs.pdf`

Here are a few of the considerations and best practices you should take into account when using VMware to virtualize these applications:

Upgrade to vSphere ESX 4   By upgrading to vSphere from an earlier version of ESX, you can gain a 10–20% performance boost on the same hardware.

Create a Computing Environment Optimized for vSphere   You should set the BIOS settings for ESX hosts accordingly. These recommendations include the following:

◆ Enable virtualization technology to support running 64-bit guest OSs.

◆ Enable Turbo Mode to balance the workload over unused cores.

◆ Enable node interleaving if your system supports non-uniform memory architecture (NUMA).

◆ Enable VT-x, AMD-V, EPT, and RVI to use hardware-based virtualization support.

◆ Disable C1E Halt State to prefer performance over power saving.

◆ Disable power-saving to prevent power-saving features from slowing down processor speeds when idle.

◆ Enable HyperThreading (HT) with most new processors that support this feature.

◆ Enable Wake On LAN to support the required features for the Distributed Power Management feature.

◆ Set Execute Disable to Yes for the vMotion and Distributed Resource Scheduler features.

Optimize your OS   Remove non-vital software, and activate only required services.

Use as Few vCPUs as Possible   One of the biggest mistakes administrators make is over-allocation of resources to a VM. When you allocate four vCPUs to a VM that barely uses one vCPU, not only will the performance of the VM be degraded, but you can also seriously impact the rest of the VMs running in the same host.

Enable HT for Intel Core i7 Processors   This is a new recommendation for the Xeon 5500 family of processors. Until now, VMware had no recommendation about enabling HT.

Allow vSphere to Choose the Best Virtual Machine Monitor Based on the CPU and Guest OS Combination   Workloads like those from a database that has a large amount of page-table activity are likely to benefit from hardware assistance. But it's still best to leave the setting as above.

Use the VMXNET Family of Paravirtualized Network Adapters   The paravirtualized network adapters in the VMXNET family implement an idealized network interface that passes network traffic between the VM and the physical network interface cards with minimal overhead.

Enable Jumbo Frames for IP-Based Storage iSCSI and NFS   This will reduce load on the network switches and give a certain percentage of performance boost. Note that this feature must be enabled end-to-end (VMkernel network switch storage) in order for it to work properly.

Create Dedicated Datastores to Service Database Workloads   It's a generally accepted best practice to create a dedicated datastore if the application has a demanding I/O profile, and databases fall into this category. The creation of dedicated datastores lets you define individual service-level guarantees for different applications and is analogous to provisioning dedicated LUNs in the physical world.

It's important to understand that a datastore is an abstraction of the storage tier and, therefore, it's a logical representation of the storage tier, not a physical representation of the storage tier. So, if you create a dedicated datastore to isolate a particular I/O workload (whether log or database files) without isolating the physical storage layer as well, you won't get the desired effect on performance.

Make Sure VMFS Is Properly Aligned   We'll get into disk alignment in more detail in Chapter 6 ("Shared Storage") and Chapter 7 ("Virtual Machine Design"). But note that the performance hit of not aligning your VMFS/NFS datastores can be significant.

vCenter Server Heartbeat

As noted earlier, this product provides redundancy for an SQL database only. That database must be the only one on the server in order for this to work.

Security

Perhaps this part of the chapter should have come first, but its current position has no reflection on its importance in the design process. Nine out of 10 administrators would rank security as one of the most important considerations in your virtual infrastructure design.

How can you design your vCenter Server for security?

◆ Isolation

◆ Permissions

◆ SSL certificates

Isolation

Your vCenter Server, from a security perspective, is probably the most important component of your infrastructure. If someone compromises the vCenter Server, they can cause immense damage, from powering off VMs, to deleting data from a VM, to deleting a VM or — worse — a complete datastore.

Your vCenter Server shouldn't be accessible from all workstations in your corporate network. You can achieve this by using any of the following measures:

◆ Put the vCenter on a separate management VLAN.

◆ Put the vCenter behind a firewall.

◆ Define an access list on the network switches.

◆ Set firewall rules on the vCenter Server.

Permissions

By default, the Administrators Security group on a vCenter Server has full permissions to the entire environment. Do you always want the administrators on the vCenter to control every

VM? This isn't always the best idea. Limiting the default administrators group access to the full vCenter can be achieved by doing the following:

1. Create a local security group on the vCenter Server (vi-admins).

2. Create a local user on the vCenter Server (viadmin-local). Then if for some reason your domain account isn't available, or the vCenter can't contact the domain, at least you'll have a way of controlling your environment.

3. Create a domain user (viadmin).

4. Add both the viadmin and viadmin-local accounts to the vi-admins local group on the vCenter Server.

5. Change the administrator permissions from the default to the vi-admins group.

In addition, you should always follow the model of least-privilege permissions. Only give a user account the minimum required permissions needed to perform a task. There is no need to give a user the Administrator role if all they need is to access the VM console. It's a better idea to create a custom role that contains only the relevant permissions needed for the task and then assign that permission to that user.

VIRTUAL MACHINE ACCESS

Would you give any user who asked you the code for the server room so they could power on a server if they wanted to? That wouldn't be wise.

You should view your vCenter Server as a secure area of your datacenter. Not everyone should have access to the vSphere infrastructure. If you want to give users access to the server, they should access it either through Remote Desktop or an SSH session (depending on the OS).

It isn't recommended that you enable a VNC client on a VM; this requires additional configuration on each and every ESX to allow for such remote management. In such a case, you're better off with a custom role.

SSL Certificates

Client sessions with vCenter Server may be initiated from any vSphere API client, such as vSphere Client and PowerCLI. By default, all traffic is protected by SSL encryption, but the default certificates aren't signed by a trusted certificate authority and therefore don't provide the authentication security you may need in a production environment. These self-signed certificates are vulnerable to man-in-the-middle attacks, and clients receive a warning when they connect to the vCenter Server.

If you intend to use encrypted remote connections externally, consider purchasing a certificate from a trusted certificate authority, or use your own PKI infrastructure in your domain to provide a valid certificate for your SSL connections.

You can locate the official Replacing vCenter Server Certificates guidelines here:

```
www.vmware.com/files/pdf/vsp_4_vcserver_certificates.pdf
```

Summary

The factors involved in the design of your vCenter Server shouldn't be taken lightly. You'll need to design for scale, redundancy, and, last but not least, security.

Take into account how many hosts and VMs you have and what kind of statistics you'll need to maintain for your environment.

Size your server correctly from the ground up, so you won't need to redeploy when you outgrow your environment.

Remember that your vCenter Server should be separated from your database server, providing a separation of duties for the different components of the infrastructure. You should plan for redundancy for both components and take into account what kind of outage you can afford to sustain. When you have that information, you can plan the level of redundancy you need.

Don't be afraid to run your vCenter as a VM. In certain cases, you can provide a greater level of resilience, with more ease, than you can with a physical server.

Your vCenter is the key to your kingdom. Leaving it exposed places your kingdom out in the open. A great number of attacks today are carried out from with the network, for a number of reasons: disgruntled employees, malicious software, and so on. Protect that key with the methods we've discussed.

Chapter 4

Server Hardware

All vSphere hosts rely on the underlying hardware to provide a suitable environment to run the ESX or ESXi hypervisor and the guest VMs. The server hardware is the most significant factor that affects the host's capabilities, performance, and cost. A vSphere design will never be successful if the server hardware isn't fit for the task.

Often, during the initial stages of a design, hardware procurement is on the critical path, because the process of selecting, approving, and ordering hardware and having it delivered can take several weeks. However, as this chapter investigates, you must review many considerations before embarking on the right server choice.

The chapter is split into the following sections:

◆ The importance of hardware, and the factors that influence and constrain your choices

◆ How vendors differ and the options to consider when choosing among them

◆ Which server components are most important to a vSphere installation and why

◆ Scale up a design with large powerful servers, or scale out with more agile servers

◆ Choosing between rack servers and blade servers

◆ Understanding new consolidated datacenter approaches

◆ Alternatives to buying servers

Hardware Considerations

A host's hardware components are critical to the capabilities of your vSphere environment. Selecting the correct mix and ensuring sufficient capacity will determine how much guest consolidation is possible. Unlike most of the other chapters in this book, which discuss software options, this chapter examines hardware, which is much more difficult to change after the initial implementation. Most software choices can be reconfigured after the fact, albeit with perhaps short outages, if something doesn't work as expected or you find an improvement to the design. With hardware selection, however, it's crucial that the architecture can survive not only the proposed requirements but any likely changes.

A design that tries to plan for any eventuality will end in overkill. You can't expect to cover every possible variant. Your goal should be a design that isn't overly specific but that covers a few of the most likely contingencies. This section will help you think about what is required before you start to select individual components.

Frequently, in a vSphere project, the first item addressed is the purchase of hardware. When any project starts and new hardware is needed, a whole procurement cycle must begin. A basic design is provided, along with the justification; project managers push it forward and managers who control budgets are involved. Often, due to the large expense associated with server hardware, several nontrivial levels of approval are required, requests for tender follow and vendor negotiations ensue. The cycle repeats until everyone is satisfied. But that's usually only the start.

Once the servers are ordered, it's often several weeks before they're delivered. Then, the server engineers need to test them and then configure them. Prior to that, a pilot may be required. The hardware must be moved to the appropriate datacenter, racked, and cabled. Power, network, and storage need to be connected and configured appropriately. All this installation work is likely to involve several different teams, and possibly coordination among several companies.

This potentially drawn-out hardware procurement cycle can take months from start to finish. This is one of the reasons virtualization has become so popular. Many managers and solutions architects are beginning to forget how long and painful this process can be, thanks to the advent of virtual hardware and the subsequent almost-immediate provisioning that is now possible.

For this reason, server hardware is nearly always on the critical path of a vSphere deployment. It's important to start this process as quickly as possible to avoid delays. But so much relies on the hardware that until you make many of the other decisions covered in this book, it's impossible to correctly design the server configurations. Buying incorrectly specified server hardware is likely to cause a vSphere design to fail to meet expectations, and this issue can be very difficult to recover from. Probably more than any other factor, the server hardware must be designed properly before you rush forward.

It's possible to identify certain do's and don'ts for server hardware that reduce the likelihood of ordering the wrong equipment. The next section looks at what is likely to determine these choices in your individual circumstances.

Factors in Selecting Hardware

The physical hardware of vSphere servers plays an important role in several areas. These roles and their importance in a specific environment will shape the hardware's design. Some are hard requirements, such as particular hypervisor features that need an explicit piece of equipment or functionality in order for the feature to be available. Others are quantitative options that you can select and weigh against each other, such as the amount of RAM versus the size or speed of the hard drives.

FEATURES

Several vSphere 4 features have specific hardware requirements. These features may not be available or may not run as efficiently if the correct underlying hardware isn't present. It's therefore critical to review these features and decide whether you need any of them now or are likely to need them, prior to purchasing equipment. Purchasing servers without the capability of running a required feature could be an expensive mistake.

These features are discussed in more depth in the subsequent chapters, but at this stage it's important for you to understand their hardware requirements:

vMotion vMotion relies on hosts having a level of similarity. The CPUs must be from the same vendor (either Intel or AMD) and of the same family providing the same hardware flags. This compatibility is particularly important within vCenter clusters, because this is the level at which many of the additional features that use vMotion (such as distributed resource scheduling [DRS]), operate. vMotion is available between hosts in the same datacenter, even if they're in different clusters, so there is merit to host hardware consistency beyond the cluster if at all possible.

The following VMware article lists Intel CPU compatibility:

> `http://kb.vmware.com/kb/1991`

And this VMware article lists AMD CPU compatibility:

> `http://kb.vmware.com/kb/1992`

Chapter 8, "Datacenter Design," examines a technique known as Enhanced vMotion Compatibility (EVC), which can make servers with somewhat dissimilar CPUs be vMotion compatible.

Fault Tolerance   VMware's fault tolerance (FT) has a number of hardware limitations. These are listed in detail in Chapter 8, "Datacenter Design," but it's important to know that there are some strict CPU requirements.

The following VMware article lists CPUs compatible with FT:

> `http://kb.vmware.com/kb/1008027`

Distributed Power Management   DPM must have access to either Intelligent Platform Management Interface (IPMI), Hewlett Packard's Integrated Lights Out (iLO), or a network adapter with Wake-On LAN (WOL) capabilities, to power on the server when the cluster requires it.

VMDirectPath   VMDirectPath allows a special I/O passthrough to a VM from the NIC or possibly a storage host bus adapter (HBA). This feature relies on specific Peripheral Component Interconnect (PCI) cards being used; but more important, the CPU must support either Intel's VT-d or AMD's IOMMU.

PERFORMANCE

The hypervisor's performance relates directly to the hardware. Other elements can have an effect, but the most significant performance enabler is derived from the hardware itself. The general premise of *more and faster* is better; but with other limiting constraints, you must usually choose what hardware gives the most performance bang for your buck.

In a vSphere design, the main performance bottlenecks revolve around CPU, memory, and I/O (particularly storage I/O). Therefore, in a server's hardware, the CPU and memory are critical in terms of its scalability. Most other server components are required in order to provide functionality, but they don't tend to limit the performance the same way. The CPU and memory rely on each other, so a good balance is required. The question of smaller but more numerous servers, as opposed to fewer servers that are more powerful, is examined in a later section in this chapter; but either way, the server's CPU and memory ratio should correlate unless you have a particular need for more of one.

Other elements can limit performance, but most newly purchased up-to-date servers from mainstream vendors avoid the obvious bottlenecks unless you have unusual cases that demand special attention. This chapter looks closely at both CPUs and memory.

RELIABILITY

The vSphere server hardware is likely to be a critical infrastructure piece in the datacenter and has the potential to make up a large part of a company's compute resources. It's obvious that the server's stability is paramount. Therefore it's important when you're selecting hardware that each component be thoroughly reliable. Although it's possible to find whitebox equipment that works with ESX or ESXi, which may even be listed on the HCL, it's important to consider the server's reliability.

Servers for a production environment should be from a reputable vendor with a proven track record. Many companies avoid the first-generation series of a new server line, even from a recognized top-tier server vendor, because this is where any stability quirks in the BIOS code or hardware agents are most likely to be found.

Additionally, with each new server, a period of testing and *bedding-in* is normal and is part of checking for stability issues. Common approaches are discussed later in the chapter.

REDUNDANCY

Along with general reliability, a server's components should provide sufficient redundancy to avoid outages during hardware failures. All components, even the most reliable, will fail periodically. However, a well-designed server can mitigate many of these failures with redundant parts. You should choose servers that are designed to take redundant parts and ensure that you order them with the extra parts to make them redundant.

These are the most common server parts that should be offered with redundancy:

◆ Hard drives with both RAID protection and hot spares

◆ Power supply units (PSUs) that not only protect from a failure of the PSU but also let you split the power supply across two separate circuits

◆ Multiple network and storage interfaces/cards, allowing connections to separate switches

◆ Several fans that prevent overheating, should one fail

UPGRADABILITY AND EXPANDABILITY

An important element, particularly in vSphere hosts, is the ability to expand the server's hardware options at a later stage. Server hardware is often purchased with an expected life cycle of three to five years, but rapid advances in hardware and software, and continuously falling prices, often make upgrading existing servers an attractive option.

It's somewhat unrealistic to expect to upgrade a server's CPU at a later stage, because the increase in performance is likely to be minimal in comparison to the additional cost. And you're unlikely to buy a server with excess sockets that aren't filled when the server is first purchased (aside from the difficulty of finding the exact same CPU to add to the server). However, RAM tends to drop significantly in price over time, so it's feasible that you could consider a replacement memory upgrade. Larger servers with extra drive bays offer the option for more local storage, although this is rarely used in vSphere deployments other than locations without access to any shared storage facilities.

The most likely upgrade possibilities that you may wish to consider when purchasing servers is the ability to fit extra PCI-based cards. These cards can add network or storage ports, or provide the potential to later upgrade to a faster interface such as 10GbE or CNAs. This is one of the reasons some companies choose 2U based server hardware over 1U based rack servers. If space isn't an issue in the datacenter, these larger servers are usually priced very similarly but give you considerably more expandability than their smaller 1U counterparts.

Computing Needs

It's important to look carefully at the computing needs of the vSphere environment before you create a detailed shopping list of server parts. Although generalizations can be made about every vSphere deployment, each one will differ, and the hardware can be customized accordingly.

HARDWARE COMPATIBILITY LIST

VMware has a strict Compatibility Guide, which for hypervisor servers is colloquially known as the hardware compatibility list (HCL). It's now a web-based tool, which you can find at www.vmware.com/go/hcl. This is a list of certified hardware that VMware guarantees will work properly. Drivers are included or available, the hardware will be supported if there's an issue, and VMware has tested it as a proven platform.

Choosing hardware that isn't on the HCL doesn't necessarily mean it won't work with vSphere; but if you have issues along the way, VMware may not provide support. If a component that isn't on the HCL does work, you may find that after a patch or upgrade it stops working. Although the HCL is version-specific, if hardware has been certified as valid, then it's likely to be HCL compatible for at least all the subsequent minor releases.

For any production environment, you should use only HCL listed hardware. Even test and development servers should be on the HCL if you expect any support and the business needs any level of reliability. If these nonproduction servers mimic their production counterparts, this has the advantage that you can test the hardware with any changes or upgrades to the vSphere environment that you plan to introduce.

WHICH HYPERVISOR?

Chapter 2, "ESX vs. ESXi," discussed the choice of hypervisor between ESX classic and ESXi. Despite their similarity, the hypervisor you choose will have some impact on the hardware. ESXi is less reliant on local storage but can still use it if required. ESX and ESXi have different HCLs, so you should check to ensure that any proposed solution is compliant.

ESXi combines the Service Console and VMkernel network interfaces into one management network, so you may need one less NIC if you use 1GbE. ESXi also uses particular CIM providers, which allows for hardware monitoring. If you're using ESXi, you should confirm the availability of CIM providers for the hardware being used.

ESXi has Installable and Embedded versions. If you want to use ESXi Embedded, it will probably have a significant effect on your hardware selection, because vendors sell specific servers that include this. In addition, the HCL for ESXi Embedded is much smaller than the HCL for Installable, so it may limit your choices for adding hardware.

Minimum Hardware

The minimum hardware requirements for each hypervisor also differs, so be sure to consult the appropriate checklist. Most designed solutions are unlikely to come close to the required minimums, but occasional specific use cases may have minimal custom needs. You still need to hit VMware's minimums in order for the hypervisor to be VMware supported.

Purpose

It's worth considering the type of VMs that will run on the hypervisors. vSphere servers can be used not only to virtualize general-purpose servers but also for a variety of other roles. A server may be destined to host virtual desktops (VDI), in which case servers should be designed for very high consolidation ratios. Alternatively, the hypervisor may host only one or two very large VMs, or VMs with very specific memory or CPU requirements. Some VMs need high levels of storage or network I/O; you can fit more capable controller cards to provide for the VM's needs, with high I/O ratings or the ability to do hardware passthrough. The servers may need to host old P2Ved servers that have specific hardware requirements such as serial or parallel ports for software dongles, or access to old equipment like facsimile modems or tape backup units.

SCALING

Buying the right hardware means not only getting the right parts but also scaling properly for your capacity and performance needs. If you buy too much, then resources will lie idle and money will have been wasted. If you buy too little, then resources will be constrained and the servers won't deliver the expected levels of performance and may not provide the required level of redundancy. No one likes to waste money, but an under-resourced environment means trouble. First impressions last, and if virtualized servers are a new concept to a business, then it's important that it perform as expected, if not better.

Not every design needs its hardware requirements planned from the outset. If your company's procurement process is sufficiently flexible and expeditious, then you can add server nodes as they're demanded. This way, the quantity should always be suitable for the job. Despite the planning and testing you conduct beforehand, you're always making a best estimate with a bit added for good measure.

HARDWARE CONSISTENCY

If you're purchasing new servers to supplement existing equipment, it's important to ensure that certain components are sufficiently similar. This is particularly significant if the new hardware will coexist in the same cluster, because this is likely where VMs frequently migrate.

Consistency within the same hardware generation is also important, so wherever possible it's advisable to set a standard level of hardware across the servers. If some situations require more or less compute resources, then you may want to implement two or three tiers of hardware standards. This consistency simplifies installation, configuration, and troubleshooting, and it also means that advanced cluster functions such as DRS, high availability (HA), and distributed power management (DPM) can work more efficiently.

Consistency within the same type of servers is beneficial, such as populating the same memory slots and the same PCI slots. You should try to use the same NICs for the same purpose and ensure that the same interface connects to the same switch. This makes managing the devices much easier and a more scalable task.

Server Constraints

In any server design, you must consider a number of constraints that limit the possible deployment. Any datacenter will be restricted primarily by three physical factors: power, cooling, and space. vSphere servers have traditionally put a strain on I/O cabling, and host licenses can restrict what server hardware is utilized.

RACK SPACE

The most apparent physical constraint faced in any server room is that of rack space. Even though virtualization is known to condense server numbers and may alleviate the problem, you still can't fit servers where there is no available space. Co-locating datacenters is common these days, and customers are often billed by the rack or down to the single U; even if it isn't your datacenter to manage, it still makes sense to pack in as much equipment as possible.

Aside from virtualizing, there are two common approaches to maximizing space: minimize the height of the rack servers or switch to blade servers. Rack servers are traditionally multi-U affairs, with sufficient height to stack ancillary cards vertically. But all mainstream vendors also sell 1U servers to reduce space. Many opt for blade servers as a way to fit more servers into a limited amount of rack space. A regular rack can take up to 42 1U servers, but most vendors sell 10U chassis that can fit 16 half-height blades, meaning at least 64 servers with 2U to spare. Both thin rack servers and half-height blades are normally sold only as dual-socket servers, so these methods align themselves more closely with a scale-out model. Both rack versus blade and scale-up versus scale-out are debated later in this chapter.

POWER

With denser hardware configurations and virtualization increasing consolidation levels, power and cooling become even more important. Smaller, more heavily utilized servers need more power and generate more heat. Cooling is discussed separately later in this section; but be aware that increased heat from the extra power used must be dissipated with even more cooling, which in turn increases the power required. Older datacenters that weren't designed for these use cases will likely run out of power well before running out of space.

As energy prices go up and servers use more and more power, the result can be a significant operating expense (OPEX). Power supply can be limited, and server expansion programs must consider the availability of local power.

Most of the world uses high-line voltage (200–240V AC) for its regular power supply, whereas North America's and Japan's standard for AC supply is low-line voltage (100–120V AC). Most datacenter customers in North America then have the option of being supplied with either low-line or high-line for server racks. Vendors normally supply servers with dual-voltage PSUs that are capable of automatically switching. High-line is considered more stable and efficient, can reduce thermal output, and allows for more capacity. However, whatever the available power supply is, you should check all server PSUs, uninterruptible power supplies (UPSs), and power distribution units (PDUs) to be sure they're compatible. Some very high-performance servers may require three-phase high-line power to operate.

The power input for each server is often referred to as its volt amperes (VA), and this is cumulatively used to calculate the power required in a rack for PDU and UPS capacity. PDUs shouldn't provide more than half of its capacity in normal operations to ensure that it can handle the excess required if one circuit fails. Also consider the number and type of sockets required on each PDU. Vertical PDUs help save rack space.

It isn't just the make and model of servers that affect the power estimate, but also how fully fitted the server is with CPUs, RAM, disks, I/O cards, and so on. The hypervisor's load affects power usage, so if you expect to run the servers at 40% or 80% utilization, that should be factored in. Most hardware manufacturers have downloadable spreadsheets or online calculators you can use to make more accurate estimates of server power and cooling requirements. Figure 4.1 shows an example of one offering, but all vendors have their own versions.

FIGURE 4.1

Example of a power and cooling estimation tool

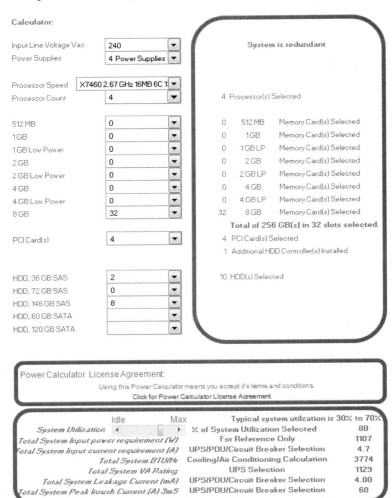

Courtesy of HP

Server PSUs should come with inrush surge protection, because when power is initially applied to a server, it draws power momentarily on full load. This normally lasts only a few seconds but can use several times more current than normal. It's important to think about this with multiple servers in a cluster. Following a power outage, if all the servers in a cluster try to power back on at the same time, the result may be an inrush that can affect the whole room. When you're powering servers back on, consider waiting at least 10 seconds between servers. Most servers have power settings to automatically start up after a power failure, but look for those that can use a random time offset to help prevent inrush issues.

Power-design calculations are often made at the start of an initial deployment—for example, when a blade chassis is fitted and only semipopulated with blades. As time goes on, more blades are added. But because no extra power cables need to be fitted, the additional power requirements are forgotten. If you're fitting a blade enclosure, then for design purposes, imagine it's fully populated.

UPS

UPSs are necessary to provide a clean, continuous supply of power to vSphere host servers. Any type of power failure or minor fluctuation can cause a shutdown. UPSs are designed to bridge the gap, automatically switching over to a battery bank until power is restored. UPSs can also filter out power spikes or sags, which can not only power off servers but also damage the PSUs and internal components. Many UPS systems provide automatic monitoring and alarming and can help with power capacity planning.

UPSs should be sufficiently rated to keep the servers powered on long enough to at least allow a clean shutdown of all VMs and hosts. Unlike regular servers, which only need to shut down one OS, hypervisors can be running tens of guests, which when all instructed to shut down at the same time can take several minutes to do so. Therefore, it's important to think about how long it may take banks of vSphere servers and all their VMs to cleanly go down.

For environments where uptime is absolutely crucial, UPS systems may only need to be enough to tide things over until a backup generator starts up. You should test any UPSs and standby power supply to ensure that all the equipment is suitably balanced and will be ready when required.

COOLING

All server hardware produces a lot of heat, which must be constantly dissipated to prevent the equipment from overheating. Cooling makes up a substantial amount of the power used in a datacenter, often over half the total power bill. Making that cooling more efficient means less cooling is required. Making the server's power usage more efficient also reduces cooling needs.

COOLING MEASUREMENTS

Server heat is usually thought of in either watts (W), which is the amount of input power, or British Thermal Units (BTUs), which is the amount of cooling required for the power being consumed (BTU/hr = 3.4 × watts). In North America, cooling systems are often rated in tons of refrigeration (RT), where 1 ton is equal to the heat absorption of 3.5 kWh or 12,000 BTU/hr. This measure originally came from the amount of cooling energy found in one ton of ice.

When you're trying to minimize the amount of cooling that each server needs, think about the airflow through your servers from front to back. How much airflow do the rack doors allow? Is the cabling at the back impeding the flow? Are the side doors attached, servers stacked together, and blanking covers fitted to prevent hot and cold air mixing? With server cooling systems, it's important to think of the entire room, because the air isn't contained to one server or one rack. Use hot and cold aisles, and think about the placement of AC units, perforated floor tiles, and the use of overhead conduits even if you have raised floors, to split power from other cables and leave more room for cooling.

I/O PORTS

In addition to the power cabling provided by PDUs, servers have a collection of cables that need to be connected. These can include Ethernet cables for both network and storage I/O, fiber optic cables, out-of-band management card connectors, and KVM cabling. Prior to fitting new servers, it's critical that you consider the amount of cabling and the number of ports required to connect each one. This means you need to know how many switch ports, patch panel ports, fibre switch ports, and KVM ports are free and useable. Remember, some of these types of equipment also need licensing on a per-port basis.

Proper capacity management also means thinking about the I/O loads on these connectors, to ensure that additional workloads won't prevent linear scaling.

vSphere Licensing

Although it isn't a physical constraint, vSphere licensing can be an important consideration. Many vSphere features are only available with higher tier licensing, but licensing may also restrict the hardware you can use. This is in addition to the fact that larger four- or eight-way servers need more licenses. In a new vSphere deployment, this becomes a project cost; but if you're supplementing an existing environment that already has a license agreement drawn up, your existing license may reduce your options.

vSphere licenses limit the host servers to 6 cores per physical CPU, unless you upgrade to Advanced or Enterprise Plus, which allows for up to 12 cores. All vSphere licenses restrict the hosts from seeing more than 256 GB RAM, unless you use the Enterprise Plus license.

Differentiating Among Vendors

Several vendors produce servers suitable for vSphere hypervisors. The Tier-1 companies commonly associated with ESX servers are HP, IBM, and Dell, although Fujitsu-Siemens has a limited following in Europe. Cisco, well known for their networking equipment, burst onto the scene in 2009 with its new line of servers; they can also be considered a mainstream vendor, despite their infancy in the server market. Many other companies have products listed on VMware's HCL, but they're much less well-known and arguably less trusted.

An option for the most budget-conscious business is what is known as a *whitebox server*. These are computers that aren't sold by a recognized vendor, and may even be configured from parts. Whitebox servers tend to lack the high-end features available from the main vendors, such as redundant parts and on-hand identical stocked replacements, and whitebox servers rarely scale beyond one or two CPUs. Such servers may appear on the HCL or meet the minimum requirements, but checking each part is left up to you.

It's difficult to recommend whitebox servers, although this approach has a popular community following and is frequently used for home test-lab type situations. A couple of excellent sites list tested whitebox equipment, although obviously VMware will only support those on its own HCL:

http://vm-help.com/esx40i/esx40_whitebox_HCL.php

http://ultimatewhitebox.com/systems

The vast majority of vSphere installations happen on Tier-1 supplied hardware. The relative importance of hypervisor hardware in comparison to regular servers, largely in part to its high consolidation workload, means that most companies spend the extra dollars to buy trusted equipment. Another reason these vendors are so popular with vSphere is that it's still an enterprise-dominated product. Small companies that are more likely to use whitebox equipment haven't embraced hypervisors so readily. They often don't benefit as much from consolidation and lack dedicated IT staff with the skills to implement it.

In certain circumstances, you may be unable to choose a different vendor, because your organization has an approved supplier. This may be due to pre-negotiated pricing, tender agreements, or a historical preference for one brand that makes continued support easier if everything remains the same. But given the opportunity to choose between vendors, beyond the raw computing power of their servers you may wish to consider the following points for hypervisor equipment. Many of them use the same underlying generic hardware, but these value-adds make them different and are particularly important for hypervisor servers, which usually have a very high criticality in a datacenter:

Warranty and Support   Server warranties are commonly for three years, although they often can be extended on a year-by-year basis. Warranties are obviously important should a component fail, but it's also important for Tier-1 vendors to stock exact replacement parts. For example, in a multi-CPU server, if one CPU fails, only an identical CPU can be fitted to match the existing ones. If you have a cluster full of servers, a different replacement server won't suffice.

Support agreements vary between vendors, and often each vendor has different options available. Compare how they can offer support—telephone support, instant messaging, email, and so on—and what hours they're willing to provide support (such as business hours or 24/7). If you have multinational offices, be sure the vendor provides international support. Previous experience with a vendor will often give you a feel for the level of service you can expect. Agreements should also specify onsite support, detailing how quickly the vendor will fit replacement parts or be onsite to troubleshoot issues.

HCL Investment   Top-tier vendors should be investing in ongoing certification work with VMware. Doing so ensures that their products continue to be supported under the HCL, and helps the vendors optimize their equipment for the hypervisor. This means drivers can be automatically included in vSphere build media, and the vendors have suitable hardware agents or CIM providers to enable hardware monitoring.

Technologies   A lot of the hardware included in servers is fairly generic and not usually manufactured by the vendor. However, vendors try to distinguish themselves with newer technologies, such as the ability to pack in more memory, optimize internal buses, or be the first to market with a particular CPU.

Later in the chapter, we'll consider consolidated approaches that match networking and storage options to servers to provide all-in-one packages.

Hardware Management   Most server vendors provide a centralized hardware-management tool, such as HP's System Insight Manager, IBM's Director, or Dell's OpenManager. It manages your hardware and provides reporting notification tools to trigger alerts when problems occur (such as failed disks). These tools often provide the capability to push out BIOS and agent updates from a central location. These products often come with additional licensing fees for extra functionality, although the base tool may come with the server.

Remote Management   Another important server option that can differ between vendors is the availability and functionality of out-of-band management cards. HP uses iLO, IBM uses RSA cards, and Dell has DRACs. These can offer numerous remote-access tools, but the more important ones for vSphere servers are as follows:

◆ Remote console access

◆ Power-button access

◆ Virtual optical drives

◆ Hardware status and logging

Some vendors include base functionality while licensing the more advanced ones; others sell add-on hardware cards. These management cards with remote console access are particularly useful for offsite datacenters or remote offices where onsite support is less likely to be able to deal with an ESX or ESXi console screen.

Server Components

Servers have a multitude of options available, and almost every component can be customized for your needs. vSphere host servers have particular needs; with careful consideration of each part, you can design a server to best fit its role as hypervisor. This section looks at each component important to virtualization, the impact it has, and where your budget should concentrate.

Before we explain the function of each component, remember the basic premise of type 1 hypervisors. vSphere ESX and ESXi virtualize the CPU, memory, disk, and network I/O to maximize throughput, making as few changes as possible so as to not impede performance. Most other hardware functions are emulated in software, because they don't play a critical role in performance and are referenced relatively little. How these four elements are shared among the hypervisor and guests is critical in overall performance, but any improvement in hardware that can improve the efficiency and speed of the CPU, memory, and I/O is crucial.

CPU

VMware vSphere hosts only run on top of 64-bit CPUs. The server's CPUs are critical in the performance of the VMs. Most servers come equipped with at least two CPU sockets, although four- and eight-way models are common as companies scale up. The most recent major advance is the use of multicore CPUs and the significant performance increases they can provide. CPUs used to be measured purely in MHz, but now vendors are packing in more punch by delivering CPUs with multiple cores. Two-, four-, and six-core CPUs are available now, and more are delivered in each generational refresh.

MULTICORE CPUs AND SCHEDULING

A multicore CPU consists of a single socket processor with multiple core units. These cores can share some of the cache levels, and can also share the memory bus. Each core has near-native performance to that of a single-core CPU, so a dual core is close to two single CPUs, and a quad core is close to four single CPUs or two dual-core CPUs. Sharing the same caches and buses can reduce performance when the VMs are particularly memory intensive, but otherwise multicore CPUs offer compelling performance for their modest increase in price.

Some Intel CPUs have a feature known as HyperThreading (HT) that allows each physical core to behave as two logical cores. HT allows two different threads to run on the same core at the same time. This may speed up some operations, depending on the software running at the time. The gains are likely to be marginal, and certainly not as substantial as having additional physical cores. vSphere uses HT by default, as long as it's enabled in the server's BIOS. Since Intel's Nehalem chip, HT has been referred to as simultaneous multithreading (SMT).

The VMkernel employs a complex but extremely efficient CPU scheduler. Its purpose is to equitably share CPU resources between its own needs and those of all the running VMs. With default resources allocated, a vSphere host time-slices processing power equally among all the VMs as soon as the CPU resources are overcommitted. Ordinarily, the host needs to take into account VM shares, reservations, and limits; the number of allocated vCPUs (VM CPUs); and the varying demands made by each VM. A VM should be oblivious to the fact that it's running on virtualized hardware, so the scheduler needs to give the impression to the VM that it completely owns the CPU. This becomes increasingly complicated when VMs have multiple vCPUs that expect all their processors to compute at the same time and not to have to wait on each other. This synchronous use of CPUs is maintained in the VMkernel with a technique known as *co-scheduling*. The co-scheduling algorithms have steadily evolved with each ESX (and ESXi) release, with continuous improvements being made to how the CPU scheduler deals with symmetric multiprocessor (SMP) VMs.

The CPU scheduler must take into account the number of physical CPUs and cores, whether HT is available, the placement of logical and physical cores in relation to the CPU caches and their cache hierarchy, and memory buses. It can make informed choices about which core each VM should run on, to ensure that the most efficient decisions are made. It dynamically moves vCPUs around cores to yield the most efficient configuration with regard to cache and bus speeds. It's possible to override the CPU scheduler on a VM basis by setting the CPU affinity in a VM's settings. This process is explained in Chapter 7, "Virtual Machines." By pinning vCPUs to specific cores, you can optimize a VM's usage. However, the built-in CPU scheduler is incredibly efficient, and pinning vCPUs to cores can prevent simultaneous workloads from being spread among available cores. This may lead to the VM performing worse and will interfere with the host's ability to schedule CPU resources for the other VMs.

CPU VIRTUALIZATION

CPUs from both Intel and AMD have continued to evolve alongside each other, mostly offering comparable features (albeit with each one pushing ahead of the other, followed by a quick period of catch-up). As each vendor's products are released, new features are added that can help to improve performance and capabilities while also potentially breaking compatibility with previous versions.

vSphere uses virtualization rather than CPU emulation, where everything runs in software and the underlying hardware is never touched. Virtualization is different in that it tries to pass as much as possible to the physical hardware underneath. This can result in significantly better performance and means VMs can take advantage of all the features the CPUs can offer. With regard to server hardware choices, the impact comes from compatibility between hosts. A VM runs on only one host at a time. However, when the host is a member of a cluster, the hosts must present similar CPUs to the guest VMs to allow vMotion. If a host exposes more (or fewer) features than another host in the cluster, you can't vMotion the VMs between them. This in turn affects other features that rely on vMotion, such as DRS.

You can configure clusters with Enhanced vMotion Compatibility (EVC) settings, which effectively dumbs down all the hosts to the lowest common denominator. This technically solves the incompatibility problems, but it isn't an effective use of your new CPUs and is something to avoid where possible.

Also be aware that there is currently no compatibility between Intel hosts and AMD hosts. You should split these servers into separate clusters whenever possible. Incompatible hosts can still power on VMs moved from other hosts, so you can take advantage of HA if you have no choice but to run a mixed cluster.

FT also has specific CPU requirements, which you should account for if FT is part of your design. Chapter 8 provides more details about FT requirements and how they may affect CPU decisions.

VMware uses three types of virtualization in its vSphere products:

Binary Translation   VMware's original method of virtualizing guest OSs is binary translation (BT) or, as VMware recently began calling it, *software-based virtualization*. BT attempts to pass as much as possible directly to the host's CPU; but it knows which calls shouldn't be allowed through, intercepts them, and translates them in software. Inevitably, this method uses slightly more CPU cycles than native OS calls, but very few calls need to be translated. It's surprisingly efficient and is the basic technique that VMware also uses on its hosted layer 2 products.

Paravirtualization   *Paravirtualization* is a technique that is possible when a guest VM is aware that it's virtualized and can modify its system calls appropriately. Because paravirtualization depends on guest OS cooperation, it can only be used with certain OSs. You can enable it on each VM with the Virtual Machine Interface (VMI) feature. Despite the fact that it's popular with Linux guests, Microsoft was slow to offer paravirtualized-enabled guests. With the advent of new CPUs and lack of OS support, VMware decided to discontinue support and announced that vSphere 4 would be the last major release with support for paravirtualization. VMI drivers will be removed from the Linux kernel from 2.6.36. Therefore, it's probably advisable not to design around this technique.

Hardware-Assisted Virtualization   With the advent of certain new processors, most of the system calls that can't be passed on directly can be intercepted in special hardware instead of software. This newer method of virtualization uses hardware-assisted CPU virtualization (HV). This reduces the associated CPU overhead and should improve overall processor efficiency. The introduction of HV-enabled servers has diminished the need for paravirtualization and is the main reason for it being retired.

VIRTUALIZATION ENHANCEMENTS

Subsequent generations of CPUs from both Intel and AMD offer virtualization-specific enhancements. The first generation supported CPU improvements, and the second generation of hardware advancements adds optimizations to the overhead associated with the memory management unit (MMU):

Hardware-Assisted CPU Enhancements   The hardware-assisted CPU enhancements are available in all CPUs that have the Intel VT-x or AMD AMD-V flags. These CPUs allow the use of a HV Virtual Machine Monitor (VMM), which is more efficient than BT and doesn't require guest support of paravirtualization.

Hardware-Assisted MMU Enhancements   Hardware-assisted MMU enhancements rely on a newer generation of CPUs. Intel packages this as Extended Page Tables (EPT) and AMD as Rapid Virtualization Indexing (RVI). These MMU improvements allow virtual-to-physical page mappings to occur in hardware, as opposed to being the responsibility of the hypervisor's MMU. CPUs with this feature can hold an additional level of page tables and avoid the need for the shadow page tables that the hypervisor normally maintains.

CPU Capacity

When you're selecting CPUs for your server hardware, there are several things to consider. The overall strategy of scaling up or scaling out may dictate the spread of CPUs to memory, which will be discussed in significantly more depth in the aptly named Scale Up versus Scale Out section. Because CPUs are such a significant part of a server's ability to consolidate VMs, it's important to get the most powerful processors possible.

The general premise of faster, newer, and more is reasonable and won't see you wrong; but for virtualization-specific scaling, you should look a little further. The high core count on some CPUs yields massive improvements. Get the most cores possible, because other than scaling up to more CPUs, you'll achieve the greatest improvements. Any recently purchased CPUs should have the hardware-assisted CPU and MMU additions, but this is worth checking. Paying more for incrementally faster CPUs usually won't give you the same return as additional cores.

Scaling the server to the VMs depends largely on the workload of the VMs and the number of vCPUs per VM. As an approximate guide, you should expect to get at least four vCPUs per physical core. As the number of cores per CPU increases, your vCPU consolidation may drop slightly because the cores are getting smaller proportions of the CPU bus and shared memory cache. Some workloads can comfortably fit far more vCPUs per core, so if possible test the configuration with your own environment.

RAM

In additional to CPUs, host memory is critical to the performance and scalability of the server. With the core count on most servers rising rapidly, it's increasingly important to have enough memory to balance the equation. There is little point in cramming a server full of the latest CPUs, if you have so little RAM that you can only power on a few VMs.

vSphere hypervisors are incredible efficient with memory usage and have several methods to consolidate as many VMs onto the same host as possible. In order to make the most of the limited supply, you should understand the basic ways in which guest VMs are allocated RAM.

MEMORY USAGE

vSphere hosts need memory for both the host and the VMs:

Host The host itself needs memory. It uses it to run the VMkernel processes, and the Service Console in the case of ESX hosts. This is used for the system, device drivers, and management agents.

VMs VMs have memory allocated to them that is mapped through to guests' physical memory pages for use by the OS. Each VM also carries a certain amount of overhead that depends on the RAM allotted, the number of vCPUs, the video memory (by default only 4 MB, but can be more if you need higher resolutions and multiple screens—for example, VDI workstations), and the base VM hardware. Table 4.1 shows the memory overhead incurred, over and above the memory you allocate, for the most common VM configurations.

TABLE 4.1: Memory Overheads for Common VM Configurations

ALLOCATED MEMORY	1 VCPU	2 VCPUS	4 VCPUS	8 VCPUS
512 MB	117 MB	165 MB	247 MB	426 MB
1 GB	124 MB	176 MB	258 MB	446 MB
2 GB	138 MB	198 MB	281 MB	484 MB
4 GB	166 MB	243 MB	325 MB	562 MB
8GB	222 MB	331 MB	414 MB	716 MB
16 GB	335 MB	508 MB	592 MB	1,028 MB

MEMORY MAPPING

The hypervisor maps the host's physical memory through to each powered-on VM. Ordinarily, the memory is divided into 4 KB pages and shared out to the VMs, and its mapping data is recorded using a page table. The guest OS is unaware that the memory is being translated via the hypervisor; the OS just sees one long, contiguous memory space.

vSphere can also use *large pages*. Large pages are 2 MB in size, and if a guest OS is able to and enabled to use them, the hypervisor uses them by default. Large pages reduce the overhead of mapping the pages from the guest physical memory down to the host physical memory.

HARDWARE-ASSISTED MAPPING

The memory mapping is stored in a shadow page table that is then available to the host's MMU, unless the host has CPUs that are capable of hardware-assisted memory mapping. Hardware-assisted MMU virtualization is possible if the host is fitted with either Intel's EPT support or AMD's RVI support (AMD's RVI is also occasionally referred to as Nested Paging Tables [NPT]). Using this additional hardware feature can improve performance compared to the shadow page table technique because it reduces the associated overhead of running it in software. Only some guest OSs can use hardware-assisted MMU; vSphere uses the shadow page table for those that aren't supported.

MEMORY OVERCOMMITMENT

vSphere has a unique set of features to overcommit its memory. This means it can potentially provide more memory to its guests than it physically has on board. It can transfer memory to guests that need more, improving the overall memory utilization of the server and increasing the level of consolidation possible.

Memory overcommitment is successful largely because at any one time, not all guests are using their full entitlement of allocated RAM. If memory is sitting idle, the hypervisor may try to reclaim some of it to distribute to guests that need more. This memory overcommitment is one of the reasons virtualization can use hardware more efficiently than regular physical servers.

Techniques to Reclaim Memory

Several methods exist in vSphere to reclaim memory from VMs, enabling more efficient guest memory overcommitment. These are the four primary methods used, in order of preference by the VMkernel:

Transparent Page Sharing   *Transparent page sharing* (TPS) is the process of removing identical memory blocks and replacing them with logical pointers to a single copy. The process is similar to how storage products use deduplication to reduce storage costs. When VMs use memory blocks that have the same content between them, or the same in a single VM, then only one copy needs to be stored.

Using TPS results in less host memory being used and therefore more opportunities to consolidate more running VMs on the one host. TPS doesn't compare every last byte, but instead uses a hash of each 4 KB page to identify pages that need closer inspection. Those are then compared to confirm whether they're identical. If they're found to be the same, then only one copy needs to be kept in memory. The VM is unaware that it's sharing the page.

Ballooning   When the VMware tools are installed into a guest OS, it includes a spurious device driver that is used for memory *ballooning* (more correctly known as *vmmemctl*). Ordinarily, the hypervisor is unaware of what memory is most important to the guest, and the guest doesn't know if the host is under memory pressure. The balloon driver is a mechanism the hypervisor can use to ask the guest to choose what memory should be released. The guest understands which pages are being used for what purpose and can make much better decisions about freeing up memory and swapping, so it has far less impact on performance.

When the VMkernel needs a guest to release memory, it *inflates* the balloon by telling the driver to try to consume more memory as a process in the guest. The guest OS then decides what is the least valuable to keep in memory. If the VM has plenty of free memory, it's passed to the balloon driver, and the driver can tell the hypervisor what memory pages to reclaim. If the VM doesn't have any free memory, the guest OS gets to choose which pages to swap out and begins to use its own pagefile (in the case of Windows) or swap partition/file (in the case of Linux). This means the balloon driver, and hence the hypervisor, can make full use of the guest's own memory-management techniques. It passes the host memory pressure on to the guests, which can make enlightened decisions about what pages should be kept in RAM and which should be swapped out to disk.

By default, the balloon driver only ever tries to reclaim a maximum of 65% of its configured memory. The guest must have a sufficiently large internal pagefile/swap to cover this; otherwise the guest OS can become unstable. As a minimum, you must ensure that your guests have the following available:

$$\text{Pagefile/swap} \geq (\text{configured memory} - \text{memory reservation}) \times 65\%$$

However, because there is the potential to change both the reservation and the pagefile after the VM is created, it's always advisable to make the guest's pagefile at least a large as the RAM allocated. Remember that if you bump up the VM's RAM, you need to also increase the internal guest pagefile for this reason.

Compression vSphere 4.1 introduced a memory-compression algorithm that analyzes each 4 KB page and determines whether it can compress the page down to at least 2 KB in size. If it can't compress the page that small, the page is allowed to be swapped to disk.

When the VM needs the page again, it decompresses the file back into guest memory. Despite the small latency and CPU overhead incurred by compressing and decompressing, it's still a considerably more efficient technique than host swapping. By default, the memory-compression cache is limited to 10% of guest's memory, and the host doesn't allocate extra storage over and above what is given to the VMs. This prevents the compression process from consuming even more memory while under pressure. When the cache is full, it replaces compressed pages in order of their age; older pages are decompressed and subsequently swapped out, making room for newer, more frequently accessed pages to be held in the cache.

Swapping When a VM is powered on, the hypervisor creates a separate swap file in the VM's working directory called *vmname*.vswp. It's used as a last resort to recover memory and page memory out to disk, when the host is under heavy memory contention. The VMkernel forcibly moves memory pages from RAM onto disk; but unlike the action of the balloon driver, it can't use the intelligence of the guest's memory management and grabs chunks of memory randomly.

Host swapping leads to significant performance degradation, because the process isn't selective and will undoubtedly swap out active pages. This swapping is also detrimental to the host's performance, because it has to expend CPU cycles to process the memory swapping.

If the guest is under memory pressure at the same time as the host, there is the potential for the host to swap the page to the .vswp file, and then for the guest to swap the same page to the guest's pagefile.

Host swapping is fundamentally different than the swapping that occurs under the control of the guest OS. Ballooning can take time to achieve results and may not free up enough memory, whereas despite its impact, host swapping is an immediate and guaranteed way for the host to reclaim memory.

When Memory Is Reclaimed

Memory is only reclaimed from nonreserved memory. Each VM is configured with an amount of memory. If no memory reservation is set, then when the VM is powered on, the .vswp file is created as large as the allocated memory. Any memory reservation made reduces the size of the swap file, because reserved memory is always backed by physical host memory and is never reclaimed for overcommitment. It's guaranteed memory and so is never swapped out by the host:

Swap file (vswp) = configured memory – memory reservation

Because the host never attempts to reclaim reserved memory, that proportion of memory is never under contention. The VM's shares only apply to allocated memory over and above any reservation. How much physical memory the VM receives above its reservation depends on how much the host has free and the allocation of shares among all the VMs.

The use of the memory-reclamation techniques depends on the amount of free host memory. Some processes run all the time, and others are activated as less free memory is available. If the VMkernel has more than 6% memory free, then it's considered not to be in contention. But when less than 6% is available, the host begins to compare VM shares to determine which VMs have priority over the remaining memory.

If the free memory drops lower, then as it reaches each predetermined threshold, more aggressive memory reclamation takes place. Each level is designed to get the host back to a free memory state:

Regular Cycle (Regardless of Memory State)   TPS runs regularly, even when there is no memory pressure on the host. By default, the host scans each VM every 60 minutes to find redundant pages. The one notable exception is after a Windows VM powers on, because the guest OS touches all of its memory as it boots up. vSphere runs TPS over those VMs immediately and doesn't wait until the next cycle.

However, TPS only scans 4 KB memory pages and not 2 MB large pages. This is because the large pages are far less likely to have identical contents, and scanning 2 MB is far more expensive. The one thing it does continue to do, regardless of the host's memory state, is create hashes for the 4 KB pages in the large pages.

The other process that runs regularly is the calculation of *idle memory tax* (IMT). VMs' memory shares are used when the host hits levels of memory contention, to figure out which ones should have priority. However, a VM with higher levels of shares may be allocated memory that it isn't actively using. To rebalance the shares so that those VMs that really need memory are more likely to get some, IMT adjusts the shares to account for the amount of unused memory. It "taxes" those VMs that have lots of idle memory. IMT is regularly calculated (every 60 seconds by default) despite the level of free memory on the host. Remember that the shares that are being adjusted are only taken into account when the host is in memory contention. IMT runs all the time but is used only when memory usage is above 94%.

Memory State Reaches High (94%)   When the memory state hits High, the hypervisor calls TPS immediately even if it isn't due for another run. Ideally, this brings the host back under 94%. As it rises toward the Soft limit, it preemptively starts to use the balloon driver, knowing that it can take time to reclaim memory, using the shares (adjusted by IMT) to make sure those deemed more worthy are under less pressure.

Memory State Reaches Soft (96%)   At the Soft memory state, ballooning is in full swing trying to reclaim memory from guests to recover the host back below 94%.

Memory State Reaches Hard (98%)   If the Hard memory state is reached, the host starts to forcibly reclaim memory by swapping the VMs' memory to their .vswp files. At this point, compression kicks in to try to reduce the amount of data being swapped out. In addition, large pages begin to be broken down into regular 4 KB pages so they can be shared via TPS to avoid them being swapped to disk if possible. Ideally, all these measures recover the host's memory back to a free state.

Memory State Reaches Low (99%) If the host's memory usage rises above the Low memory state, the host stops creating new pages for VMs and continues compressing and swapping until more memory is freed up and the host recovers.

Figure 4.2 shows the levels at which the different memory-reclamation techniques kick in. As less memory is available for the VMs, the VMkernel becomes more aggressive.

FIGURE 4.2
How memory is reclaimed

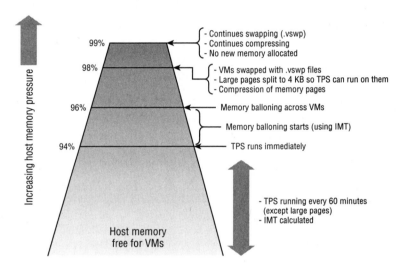

The one exception to these memory state levels is if a VM has a memory limit set. If an artificial limit is set, then when the VM reaches it, the host begins to balloon and, if necessary, swap the VM. The host does this even if it has plenty of free memory. Chapter 7 discusses the dangers of setting VM memory limits.

MEMORY CAPACITY

vSphere hypervisor servers demand more from their memory than the average general-purpose OS. Not only do they require swaths of capacity, but they often test the hardware more rigorously than other OSs.

Achieving the right balance of CPU cores to memory is important. A general rule of thumb is to make sure you have at least 4 GB RAM per core. Many of today's memory-hungry applications tilt this ratio, so you may need more memory than 4 GB per core, although this very much depends on workload. Remember, this ratio is related to the proportion of shared and reclaimed memory to the time-sliced co-scheduling of the CPU cores. It's used to understand what a balanced amount of RAM may be for an average server with a certain CPU configuration.

As the core density in modern servers grows, it can become increasingly difficult to fit in enough memory. At the time of writing, 4 GB modules are the sweet spot for memory. Jumping up to 8 GB modules can quadruple the price. However, if you have a 4-way 6-core server, you need at least 96 GB to make sure you have enough memory to back all the cores. Unless you have a server with at least 24 DIMM sockets, you'll have to pay the extra for those costly 8 GB modules.

As 8 GB modules become the norm and CPUs gain more cores, you should reevaluate this guideline for your environment. But be aware that more dense form-factor motherboards can constrain overall system performance unless more expensive memory is fitted.

Fortunately, vSphere licensing is based on CPU socket count, not RAM; if you have the slots available, buying the maximum amount of memory you can afford is probably worthwhile. Arguably, memory is the number-one scalability factor in any server. Aside from capacity, the front-side bus speed on the memory is an important element of overall server performance. The speed of the bus and the attached memory often have as much impact as the CPUs driving the instructions.

NUMA

Some servers come with non-uniform memory access (occasionally referred to as non-uniform memory architecture NUMA) enabled CPUs and motherboards. These are available on AMD Opteron, Intel Nehalem, and IBM x-Series servers.

Multi-CPU servers, particularly those with multiple cores, face a bottleneck when so many processors simultaneously try to access the same memory space through a single memory bus. Although localized CPU memory caches can help, they're quickly used up. To alleviate this issue, NUMA-enabled servers' CPUs are split into nodes that have access to localized RAM modules that have much lower latency. NUMA combines CPU and memory allocation scheduling. But if VMs need access to nonlocal memory, this can actually increase latency beyond normal SMP-style architecture and degrade performance.

vSphere can use NUMA-enabled systems and has a specially tuned NUMA CPU scheduler to manage the placement of VMs. Each VM is allocated a home node and is then given memory from the same home node. The NUMA scheduler dynamically balances the home-node allocations every 2 seconds, rebalancing them as each VM's CPU and memory requirements change.

The NUMA scheduler uses TPS memory sharing on a per-node basis to prevent shared pages being matched from nonlocal memory. You can disable this feature if memory is particularly tight on the server or if many VMs are very similar and will benefit the most from TPS.

One of the problems faced by the NUMA scheduler is VMs with more vCPUs than each node has cores. Also, if a VM is allocated more memory than a single node's local memory can provide, it must get some of its memory across an intersocket connection. vSphere 4.1 introduces *wide NUMA* scheduling to improve the placement of VMs with more vCPUs than a single node can hold, which prevents them becoming more scattered than they need to be and allocates memory as locally as possible. Of course, if you know how many vCPUs and how much RAM will be allocated to your larger VMs, you can scale your server design sufficiently to make sure that, where possible, the VMs will fit on a single NUMA node.

Often, NUMA is disabled in the BIOS. The setting Node Interleaving means that the server ignores NUMA optimizations and doesn't attempt to localize the memory. To enable the use of NUMA, make sure Node Interleaving is set to Disabled. Normally, NUMA is only enabled on hosts with at least four cores across at least two NUMA nodes.

NUMA allocation is yet another reason it's advisable to have similarly specified servers in the same DRS cluster. Otherwise, VMs can vMotion between hosts where the source has one NUMA node size but there's a different node allocation on the next. The DRS mechanism is currently unaware of NUMA calculations and sizes on each host.

Arguably, NUMA as a feature is useful but probably not enough to make you buy servers because they include it. However, if you're deploying servers that have NUMA, various design options can take advantage of the NUMA scheduling and maximize local low-latency memory access for your VMs. The physical placement of RAM modules in the motherboard slots affects which CPUs use that RAM as local memory, so normally you should follow your vendor's advice and ensure that the RAM modules are spread evenly so each CPU receives an equal share.

Motherboard

The server's motherboard, sometimes known as the mainboard or system board, dictates what components can be fitted to the server and how many of each. The motherboard is designed to cope with the hardware, so it shouldn't be a bottleneck; but different vendors try to provide competing efficiencies because the motherboard is one of the few pieces particular to them.

One of the more crucial elements on the motherboard is the chipset that provides the interface between the CPU and its front-side bus (FSB) to the memory and peripheral buses. The motherboard and its chipset mandate the number and type of CPUs, RAM slots, and PCI slots. Given sufficient space in the case, how expandable the server is depends on its motherboard.

The motherboard can also be responsible for an onboard RAID solution, although it's more common to use a separate controller card in large servers. It monitors the temperature of components and can adjust the internal fans appropriately. Motherboards also provide integrated peripherals such as serial, parallel, and USB ports and usually have onboard diagnostics.

Normally, motherboards aren't marketed as options, but they're the main differentiators between a vendor's models. Choosing a particular model of server isn't just about the form factor of the case, but primarily it's about the motherboard inside. From a vSphere design perspective, it dictates the expandability of the server and configuration maximums available. Generationally, newer boards allow you to connect newer hardware components. In addition to choosing the CPU family and number of sockets you need, along with the capacity to fit all the memory and cards required, you should look for designs with better bus speeds, the latest PCIe standards, and the largest system caches.

Storage

Storage in vSphere is a fundamental topic that is the basis for Chapter 6. From a server hardware perspective, it revolves around two different areas: the local storage that the server commonly boots from and the way in which the server connects to any shared external storage.

Local storage is most often used for the ESX or ESXi boot image. Other options exist, such as boot from SAN, which can negate the need for any local storage. The local storage can also be physically external to the server itself, in an expansion shelf connected via a SCSI cable.

If the local storage will be used to run VMs on a Virtual Machine File System (VMFS) partition, the performance of the disks is important. In this case, the speed of the disks, interface connector (SAS, SATA, and so on), RAID type, number of spindles in the RAID set, and RAID controller are all factors in the VM's performance, because disk I/O is important. Local VMFS storage is often used in small offices and remote office locations where shared storage may not be available. It tends to be significantly less expensive and so can be useful to store less important data, or as an emergency drop location if there are issues with shared storage.

If local storage is only used to boot the vSphere OS, performance is arguably less important. The ESXi hypervisor is loaded from disk entirely into memory, so apart from minor differences in boot speed, faster disks won't improve performance. Even ESX gains little from faster boot disks, and the expense in buying faster disks is probably better spent on more CPU cores or more RAM modules. For ESX in particular, it's worth considering fitting at least one spare disk, set to automatically swap in if there is a failure. Any production server should employ some sort of RAID redundancy protection, but an extra hot spare provides an inexpensive additional level of protection.

The more common storage for VMs is shared storage where the servers connect to centralized storage. The method a server uses to connect to that shared storage is dictated by the protocol and transport used by the storage array. The common connections are Fibre Channel (FC) host bus adapters (HBAs), Fibre Channel over Ethernet (FCoE) CNAs, iSCSI hardware HBAs, and Ethernet network cards for both software iSCSI and NFS. Because the speed and resilience of these connections can be paramount to VMs, the selection of the cards, their speed rating, the redundancy of ports, and the PCI connector type are all important. Select the best PCI card connection possible on the motherboard, because the storage cards should ordinarily take priority over any other I/O cards. It's advisable to buy two single-connector cards instead of one dual-port card if the budget allows, because this will help to spread the I/O across two PCI connectors and provide redundancy if a card fails or disconnects.

Network

Network I/O is also a cardinal vSphere design topic and is explained in depth in Chapter 5, "Designing Your Network," but several design choices with respect to server hardware are worth discussing at this juncture. First, although most servers have two or four onboard 1GbE network adapters, it isn't uncommon to see an extra two or even three four-port 1GbE PCI cards to cover all networking needs. If you're using any FC HBAs or CNAs, you should reserve the fastest PCI connections for them, and then use the next available fastest PCI slots for your additional network connections.

But if there is no need for other storage bandwidth-intensive cards, or you're going to use 10GbE cards to aggregate storage and network traffic, these should be in the fastest slots possible. Although using 10GbE ports is likely to reduce the number of cables used, at the time of writing no servers come with onboard 10GbE; and like storage cards, you may choose to use two one-port cards instead of a single two-port card, so you still need at least two high-speed PCI slots. Try to get cards that support NetQueue, because it can improve 10GbE performance.

If a company has specific rules about DMZ cabling or doesn't use trunked network ports, you may need even more network cards.

PCI

PCI is a standard bus used by expansion cards to connect to a motherboard. The original PCI standard has evolved through numerous versions, including the PCI-X and PCI Express (PCIe) revisions. Table 4.2 shows the increased theoretical maximum bandwidth between the standards.

TABLE 4.2:   PCI bus speeds

BUS	MAX BANDWIDTH
PCI	133 MB/s (although extended up to 533 MB/s for 64-bit at 66 MHz)
PCI-X	1,064 MB/s
PCI Express	250 MB/s per lane (8x is 2,000 MB/s, 16x is 4,000 MB/s, 32x is 8,000 MB/s)
PCI Express 2.0	500 MB/s per lane (8x is 4,000 MB/s, 16x is 8,000 MB/s, 32x is 16,000 MB/s)

The PCI-X interface became increasingly popular with 1GbE cards because the cards couldn't saturate the bus link. Now the PCI Express standard brings bus speeds closer to the FSB speeds used by CPUs today. Most new servers come with PCI Express slots, but you should check how many and of what type, because some have only one or two, may not be PCI Express version 2.0, or only offer 8x lanes. Consider the number of high-speed PCI slots against your card requirements.

VMDIRECTPATH

VMDirectPath is a technique employed by vSphere to directly connect up to two PCI devices to a VM, allowing the I/O to bypass the virtualization layer. This can potentially reduce latency and improve the performance of high-speed cards such as 10GbE and FC HBAs, but few cards are currently supported. To use VMDirectPath, the host CPU must support Intel's VT-d or, experimentally, can use AMD's IOMMU.

This method places several restrictions on the VM, such as no vMotion, Storage vMotion, FT, or snapshots. And the performance gains are thought to be so slight that unless device performance is paramount, VMDirectPath may be something you wish to avoid.

You should make sure your highest-speed slots are used for your highest bandwidth I/O cards, to avoid buses being a bottleneck. Usually, storage cards—whether FC HBAs, FCoE CNAs, or 10GbE interfaces—take precedence. If you're limited on PCI Express slots, ensure that these cards are fitted first. Less bandwidth-intensive workloads such as 1GbE network adapter cards can use less-well-specified slots. For a single-port 10GbE card, aim to use at least a PCI Express x8 slot; and for a dual-port card, use a x16 as a minimum.

PCI IRQ SHARING

No need to worry about PCI IRQ sharing anymore. Previous versions of ESX could experience issues with PCI IRQs, because the Service Console shared the IRQ allocation with the VMkernel. This resulted in some nasty performance problems for many customers. vSphere 4 eliminated this issue: the VMkernel now controls all the PCI IRQs.

One last important design consideration for host PCI slots is consistency. Ensuring that servers have the same cards in the same slots can ease installation and configuration, particularly cabling, and make troubleshooting hardware issues considerably more straightforward. This becomes increasingly important as your deployment techniques mature with greater levels of automation. If all the servers in a cluster are the same make and model, then having the same I/O cards in the same slots means that each port gets the same VMNIC or VMHBA number. If you have a multisite rollout, and you're able to purchase the same server hardware for more than one location, think about all the sites' storage and networking requirements before choosing which slot to use for which. For example, although you may only have a few sites with a FC SAN, with the rest using 1GbE-connected iSCSI or NFS devices, you may wish to always put the 1GbE cards into a slower slot. Even though at most sites you have one or two slots free that are very high performance, the 1GbE cards won't use the extra bandwidth, and you can keep all the servers consistent across the fleet.

Preparing the Server

After server hardware selection is complete, you should test the server's non-OS settings and hardware configuration prior to using them in production. You need to make several choices regarding their setup, and a good design should have a set of preproduction checks to make sure the hardware is deployed as planned. Hardware configuration and testing will affect the rollout.

Configuring the BIOS

Every server's hardware settings are primarily configured through its BIOS. Some of the default settings set by vendors are configured for general-purpose OSs and may not give you optimal performance with vSphere. To get the most from your servers, several settings should always be set:

Sockets and Cores Ensure that all occupied CPU sockets are enabled and all cores are enabled.

Hardware Assist Enable hardware-assisted virtualization features. For the CPU, this is Intel VT-x or AMD-V; for memory, it's Intel EPT or AMD RVI.

Execute Protection Enable the Execute Protection feature, because it's required for EVC. This is eXecute Disable (XD) on Intel-based servers or No eXecute (NX) on AMD.

Node Interleaving Disable node interleaving, or NUMA management won't be used. (IBM refers to this setting as Memory Interleaving.)

HyperThreading HT should be enabled.

The following are settings you may wish to consider changing:

Power Settings Servers often have power-management technologies that attempt to save power while they aren't being fully utilized. But some users report that these settings reduce vSphere's performance, stepping down the CPUs unnecessarily. Some of the newer servers now include OS Control as an option, which allows the hypervisor to control the CPU throttling. This tends to provide better results than letting the system's firmware moderate it. Consider disabling this setting, because performance should almost always be more important than saving power.

Turbo Mode Enable any Turbo Mode settings, which can temporarily increase the CPU clock speed when more performance is required and thermal limits allow. Intel uses the moniker Turbo Boost for this feature.

Extraneous Hardware Consider disabling any hardware that is unused, such as legacy serial and parallel ports. These continue to create unnecessary hardware interrupts while they're enabled and cost CPU cycles.

In general, you should aim to keep as many settings as possible at the manufacturer's default. Use the server installation as a good opportunity to update the BIOS to the latest version available. Do this first, before taking the time to change any options, because re-flashing the BIOS may reset everything. Strive to have all BIOS firmware levels and settings identical across every host in a cluster.

Other Hardware Settings

In addition to the BIOS settings, remember that you should set several other settings according to the designed environment:

RAID Controller and Disk Configuration Before installing the hypervisor, you need to configure the local disks into a usable RAID set. It's advisable to reserve one local disk as a hot spare.

I/O Cards Each I/O card, such as the network and storage PCI cards, has its own firmware that should be updated and configured. Normally, these are set up with a keystroke during the server's Power On Self Test (POST). You should consult not only the I/O card's manufacturer but also the destination device's recommended practices.

Remote Access Cards Most servers at least have the option of an out-of-band management card. Prior to being ready for production, you should set this device's IP address, hostname, password, and so on.

Burn-in

Before each server is unleashed under a production workload, you should test it extensively to ensure that any initial teething problems are identified and rectified. Most servers have a hardware diagnostic program in the BOIS, during the POST, or on a bootup CD. This utility runs a series of stress tests on each component, to make sure it can cope with a full load.

For vSphere, the server's memory is the most critical thing to test thoroughly, because it's used so much more intensively than normal. A useful free tool to test memory is Memtest86+, which you can download from www.memtest.org and burn to a CD. We recommend that you boot new servers off the CD and let the utility run its memory testing for at least 72 hours before using the server in production.

Preproduction Checks

Finally, after the server's hypervisor is installed and before the server is brought into a working cluster and allowed to host VMs, you should perform several checks:

◆   Memory and I/O cards have been fitted to the correct slots.

◆   The server is racked properly, and the cabling is correctly fitted. Using cable management arms not only helps improve airflow but also allows access to the servers without shutting them off to change hot-swap items and check diagnostic lights.

◆ The storage cards can see the correct datastores. If you're using NFS, the server has write access to each datastore.

◆ The network cards can see the correct subnets. Move a test VM onto each port group, and test connectivity.

◆ This is a good opportunity to make sure the hypervisor is patched.

◆ NTP is working properly.

◆ The server has the appropriate vSphere licensing.

Scale Up vs. Scale Out

vSphere allows administrators to spread the x86 infrastructure across multiple physical hosts, with the ability to consolidate several workloads onto each server. Each VM's hardware layer is virtualized, abstracting the underlying physical compute resources such as CPU and memory from each VM's allocation. This abstraction allows you to separate the decisions around VM scaling from those of the host servers. The process of virtualizing the guest systems gives rise to an important design decision: how much consolidation is desirable. The ever-expanding capabilities of today's hardware allows an unprecedented level of VMs to hypervisors; but as an architect of vSphere solutions it's important to understand that just because they can be larger doesn't necessarily make them the most desirable configuration for your business.

The *scale-up versus scale-out* argument has existed as long as computers have. Virtualized infrastructure has its own implications on the debate; and as hardware evolves, so do the goal posts of what scale-up and scale-out really mean. Essentially, a *scale-up* design uses a small number of large powerful servers, as opposed to a *scale-out* design that revolves around many smaller servers. Both aim to achieve the computing power required (and both can, if designed properly), but the way in which they scale is different.

The classic scale-up scenario was based around server CPU sockets; in general computing circles during the ESX virtualization era, this usually meant one or two sockets for scale-out and four or eight sockets for scale-up. But in the last few years, this definition has been significantly blurred, primarily due to a couple of hardware advances. First, the size of RAM modules in terms of gigabytes and the number of DIMM sockets per motherboard has increased massively. Even in relatively small servers with one or two sockets, the amount of memory that can be fitted is staggering. Smallish blade servers can take large amounts of RAM. For example, Cisco's UCS servers can handle up to 384 GB of RAM! Second, the number of physical sockets on a server no longer necessarily dictates the CPU processing power, because the advent of multicore CPUs means a 2-way server can have 12 CPU cores, and an 8-way server can have a colossal 48 cores.

These monstrous memory and core levels rewrite the rules on scale-up and scale-out, and reiterate the message that the design is no longer based only on socket numbers. But the underlying premise still holds true. Scale-up is a smaller number of more powerful servers; scale-out is about lots of smaller servers. It's just that the definitions of large and small change and are based on differing quantifiable means.

With regard to vSphere servers, the scale-up or scale-out debate normally revolves around CPU and memory. I/O is less of a performance bottleneck, and storage and networking requirements are more often an issue of function rather than scale. These things work or they don't; it isn't so much a matter of how well they work. We're talking about the server hardware, not the switches or the storage arrays themselves. Obviously, storage can be a performance bottleneck, as can the backplanes on the switches; but with regard to the server hardware, we mean the I/O cards, adapter ports, and transport links. These adapters rarely dictate a server's level of scalability. There can be clear exceptions to this, such as security-focused installations that require unusually large numbers of network ports to provide redundant links to numerous air-gapped DMZ switches, or hosts that need to connect to several older smaller SANs for their collective storage. Create a rule, and there will always be an exception. But generally speaking, scale-up versus scale-out server design is concerned with CPU and memory loading.

As this chapter has identified, CPU and memory are both important performance characteristics of a host server. It's important to note that for the *average* VM workload, you need to maintain a good balance of each. Even though RAM modules are inexpensive and a two-socket server can fit a very large amount of memory, they may not help much if the VMs are CPU constrained. Similarly, even if it's comparatively cheap to buy six-core CPUs instead of two-core CPUs, if you can't afford the extra memory to fit alongside them, the extra cores may be wasted. The CPU and memory requirements must normally be in balance with each other to be truly effective.

A common misconception is that scaling up means rack servers and scaling out means blades. The densities that can be achieved in both form factors mean that scaling up and out decisions aren't necessarily the same discussion. To understand a business's requirements, you should examine each independently. Although there is potential for cross-over in arguments, one certainly doesn't mean the other. Blades and rack servers have their own interesting architectural considerations, and we'll look at them in the next section.

Now that you understand the basic definitions of scaling up and out, we can compare each approach.

Advantages of Scaling Up

The advantages of scaling up are as follows:

Better Resource Management Larger servers can take advantage of the hypervisor's inherent resource optimizations, such as TPS or CPU co-scheduling (but remember that by default, TPS on NUMA servers only shares pages on the same NUMA node, not across the entire server). Although scaling out can use DRS to load balance, it doesn't make such efficient use of resources.

Larger servers can cope with spikes in compute requirements much more effectively, whereas smaller servers have to react by using load-balancing techniques that incur significant delay.

Cost This is an interesting advantage, because the classic scaling based on CPU sockets meant that scaling up used to be more expensive. Generally, a four-way SMP server was much more expensive than four one-socket servers. However, with the changes in server components, scaling up often means adding more and more cores and RAM modules; and by scaling up instead of buying more and more smaller servers, you're likely to achieve some savings. By scaling up, the RAM or processors need not be more expensive, so scaling can be linear, and you save on the number of PSUs, I/O cards, case components, and so on.

Fewer Hypervisors With fewer servers loaded with ESX or ESXi, you have fewer hypervisors to manage. Despite the number of VMs running, each physical server needs to have its hypervisor OS installed, maintained, patched, upgraded, monitored, and so on. Scaling up means fewer instances to manage.

Lower Software Licensing Costs   VMware licenses its software on a socket basis, so having servers with more cores and more memory means fewer socket licenses to buy. This makes scaling up an attractive option when your business is paying for every server it adds.

Additionally, many businesses license their guest OS software on physical servers. You can buy Microsoft server licensing to cover unlimited guest copies per host hypervisor. The fewer hosts, the fewer licenses needed.

Larger VMs Possible   Large servers give you more flexibility with VM scaling. A two-way dual-core server can only accommodate a VM with four vCPUs, and even that isn't particularly desirable. If you stick to the rule that you should always have more cores than the largest VM has vCPUs, then such a server should only host VMs with two vCPUs. If you can feasibly think that some elements of your business will need VMs with 8 vCPUs, then you may want to consider hosts with at least 12 cores (2-way 6 cores, or 4-way with quad cores).

Less I/O Cabling   Each vSphere host is likely to need a similar number of network and storage cables attached. By using fewer but more powerful servers, you cut down the switch ports, fabric ports, and cabling needed. This in itself may reduce the number of fabric switches or switch blades, further reducing the amount of infrastructure provisioning required. The network team has fewer server ports to manage, and the storage team doesn't need to maintain so many zones, masks, redundant links, and so on.

Less Power and Cooling   Generally speaking, scaling up uses less power per VM, and needs less cooling, than a scale-out approach. Although smaller servers use fewer watts, a server with half the number of cores or RAM won't reduce the power consumption by 50%.

Advantages of Scaling Out

In comparison to larger servers, more servers that are less powerful have the following advantages:

Less Impact During a Host Failure   Having fewer VMs per server reduces the risk if a physical host failure should occur. The old adage of not putting all your eggs in one basket is the point here, and this is one of the predominant advantages to scaling out.

Arguably, having twice as many servers, each with half the parts, should mean that you get twice the number of failed hosts on average. But the reality is that you'll have fewer outages per VM. Hardware failures are likely to account for relatively few hosts failures. Server components are so reliable and are backed by so many redundant subsystems that they don't often collapse in a heap. User error is far more likely cause of host failure these days.

Although scaling out may reduce overall VM outages per year, that's not the main point. The real importance of scaling out is the impact of a single host failure. When a host fails, and they will fail occasionally, fewer VMs will fail at once. One of the greatest worries that companies have about virtualization is that host failures can have such a significant effect on services. By scaling out to many more servers, fewer VMs are affected at once.

Although HA is a great recovery mechanism, reducing the time VMs are offline, it doesn't prevent VM outages when a host fails. With fewer VMs per host, HA should recover those VMs far more quickly. In a scale-out situation, if a host fails, HA has fewer VMs to recover and also has more hosts on which to recover them. Generally, the VMs are up and running again much more quickly. After the VMs are brought back up, DRS can load-balance those VMs more effectively than if there is a much smaller pool of hosts.

Less Expensive Host Redundancy   Most companies have a policy of host redundancy of at least *n+1*. With a scale-out approach, this is significantly cheaper to accomplish.

Easier Continuation of Scaling over Time   When the servers are small, it's more straight-forward to add nodes as demanded. The significant cost of scale-up hosts can make it difficult to add another host; but a scale-out host gives you more granularity, meaning you can slowly add hosts as you go. Scale-up clusters are more likely to be replaced wholesale after they reach their useful limit.

More Efficient Bus I/O   With an increase in the number of cores and the amount of RAM in each server, the various internal buses come under increasing pressure. Larger servers have solutions such as NUMA to try to deal with this issue, but that can create significant performance compromises for the hypervisor. Smaller servers have more bandwidth available on these buses for throughput, which can lead to reduced latency for the CPU to memory bus. Despite a reduction in possible TPS and CPU co-scheduling opportunities, more scaled-out servers may provide better performance in your environment.

Scaling Is a Matter of Perspective

The classic picture of scale-up and scale-out being one to two sockets versus four or eight isn't appropriate in many situations. It's all about the interpretation of what is *large* and what is *small*. For example, compared to six one-socket servers, three two-socket servers is scaling up. And instead of four eight-way servers, using eight four-way servers is scaling out. The same can be said of cores versus sockets or the size of the RAM modules. It's all a matter of perspective.

Whatever a business considers scaling up or out is always tempered somewhat by their VM requirements. It's often not out or up, but what is right for them. It's unlikely that any company will only opt for two very large servers, because if it's hoping to have *n+1* redundancy, it effectively needs two hosts that are so large the company could run everything from one. That means buying double the capacity the company needs. Neither is a company likely to decide that 32 hosts per cluster is a good idea, because the company will lose any efficiencies of scale, and such a solution doesn't leave any room for host growth in the cluster.

Sizing hosts appropriately depends on the work you expect. Hosts will vary if you're going to run hundreds of workstation VDI desktops, or a handful of very large Tier-1 multi-vCPU workhorses. Generally, large VMs need large hosts, and lots of small VMs work best with scaled-out hosts.

Risk Assessment

The biggest fear with a scaled-up architecture is the large impact created by a single host failure. This risk is largely dependent on the business and the applications running on the hosts. Is such aggressive consolidation worth the associated risk? If the server hosts business-critical VMs, then perhaps reducing the consolidation ratio to limit the risk of an outage is justified. Some companies split their resources so that most VMs run in large consolidated scaled-up hosts; other, more important VMs run in a cluster that is designed with smaller hosts that have consolidation ratios normally found in a scale-out approach.

You should consider the risk of a failure of a particularly heavily loaded host in the context of its likelihood. Yes, there is always the chance that a host will fail. However, think of some of your organization's other critical infrastructure pieces. For example, many businesses run all of their main datacenter's VMs from a single storage array. That one array is stacked full of redundant parts, but it's still a single infrastructure piece. Unfortunately, servers don't have the same level of redundancy. But if you manage your hosts properly, with good maintenance and change-control procedures, host failures should be very rare.

Fear still drives a lot of companies away from scale-up designs. If an application is that critical to the business, much more than server hardware redundancy and vSphere HA should be in place to protect it. With the correct level of software insurance, only the most extremely risk-averse situations should shy away from scale-up servers for fear of host outages. Many options exist, such as VMware's FT, guest OS-based clustering, and failover written into applications. These extra levels of protection should supplement the most important VMs.

It's important to think about how applications interoperate, as well. There is little point in having clustered VMs run across servers that are scaled up so much that a single server failure will apply enough pressure on the remaining nodes that the application becomes unusable. On the other hand, scaling out servers to minimize the risk to an application won't help if all the VMs need to be online for the application to work. A single host failure, however scaled out, will still bring down the entire system. This is where you can design VM affinity and anti-affinity rules, along with host sizing, to protect your VMs.

If you're less concerned with the potential risk of large hosts, it's worth considering that these days, application owners think less and less about redundancy and failover. This is largely due to the success of virtualization and improvements to hardware and guest OS stability. In the days before mainstream x86 virtualization, application owners thought carefully about hardware redundancy and what would happen if a server were to fail. But with the ease of provisioning new virtual servers, and the belief that vSphere hosts with DRS and HA features are infallible, many application designers assume that their failover needs are taken care of. They don't realize that hosts can still fail—and that when they do, their VMs will go down. This means that more and more, it's down to those designing the vSphere layer to understand the applications that run on it and the level of risk associated with an outage.

Choosing the Right Size

Getting the right scaled hosts is usually a good balance of risk versus cost efficiencies. Scaling up saves money on OPEX and licensing. Larger servers used to be prohibitively expensive, but this is no longer the case. Most costs are fairly linear. Adding more cores is now often cheaper than scaling out; and because servers have increasingly large DIMM banks, there is less need to buy very expensive RAM modules. CAPEX-wise, price your scale-up and scale-out options, because it will depend on your definition of *up* and *out*. You may be surprised to find that scaling up is no longer the more expensive option.

Another issue that used to plague scale-up solutions was rack space, because most four-socket servers were at least 3Us, and often 4Us or 5Us. Today, with such dense core packages on the processors, your scale-up option may be on a 1U server or even a blade.

Look at the VM workload and the number of VMs, and consider what you think the pain points will be. Sometimes different situations require solutions that most would consider lopsided. You may have very high CPU requirements or unusually high memory requirements. The scale-up and scale-out approaches may also differ within an organization. The company's main datacenter probably has very different compute requirements than one of its branch offices. For example, a design that chooses a scale-out approach in the datacenter may want a scale-up for its smaller sites. The fact that the scaled-out servers are larger than the remote office's scaled-up servers is a product of the situation.

When you're considering the desirable consolidation ratio for VMs on each host, it's important to remember that after a design is implemented, the ratio will very likely change naturally. Undoubtedly, more VMs will appear, and it may be some time before the hosts are scaled up or out further to accommodate the extra VMs. Consolidation ratios should be designed with the expectation that they will be stretched.

It's easy for this to become a "religious" debate, and all too often architects have strong opinions one way or the other. These preferences can often cloud the best decision for a business, because every situation is different. Each company has its own unique requirements, and only by revisiting the base differentiators can you make an objective agnostic decision every time. It's important to remember that as hardware capabilities constantly change and evolve, this decision should be continually reviewed. Although you had a preference for scale-out last year, this year you may think differently for the same business and opt with scale up (or vice versa).

Blade Servers vs. Rack Servers

In addition to the continual debate over scaling up or out, the intertwined argument over blade or rack servers continues unabated. This is also a contentious issue, but slightly more quantitative. There are different opinions about what a scale-up or scale-out solution is, but a server is definitively either a blade or a rack. Each manufacturer has its own twist, but generally a rack server is a standalone unit that is horizontally mounted. A blade server uses a chassis or enclosure, with certain shared components such as power, backplane, and I/O units. It's common to see the blade servers mounted vertically with half- or full-height options.

The blade versus rack discussion used to be far more closely aligned with scale-up and scale-out solutions, because blades were always considered to be a very dense, lower-performing option. But these days, that categorization isn't as applicable. You can find blade servers in four-way configurations with potential for several hundred gigabytes of memory. Also, some manufacturers are beginning to produce rack servers that can compete with blades on power efficiency and reduced cabling.

With that caveat understood, you can generalize about blades and take them as a scale-out option, the advantages and limitations of which we covered in the last section. Our discussion here will focus on the differences inherent in the two form factors.

Servers have also long come in tower models. Towers serve a purpose and shouldn't automatically be discounted even by large enterprises. But their large size usually prevents them from being space efficient enough in all but the smallest deployment. Also, remember that tower servers should be specified just like any other production server with adequate hardware redundancy and quality components. Towers aren't often used in virtualization environments because they tend to be very underpowered; but if a small branch office needs a stand-alone server, and you want to consolidate its small workload on a hypervisor, a tower can prevent the cost and space requirements that come with a half-height rack installation.

Blade Servers

Both blades and racks are viable options with vSphere. Despite a blade's limitations, you can make it work in a virtualized environment. Although rack servers are very much the predominant force in the server market, blades have always attracted those interested in hypervisors. Often, the same people who can see the distinct advantages of consolidation, energy efficiency, and modular hardware options in vSphere can see obvious synergies with blade servers as their form factor of choice.

However, those who dabbled with blades when they first arrived were often hit by first-generational teething problems: poor redundancy, lack of management tools, BIOS issues, no training, excessive heat, and so on. This has tarnished the view of many server engineers, and some are vehemently opposed to using blades. But in many situations, using blade servers offers real gains.

The Case for Blade Servers

After a blade chassis has been fitted to a rack and cabled in, adding/removing/replacing blades is trivial. It takes only minutes to fit or unrack a server and move it to new chassis. The modular design is one of its key strengths. This can be one of most obvious OPEX cost-reduction effects of using blade servers.

Their combined midplane reduces the amount of cabling, which not only reduces the OPEX but can also reduce the CAPEX resulting from cabling costs in a datacenter. Fewer power cables are required in racks and therefore fewer PDU connectors. The reduction in the number of Ethernet and FC cables going to the next hop switch cuts cabling costs and can also substantially reduce the number of ports on network and storage switching equipment.

Blade chassis can potentially allow for a reduction in rack-space usage. You can typically fit at least 50% more servers into the same area than even 1U rack servers. If you lease your rack space, this can be quite a cost saving. Most of the current generation chassis offer very advanced management tools, which can surpass those found on rack servers; and unlike the rack equivalents, which can be licensed extras, the blade's tools are usually included in the price of the chassis. These advanced management tools can provide remote management (power options and remote consoles), virtual hardware device emulation (mounting remote media), midplane configuration, BIOS management, automated provisioning, and so on.

Traditionally, blade servers have offered power efficiency savings. By combining several servers' PSUs together, a chassis can reduce the number of PSUs well below the normal minimum of two per rack server and still provide hardware redundancy. Modern blade chassis use incredibly efficient PSUs, to try to reduce heat generation as much as possible. They can automatically step down their power consumption depending on how full the enclosure is.

With the increasing use of 10GbE in servers, storage, and networking equipment, blades become even more viable. The additional bandwidth they can provide means that much higher I/O is possible down to each server. The interconnects on many of the chassis backplanes are 10GbE, with extremely fast interserver traffic possible. This removes one of the biggest drawbacks that blades posed, particularly to virtualized workloads that needed excessive Ethernet cabling.

With the increase in CPU core density, the availability of four-way blades, and large DIMM socket density, it's possible to build very powerful blade servers. Considering that vSphere servers aren't usually built to depend heavily on local storage, blades can make excellent hypervisors.

Additionally, often companies don't virtualize everything they have, and it's possible to mix non-ESX servers into chassis to spread the HA and I/O load.

THE CASE AGAINST BLADE SERVERS

One of the biggest constraints with blade servers that deters many companies is the much higher initial entry cost. Before deploying your first blade server, you must buy and fit a full chassis with power supplies, network, and possibly FC mezzanine. This can effectively make the first server very expensive. If you buy several blades at once, this cost can be absorbed. Either you need a flexible budget in which you can offset CAPEX investments for subsequent blades, or you must plan to purchase quite a few blades in the first order to make the cost more palatable. The tipping point for blade servers is usually somewhere around seven or eight per chassis, at which point you can begin to see reasonable unit costs per server. Anything less means each server will seem very expensive.

Server technology churns frequently, with new models and features arriving all the time, so you shouldn't expect to wait several years to fill each chassis—those empty slots may become useless because the new blades may need newer chassis. Make sure the chassis, all its integrated equipment, and the change in infrastructure provide a suitable ROI. The chassis are proprietary to the vendor, so you're locked into those blades and their add-on options after you buy the chassis. You're entirely reliant on the vendor's hardware plans, so in the future you may be limited to the technology roadmap the vendor chooses. If it delays moving to the next CPU architecture, doesn't offer the latest chipset options, or doesn't provide a new I/O protocol or transport, there is little you can do.

Another frequently quoted concern about blades is the chance of an entire chassis failure. Such failures are regarded as very rare, but the thought is enough to dissuade many businesses. If you've ever experienced a complete chassis outage that takes all the blades down at once, it's likely to make you think twice about purchasing blades again. People dismiss scaling up their vSphere servers to two or three times their usual size, for fear of losing all their VMs in one go. Imaging losing 16 scaled-out servers for a period of time. Although vendors describe chassis failures as extremely unlikely, there are always single points of failure involved; and if that risk is too much, this is a very real barrier to adopting blades.

This possibility of a single point of failure also influences certain aspects of your vSphere design. For example, as discussed in Chapter 8, the HA feature currently nominates five cluster hosts to be primaries. Should all five primary HA servers fail at once, then none of the secondary servers will be promoted, and no VMs will be recovered. You should carefully spread primaries across chassis, which unfortunately isn't easy to accomplish.

If you've ever stood behind several fully loaded blade chassis, then you know the tremendous amount of heat they can generate. Although high server density is an obvious advantage of using blade servers, you need to be prepared for the very high power and subsequent cooling requirements. Today's datacenters are struggling to keep up with these physical demands, and the power or cooling available to you may be limited. Although blades shouldn't produce any more heat than their rack equivalents, they allow increased concentration. If you expect to take the same amount of space and fill it with blade servers, then you'll need more power and more cooling. Think about the hot spots blades can create and how they affect your hot and cold aisle distribution. You may need additional cooling units and extractors over particular areas to account for uneven heat distribution.

When introducing blades, especially in larger environments, you may find that internal teams need to work more closely than they're accustomed to. If there are separate server, storage, and networking teams, you will need buy-in from all parties. They may be accustomed to physical separation of equipment, but with blades chassis, the management tools and rack space are shared. You may have to change internal processes for teams that are used to being independent. Often, these teams have disparate purchasing cycles and separate budgeting models, so the financial logistics may need to change. To make this happen, a cultural shift is often required, which can more difficult to achieve than you expect. Or, as sometimes happens, the server guys may need to come up to speed with network switches and storage equipment very quickly.

One often-overlooked aspect of using blades is training. Rack servers are a known entity, and it's fairly straightforward for an engineer to maintain a new model or even move to a new vendor's equipment. But blade servers are different beasts and need a lot of internal management that may require additional training. Even moving from one blade vendor to another can involve an uphill learning curve, because blades are much more proprietary than rack servers. A deeper understanding of network and storage switches is often needed, and non-server engineers may have to familiarize themselves with new management tools.

Blade chassis used to suffer terribly from a lack of I/O in comparison to their corresponding rack server models. 10GbE has resolved many of these issues; but unless you already have a 10GbE uplink switch to connect to, this can require expensive upgrades to your switching infrastructure. Most vendors should have 10GbE and FC mezzanine cards available, but you may not always find the 8 Gbps FC option, CNA cards, or even a compatible connector for your requirements. Even when it comes to changing from one standard to another, you normally have to do it en masse and exchange the entire chassis's I/O options at once.

Even with 10GbE, you'll still find I/O limitations with vSphere. You'll almost certainly need to rely on VLANing to separate the traffic to reduce the broadcast domains and provide basic security segregation. vSphere 4.1 introduced the network I/O control (NIOC) feature, which can help provide simple quality of service (QoS) while aggregating the traffic onto a smaller number of cables and maintaining redundant links. But blade servers can never match rack servers with their full PCI slots for I/O expansion options.

Despite the fact that the blades have access to very fast interconnects, chances are that most of the traffic will still exit each blade, go out through the network cards, and hit a physical network switch where the default gateway sits. Localizing traffic in a chassis usually depends on the network cards' functionality and how capable and interested the network team is.

Blades are considerably more powerful than they used to be, with four-socket CPU configurations possible and many more DIMM slots than previously. The increase in core density has also improved the viability of blades, increasing the compute density. However, even though some blades offer up to 16 DIMM sockets, to really scale out in terms of some of the large four-way rack servers is very expensive, because you have to use large, costly memory modules. It's difficult to fit enough memory to keep up with the number of cores now available. Even the most powerful blades can't compete with the levels of scalability possible with rack servers. For your most ambitious scale-up architectures and your most demanding Tier-1 applications, you may find that blades don't measure up.

Rack Servers

An often lauded downside of rack servers is that they consume more physical rack space. You literally can't squeeze as many of them into as small a space as you can with dense blade servers. However, if you're not space constrained, this may not be such a disadvantage. Blades tend to increase heat and power usage in certain areas in your datacenter, creating hotspots. Often, virtualization projects free up space as you remove less powerful older servers and consolidate on fewer, smaller, and often more energy-efficient servers that take up less space than their predecessors. If you have plenty of space, why not spread out a little?

One advantage of rack servers is that they can be rolled out in small numbers. Unlike blades, which need several servers to be deployed at a minimum to make them economical, rack servers can be bought individually. In small offices that need one or two vSphere servers, you wouldn't even consider a blade chassis purchase. By choosing rack servers to also use in your larger datacenters, you can standardize across your entire fleet. If you don't need to manage two different form factors, then why would you?

You can also redeploy rack servers to different locations without having to provide an accompanied chassis. They're standalone units, so you can more easily redistribute the equipment. Rack servers also provide opportunities for upgrading, because they're much more standardized and usually take standard PCI cards. If you need to add the latest I/O card to support new network or storage technologies, then doing so will always be easier, and probably cheaper, on a set of rack servers.

If you need to be able to scale up, then rack servers will always be the obvious choice. Although blades can scale up to respectable levels these days, they can never match the options with rack servers. Many datacenter backbones are still 1GbE, and it isn't uncommon to see vSphere host servers with the need for two quad NIC cards and a pair of FC HBA ports. In addition to the number of ports, if you have very heavy I/O loads and bandwidth is particularly important, you're likely to opt for rack servers, because blades can't offer the same level of bandwidth across the entire chassis. Most blades still come as two sockets, so even four-way servers are usually rack servers, not blades. If you need to scale up beyond four sockets, rack servers are really the only option.

Blade servers have long been admired for their cable consolidation, but with 10GbE PCI cards, you can consolidate all networking and storage demands down to similarly small numbers on rack servers as well. Even some of the advanced management features that blade chassis enjoy are starting to be pushed back up, allowing the management of rack servers in common profile configurations.

Form-Factor Conclusions

Both blades and rack-mounted servers are practical solutions in a vSphere design. Blades excel in their ability to pack compute power into datacenter space, their cable minimization, and their great management tools. But rack servers are infinitely more expandable and scalable; and they don't rely on the chassis, which makes them ultimately more flexible.

Rack servers still dominate, holding more than 85% of the worldwide server market. Blades can be useful in certain situations, particularly in large datacenters or if you're rolling out a brand-new deployment. Blades are inherently well suited to scale-out architectures, whereas rack servers can happily fit either model. Blades compromise some elements. But if you can accept their limitations and still find them a valuable proposition, they can provide an efficient and effective solution.

A reasonable approach may be to use a mixture of small rack-mounted servers in your smaller offices, have some blade chassis making up the majority of your datacenter needs, and use a few monster rack servers to virtualize your largest Tier-1 VMs. After the blade chassis are filled, the cost per VM works out to be very similar. Neither blades nor racks are usually very different in cost per vCPU and gigabyte of memory. As long as each solution can provide sufficient processing power, memory, I/O, and hardware redundancy, either form factor is acceptable. Much of the decision comes down to personal preference drawn from previous experiences and seeing what works and doesn't work in your environment.

Alternative Hardware Approaches

Before trotting down to your local vendor's corner store with a raft of well-designed servers on your shopping list, you may wish to consider a couple of alternatives: cloud computing and converged hardware. Both approaches are in their relative infancy, but momentum is starting to grow behind each one. Although neither is likely to displace the role of traditional server purchases any time soon, it's worth considering where you might benefit and look at how they could replace elements of your existing design.

Cloud Computing

Much is being made of the term *cloud computing* these days, but confusion often remains about its place in traditional infrastructure models. Cloud computing is really a generic term used to describe computing services provided via the Internet. Rather than buying servers, storage, and networking in-house, you work with an external company that provides a service offering. Such offerings can usually be classified into three common models:

Infrastructure as a Service   Infrastructure as a Service (IaaS) provides the basic hardware infrastructure required, so you can install your own OS and applications. This typically includes servers, storage, datacenter space, networking equipment, and bandwidth.

You may be offered two different versions of IaaS. With the first, the hosting company provides you with a dedicated physical server, and you're responsible for the hypervisor, the VMs, the guest OSs, and the applications (similar to the traditional hosted model). With the second type of IaaS, you get only the virtual infrastructure. The hosting company manages the virtualization layer, and you control your VMs and templates on the provided hypervisor or transfer them from your existing infrastructure.

Platform as a Service   Platform as a Service (PaaS) gives you everything up to a working OS and may offer preinstalled frameworks. Most companies offer either basic Linux or Windows platforms. You can log in to your server and install and configure your software. Examples of current PaaS offerings are Microsoft Azure and Google App Engine.

Software as a Service   Software as a Service (SaaS) is the most hands-off approach. The external company runs everything behind the scenes, and your users merely have the ability to log in to the remote software and use it via their web browser. SaaS is particularly popular for CRM, accounting, ERP, HR, and financial software. Examples of SaaS products are Google Docs, Salesforce, and Microsoft Exchange Hosted Services and Office 365.

Clearly IaaS has an obvious correlation to an existing or a newly designed vSphere environment. When you're considering new hardware, it's becoming more feasible to consider external providers to provide that hardware and manage it for you. VMware's own vCloud Director is a product that gives external service providers the tools to provide these IaaS services around the vSphere hypervisor more easily.

Amazon is the clear market leader with its Xen-based Elastic Compute Cloud (EC2) model. Some of the other prominent players in this IaaS space currently are the large web-hosting companies such as Rackspace and AT&T.

IaaS can be a boon for small business and startups, because minimal technical knowledge is needed to get going. It can be instantly deployed and accessed worldwide. It's completely self service, so users can create instances themselves. IaaS is usually pay-as-you-go, so you only need to pay for the time it's been used—you don't need to justify it through an entire hardware lifecycle. And IaaS is instantly scalable; if you need more compute power, you just add more.

The biggest concern for any company regarding these cloud computing offerings is security. Most businesses are rightfully wary of giving up all their precious data to sit in someone else's datacenter, relying on their backups and entrusting an external company with the keys.

Despite the considerable hype surrounding cloud computing and the ongoing growth in this sector, there will always be a substantial need for in-house vSphere deployments on privately owned servers. Don't worry: despite the pundits' warnings, our jobs are safe for now. However, this is an increasingly interesting market, which gives you more options when designing how to deploy VMs. You may wish to investigate external hardware IaaS solutions prior to making any large investment, to compare costs and see if IaaS is a viable option.

Converged Hardware

Most server vendors are starting to come to market with their versions of a converged solution that combines servers, virtualization, networking, and storage in various ways. This may be a combination of the vendor's own home-grown equipment, because some vendors have expanded or bought their way into diversified markets; or it may be the result of a coalition between hardware partners. The coalitions are often the outcome of *coopetition*, where companies in related fields such as servers, storage, and networking work together in some parts of the market where they don't directly compete, but continue to vie with each other in other areas.

For example, here are some of the more popular current examples of these converged market products:

Vblocks   Vblocks are a product of the Virtual Computing Environment (VCE) coalition. VCE involves Cisco and EMC selling their combined products, with Cisco networking gear and servers, and EMC storage, for VMware-specific markets.

Vblocks are predesigned systems that have a fixed hardware makeup. They're sold in tiered units, scaled for particular purposes, and come prebuilt as new equipment, racked and ready to install. They provide an easy, quick way to deploy new environments. You're literally purchasing capacity en masse.

NetApp/Cisco SMT   Secure multi-tenancy (SMT) was NetApp's initial response to EMC's VCE coalition. Rather than a prebuilt system, SMT is a reference architecture using NetApp storage and Cisco network and server equipment for vSphere roles.

Unlike Vblocks, SMT is something you need to design and build yourself. Doing so in accordance with the SMT reference architecture produces a combined, supportable solution. It's more customizable; and because it isn't sold as a unit, it gives you the opportunity to reuse some existing equipment. This makes the SMT solution more flexible but also more complex to build.

SMT is aimed primarily at large organizations and service providers that need to host multiple customers on the same equipment. Arguably, this puts it in an overlapping and competing market with Vblocks.

At the time of writing, NetApp just announced its FlexPod for VMware offering, which provides presized hardware solutions to more closely compete with VCE's Vblocks. Unfortunately, at the moment, not enough product detail exists to draw up a comparative analysis.

Cisco UCS Servers   Cisco's Unified Computing Systems (UCS), not to be confused with its Unified Communications System, is a play from the world's largest networking hardware provider to expand into the server market. The company's blade enclosures move a lot of the management from the blade chassis up to a top-of-the-rack management switch. Cisco is also expanding into rack servers.

HP   HP as a server vendor has long been expanding into several lateral markets. It has its own storage lines, such as MSAs and EVAs, and it recently bought out LeftHand's virtualized storage and 3PAR. HP also has ProCurve network switches and has bought several high-profile networking manufactures such as 3Com. HP has a very complete product offering in the converged market space.

Oracle   When Oracle bought out Sun Microsystems, it became another big player among the converged equipment providers. It owns a large stack from servers to storage, a Unix OS (Solaris), and virtualization products based on Xen and VirtualBox. In addition to its sizable existing middleware and database software products, Oracle added on Java and MySQL.

Dell   Dell obviously sells servers, but it also sells its own LSI-based storage along with the popular EqualLogic brand of devices and resells EMC storage. In addition, Dell sells rebranded networking equipment under the PowerConnect brand.

IBM   IBM has long sold servers and its own LSI-based storage devices. It also rebrands storage from NetApp and resells networking equipment.

HDS   HDS, known for its SAN equipment, is now expanding into blade servers.

These are just some of the more popular and well-known examples of continuing converged solution sets from vendors. Buying equipment this way has the advantage of being generally a more simplified total solution that needs less design and that provides end-to-end accountability with components that are certified to work together.

A converged solution reduces the amount of homework you need to do to get something on the ground if you need to produce a more immediate solution with less risk. However, by purchasing your equipment this way, you risk the dreaded vendor lock-in, making it harder to switch out to a competitor when you want to. You have to accept the vendor's opinion regarding the correct balance of equipment. If your needs are less typical, then a preconfigured arrangement may not fit your workload. When buying converged packages, you'll always have an element of compromise: you reduce the opportunity to get the best of breed for your environment in each area. Such solutions are useful for new greenfield deployments or companies that need to scale up with a new solution very quickly.

At the end of the day, converged equipment is just another way for vendors to sell you more *stuff*. It can simplify the procurement process; and if you're already tied to a vendor, or you have a particularly good relationship with one (that is, they offer you a substantial discount over the others), it can make sense to explore these options as alternatives to server hardware in isolation.

Summary

Server hardware defines the capabilities, the performance, and a large proportion of the CAPEX of a vSphere implementation. It's crucial that you don't rush into the purchase, but first consider all the elements of your design. CPU, memory, and I/O requirements are fundamental to hypervisor servers, but more options exist and need to be thought out. Don't try to make the design fit the servers, but create the design around your needs and then figure out exactly what hardware is required. Some architects have very fixed opinions about scaling up or out, or blade versus rack servers, but each situation is different and demands its own solution.

If possible, standardize the hardware across your fleet. You may need to provide a tiering of two or three levels to accommodate more or less demanding roles. You may even be able stick to one model while scaling up or down with more or fewer cores or memory modules. Try to select common I/O cards across the board and think of other ways you can simplify deployment, configuration, or management to reduce OPEX.

When comparing vendors or models, get a hold of sample equipment and test it during any pilot phases. Most vendors will be only too happy to lend such equipment, and often you can learn a lot by spending some hands-on time with it. Make sure you double-check the HCL for all server equipment you order.

Despite any preconceptions you have with regard to hardware, try to think about your overall strategy and whether you want to generally scale up or out. Choose the approach you want for the size of servers before you even think about whether you want rack or blade servers. Your hardware needs can then influence your form-factor decision. Trying to fit your design to a pre-chosen vendor, form factor, or server capacity will only result in a compromise. Design first, and then choose your servers.

Chapter 5

Designing your Network

Have you ever tried to make a cell-phone call in an elevator? Were you shocked when the call dropped in the middle? Some people get annoyed when that happens. But others plan ahead. They know the call will drop due to the lack of reception, so they end the call before they step into the elevator and continue it when they get out. That is called *proper planning*.

We won't go into the reasons why cell-phone coverage is bad in general or why you have to hold your phone a certain way (sorry, iPhone) when you talk. What we'll examine in this chapter are the factors you need to take into account when designing the infrastructure for virtualization. We guarantee that if your servers go down due to a network outage resulting from bad planning, more than one person will be annoyed!

The topics we'll discuss in this chapter include:

◆ Redundancy (at all levels)

◆ Security (this time, it's moved higher in the list)

◆ Networking considerations for the different vSphere components (HA, IP storage, FT, and so on)

◆ Sizing: which NICs to use for which purpose

◆ Virtual switches

◆ Naming conventions

◆ Design scenarios

Designing with Redundancy

The dictionary definition of *redundant* is as follows: "Serving as a duplicate for preventing failure of an entire system (as a spacecraft) upon failure of a single component."

When you design your environment, you don't want it to include a single point of failure (SPOF). That is why you have two hard disks for mirroring, two power supplies, and two NICs — two and two and two. Of course, in reality the environment will be much more complicated and expensive, because you should have redundant storage arrays (or storage processors) and a redundant location (a disaster recovery/business continuity planning [DR/BCP] site) to bring everything up if one site fails.

In this section we'll discuss the virtual infrastructure and its strong dependency on your network infrastructure. The components we'll deal with are:

- Hosts
- Network switches

Hosts

Show me a server (a brand name) that you can buy today that has one NIC — we'll bet you can't do it. The same goes for a server with Ethernet ports that are less than 1Gb. Soon it will be the standard for all servers to have dual-10Gb ports. Vendors know that redundancy on the network is a must; but for an ESX host, sometimes (actually, almost always) two ports aren't enough.

How many ports do you need for your host? Here comes the great IT answer: "It depends." It depends on what your needs are.

Host networking is divided into the following components:

- Service Console (management network)
- Virtual machine port groups
- IP storage (NFS/iSCSI, FCoE)
- vMotion
- Fault tolerance

Let's start with the basics.

SERVICE CONSOLE

Your Service Console/management network is the lifeline into your host. If that lifeline goes down, you can't remotely manage that host. The host will think it has lost connectivity and may power down all the VMs it has running. The other hosts in the cluster may think your host is down and try to restart the VMs that were running. In a nutshell, bad things happen. You should never leave your Service Console on a single NIC.

WARNING   If your Service Console/management network becomes isolated, you lose management to the ESX host, and rightly so. The other hosts in the cluster think so as well, which causes a failover event.

You have two options for planning for the redundancy of your Service Console. You can have either two management network ports on two separate vSwitches or one management network port with redundant NICs on the same vSwitch. Let's start with an example of the first option, as shown in Figure 5.1.

The first management network port is named *Management Network*. It has an IP address of 192.168.165.1 configured on vSwitch0, which uses vmnic0. The second management network port is named *Management Network 2* and has an IP of 192.168.166.1, on vSwitch1 using vmnic1. By providing two management points into your ESX host, you mitigate the risk of a SPOF for the management network.

FIGURE 5.1
ESX host with two
management ports

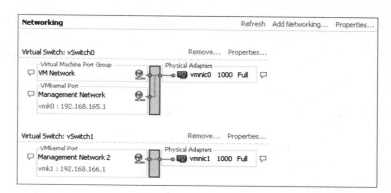

A certain amount of additional overhead is required in such a scenario. You need to apply some configuration changes to your cluster to accommodate such changes. These changes are as follows:

`das.isolationaddress[x]`   This option specifies that you now have more than one possible isolation address that should be available in the event of loss of network on one of the management ports. By default, with one Service Console, `das.isolationaddress` is set to the default gateway of the management port (in the previous case, `192.168.165.254`). In this case, the correct settings are:

```
das.isolationaddress[0] 192.168.165.254
das.isolationaddress[1] 192.168.166.254
```

`das.failuredetectiontime`   This option defines the interval that trigger a HA failure if there is no network connection during that period. The default setting is 15,000 milliseconds. In order to prevent the case of a false positive and having HA invoked because of an error, you should increase this to 30,000 ms:

```
das.failuredetectiontime 30000
```

Now, let's look at the second option the redundancy of your Service Console, illustrated in Figure 5.2.

FIGURE 5.2
ESX host with one
management port
using two NICs

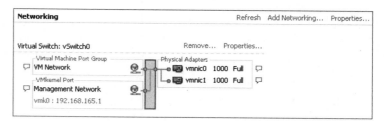

Here you use only one vSwitch and only one management port. This makes the configuration slightly easier and less complex. You don't need an additional IP address for the management ports, and you don't have to configure the additional settings required in the first option. You use two NICS that are set in an active-passive configuration. Each VMNIC should be connected to a separate physical switch, so that if one goes down, the other will continue to provide the management network for the ESX host.

The following settings are recommended on the vSwitch, as shown in Figure 5.3:

- ◆ Failback: Yes
- ◆ Load Balancing: Route Based on the Originating Virtual Port ID

FIGURE 5.3
Recommended settings for a vSwitch with redundant NICs

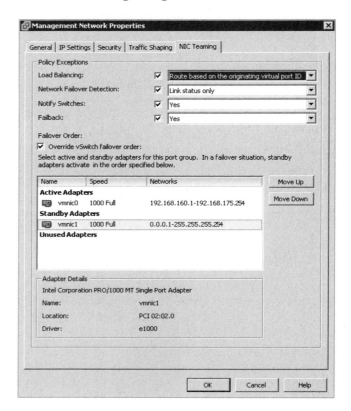

You should also set das.failuredetectiontime to 30000. Doing so prevents the occurrence of a false positive, which can cause you to end up with the VM being powered off (if you've set the configuration this way on your cluster settings) and not powered back up because the host no longer detects that it's isolated.

What is the preferred configuration: two management ports or one (redundant management ports or redundant NICs)? That depends on a number of factors:

- ◆ How many NICs per host? If you're limited in the number of NICS available to you, then you probably can't dedicate two NICs to a management port.
- ◆ Can you make better use of the configuration by adding functions to the vSwitch (vMotion, for example)?
- ◆ Does your security policy allow for the mixture of management VLANs and other purposes (vMotion, IP storage, and VM traffic)? If not, then you'll need to use dedicated NICs.

In the end, it's a question of choices that depend on your environment.

VIRTUAL MACHINE TRAFFIC

Each ESX host can run a multitude of VMs — the exact number always depends on the consolidation ratio you want to achieve and the capabilities of your infrastructure. A good portion of these VMs will need network connectivity outside the host onto your corporate network. So, when you're designing this portion of your infrastructure, you shouldn't be dependent on a single NIC or the connection to a single physical switch. You'll need to plan for the redundancy of the VM traffic.

Most modern network infrastructures have the option to trunk different VLANs on the same network port. This is called *VLAN tagging* (IEEE 802.1Q). A header is attached to a network packet, identifying which VLAN it belongs to; the software on the other side knows how to decipher the packet.

In the ESX case, the vSwitch fully supports VLAN tagging. How does this help you? Instead of having to provide a separate network card for every VLAN you're connecting into your ESX server, you can trunk them all onto the same physical NIC. Doing so can significantly reduce TCO for your infrastructure from day one and in the long run.

Providing redundancy for the vSwitch is also extremely simple. There are four options:

◆ Route based on the originating virtual port ID

◆ Route based on an IP hash

◆ Route based on the source MAC hash

◆ Explicit failover order

The most commonly used option is the first (it's the default for all vSwitches). A number of VMs are connected to a vSwitch that uses two or more physical NICs (pNICs). You use all of these pNICs in an active-active configuration. If you lose a pNIC, traffic automatically travels over one of the other pNICs in the vSwitch.

Each time a VM is powered on, it's assigned to a pNIC and continues to operate from that NIC until it's power-cycled or until the pNIC fails and network traffic is passed to the other pNICs in the vSwitch. This setup doesn't provide efficient load balancing over all the pNICs in the vSwitch and can become unbalanced in certain cases; but in the majority of scenarios, it's suitable because it's the default configuration of an ESX host.

IP STORAGE (NFS/iSCSI)

This has been mentioned before, and we can't stress it enough: *don't rely on one pNIC*, especially when you're using pNICs to provide storage. You should provide at least two pNICs in the vSwitch used for IP storage.

vMOTION

Why should you have redundancy for your vMotion interface? You may think this isn't an essential part of your enterprise. Well, you're wrong. Without a working vMotion interface, you can't balance your cluster properly, you can't evacuate your host if you need to perform maintenance, and more. You definitely need redundancy for your vMotion interface.

Does this mean you must have two dedicated pNICs for this purpose? Probably not. You can use one of the NICs from your management network or VM network to provide redundancy in the case of failover. Usually the degradation in performance is acceptable for the short time until you restore the primary pNIC used for vMotion.

FT

Fault tolerance (FT) is a relatively new feature that was made available in vSphere 4.0. Later in the chapter, we'll go into more detail about how FT works and the considerations for designing a network for FT. But for now, let's deal with redundancy.

In order for FT to work, you need a dedicated pNIC that replicates the state of the VM from one host to another. You can't afford to have that pNIC fail — if that happens, your VM will no longer be protected; and in the case of host failure, the secondary VM won't be available. Therefore, in the case of FT, you should have two dedicated pNICs (and preferably, they should be 10GbE NICs — you'll see the rationale behind this later in the chapter).

Network Switches (pSwitches)

All the hard work of providing redundancy on your ESX host will do you little good if your pNICs are connected to the same pSwitch. If the pSwitch goes down, then your network connectivity will go down with it. Let's look at the example in Figure 5.4.

FIGURE 5.4
Both physical NICs are connected to the same physical switch.

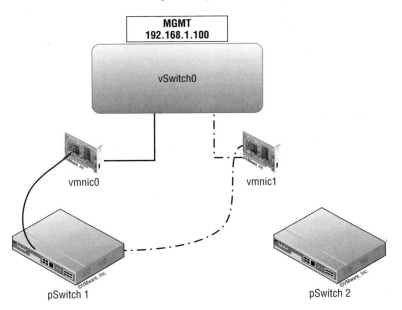

Here you have an ESXi host with multiple pNICs to provide redundancy to the management network and the VM port groups — but they're all connected to the same pSwitch. This is a SPOF. The proper way to provide redundancy is to connect the different pNICs in each vSwitch to a different pSwitch, as shown in Figure 5.5.

Of course, you could provide redundancy in your network infrastructure by creating network stacks, but that's beyond the scope of this book. Cisco provides a best practices document for VMware environments:

    www.vmware.com/files/pdf/vmi_cisco_network_environment.pdf

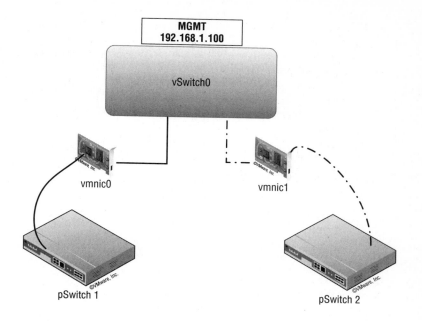

FIGURE 5.5
Each physical NIC
is connected to a
different physical
switch.

Security

You should also take the time to look at the components of your design from the point of view of security. Always consult the VMware site for updated recommendations on securing your vSphere infrastructure. VMware currently offers a vSphere 4.0 Security Hardening Guide:

```
http://communities.vmware.com/servlet/JiveServlet/downloadBody/12306-102-4-12833/
vSphere%20Hardening%20Guide%20April%202010.pdf
```

We'll be discussing the following kinds of traffic in this section:

◆ Management network traffic

◆ Virtual machine traffic

◆ IP storage traffic

◆ vMotion and FT traffic

Management Network

Do your domain controllers and mail servers sit on the same subnet as your desktop computers? We hope not! They shouldn't, because your corporate servers should be separate from your end users. This arrangement provides the option to protect your server farm from outside attacks. We don't mean attacks from outside your network but rather from inside your network due to a computer being compromised and acting as an attack point into the server farm. Some enterprise organizations have their server farms behind a firewall with IPS and IDS systems protecting their critical servers.

Your vSphere environment should definitely be treated as a critical server. The risk of the environment being exploited if it's compromised is potentially disastrous. If someone takes control of your vCenter server, they gain control of every VM in your environment. If they take control of one host, they have control of every VM running on that host.

Therefore, your management network should be separate from the rest of your virtual environment. And it isn't the only element that should be separated. vMotion, IP storage, and FT should be as well; we'll get to those later in the chapter.

How do you separate your management network? Dedicate a network segment specifically for this purpose. Some enterprises have dedicated subnets for out-of-band (OOB) management devices such as iLO ports. Some define the management network on an ESX host as an OOB port, because the Service Console is there only to provide management to either the vSphere client or the vCenter Server on that host. You can also provide a new dedicated subnet, depending on your corporate policy.

With this segregation, you can provide the correct network-access lists on this segment to secure your environment even further.

Virtual Machine Traffic

When you start, you'll be hosting a few VMs. Then the number will grow. In the not-too-distant future, you'll be providing virtualization services for a great number of VMs. You don't want to have all those VMs (production servers, desktops, lab machines, test and development machines, and so on) on the same subnet. The way you'd segregate traffic on the physical network is exactly the same way you should separate it on a virtual network: production servers on this subnet, desktops here, and so on. VMware makes this extremely easy with VLAN tagging on VM port groups. All the VMs may be running on the same two pNICs, but they're on different VLANs with different IP addresses.

You must make sure that all the VLANs are trunked correctly to the appropriate ports on the pSwitch and that the port groups are defined on all the hosts that are in the same cluster. Otherwise, the VMs will disconnect from the network if a pNIC fails or they're migrated to another host.

You should work with your network team to define a solid policy that will work well in your environment. The option of assigning all VLANs up front to every port is very appealing because it would require a one-time configuration for each ESX host. But in some environments, having all the VLANs open on the pNICs will cause problems. Multicast network traffic is a good example.

IP Storage Network Traffic

When we say *IP storage*, we're talking about NFS or iSCSI. There are good use cases for both network protocols, but this traffic isn't encrypted, and it travels over the wire. Anything that travels over the wire can potentially be tapped with a packet sniffer — and may compromise your security.

How can you protect this traffic? We'll discuss three ways. They aren't either/or solutions but can be used together in the appropriate use cases:

- VLAN isolation and a non-routable VLAN

◆ NFS export (`/etc/export`)

◆ iSCSI CHAP authentication

VLAN SEPARATION

This approach is valid for both iSCSI and NFS. Your IP storage should be on a separate network segment. This helps by segregating IP storage from the rest of your network and thus limiting the attack surface to only that segment. An attacker must have an interface on that segment to eavesdrop on the traffic.

To extend this concept, the VLAN should be nonroutable. This ensures that only interfaces on the same network can reach the VMkernel and IP storage interfaces.

NFS EXPORTS

This approach applies only to NFS. When you create the NFS export on your storage, be it an enterprise-grade storage array or a Linux server providing NFS, you should always limit the hosts that are allowed access to NFS shares. Doing so limits who can access the file systems where your VMs are stored.

You do this using the exports file. The `/etc/exports` file specifies remote mount points for the NFS mount protocol per the NFS server specification. On some arrays, you use the GUI rather than configuring the file itself.

Let's look at an example. If you want to define the export to folder `/vol/nfs1` to all the hosts on the 192.168.0.0/24 segment (254 hosts), you configure the export as shown here:

```
192.168.0.0/255.255.255.0 (rw,no_root_squash)
```

To export `/vol/nfs2` only to a host that has IP address 192.168.0.45, configure the export as follows:

```
192.168.0.45 (rw,no_root_squash)
```

In this case, any other IP trying to mount the NFS share will be denied access.

CHAP AUTHENTICATION

This approach is relevant only to iSCSI. For the most part, iSCSI operates as a clear-text protocol that provides no cryptographic protection for data in motion during SCSI transactions. Because of this, an attacker can listen in on iSCSI Ethernet traffic and potentially do the following:

◆ Rebuild and copy the files and file systems being transferred on the network

◆ Alter the contents of files by injecting fake iSCSI frames

◆ Corrupt file systems being accessed by initiators and exploiting software flaws

ESX supports bidirectional CHAP authentication. This means the target and the host initiators authenticate with each other, providing a higher level of security to the IP storage protocol.

vMotion and FT Traffic

vMotion of a VM between hosts is a necessity for most enterprise environments, whether for planned maintenance or to balance machines with distributed resource scheduling (DRS).

When you migrate the machine from one host to another, the VM disk isn't migrated over the network — only the VM's live running state (CPU execution, memory contents, and network). None of this traffic is encrypted, so someone could eavesdrop on the traffic and acquire the information flowing at that time, which could be a security risk.

If you're performing a storage vMotion, which takes much longer, the powered-off VM is transferred over the network (unless your array supports vStorage API for Array Integration [VAAI]). This information can also be compromised.

In this case, the earlier solution of network segregation and a nonroutable VLAN will minimize the attack surface and provide a level of protection. This segregation should also be done with FT traffic.

Performance

What speed should your NICs be? The question should more accurately be, what ports should your NICs be connected to? Ideally, as fast as possible for everything, but that isn't practical. You could have a 10GbE NIC for your Service Console, another for redundancy, two (or four) for IP storage, more for your VMs, and others for vMotion, but that would probably be extreme overkill.

Why should you care? Because each port has a cost. Here's an example. Suppose your server racks are equipped with a patch panel that goes to your corporate Tier-1 switches, and in addition an older Tier-2 10/100Mb managed switch is used for all the remote-control cards and backup ports for each server. The NICs connected to Tier-1 ports are more expensive than Tier-2. In most cases a 10/100Mb port will be more than sufficient for remote-control cards, management ports, and backup NICs in a team that are mostly dormant. Your regular production traffic will go over the Tier-1 ports and in the case of an outage on the primary NIC/port it will failover to the Tier-2 port.

But what do you actually need? Let's look at the following components:

◆ Service Console

◆ vMotion

◆ IP storage

◆ Virtual machine networking

Service Console

What level of traffic goes through your management port? If it's a dedicated management port used only for the Service Console, then not that much. In theory, a 10Mb port would be more than enough, but finding such a port today is relatively impossible. You'll probably go for a 100Mbps port.

But you can easily saturate the throughput of a 100Mbps NIC. There are several ways of doing that. You could run a backup agent on the Service Console that uses all the bandwidth on the management port. This isn't likely and is probably impossible because ESX is moving away from the full Service Console in favor of ESXi. A much easier (and not well known) way to saturate throughout is to convert a VM into your environment. The process when you're importing or converting a VM uses the bandwidth on the Service Console.

Figure 5.6 is an example of an ESX host running without any unusual load on vmnic0 (the management port).

FIGURE 5.6
esxtop example of normal network load on a host

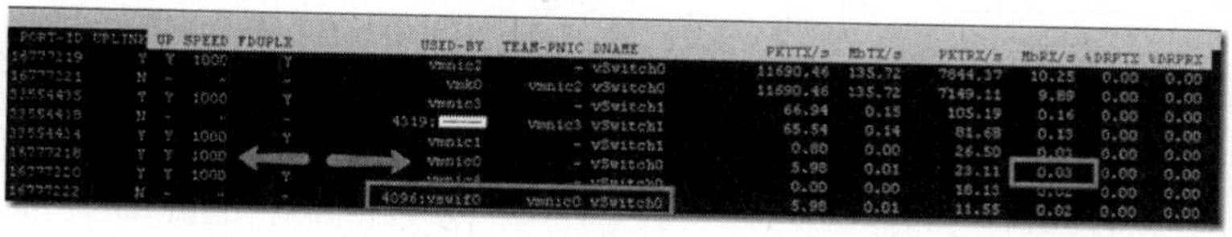

When you begin an import process on a VM through the Enterprise Converter or the VMware stand-alone converter, all import traffic goes through the management port. As you can see in Figure 5.7, the traffic on that port can easily hit 200Mbps, in which case a 100Mbps port won't be sufficient.

FIGURE 5.7
esxtop output during import of a VM to a host

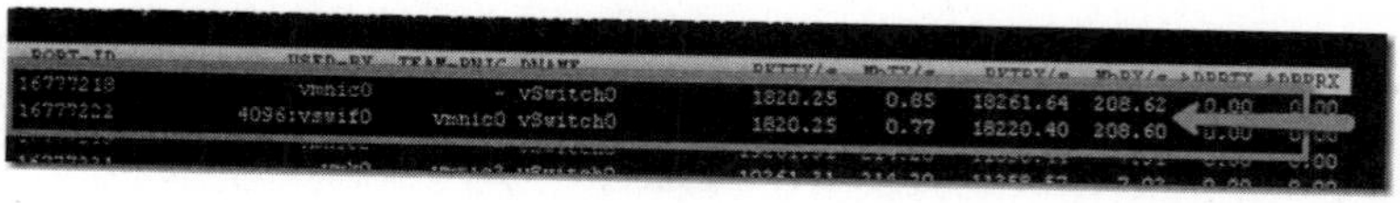

If you're planning to convert a number of servers into your environment or you plan to perform a large number of physical to virtual (P2V) conversions, you should definitely allocate a 1Gb port for the management port.

vMotion

How fast do you want your host evacuated? How fast do you want your migrations to work?

Let's consider the following scenario. One of the hosts in your cluster just reported that a power supply failed. If you planned correctly, you have two in your host, so the server can run with only one power supply for a while; but server redundancy is now degraded, and you don't want to leave your server vulnerable. You should evacuate the host as soon as possible. So, you start to vMotion off your VMs (you have 60 on the host). Running on a 1Gb NIC, you can perform four simultaneous migrations. Each migration takes 1 minute; that means you can vacate the host in 15 minutes, which is more than acceptable in our book. But using a 100Mb NIC, that number will be more like 150 minutes, which isn't so acceptable.

You want the migration to go as quickly as possible. So, you could go for 10Gb, but you should take into account the following. Starting with 4.1, the number of concurrent vMotions was raised to eight from four, and the speed cap on a 10Gb link for vMotion was raised to 8Gbps. If you aren't careful, you may saturate the 10Gb NIC with only vMotion. This isn't a good thing. You'll generally be using the NIC for other purposes as well (VM traffic or IP storage). If this is the case, you'll have to incorporate some kind of network QOS on the NIC to ensure that the vMotion interfaces don't saturate the interface.

IP Storage

IP storage has grown from being a second-level storage platform to being a more mainstream enterprise-grade storage platform.

The I/O performance you can achieve from a 10Gb NIC is no worse than the speeds that you can achieve with Fibre Channel (FC) storage. But the number of 1Gb NICs needed to achieve performance equal to FC is considerably higher, and the configuration is much more complex to achieve the same results.

Therefore, the default choice for IP storage should be 10Gb NICs to maximize performance and options for growth in your datacenter. This, of course, assumes you have the infrastructure in place — if not, then you should plan to make this your standard for the future.

Virtual Machine Network

Each VM needs a certain amount of bandwidth, and there is no one-size-fits-all solution. You'll have do your homework and measure (or estimate) the amount of network traffic each VM will use. If you're converting a physical server, then collecting the data beforehand should be part of your policy before you migrate the server.

We won't go into the details of how this can/should be performed on Windows/Linux servers; we'll leave that to you and your corporate policies and procedures. But when you have this data, you can estimate how many VMs can reside on each NIC. You then size your host accordingly, taking into account the network information. It may be that one 1Gb NIC will suffice for your environment, or it may be that two 10Gb NICs won't suffice.

The bottom line is to plan according to your sizing needs. ESX will be able to accommodate your needs regardless of the speed of your NIC.

Teaming Options

In this section, we'll discuss in more detail the options for pooling (teaming) the networking interfaces on your host. We'll deal with the following topics:

◆   Guest OS network teaming (why it isn't needed) and VM port groups

◆   IP storage

Guest OS Network Teaming and Virtual Machine Port Groups

All systems administrators know that when they buy a server, they get two NICs built in, for redundancy. The NICs are then teamed either for load balancing or for redundancy: basically, two network cables run into the server.

Time and time again, people try to provide better throughput or load balancing to the guest OS by attempting to team the virtual NICs in the guest OS, as shown in Figure 5.8.

The proper way to achieve this is to provide the network redundancy on the port group/vSwitch. We already touched briefly on the options for ESX Network Load Balancing (NLB) when we discussed redundancy; the default and preferred option on a VM port group is route based on the originating virtual port ID. The configuration provides sufficient load-balancing for the VM.

IP Storage

We need to differentiate between iSCSI and NFS. iSCSI allows for multiple connections per session to the storage processor. NFS allows for only one connection per session per datastore, but you can aggregate connections with multiple datastores.

Now we'll go into more detail about these differences and what design considerations you should take into account when planning your infrastructure.

FIGURE 5.8
Providing teaming
to a VM, the wrong
way

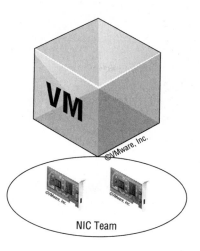

iSCSI

As we mentioned, iSCSI allows for multiple connections per session to the storage processor, which essentially allows for multipathing. You can have multiple TCP connections from the same session when using the iSCSI initiator.

What does this mean? When your ESX iSCSI initiator connects to the iSCSI target (storage), a session is created, and traffic is passed from one pNIC to the storage. From then on, SCSI commands are communicated between the initiator and the target can be sent over different paths (that is, different pNICs). This allows for better load-balancing of the IP storage traffic over the pNICs and perhaps better performance overall.

Depending on which vendor you're using for your storage, you'll have to set up your VMkernel network configuration accordingly. You also need to configure several settings on the Command Line Interface (CLI) to allow multipathing to work correctly.

NFS

NFS (in its current supported version) differs from iSCSI in that after you open a connection to the storage processer (NFS export), all traffic travels over that connection for the life of the session. When the datastore is mounted, all IP storage traffic continues on the same pNIC, which makes load-balancing more complicated. There aren't multiple paths to the storage processor as there are with iSCSI, and load-balancing requires human intervention.

Again, your vendor can provide the exact best practices for your specific environment. But you'll have to adapt to the environment, taking into account how your network stack is set up.

pSwitches Support EtherChannel

Suppose your goal is to have your ESX host access more than one storage controller from different pNICs. In this case, you have to set up multiple IP addresses in the storage controller and configure Link Aggregation Control Protocol (LACP) load-balancing on your storage array. Figure 5.9, courtesy of NetApp, illustrates an example of such a setup.

FIGURE 5.9

Load balancing using LACP on the storage array

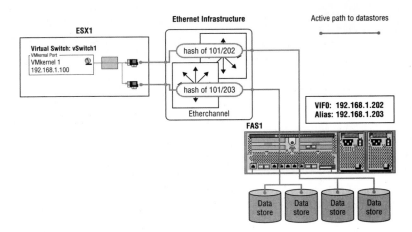

In this example, vmk0 (configured with two VMNICs) uses IP 192.168.1.101 and connects through an EtherChannel to a storage controller with two IP addresses (192.168.1.202 and 192.168.1.203). The vSwitch configuration is set to Route Based on IP Hash. The hash of the VMkernel IP and each of the storage controllers' IPs aren't the same. A hash is created based on the source and destination IP addresses. In this case, the two IP addresses of the storage controller don't have to be on different subnets: they can reside on the same subnet.

pSwitches Don't Support EtherChannel

Now suppose the goal is the same, but the situation is more complicated than in the previous example. Again, the storage controller must be set with multiple IP addresses, but they have to be on separate subnets as well. Figure 5.10 gives an example of such a configuration.

FIGURE 5.10

Providing load balancing with multiple datastores and multiple VMkernel interfaces

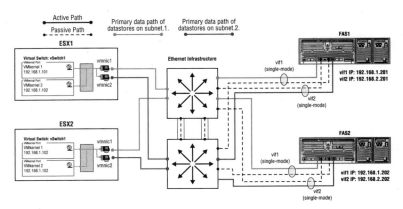

Why the need for multiple VMkernel interfaces, and why do they have to be on separate subnets?

Using separate subnets forces the NFS traffic to go out from one specific pNIC and not through the other. And why on separate subnets? Because each VMkernel connects to the datastore on that subnet.

The configuration options are vast. Consult your storage provider about the best practices for your particular environment. You should look to provide the maximum number of paths to your storage array, regardless of the storage protocol.

Jumbo Frames

ESX supports jumbo frames out of the box. The term *jumbo frames* means that the size of the largest Ethernet frame passed between one host and another on the Ethernet network is larger than the default of 1500 bytes. Jumbo frames are often set to 9000 bytes, the maximum available for a variety of Ethernet equipment.

The idea is that larger frames represent less overhead on the wire and less processing required at each end to segment and then reconstruct Ethernet frames into the TCP/IP packets used by network protocols. Even though enhancements in the ESX network stack keep reducing the CPU cycles needed to deal with jumbo frames, they're still often configured to extract even the slightest improvement in performance. You should always test your specific workloads and environment to see if the use of jumbo frames will give you added value and performance.

You must do two important things when working with jumbo frames:

Configure End to End   Configuration has to be done on the ESX host *and* the network switch *and* the storage controller in order for it to work. If even one component isn't configured, the jumbo frames configuration will cause more harm than good.

Define VMkernel Interfaces Manually   Setting an MTU of 9000 on a vSwitch, port group, or VMkernel interface must be done at the command line of the ESX host. There is no option to do it through the GUI.

You must do the configuration both at the vSwitch level and at the port group/VMkernel. This example creates a vSwitch named vSwitch1 and sets the MTU to 9000:

```
esxcfg-vswitch -a vSwitch1 -m 9000

Switch Name     Num Ports   Used Ports   Configured Ports   MTU     Uplinks
vSwitch1        64          1            64                 9000

  PortGroup Name        VLAN ID  Used Ports   Uplinks
```

When you create a VMkernel interface in the ESX GUI, it's automatically created with an MTU of 1500. This can't be changed:

```
esxcfg-vswitch -A VMKernel vSwitch1
esxcfg-vmknic -a -i 192.168.1.9 -n 255.255.255.0 VMKernel
vmk2        VMKernel            IPv4        192.168.1.9
255.255.255.0   192.168.1.255   00:50:56:77:60:1c 1500     65535      true     STATIC
```

To change it, you have to remove the VMkernel interface and re-create it with the correct MTU:

```
esxcfg-vmknic -d VMKernel
esxcfg-vmknic -a -i 192.168.1.9 -n 255.255.255.0 VMKernel -m 9000
vmk2        VMKernel            IPv4        192.168.1.9
255.255.255.0   192.168.1.255   00:50:56:77:60:1c 9000     65535      true     STATIC
```

Each vendor will have instructions on how to configure jumbo frames on their storage controllers. It's best to consult their documentation.

Fault Tolerance

vSphere 4.0 introduced VMware FT, which allows you to provide an extra dimension to the redundancy of the VM. Until now, you used HA to provide redundancy for VMs in case of hardware failure. But in such cases the VM would crash and would have to be restarted on another host. This caused downtime — a minimal amount, but downtime nonetheless. Certain systems can't allow for such downtime. Enter VMware FT.

FT relies on VMware vLockstep technology to establish and maintain an active secondary VM that runs in sync with the primary VM. The secondary VM resides on a different host and executes exactly the same sequence of virtual (guest) instructions as the primary VM. The secondary VM receives the same inputs as the primary and is ready to take over at any time without any data loss or interruption of service should the primary VM fail due to host failure. Both VMs are managed as a single unit but run on different physical hosts.

vLockstep guarantees that the states of the primary and secondary VMs are identical at any point in the execution of instructions running in the VM. vLockstep accomplishes this by having the primary and the secondary execute identical sequences of x86 instructions. These instructions are sent across a logging network to the secondary VM. The secondary VM uses the logs received over the logging network to replay the instructions in a manner identical to the actions of the primary. The secondary thus executes the same series of instructions as the primary.

Because both the primary and secondary VMs execute the same instruction sequence, they both initiate I/O operations. The main difference between them is how the output from each VM is treated. Operations are committed to disk and network packets are transmitted on the primary VM. All output of the secondary is suppressed by the hypervisor. The outside world isn't aware of the secondary, and an FT VM is treated as a single workload.

When the primary VM fails, the secondary VM continues to provide the same services and becomes the primary VM; in turn, a new secondary VM is created to provide redundancy again.

WARNING   FT doesn't replace application clustering. You shouldn't use VMware FT to replace a Microsoft/Red Hat application cluster. FT doesn't protect the primary VM from an operating system failure.

If the application service fails, then the same instructions are shipped to the secondary VM and won't work from that side either.

We mentioned a logging network: hence this section of the chapter. VMware's minimum requirement for FT is a dedicated 1Gb NIC. As we said at the beginning of the chapter, this link has to be redundant.

The question is, how much traffic will travel over this link? It depends on the number of non-deterministic events and external inputs that are recorded at the primary VM. Because the bulk of this traffic usually consists of incoming network packets and disk reads, you can estimate the amount of networking bandwidth required for VMware FT logging using the following formula:

```
VMware FT logging bandwidth ~= (Avg disk reads (MB/s) × 8 + Avg network input
(Mbps)) × 1.2 [20% headroom]
```

Let's take an example of a VM that is using on average 25Mbps on disk reads and has an average of 100Mbps network traffic:

```
360Mbps = ((25 × 8) + 100) × 1.2
```

You can see that the traffic predicted to travel on the NIC won't be enough for more than three VMs. At the moment, FT has certain strict limitations (CPU compatibility, 1vCPU), but these will be removed in the not-too-distant future. When this happens, FT will be used more and more. Thus you shouldn't limit yourself to 1Gb NICs and will be better off going with 10GbE NICs for FT.

10GbE

Several considerations come to mind when you're planning the infrastructure and using 10GbE:

- Physical network cable
- pSwitches
- Network modules

Physical Network Cable

10GbE should be deployed on Cat-6A cables. It will work on Cat-6, but because you're building your enterprise infrastructure, you should go with nothing less than the top of the line.

Switches

Several vendors provide 10GbE-capable switches today. When you're designing your virtual infrastructure, you should take into account your current environment and how these network components will fit into it. Usually, your network team will manage these components, so they should be brought on board and be part of the network-design process.

Network Modules

Suppose you've opted to go for 10GbE, but you don't necessarily want to allocate 10GbE for vMotion or IP storage. The ideal approach is to split this extra bandwidth over the different network components in your ESX host:

- 1Gb — Management port
- 1Gb — vMotion
- 2Gb — VM traffic
- 2Gb — FT
- 4Gb — IP storage

That would make proper use of your NIC.

At present, hardware vendors only offer this kind of functionality on Blade enclosures, whether HP's Flex-10 Module or IBM's Virtual Fabric. This can't be done with a standard rack-mount server and a 10GbE adapter.

An emerging technology called *I/O virtualization* is essentially a virtual LAN in a box. You connect a hardware network component at extreme speeds to the backbone (for example, 780Gbps); the network component serves as a robust I/O gateway for dozens of servers.

Using this technology, you can provide virtual HBA and NICs and present them to the host with a considerable amount of bandwidth. You can create profiles and allocate QOS to each vNIC and vHBA presented to the host. An example of such a vendor is Xsigo (`www.xsigo.com`), which offers this technology with its products.

vSwitches and vDSs

First and foremost, vSwitches are available in every ESX version from the vSphere hypervisor (free ESXi) all the way up to ESX Enterprise Plus. vDSs are only available on ESX Enterprise Plus.

Let's start by comparing vNetwork standard switches to vNetwork distributed switches (vDS). The following features are available on both types of virtual switches:

◆ Can forward L2 frames

◆ Can segment traffic into VLANs

◆ Can use and understand 802.1q VLAN encapsulation

◆ Can have more than one uplink (NIC teaming)

◆ Can have traffic shaping for the outbound (TX egress) traffic

The following features are available only on a distributed vSwitch:

◆ Can shape inbound (RX ingress) traffic

◆ Has a central unified management interface through vCenter

◆ Supports Private VLANs (PVLANs)

We'll go into more detail about some points related to these features:

◆ Central management

◆ PVLANs

◆ VM port groups, VMkernel, and management ports

Central Management

The larger your environment grows, the more dynamic it becomes, and the harder it gets to manage the network configuration and keep it consistent across all the hosts in your cluster. This is especially difficult with cloud computing, for which VMware specifically recommends using a vDS to support the advanced networking now available in the VMware vCloud Director (vCD) product.

The vDS eases the management overhead per host and virtual switch configuration management by treating the network as an aggregated resource. Individual, host-level virtual switches are abstracted into a single large vDS that spans multiple hosts at the datacenter level. Port groups become distributed virtual port groups (dvport groups) that span multiple hosts and ensure configuration consistency for VMs and virtual ports necessary for such functions as VMotion and network storage.

Private VLANs

A PVLAN a mechanism to divide a broadcast domain into several logical broadcast domains. PVLAN support enables broader compatibility with existing networking environments using PVLAN technology. PVLANs enable users to restrict communication between VMs on the same VLAN or network segment, significantly reducing the number of subnets needed for certain network configurations.

Private VLAN is an extension to the VLAN standard, already available in several (most recent) physical switches. It adds a further segmentation of the logical broadcast domain to create private groups. *Private* in this case means that hosts in the same PVLAN can't be seen by the others, except those selected in a promiscuous PVLAN.

A PVLAN is divided into these two groups:

Primary PVLAN   The original VLAN that is being divided into smaller groups is called the primary. All the secondary PVLANs exist only inside that primary.

Secondary PVLANs   The secondary PVLANs exist only inside the primary. Each secondary PVLAN has a specific VLAN ID associated with it. Each packet traveling through it is tagged with a VLAN ID as if it were a normal VLAN. The physical switch associates the behavior (isolated, community, or promiscuous) depending on the VLAN ID found in each packet.

Secondary PVLANs are further divided into these three groups:

Promiscuous   A node attached to a port in a promiscuous secondary PVLAN may send and receive packets to any node in any other secondary VLAN associated with the same primary. Routers are typically attached to promiscuous ports.

Isolated   A node attached to a port in an isolated secondary PVLAN may only send packets to and receive packets from the promiscuous PVLAN.

Community   A node attached to a port in a community secondary PVLAN may send packets to and receive packets from other ports in the same secondary PVLAN, as well as send to and receive from the promiscuous PVLAN.

Figure 5.11 shows these three groups.

Port Groups, Management, and VMkernel

A vDS is suitable for any and all of the types of networking we've discussed. They're all supported. However, we must address one caveat. The vDS is managed by your vCenter Server, and if that isn't available, you'll have great difficulty managing the vDS ports on any of the servers.

And what if one of those ports happens to be the management port — your lifeline into the ESX host? This is even more relevant if you're running your vCenter Server as a VM on one of your ESX hosts connected to a port group on a vDS. This is another chicken-and-egg situation like the one we mentioned when discussing how to choose physical or virtual for your vCenter Server.

It's wise to leave the management port out of your vDS, to prevent really bad results when things hit the fan.

FIGURE 5.11
Private VLAN
groups on a vDS

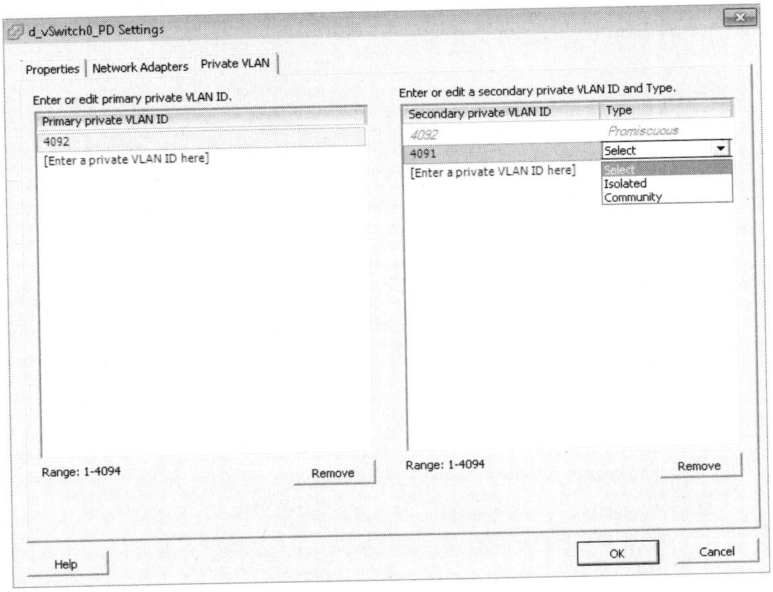

Naming and IP Conventions

It would be great if we could give any names we wanted to network components. After all, we name our children the way we want, give our pets names, and perhaps name a boat. But a network isn't the same as a family. Naming VLANs Tom, Dick, and Harry may be amusing, but it isn't the way to do things in the enterprise.

You should label your network components properly. They should be clearly identifiable even for those who don't manage the environment on a day-to-day basis. Here are a few examples:

- iSCSI_VLAN_765
- VM_VLAN_55
- 755_NFS
- 123_vMOTION
- Mgmt_1

Choose names that that can be recognized easily and associated with the appropriate VLAN.

In addition, be sure to create IP addresses in a consistent manner across all of your hosts. Table 5.1 shows an example of how *not* to do it.

TABLE 5.1:   How *not* to assign IP addresses

	IP ADDRESS
MGMT	192.168.1.4
NFS	192.168.6.54
vMotion	192.168.4.20
iSCSI	192.168.20.222

This list has no standardization. When the environment grows, you won't be able to manage anything.

How about the example in Table 5.2?

TABLE 5.2:   Standardized IP addresses

	HOST 1	HOST 2
MGMT	192.168.1.1	192.168.1.2
NFS	192.168.6.1	192.168.6.2
vMotion	192.168.4.1	192.168.4.2
iSCSI	192.168.20.1	192.168.20.2

We hope you can see the difference and how much easier it is when you keep things nice and tidy.

Design Scenarios

Last but not least in this chapter, we'll provide some scenarios of ESX host configuration with 2, 4, 6, 8, or 10 NICs. Each host has the following:

◆ Management port

◆ VMkernel for IP storage

◆ VMkernel for vMotion

◆ VM port group 1

◆ FT port

Two NICs

This isn't a good idea. You can't provide proper performance, security, isolation, or redundancy with only two NICs. With that off our chest, let's start.

VM traffic goes through vmnic1, MGMT vMotion, VMkernel, and FT on vmnic0, as you can see in Figure 5.12.

FIGURE 5.12
Configuration with two NICs

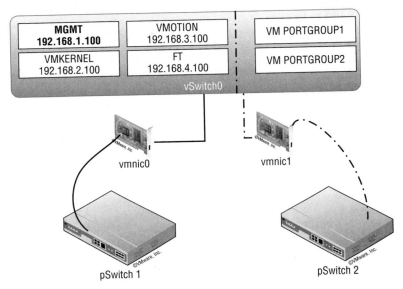

Four NICs

In this case, VM traffic goes through vSwitch1 (vmnic2 and vmnic3, both active). On vSwitch0, it goes through MGMT, VMkernel on vmnic0 (active; vmnic1 on standby), vMotion, and FT on vmnic1 (active; vmnic0 on standby), as you can see in Figure 5.13.

FIGURE 5.13
Configuration with four NICs

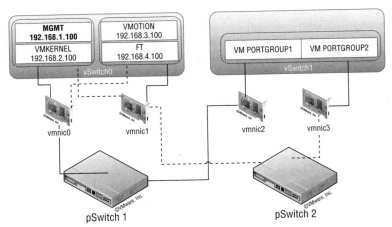

The solid lines represent the primary links for each component, and the dotted lines represent the backup links. Here you provide redundancy for the VM traffic and some sort of redundancy for console and other traffic. This isn't ideal because too many components are competing for the same resources on vSwitch0.

Six NICs

Here, VM traffic goes through vSwitch1 (vmnic2 and vmnic3, both active). On vSwitch0, it goes thorough MGMT on vmnic0 (active; vmnic1 on standby) and vMotion on vmnic1 (active; vmnic0 on standby). On vSwitch2, it goes through VMkernel on vmnic4 (active; vmnic5 on standby) and FT on vmnic5 (active; vmnic4 on standby), as you can see in Figure 5.14.

FIGURE 5.14
Configuration with six NICs

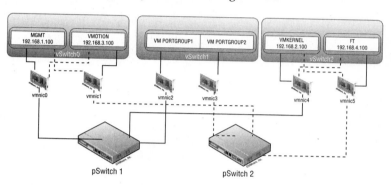

You have redundancy for all components, but the FT and VMkernel traffic have only one NIC each. This usually won't provide enough throughput for either of the two functions.

Eight NICs

In this scenario, VM traffic goes through vSwitch1 (vmnic2 and vmnic3, both active). On vSwitch0, it goes through MGMT on vmnic0 (active; vmnic1 on standby) and vMotion on vmnic1 (active; vmnic0 on standby). On vSwitch2, it goes through VMkernel on vmnic4, vmnic5, and vmnic6 (all active; vmnic7 on standby) and FT on vmnic7 (active; vmnic6 and vmnic5 on standby), as you can see in Figure 5.15.

FIGURE 5.15
Configuration with eight NICs

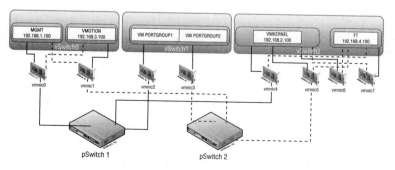

Here you have redundancy for all components, and VMkernel traffic has reasonable throughput using three NICS. FT is limited to one NIC, which will limit the number of FT VMs you can host.

Two 10GbE NICS

Now we'll assume that you have some kind of I/O virtualization component that lets you split the pipe into smaller chunks. VM traffic goes through (2 × 1Gb) vSwitch1 (vmnic2 and vmnic3, both active). On vSwitch0, it goes through MGMT on vmnic0 (1Gb, active; vmnic1 on standby) and vMotion on vmnic1 (1Gb, active; vmnic0 on standby). On vSwitch2, it goes through VMkernel on vmnic4 and vmnic5 (2Gb and 2Gb, both active; vmnic6 [1Gb] and vmnic7 [1Gb] on standby) and FT on vmnic6 (active; vmnic7 on standby), as you can see in Figure 5.16.

FIGURE 5.16
Configuration with
two 10GbE NICs

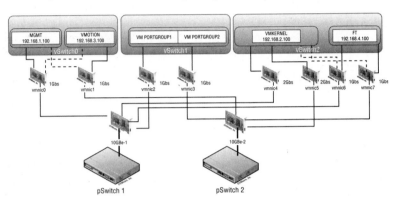

Here you have redundancy for all components. VMkernel traffic has reasonable throughput using two (2Gb) NICS. FT is limited to one NIC, which will limit the number of FT VMs you can host.

Four 10GbE NICS

Again, let's assume you have some kind of I/O virtualization component that allows you to split the pipe into smaller chunks. VM traffic goes through (2 × 2Gb) vSwitch1 (vmnic2 and vmnic3, both active). On vSwitch0, it goes through MGMT on vmnic0 (1Gb, active; vmnic1 [1Gb] on standby) and vMotion on vmnic4 (3Gb, active; vmnic5 [3Gb] on standby). vSwitch2 has VMkernel on vmnic6 and vmnic7 (4Gb, 4Gb, both active; vmnic8 [4Gb] and vmnic9 [4Gb] on standby) and FT on vmnic8 (active; vmnic9 on standby), as you can see in Figure 5.17.

FIGURE 5.17
Configuration with
four 10GbE NICs

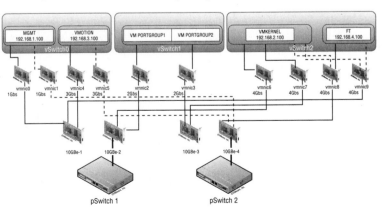

Here you have redundancy for all components. VMkernel traffic has good throughput using two (3Gb) NICS. FT has two (2Gb) links, which should provide adequate breathing room.

Summary

Designing any part of your virtual infrastructure isn't easy. It's a lengthy and complicated process, with many parameters that have to be taken into account.

Plan for that rainy day when things go bad. You may receive a small token of appreciation if you save a few bucks, but we assure you that you won't receive flowers if your environment crashes because you don't have the proper redundancy measures in place.

You must consider your network standard — 1Gb or 10GbE — and learn the best way to set up your network for your specific environment.

Now, we'll move on to another critical part of the infrastructure: storage.

Chapter 6

Storage

When you're considering the design of a vSphere environment, the storage component is commonly regarded as one of the most crucial to overall success. It's fundamental to the capabilities of virtualization. Many of the benefits provided by VMware's vSphere wouldn't be possible without the technologies and features offered by today's storage equipment.

The storage design topics discussed in this chapter are:

◆ Primary storage design factors to consider

◆ What makes for an efficient storage solution

◆ How to design your storage with sufficient capacity

◆ How to design your storage to perform appropriately

◆ Whether local storage is still a viable option

◆ Which storage protocol you should use

◆ Using multipathing with your storage choice

Dimensions of Storage Design

In the past those who designed, built, configured, and, most important, paid for server storage were predominately interested in how much space they could get for their dollar. Servers used local direct attached storage (DAS), (with the occasional foray into two node clusters) where performance was limited to the local bus, the speed of the disks, and the RAID configuration chosen. These configurations could be tweaked to suit all but the most demanding of server-room requirements. If greater performance was required, companies scaled-out with multiple servers; or if they had the need (and the cash!), they invested in expensive dedicated Fibre Channel storage area network devices (SANs) with powerful array technologies. Times were relatively simple. CIOs cared about getting the most bang for their buck, and $/GB (cost per gigabyte) was what was on the storage planning table.

With the advent of virtualization, storage is now much more than just capacity. Arguably, the number of terabytes (TBs) that your new whizzy storage array can provide is one of the lesser interests when you're investigating requirements. Most shared storage units, even the more basic ones, can scale to hundreds of TBs.

Some of the intrinsic vSphere capabilities mean that storage is significantly more mobile than it was previously. Features such as Storage vMotion help abstract not just the server hardware but also the storage. Upgrading or replacing storage arrays isn't the thing of nightmares anymore; and the flexibility to switch in newer arrays make the situation far more dynamic. Rather than intimidating or constraining the vSphere architect in you, this should open your mind to a world of new possibilities. Yes, there are more things to understand and digest, but they're all definable. Like any good design, storage requirements can still be planned and decisions made using justifiable, measurable analysis. Just be aware that counting the estimated number and size of all your projected VMs won't cut the mustard for a virtualized storage design anymore.

Storage Design Factors

Storage design comes down to three principle factors:

◆ Availability

◆ Performance

◆ Capacity

These must all be finely balanced with the ever-present fourth factor:

◆ Cost

AVAILABILITY

Availability of your vSphere storage is crucial. Performance and capacity issues aren't usually disruptive and can be dealt with without downtime if properly planned and monitored. However, nothing is more noticeable than a complete outage. You can (and absolutely should) build redundancy in to every aspect of a vSphere design, and storage is cardinal in this equation. In a highly available environment, you wouldn't have servers with one Power Supply Unit (PSU), standalone switches, or single Ethernet connections. Shared storage in its very nature is centralized and often solitary in the datacenter. Your entire cluster of servers will connect to this one piece of hardware. Wherever possible, this means every component and connection must have sufficient levels of redundancy to ensure that there are no single points of failure.

Different types of storage are discussed in this chapter, and as greater levels of availability are factored in, the cost obviously rises. However, the importance of availability should be overriding in almost any storage design.

PERFORMANCE

Performance is generally less well understood than capacity or availability, but in a virtualized environment where there is significant scope for consolidation, it has a much greater impact. You can use several metrics, such as input/output operations per second (IOPS), MBps, and latency, to accurately measure performance. These will be explained in greater depth later in the chapter.

This doesn't have to be the black art that many think it is — when you understand how to measure performance, you can use it effectively to underpin a successful storage design.

CAPACITY

Traditionally, capacity is what everyone thinks of as the focus for a storage array's principle specification. It's a tangible (as much as ones and zeros on a rusty-colored spinning disk can be), describable, quantitative figure that salesmen and management teams love. Don't misunderstand: it's a relevant design factor. You need space to stick stuff. No space, no more VMs. Capacity needs to be managed on an ongoing basis, and predicted and provisioned as required. However, unlike availability and performance, it can normally be augmented as requirements grow.

It's a relatively straightforward procedure to add disks and enclosures to most storage arrays without incurring downtime. As long as you initially scoped the fundamental parts of the storage design properly, you can normally solve capacity issues relatively easily.

Cost

Costs can be easy or difficult to factor in, depending on the situation. You may be faced with a set amount of money that you can spend. This is a hard number, and you can think of it as one of your constraints in the design.

Alternatively, the design may need such careful attention to availability, performance, and/or capacity that money isn't an issue to the business. You must design the best solution you can, regardless of the expense.

Although you may feel that you're in one camp or the other, cost is normally somewhat flexible. Businesses don't have a bottomless pit of cash to indulge infrastructure architects (unfortunately); nor are there many managers who won't listen to reasoned, sensible explanations as to why they need to adjust either their budget or their expectations of what can be delivered.

Normally, the task of a good design is to take in the requirements and provide the best solution for the lowest possible cost. Even if you aren't responsible for the financial aspects of the design, it's important to have an idea of how much money is available.

Storage Efficiency

Storage *efficiency* is a term used to compare cost against each of the primary design factors. Because everything relates to how much it costs and what a business can afford, you should juxtapose solutions on that basis.

Availability Efficiency

You can analyze availability in a number of ways. Most common service level agreements (SLAs) use the term *9s*. The 9s refers to the amount of availability as a percentage of uptime in a year, as shown in Table 6.1.

TABLE 6.1:   The 9s

AVAILABILITY %	DOWNTIME PER YEAR
90%	36.5 days
99%	3.65 days
99.5%	1.83 days
99.9%	8.76 hours
99.99%	52.6 minutes
99.999% ("5 nines")	5.26 minutes

Using a measurement such as 9s can give you a quantitative level of desired availability; however, the 9s can be open to interpretation. Often used as marketing terminology, you can use the 9s to understand what makes a highly available system. The concept is fairly simple.

If you have a single item for which you can estimate how frequently it will fail (mean time between failures [MTBF]) and how quickly it can be brought back online after a failure (mean time to recover [MTTR]), then you can calculate the applicable 9s value:

Availability = ((minutes in a year − average annual downtime in minutes) / minutes in a year) * 100

For example, a router that on average fails once every 3 years (MTBF) and that takes 4 hours to replace (MTTR) can be said to have on average an annual downtime of 75 minutes. This equates to:

Availability = ((525600 − 75) / 525600) * 100 = 99.986%

As soon as you introduce a second item into the mix, the risk of failure is multiplied by the two percentages. Unless you're adding a 100 percent rock-solid, nonfallible piece of equipment (very unlikely, especially because faults are frequently caused by the operator), the percentage drops, and your solution can be considered less available.

As an example, if you have a firewall in front of the router, with the same chance of failure, then a failure in either will create an outage. The availability of that solution is halved: it's 99.972 percent, which means an average downtime of 150 minutes every year.

However, if you can add additional fail-over items in the design, then you can reverse the trend and increase the percentage for that piece. If you have two, then the risk may be halved. Add three, and the risk drops to one-third. In the example, adding a second fail-over router (ignoring the firewall) reduces the annual downtime to 37.5 minutes; a third reduces it to 25 minutes.

As you add more levels of redundancy to each area, the law of diminishing returns sets in, and it becomes less economical to add more. The greatest benefit is adding a second item, which is why most designs require at least one fail-over item at each level. If each router costs $5,000, the second one reduces downtime from a 1-router solution by 37.5 minutes (75 – 37.5). The third will only reduce it by a further 12.5 minutes (37.5 – 25), even though it costs as much as the second. As you can see, highly available solutions can be very expensive. Less reliable parts tend to need even more redundancy.

During the design, you should be aware of any items that increase the possibility of failure. If you need multiple items to handle load, but any one of them failing creates an outage, then you increase the potential for failure as you add more nodes. Inversely, if the load is spread across multiple items, then this spreads the risk; therefore, any failures have a direct impact on performance.

Paradoxically, massively increasing the redundancy to increase availability to the magic "five nines" often introduces so much complexity that things take a turn south. No one said this design thing was easy!

You can also use other techniques to calculate high availability, such as MTBF by itself.

NOTE Remember that to a business, *uptime* may not mean the same thing as *availability*. For example, if performance is so bad as to make a solution unusable, then no one will be impressed by your zero-downtime figures for the month.

Also worthy of note is the ability to take scheduled outages for maintenance. Does this solution really need a 24/7 answer? Although a scheduled outage is likely to affect the SLAs, are there provisions for accepted regular maintenance, or are all outages unacceptable? When absolute availability is needed, things tend to get very costly.

This is where availability efficiency is crucial to a good design. Often, there is a requirement to propose different solutions based on prices. Availability efficiency usually revolves around showing how much the required solution will cost at different levels. The 9s can easily demonstrate how much availability costs, when a customer needs defined levels of performance and capacity.

PERFORMANCE EFFICIENCY

You can measure performance in several ways. These will be explained further in this chapter; but the most common are IOPS, MBps, and latency in milliseconds (ms).

Performance efficiency is the cost per IOPS, per MBps, or per ms latency. IOPS is generally the most useful of the three; most architects and storage companies refer to it as $/IOPS. The problem is, despite IOPS being a measureable test of a disk, many factors in today's advanced storage solutions — such as RAID type, read and write cache, and tiering — skew the figures so much that it can be difficult to predict and attribute a value to a whole storage device.

This is where lab testing is essential for a good design. To understand how suitable a design is, you can use appropriate testing to determine the performance efficiency of different storage solutions. Measuring the performance of each option with I/O loads comparable to the business's requirements, and comparing that to cost, gives the performance efficiency.

CAPACITY EFFICIENCY

Capacity efficiency is the easiest to design for. $/GB is a relatively simple calculation, given the sales listings for different vendors and units. Or so you may think.

The "Designing for Capacity" section of this chapter will discuss some of the many factors that affect the actual useable space available. Just because you have fifteen 1 TB disks doesn't mean you can store exactly 15 TB of data. As you'll see, several factors eat into that total significantly; but perhaps more surprising is that several technologies now allow you to get more for less.

Despite the somewhat nebulous answer, you can still design capacity efficiency. Although it may not necessarily be a linear calculation, if you can estimate your storage usage, you can predict your capacity efficiency. Based on the cost of purchasing disks, if you know how much useable space you have per disk, then it's relatively straightforward to determine $/GB.

OTHER EFFICIENCIES

Before moving on, it's worth quickly explaining that other factors are involved in storage efficiencies. Availability, performance, and capacity features can all be regarded as capital expenditure (CAPEX) costs; but as the price of storage continues to drop, it's increasingly important to understand the operational expenditure (OPEX) costs. For example, in your design, you may wish to consider these points:

Watts/IOPS. How much electricity does each disk use? Flash drives, although more expensive per GB, are not only cheaper per IOPS but also use significantly less electricity per IOPS.

Rack Usage.   Now that it's more common to use co-lo facilities, businesses are aware how much each U in a rack costs. Solutions that can combine very dense capacity (SATA) and very dense performance (flash) in the required mix can save leased space.

Management Overhead.   The cost of managing the storage may be difficult to quantify, but it can have a significant effect on the OPEX associated with a storage design. Later, this chapter discusses different designs and protocol choices. As you'll see, the protocol you opt for often comes down to its integration in your existing environment.

Flexibility.   One thing is certain: your design will never be perfect and must remain flexible enough to adapt to an ever-changing environment. Can the design accommodate more disks, different disks, multiple protocols and transport, upgrades, more hosts, and so on? If not, future OPEX costs may be more expensive than previously planned.

Designing for Capacity

An important aspect of any storage design involves ensuring that it has sufficient capacity not just for the initial deployment but also to scale up for future requirements. Before discussing what you should consider in capacity planning, let's review the basics behind the current storage options. What decisions are made when combining them into usable space?

RAID Options

Modern servers and storage arrays use Redundant Array of Independent/Inexpensive Disks (RAID) technologies to combine disks into logical unit numbers (LUNs) on which you can store data. Regardless of whether we're discussing local storage; a cheap, dumb network-attached storage (NAS) or SAN device; or a high-end enterprise array, the principles of RAID and their usage still apply.

The choice of which RAID type to use, like most storage decisions, comes down to availability, performance, capacity, and cost. In this section, the primary concerns are both availability and capacity. Later in the chapter in the "Designing for Performance" section, we discuss RAID to evaluate its impact on storage performance.

Many different types of RAID (and non-RAID) solutions are available, but these examples cover the majority of cases that are used in VMware solutions. Figure 6.1 compares how different RAID types mix the data-to-redundancy ratio.

RAID 0

RAID 0 stripes all the disks together without any parity or mirroring. Because no disks are lost to redundancy, this approach maximizes the capacity of the RAID set. However, with no redundancy, just one failed disk will destroy all of your data. For this reason, RAID 0 isn't suitable for a VMware (or almost any other) production setting.

RAID 10

RAID 10 describes a pair of disks, or multiples thereof, that mirror each other. From an availability perspective, this approach gives an excellent level of redundancy, because every block of data is written to a second disk. Multiple disks can fail as long as one copy of each pair remains available. Rebuild times are also short in comparison to other RAID types. However, capacity is effectively halved; in every pair of disks, exactly one is a *parity* disk. So, RAID 10 is the most expensive solution.

FIGURE 6.1
Capacity versus redundancy

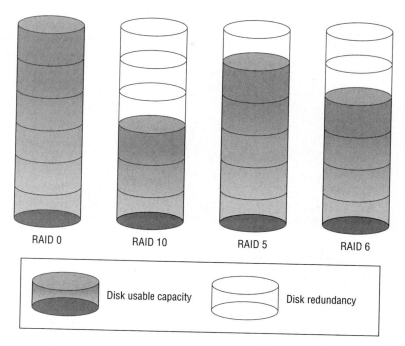

Without considering performance, RAID 10 is useful in a couple of vSphere circumstances. It's often used in situations where high availability is crucial. If the physical environment is particularly volatile — for example, remote sites with extremes of temperature or humidity, ground tremors, or poor electrical supply — or if more redundancy is a requirement due to the importance of the data, then RAID 10 always provides a more robust solution. RAID 1 (two mirrored disks) is often used on local disks for ESX's OS, because local disks are relatively cheap and capacity isn't normally a requirement when shared storage is available.

RAID 5

RAID 5 is a set of disks that stripes parity across the entire group using the equivalent of one disk (as opposed to RAID 4, which assigns a single specific disk for parity). Aside from performance differences, RAID 5 is a very good option to maximize capacity. Only one disk is lost for parity, so you can use $n - 1$ for data.

However, this has an impact on availability, because the loss of more than one disk at a time will cause a complete loss of data. It's important to consider the importance of your data and the reliability of the disks before selecting RAID 5. The MTBFs, rebuild times, and availability of spares/replacements are significant factors.

RAID 5 is a very popular choice for SCSI/SAS disks that are viewed as fairly reliable options. After a disk failure, RAID 5 must be rebuilt onto a replacement before a second failure. SCSI/SAS disks tend to be smaller in capacity and faster, so they rebuild much more quickly. Because SCSI/SAS disks also tend to be more expensive than their SATA counterparts, it's important to get a good level of capacity return from them.

With SAN arrays, it's common practice to allocate one or more spare disks. These spare disks are used in the event of a failure and are immediately moved in as replacements when needed. An advantage from a capacity perspective is that one spare can provide additional redundancy to multiple RAID sets.

If you consider your disks reliable, and you feel that two simultaneous failures are unlikely, then RAID 5 is often the best choice. After all, RAID redundancy should never be your last line of defense against data loss. RAID 5 provides the best capacity, with acceptable availability given the right disks and hot spares.

RAID 6

An increasingly popular choice among modern storage designs is RAID 6. It's similar in nature to RAID 5, in that the parity data is distributed across all member disks, but it uses the equivalent of two disks. This means it loses some capacity compared to RAID 5 but can withstand two disks failing in quick succession. This is particularly useful when you're creating larger RAID groups.

RAID 6 is becoming more popular as drive sizes increase (therefore increasing rebuild times), because MTBF drops as physical tolerances on disks become tighter, and as SATA drives become more pervasive in enterprise storage.

OTHER VENDOR-SPECIFIC RAID OPTIONS

The basic RAID types mentioned cover most scenarios for vSphere deployments, but you'll encounter many other options when talking to different storage vendors. Many of these are technically very similar to the basic types, such as RAID-DP from NetApp. RAID-DP is similar to a RAID 6 group, but rather than the parity being distributed across all disks, RAID-DP uses two specific disks for parity (like RAID 4). The ZFS file system designed by Sun Microsystems (now Oracle), which includes many innovative storage technologies on top, uses a self-allocating disk mechanism not dissimilar to RAID 5, called RAID-Z. Although it differs in the way it writes data to disks, it uses the premise of a disk's worth of parity across the group like RAID 5.

Some storage arrays effectively make the RAID choices for you, by hiding the details and describing disks in terms of pools, volumes, aggregates, and so on. They abstract the physical layer and present the storage in a different way. This allows you to select disks on more user-friendly terms, while hiding the technical details. This approach may reduce the level of granularity that storage administrators are used to, but it also reduces complexity and arguably makes default decisions that are optimized for their purpose.

BASIC RAID STORAGE RULES

The following are some additional basic rules you should follow in vSphere environments:

- Ensure that spares are configured to automatically replace failed disks.

◆ Consider the physical location of the hardware and the warranty agreement on replacements, because they will affect your RAID choices and spares policy.

◆ Follow the vendor's advice regarding RAID group sizes and spares.

◆ Consider the importance of the data, because the RAID type is the first defense against disk failures (but definitely shouldn't be the only defense). Remember that availability is always of paramount importance when you're designing any aspect of storage solutions.

◆ Replace failed disks immediately, and configure any phone-home options to alert you (or the vendor directly) as soon as possible.

◆ Use predictive failure detection if available, to proactively replace disks before they fail.

Estimating Capacity Requirements

Making initial estimates for your storage requirements can be one of the easier design decisions. Calculating how much space you really need depends on the tasks ahead of you. If you're looking at a full virtualization implementation, converting physical servers to VMs, there are various capacity planners available to analyze the existing environment. If the storage design is to replace an existing solution that you've outgrown, then the capacity needs will be even more apparent. If you're starting anew, then you need to estimate the average VM, with the flexibility to account for unusually large servers (file servers, FTP, databases, and so on).

In addition to the Virtual Machine Disk Format (VMDK) disk files, several additional pieces need space on the datastores:

VM Swap Space   By default, a VM uses some disk space to create a swap area that is equal to the size of the VM's allocated RAM. Technically, if you a set a memory reservation on the VM, this swap allocation is reduced. This topic will be discussed more in Chapter 7, "Virtual Machines," but for the purposes of capacity planning, you can ignore the reservation.

Snapshots   Many advanced features in vSphere use snapshotting functionality in addition to manually created snapshots. Backup tools, Storage vMotion, and others also create snapshots, which use extra space in the datastores. Regardless of which datastores a VM's disks are spread across, all snapshots are held in the same Virtual Machine File System (VMFS) volume as the VM's configuration file.

Templates and ISOs   For even the smallest deployments, the use of templates provides a convenient method of creating new VMs and consistent builds. Storing the templates and ISO files on shared storage allows for all hosts in a cluster to use a single set, minimizing the need for individual copies on every host (which would increase the maintenance overhead).

TIP   A good rule of thumb for estimating overhead is to add 25 percent to the size of the datastore to account for this overhead.

VMFS Capacity Limits

VMFS isn't the only storage option available for VMs, but it's by far the most popular. You can make different assumptions when using Network File System (NFS) datastores, and they will be discussed later in the chapter in "Choosing a Protocol." Using raw device mapping disks (RDMs) to store VM data is another option, but this is out of the scope of this chapter. Chapter 7 will look at RDMs in more detail; for the purposes of capacity planning for a storage array, consider their use frugally and note the requirement for separate LUNs for each RDM disk where needed.

VMFS volumes can be up to 2 TB in size (less 512 bytes). You can use VMFS *extents*, which are effectively a concatenation of additional partitions to the first VMFS partition. VMFS version 3 (the version available with vSphere 4) allows for up to 32 extents, meaning a total maximum VMFS volume size of $\approx$ 64 TB. Considering that a VM doesn't need to be tied to a single datastore, you can see that vSphere will accommodate all but the most extreme VM capacity requirements.

VMFS extents have historically been regarded as an emergency measure only, when the datastore unexpectedly fills to capacity. However, this aversion to VMFS extents is somewhat misplaced, and there are good technical arguments why their use can be part of a design. The stigma regarding extents arose partially because they were used in cases where planning didn't happen properly, and somewhat from the belief that they would cause performance issues. In reality, extents can improve performance when each extent is created on a new physical LUN, thereby reducing LUN queues, aiding multipathing, and increasing throughput. Any additional LUNs should have the same RAIDing and use similar disk types (same speed and IOPS capability).

However, despite any potential performance benefits, there are still pitfalls involving extents that make them difficult to recommend. You must take care when managing the LUNs on the array, because taking just one of the extent LUNs offline is likely to affect many (if not all) of the VMs on the datastore. When you add LUNs to the VMFS volume, data from VMs can be written across all the extents. Taking one LUN offline can crash all the VMs stored on them — and pray that you don't delete the LUN as well. Most midrange SANs can group LUNs into logical sets to prevent this situation, but it still remains a risk that a single corrupt LUN can affect more VMs than normal. The "head" LUN (the first LUN) contains the metadata for all the extents. This one is particularly important, because a loss of the head LUN corrupts the whole datastore. This LUN attracts all the SCSI reservation locks.

For most VM use cases, 2 TB is more than sufficient for datastores. In reality, other performance factors will likely mean that most datastores are smaller than this. If very large datastores are a requirement, such as for virtual desktops, then NFS is a better solution.

Large or Small Datastores?

Just how big should you make your datastores? There are no hard-and-fast rules, but your decision relies on several key points. Let's see why you would choose one or the other:

A Few Large Datastores   At first glance, having a few very large datastores would seem an obvious choice:

◆ You have fewer datastores and array LUNs to manage.

◆ You can create more VMs without having to make frequent visits to the array to provision new LUNs.

◆ Large VMDK disk files can be created.

◆ It allows more space for snapshots and future expansion.

A Lot of Small Datastores   There are also some very good reasons not to max out every datastore at 2 TB:

- Better control of the space.

  - Having fewer VMs in each datastore means you have more granularity when it comes to RAID type.
  - Disk shares can be apportioned more appropriately.
  - ESX hosts can use the additional LUNs to make better use of multipathing.

- There is less contention on individual LUNs and storage processors (SPs), making for more balanced use of array performance.

- It lowers the likelihood that an out-of-control snapshot will take down large numbers of VMs.

- Arguably, you waste less space if the datastores are created more specifically for VMs. But depending on how you reserve space for snapshots, this can be negated by the requirement to keep a certain percentage or amount free on each datastore.

In reality, like most design decisions, the final solution is likely to be a sensible compromise of both extremes. Having one massive datastore would likely cause performance issues, whereas having a single datastore per VM would be too large an administrative overhead for most, and you'd soon reach the upper limit of 256 LUNs on a host.

The size of your datastores will ultimately be impacted primarily by two elements:

Size of the VM's Disk Files   If your VMs are very large, you'll need larger datastores. Smaller VMs need smaller datastores; otherwise, you might see overcommitment-based performance issues.

I/O Levels of Your VMs   If you have VMs that use elevated amounts of I/O — for example, databases or Exchange or SharePoint servers — then you should reduce the number of VMs on each datastore (and in turn reduce their size).

Previous versions of vSphere advised you to limit your datastores to 16 VMs. With vSphere 4, the number has increased to 32; but consider that an upper limit and not the number of VMs around which to create an initial design. Look at your VMs, taking into account the previous two factors, and estimate a number of VMs per datastore that you're comfortable with. Then, multiply that number by your average estimated VM size. Finally, add a fudge factor of 25 percent to account for short-term growth, snapshots, and VM swap files, and you should have an average datastore size that will be appropriate for the majority of your VMs. Remember, you may need to create additional datastores that are specially provisioned for VMs that are larger, are more I/O intensive, need different RAID requirements, or need increased levels of protection.

Fortunately, with the advent of Storage vMotion, moving your VMs to different-sized datastores no longer requires an outage.

VMFS Block Sizes

This is a simple decision. When you create VMFS volumes, you're given the choice of selecting the partitioning block size, as shown in Figure 6.2. This varies from 1 MB blocks up to 8 MB blocks. With most file systems, there is a tradeoff. If you pick a large block size, then every file that's created, no matter how small, uses an entire single block. Ordinarily, a file system has to hold potentially millions of files, which can lead to excessive waste if you choose a block size that's too large for your needs.

FIGURE 6.2
VMFS block-size
selection

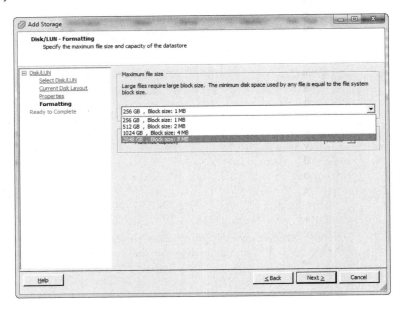

However, VMFS is designed specifically for storing VMs, and as such the number of files is usually in the hundreds at most. Additionally, VMFS 3 can use sub-block allocation for files smaller than 1 MB by splitting blocks into 64 KB chunks. This reduces the impact that ordinary file systems suffer from when storing lots of small files.

If you select a small block size, you limit your options to grow VMs beyond the limit imposed by the smaller block size (for example, datastores with a 1 MB block size can only hold files up to 256 GB in size). This can prevent future growth and can cause problems if committing snapshots causes the disk to grow over the allowable size. Also, after you create the partition, you can't change it. To make a datastore bigger, you must evacuate everything first and then delete and re-create the entire datastore.

Design decision made: create all datastores with an 8 MB block size. It has been proven that there is no appreciable performance benefit from making the size smaller, and you won't hit any file limits with a large block size.

Thin Provisioning

vSphere 4 introduced the ability to thin-provision VM disks from the vSphere client GUI. You can also convert existing VMs to thinly provisioned ones during Storage vMotions. Chapter 7 explains in more depth the practicalities of thin-provisioning VMs, but you need to make a couple of important design decisions when considering your storage as a whole.

Thin provisioning has been available on some storage arrays for years. It's one of the ways to do more for less, and it increases the amount of usable space from disks. Since the support of NFS volumes, thin provisioning has been available to ESX servers. Basically, despite the guest operating system (OS) seeing its full allocation of space, the space is actually doled out only as required. This allows all the spare (wasted) space within VMs to be grouped together and used for other things (such as more VMs).

The biggest problem with any form of storage thin-provisioning is the potential for overcommitment. It's possible — and desirable, as long as it's controlled properly — to allocate more storage than is physically available (otherwise, what's the point?). Banks have operated on this premise for years. They loan out far more money than they have in their vaults. As long as everyone doesn't turn up at the same time wanting their savings back, everything is okay. If all the VMs in a datastore want the space owed to them at once, then you run into overcommitment problems. You've effectively promised more than is available.

To help mitigate the risk of overcommiting the datastores, you can use both the Datastore Disk Usage % and Datastore Disk Overallocation % alarm triggers in vSphere. Doing so helps proactively monitor the remaining space and ensures that you're aware of potential issues before they become a crisis. In the vSphere Client, you can at a glance compare the amounts provisioned against the amounts utilized and get an idea of how thinly provisioned your VMs are.

Why do this? At any one time, much of the space allocated to VMs is sitting empty. You can save space, and therefore money, on expensive disks by not providing all the space at once. It's perfectly reasonable to expect disk capacity and performance to increase in the future and become less expensive, so thin provisioning is good way to hold off as long as possible. As VMs need more capacity, you can add it as required. But this needs careful monitoring to prevent problems.

SHOULD YOU THIN-PROVISION YOUR VMS?

Sure, there are very few reasons not to do this, and one big, fat, money-saving reason to do it. As we said earlier, thin provisioning requires careful monitoring to prevent out-of-space issues on the datastores. vCenter has built-in alarms that you can easily configure to alert you of impending problems. The trick is to make sure you'll have enough warning to create more datastores or move VMs around to avert anything untoward. If that means purchasing and fitting more disks, then you'd better set the threshold suitably low.

As we've stated, there are a few reasons not to use vSphere thin provisioning:

◆ It can cause overcommitment.

◆ It prevents the use of eager zeroed thick VMDK disks which can increase write performance (Chapter 7 explains the types of VM disks in more depth).

◆ It creates higher levels of consolidation on the array, increasing the I/O demands on the SPs, LUNs, paths, and so on.

◆ Converting existing VMs to thin-provisioned ones can be time-consuming.

◆ You prefer to use your storage array's thin provisioning instead.

There are also some situations where it isn't possible to use thin-provisioned VMDK files:

◆ Fault-tolerant (FT) VMs.

◆ Microsoft clustering shared disks.

Does Thin Provisioning Affect the VM's Performance?

vSphere's thin provisioning of VM disks has been shown to make no appreciable difference to their performance, over default VMDK files (zeroed thick). It's also thought that thin provisioning has little impact on file fragmentation of either the VMDK files or their contents.

If Your Storage Array Can Thin-Provision, Should You Do It on the Array, in vSphere, or Both?

Both array and vSphere thin provisioning should have similar results, but doing so on the array can be more efficient. Thin provisioning on both is likely to garner little additional saving (a few percent, probably), but you double the management costs by having to babysit two sets of storage pools. By thin-provisioning on both, you expedite the rate at which you can become oversubscribed.

Data Deduplication

Some midrange and enterprise storage arrays offer what is known as *data deduplication*. This feature looks for common elements that are identical and records one set of them. The duplicates can be safely removed and thus save space. This is roughly analogous to the way VMware removes identical memory blocks in its transparent page sharing (TPS) technique.

There are two types of deduplication:

File-Level Deduplication   The more rudimentary type of array deduplication is known as *file-level* or *single-instance* storage. This looks for identical (not similar — absolutely identical) files spread across the file system and removes duplicate copies. This is similar to hard links on a Unix file system, except that each copy of the file is considered a separate entity.

As an example, a company's file server may have 10 copies of the same 5 MB newsletter in 10 separate home folders. File-level deduplication recognizes them as identical files and only needs to store one 5 MB instance instead of the original 50 MB. Microsoft Exchange has been using this technique from version 5.5 through 2007 on its mailbox stores, to dedupe large email attachments that are replicated many times (interestingly, this functionality has been removed from Exchange 2010 because Microsoft felt it affected performance too much).

In a VMware-centric world, file-level deduplication is usually fairly unhelpful. The arrays look on the file system (NFS in the vSphere context) and find very large VMDK files that despite containing somewhat similar data are almost never exactly identical.

Block-Level Deduplication   This more advanced type of deduplication can work at the block-level. It has the same idea of finding identical chunks of disk but does so at a much lower level. Block-level deduplication doesn't need to understand the file system, so the technique can usually be applied to block and file storage, and can see inside VMDK files.

In a vSphere setup, where VMs are often provisioned from a small set of templates, block-level deduplication can normally provide good space reductions. It isn't uncommon to remove from 25 percent to even 50 percent or more on some datastores. VMs that are very similar — for example, virtual desktops — can benefit greatly from this type of deduplication, with savings of more than 75 percent.

Deduplication can be done inline or post process. *Inline* means the data is checked for duplicates as it's being written. This creates the best levels of space reduction; but because it has a significant impact in I/O performance, it's used only in backup and archiving tools. Storage arrays use post-process deduplication, which runs as a scheduled task against the data. Even post-process deduplication can tax the arrays' CPUs and affect performance, so you should take care to schedule these jobs only during times of lighter I/O.

It's also worth noting that thin provisioning can negate some of the benefits you see with block-level deduplication, because one of the big wins normally is deduplicating all the empty zeros in a file system. It isn't that you don't see additional benefits from using both together; just don't expect the same savings as you do on a thickly provisioned LUN or VMDK file.

Array Compression

Another technique to get more capacity for less on storage arrays is compression. This involves algorithms that take objects (normally files) and compress them to squash out the repeating patterns. Anyone who has used WinZip or uncompressed a tarball will be familiar with the concept of compression.

Compression can be efficient in capacity reduction, but it does have an impact on an array's CPU usage during compression, and it can affect the disk-read performance depending on the efficiency of the on-the-fly decompression (but shouldn't affect the disk-writes, because compression is normally done as a post process). Due to the performance cost, the best candidates for compression are usually low I/O sources such as home folders and archives of older files.

Downside of Saving Space

There is a downside to saving space and increasing your usable capacity? You may think this is crazy talk; but as with most design decisions, you must always consider the practical impacts. Using these newfangled technological advances will save you precious GB of space, but remember that what you're really doing is consolidating the same data but using fewer spindles to do it. Although that will stave off the need for more capacity, you must realize the potential performance repercussions. Squeezing more and more VMs onto a SAN puts further demands on limited I/O.

Designing for Performance

Often, in a heavily virtualized environment, particularly one that uses some of the space-reduction techniques just discussed, a SAN will hit performance bottlenecks long before it runs out of space. If capacity becomes a problem, then you can attach extra disks and shelves. However, not designing a SAN for the correct performance requirements can be much more difficult to rectify. Upgrades are usually prohibitively expensive, often come with outages, and always create an element of risk. And that is assuming the SAN can be upgraded.

Just as with capacity, performance needs are a critical part of any well-crafted storage design.

Measuring Storage Performance

All the physical components in a storage system plus data characteristics combine to provide the resulting performance. You can use many different metrics to judge the performance levels of a disk and the storage array, but the three most relevant and commonly used are:

Disk Latency   Latency is measured in ms and shows the time from the storage request being made to the data then being read or written. A disk's latency is determined by the spin-up time, the seek time, and the rotational latency of the disk.

Bandwidth Bandwidth is normally measured as MBps, and it shows the peak rate at which data can move to and from the storage. How quickly data can be read from and written to disk or cache is the most fundamental issue, although storage arrays have a number of optimizations that can significantly increase the numbers.

IOPS IOPS is probably the most-quoted storage performance statistic. In its most basic form, it's a benchmark of how many read and write commands can be executed in a second, although as you'll see, it can be affected by many other factors. Latency, throughput, and the rotational speed of the disks all affect the IOPS value. This allows you to predict the performance results of disks and to design the storage accordingly.

How to Calculate a Disk's IOPS

To calculate the potential IOPS from a single disk, use the following equation:

IOPS = 1 / (rotational latency + average read/write seek time)

For example, suppose a disk has the following characteristics:

Rotational latency: 2 ms

Read latency: 4 ms

Write latency: 5 ms

If you expect the usage to be around 75 percent reads and 25 percent writes, then you can expect the disk to provide an IOPS value of:

1/(0.002 + 0.00425) = **160 IOPS**

What Can Affect a Storage Array's IOPS?

Looking at single-disk IOPS is relatively straightforward. However, in a vSphere environment, single disks don't normally provide the performance (or capacity or redundancy) required. So, whether the disks are local DAS storage or part of a NAS/SAN device, they will undoubtedly be aggregated together. Storage performance involves many variables. Understanding all the elements and how they affect the resulting IOPS available should clarify how an entire system will perform.

DISKS

The biggest single affect on an array's IOPS performance comes from the disks themselves. They're the slowest component in the mix, with most disks still made from mechanical moving parts. Each disk has its own physical properties, based on the number of platters, the rotational speed (RPMs), the interface, and so on; but disks are predicable, and you can estimate any disk's IOPS.

The sort of IOPS you can expect from a single disk is shown in Table 6.2.

TABLE 6.2:   Average IOPS per disk type

RPM	IOPS
SSD (SLC)	6000–30000
SSD (MLC)	1000–2000
15K (normally FC/SAS)	180
10K (normally FC/SAS)	130
7.2K (normally SATA)	80
5.4K (normally SATA)	50

Solid-state drive (SSD) disks, sometimes referred to as flash drives, are viable options in storage arrays these days. The prices are dropping rapidly, and most vendors provide hybrid solutions that include them in modern arrays. The IOPS value can vary dramatically based on the generation and underlying technology such as multi level cell (MLC) or the faster, more reliable single level cell (SLC). If you're including them in a design, check carefully what sort of IOPS you'll get. The numbers in Table 6.2 highlight the massive differential available.

Despite the fact that flash drives are approximately 10 times the price of regular hard disk drives, they can be around 50 times faster. So, for the correct usage, flash disks can provide increased efficiency with more IOPS/$. Later in this section, we'll explore some innovative solutions using flash drives and these efficiencies.

RAID CONFIGURATION

Creating RAID sets not only aggregates the disks' capacity and provides redundancy, but also fundamentally changes their performance characteristics (see Figure 6.3):

RAID 0   The simplest example is for RAID 0. Suppose you take two identical disks, each with an IOPS value of 150, and create a RAID 0 group. (For simplicity, let's assume that the read and write IOPS are the same. Normally, writes are more expensive, so the write IOPS are usually lower.) The result is a disk set that can provide 300 IOPS for both reads and writes. A RAID 0 set of 6 disks gives 900 IOPS (n × IOPS). But not so fast. Remember, you shouldn't use RAID 0 anywhere near your vSphere environment, because there is no redundancy. If one disk is lost, then so is all the data on all the disks.

RAID 10   RAID 10 provides excellent read performance, which generally goes up in a linear fashion according to the number of disks. With mirrored copies of the data, it can read from the mirrored disks in parallel. With the data striped across the mirrors, you can expect read IOPS approximately equal to the number of disks.

FIGURE 6.3
Performance examples

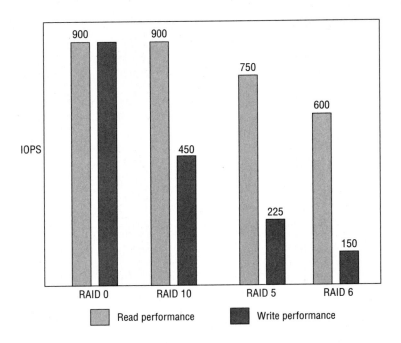

When writing to disk, RAID 10 needs to write to only two disks at a time. The data can still be striped, so you should see performance at around the combined IOPS of half the disks in a set.

For the previous example, if you have a RAID 10 set of 6 disks, it will in theory give you approximately 900 read IOPS (n × IOPS) but only 450 write IOPS ((n × IOPS) / 2). If you understand your split of reads and writes, you can apportion them appropriately and work out the IOPS value depending on different disk amounts.

RAID 5 RAID 5 is often used because it's a good compromise for the sake of capacity: only one disk is lost to parity. Performance for reads remains good, because all but one of the disks can be simultaneously read from. However, RAID 5 write performance is much lower, because for every write I/O, it needs four actual operations. It needs to read the old data, then read the parity, then write the new data, and then write the new parity. This is known as the *RAID write penalty*.

For example, if you have 150 IOPS disks in a set of 6 disks as RAID 5, you should see read performance of 750 IOPS ((n − 1) × IOPS) but write performance of only 225 IOPS ((n × IOPS) / 4).

Additionally, when a disk fails, the set has to run in a degraded mode. Performance tapers off because all the blocks from the failed disk have to be calculated through the parity until the failed disk is replaced and rebuilt. After the failed disk is replaced, all the parity bits must be updated. This explains why failed RAID 5 disks take much longer to replace than failed disks in a mirrored set. Also remember that as the disk sizes increase and the RAID set contains more disks, rebuild times become even longer.

RAID 6   RAID 6 has even less performance than RAID 5 but offers greater protection. In the same example of 6 disks, RAID 6 gives 600 read IOPS ((n − 2) × IOPS) but only 150 write IOPS (a penalty of 6 operations for every I/O) ((n × IOPS) / 6). Despite this, RAID 6 is becoming increasingly popular, because it provides reasonably good capacity and provides better protection than RAID 5. With the increased strain that a RAID 5 rebuild puts on the remaining disks, in conjunction with much larger disks (causing even longer rebuild times) and the use of cheaper SATA disks, more and more vendors are recommending RAID 6 as a standard.

INTERFACES

The *interface* is the physical connection from the disks. The disks may be connected to a RAID controller in a server, a storage controller, or an enclosure's backplane. Several different types are in use, such as IDE, SATA, SCSI, SAS, and FC, and each has its own standards with different recognized speeds. For example, SATA throughput is 1.5 Gbps, but SATA II is backward compatible but qualified for 3 Gbps (with 6 Gbps coming next).

CONTROLLERS

Controllers sit between the disks and servers, connected via the disk (and enclosure) interfaces on one side and the connectors to the server on the other. Manufacturers may refer to them as *controllers*, but the terms *SPs* and *heads* are often used in SAN hardware. Redundancy is often provided by having two or more controllers in an array.

Controllers are really mini-computers in themselves, running a customized OS. They're responsible for most of the special features available today, such as deduplication, failover, multipathing, snapshots, replication, and so on. Onboard server controllers and SAN controllers present their storage as block storage (raw LUNs), whereas NAS devices present their storage as a useable file system such as NFS. However, the waters become a little murky as vendors build NAS facilities into their SANs and vice versa.

Controllers almost always use an amount of non-volatile memory to cache the data before destaging it to disk. This memory is orders of magnitude faster than disks and can significantly improve IOPS. The cache can be used for writes and reads, although write cache normally has the most significance. Write cache allows the incoming data to be absorbed very quickly and then written to the slower disks in the background. However, the size of the cache limits its usefulness, because it can quickly fill up. At that point, the IOPS are again brought down to the speed of the disks, and the cache needs to wait to write the data out before it can empty itself and be ready for new data.

Controller cache helps to alleviate some of the affect of RAID write penalties mentioned earlier. It can collect large blocks of contiguous data and write them to disk in single operation. The earlier RAID calculations are often changed substantially by controllers; they can have a significant effect on overall performance.

TRANSPORT

The term *transport* in this instance describes how data gets from the servers to the arrays. If you're using a DAS solution, this isn't applicable, because the RAID controller is normally mounted directly to the motherboard. For shared storage, however, a wide variety of technologies (and therefore design decisions) are available. Transport includes the protocol, the topology, and the physical cables/connectors and any switching equipment used. The protocol you select determines the physical aspects, and you can use a dizzying array of methods to get ones and zeros from one rack to another.

Later in the chapter in "Choosing a Network Protocol," we'll examine the types of protocols in more depth, because it's an important factor to consider when you're designing a storage architecture. Each protocol has an impact on how to provide the required redundancy, multipathing options, throughput, latency, and so on. But suffice it to say, the potential storage protocols that are used in a vSphere deployment are Fibre Channel (FC), iSCSI, and NFS.

OTHER PERFORMANCE FACTORS TO CONSIDER

In addition to the standard storage components we've mentioned, you can customize other aspects to improve performance.

Queuing

Although block storage, array controllers, LUNs, and host bus adapters (HBAs) can queue data, there can still be a bottleneck from outstanding I/O. If the array can't handle the level of IOPS, the queue fills faster than it can drain. This queuing causes latency, and excessive amounts can be very detrimental to overall performance. When the queue is full, the array sends I/O-throttling commands back to the host's HBAs to slow down the traffic. The amount of queuing, or *queue depth*, is usually configurable on devices and can be optimized for your requirements. The QUED column in esxtop shows the queuing levels in real time.

Each LUN gets its own queue, so changes to HBA queue depths can affect multiple LUN queues. If multiple VMs are active on a LUN, you also need to update the `Disk .SchedNumReqOutstanding` value. This is the level of active disk requests being sent to the LUN by the VMs. Normally, that value should equal the queue-depth number. (VMware's Knowledge Base article 1267 explains how to change these values: `http://kb.vmware.com/kb/1267`.)

The default queue-depth settings are sufficient for most user cases. However, if you have a small number of very I/O-intensive VMs, you may benefit from increasing the queue depth. Take care before you decide to change these values; it's a complex area where good intentions can lead to bigger performance issues. Increasing queue depth on the hosts unnecessarily can create more latency than needed. Often, a more balanced design, where VM loads are spread evenly across HBAs, SPs, and LUNs is a better approach than adjusting queue-depth values. You should check the array and the HBA manufacturer's documentation for their recommendations.

Partition Alignment

Aligning disk partitions can make a substantial difference — up to 30 percent in the performance of some operations. When partitions are aligned properly, it increases the likelihood that the SAN controller can write a full stripe. This reduces the RAID write penalty that costs so much in terms of IOPS.

You need to address partition alignment on vSphere in two areas: the VMFS volume and the guest OS file system. When you create VMFS datastores from within the vSphere client, it aligns them automatically for you. Remember that if you create additional VMFS volumes during the initial build, the anaconda-based installer won't align them properly. In most cases, local VMFS isn't used for performance-sensitive VMs; but if you're planning to use this storage for such tasks, you should re-create the partition in the client after the build.

The most likely place where partitions aren't aligned properly is in the guest OSs of the VMs. Chapter 7 will have a more in-depth examination of this topic and how to align or realign a VM's partitions.

Storage I/O Control

Storage I/O Control (SIOC) is a feature that was introduced in vSphere 4.1 to improve the spread of I/O from VMs across a datastore. It provides for a level of quality of service by enforcing I/O shares and limits regardless of which host is accessing them. SIOC works by monitoring latency statistics for a datastore; when a predetermined level is reached, SIOC scales back I/O via allotted shares. This prevents any one VM from saturating the I/O channel and allows other VMs on the datastore their fair share of throughput.

Just as CPU and memory shares only apply during contention, SIOC will only balance the I/O spread when the latency figures rise above the predefined levels. SIOC enforces I/O with the set IOPS limits for each VM disk and distributes load depending on the datastore's total shares. Each host with VMs on the datastore uses an I/O queue slot relative to the VM's shares, which ensures that high-priority VMs receive greater throughput than lower-priority ones.

This feature is currently available only on block-based storage: NFS datastores and RDM disks aren't supported. Also, each datastore enabled for SIOC can have only one extent.

To configure SIOC, do the following:

1. Enable the SIOC feature within the datastore's properties.

2. Set the shares and IOPS level for each VM disk on the datastore.

It's possible to adjust the threshold value. By default, it's set to 30 ms, but you can use a value from 10 ms up to 100 ms. The default value is appropriate in most circumstances; but if you want to fine-tune it to a specific disk type, then SSDs should be around 10–15 ms, FC and SAS disks 20–30 ms, and SATA disks 30–50 ms. Setting the value too high reduces the likelihood that SIOC will kick in to adjust the I/O queues. Setting it too low means shares are enforced more frequently, which can unnecessarily create a negative impact on the VMs with lower shares.

Workload

Every environment is different, and planning the storage depends on what workloads are being generated. You can optimize storage for different types of storage needs: the ratio of reads to writes, the size of the I/O, and how sequential or random the I/O is.

Writes always take longer than reads. Individual disks are slower to write data than to read them. But more important, the RAID configurations that have some sort of redundancy always penalize writes. As you've seen, some RAID types suffer from write penalties significantly more than others. If you determine that you have a lot of writes in your workloads, you may attempt to offset this with a larger controller cache. If, however, you have a negligible number of writes, you may choose to place more importance on faster disks or allocate more cache to reads.

The size of I/O requests varies. Generally speaking, larger requests are dealt with more quickly than small ones. You may be able to optimize certain RAID settings on the array or use different file-system properties.

Sequential data can be transferred to disk more quickly than random data because the disk heads don't need to move around as much. If you know certain workloads are very random, you can place them on the faster disks. Alternatively, most controller software attempts to de-randomize the data before it's de-staged from cache, so your results may vary depending on the vendor's ability to perform this efficiently.

VMs

Another extremely important aspect of your design that impacts your storage performance is the VMs. Not only are they the customers for the storage performance, but they also have a role to play in overall speed.

Naturally, this will be discussed in more depth in Chapter 7, but it's worth noting the effect it can have on your storage design. How you configure a VM affects its storage performance but can also affect the other VMs around it. Particularly I/O-intensive VMs can affect other VMs on the same host, datastore (LUN), path, RAID set, or controller. If you need to avoid IOPS contention for a particular VM, you can isolate it, thus guaranteeing it IOPS. Alternatively, if you wish to reduce the impact of I/O from VMs on others, you can spread the heavy hitters around, balancing the load. Chapter 8 also looks at how disk shares can spread I/O availability.

We've already mentioned guest OS alignment, but you can often tune the guest OS to the environment for your storage array. The VM's hardware and drivers also have an impact on how it utilizes the available storage. How the data is split across VMDKs, whether its swapfile is segregated to a separate VMDK, and how the balance of different SAN drive types and RAIDing are used for different VM disks all affect the overall storage design.

NEWER TECHNOLOGIES TO INCREASE EFFECTIVE IOPS

Recently, many SAN vendors have been looking at ways to improve the performance of their arrays. This is becoming important as the density of IOPS required per disk has risen sharply. This jump in the need for IOPS is partly because of the consolidation that vSphere lends itself to, and partly due to some of the advancements in capacity optimizations such as deduplication.

Write Coalescing

Coalescing is a function of some SPs that can improve the effective IOPS. It attempts to take randomized I/O in the write cache and reorganize it quickly into more sequential data. This allows it to be more efficiently striped across the disks and cuts down on write latency. By its very nature, coalescing doesn't help optimize disk reads, so it can only help with certain types of I/O.

Large Cache

Today's controller cache can vary from perhaps around 256 MB on a server's RAID controller to tens of gigabytes on larger enterprise SANs.

However, some SAN vendors have started to sell add-on cards packed with hundreds of gigabytes of nonvolatile memory. These massive cache cards particularly help in situations where the data is being compressed heavily and IOPS/TB are very high. A good example is virtual desktop infrastructure (VDI) workloads such as VMware View deployments.

Another approach is to augment the existing controller cache with one or more flash drives. These aren't as responsive as the onboard memory cache, but they're much less expensive and can still provide speeds that are exponentially (at least five times) more than the SAS/SATA disks they're cache for. This relatively economical option means that you can add terabytes of cache to SANs.

These very large caches are making massive improvements to storage array's IOPS. But these improvements can only be realized in certain circumstances, and it's important that you consider your own workload requirements.

The one criticism of this technique is that it can't preemptively deal with large I/O requests. Large cache needs a period of time to *warm up* when it's empty, because although you don't want to run out of cache, it isn't very useful if it doesn't hold the data you're requesting. After being emptied, it takes time to fill up with suitable requested data.

Cache Pre-Fetch

Some controllers can attempt to pre-fetch data in their read caches. They look at the blocks that are being requested and try to anticipate what the next set of blocks might be, so they're ready if a host subsequently requests it. Vendors use various algorithms, and cache pre-fetch relies on the sort of workloads presented to it. Some read the next set of blocks; others do it based on previous reads. This helps to deliver the data directly from the cache instead of having to wait for slower disks, thus potentially improving response time.

Cache Deduplication

Cache deduplication does something very similar to disk deduplication, in that it takes the contents of the cache's data and removes identical blocks. It effectively increases the cache size and allows more things to be held in cache. Because cache is such a critical performance enhancement, this *extra* cache undoubtedly helps improve the array's performance. Cache deduplication can be particularly effective when very similar requests for data are being made, such as VDI boot storms or desktop recomposes.

Tiering

Another relatively new innovation on midrange and enterprise SANs is the tiering of disks. Until recently, SANs came with 10 K or 15 K drives. This was the only choice, along with whatever RAIDing you wanted to create, to divide the workload and create different levels of performance. However, SATA disks are used increasingly, because they have large capacity and are much less expensive. Add to that the dramatic drop in prices of flash drives, which although smaller provide insane levels of performance, and you have a real spread of options. All these can be mixed in different amounts to provide both the capacity and the performance required.

Initially, only manual tiering was available: SAN administrators created disk sets for different workloads. This was similar to what they did with drive speeds and different types of RAID. But now you have a much more flexible set of options with diverse characteristics.

Some storage arrays have the ability to automate this tiering, either at the LUN level or even down to the block level. They can monitor the different requests and automatically move the more frequently requested data to the faster flash disks and the less requested to the slower but cheaper SATA disks. You can create rules to ensure that certain VMs are always kept on a certain type of disk, or you can create schedules to be sure VMs that need greater performance at set times are moved into fast areas ahead of time.

Automatic tiering can be very effective at providing extra IOPS to the VMs that really need it, and only when they need it. Flash disks helps to absorb the increase in I/O density caused by capacity-reduction techniques. Flash disks reduce the cost of IOPS, and the SATA disks help bring down the cost of the capacity. It's like DRS for your storage array.

Storage Hardware Acceleration

vStorage API for Array Integration (VAAI) is a new set of storage APIs that VMware introduced in vSphere 4.1. To use the capabilities of the API, the storage array must include appropriate support. NFS NAS devices can't integrate with VAAI at this time.

VAAI integration with an array means you can offload directly to the array some of the storage tasks that are normally performed by the host. Doing so reduces host CPU, memory, network, and fabric loads and performs operations more efficiently and quickly. VAAI currently uses three techniques to offload tasks:

Full Copy   Full Copy uses SAN technologies to perform data copies, without requiring the hosts to read and write everything. It reduces the time and overhead of Storage vMotions, template deployments, and VM clones.

Block Zeroing   Block Zeroing allows the SAN to zero out disks for eager zero thick disks. This significantly reduces the time required to create these disks, which are used by FT-enabled VMs and advised for use with VMs that need high disk performance.

Hardware Assisted Locking   Hardware Assisted Locking provides a better locking mechanism than the existing SCSI reservations normally used. This can help improve datastore access efficiency and scalability.

Storage hardware acceleration provides some useful benefits. Check the VMware storage hardware compatibility list (HCL) for compatibility with different arrays. Some arrays may require a firmware upgrade to support this feature.

Measuring Your Existing IOPS Usage

When you know what affects the performance of your storage and how you can improve the design to suit your environment, you should be able to measure your current servers and estimate your requirements.

Various tools exist to measure performance:

◆ *Iometer* (www.iometer.org/) is an open source tool that can generate different workloads on your storage device. It lets you test your existing storage or generate suitable workloads to test new potential solutions.

◆ To monitor existing VMs, start with the statistics available in the vSphere client. You can also use *esxtop* to look at the following statistics:

  ◆ *DAVG* — Disk latency at the array

  ◆ *KAVG* and *QUED* — Queue-depth statistics showing latency at the VMkernel

◆ For very in-depth VM monitoring, the *vscsiStats* tool provides a comprehensive toolset for storage analysis.

◆ Windows VMs and physical servers can be monitored for IOPS with the *perfmon* tool. Just add the counters Disk Reads/sec and Disk Writes/sec from the Physical Disk performance objects to view the IOPS in real time. These can then be captured to a CSV file so you can analyze typical loads over time.

◆ Linux/Unix VMs and physical servers can use a combination of *top* and *iostat* to perform similar recordings of storage usage.

When you're testing VMs, it's worth noting that the hypervisor can create some inaccuracies in guest-based performance tools such as perfmon due to timing issues, especially when the CPU is under strain. Remember to take into account the requirements of nonvirtual servers that may use the same storage, because they may affect the performance of the VMs.

vSphere 4.1 has added new host and VM performance metrics in both the vSphere Client and in esxtop/resxtop. These additional statistics cover both real-time and trending in vCenter, and bring the NFS data on par with the existing block-based support. So to make the most of the tools, use the latest host software available.

Local Storage vs. Shared Storage

Shared storage, aka SANs or NAS devices, have become so common place in vSphere deployments that local storage is often disregarded as an option. It's certainly true that each new release of VMware's datacenter hypervisor layers on more great functionality that takes advantage of shared storage. But local storage has its place and can offer some tangible advantages. Each design is different and needs to be approached with an open mind. Don't dismiss local storage before you identify the real needs of your company.

Local Storage

Local storage, or DAS, can come in several forms. Predominantly, we mean the disks from which you intend to run the VMs, mounted as VMFS datastores. These disks can be physically inside or attached to the host's disk bays. The disks can also be in a separate enclosure connected via a SCSI cable to an external-facing SCSI card's connector. Even if externally mounted, it's logically still local host storage. With local storage, you can mount a reasonable amount of capacity via local SCSI.

You can install vSphere 4 on IDE, ATA, SCSI, SAS, and SATA disks, although your mileage may vary if the disk controller isn't listed on VMware's approved HCL. But ATA disks can't support VMFS volumes, so although you can install ESX, you won't be able to run VMs from those disks.

First, let's identify more clearly when you *don't* want to deploy VMs on local storage. Certain features need storage that multiple hosts can access, and if these will be part of your solution, you'll need at least some shared storage. Make no mistake, there are definite advantages to using shared storage (hence its overwhelming popularity):

◆ vMotion needs shared storage. This also means local storage can't take advantage of DRS.

◆ High-availability (HA) hosts need to be able to see the same VMs to recover them when a protected host fails.

◆ FT hosts need a second host to access the same VM, so it can step in if the first host fails.

◆ RDM disks can't use local storage. In turn, this excludes the use of Microsoft clustering across multiple hosts.

- ◆ Shared storage has the great advantage of allowing you to patch and schedule hardware outages with no downtime to the VMs using vMotion techniques.

- ◆ When you use shared storage, you can recover from host failures far more easily. If you're using local storage and a server fails for whatever reason, the VMs will be offline until the server can be repaired. This often means time-consuming backup restores. With shared storage, even without the use of HA, you can manually restart the VMs on another cluster host.

- ◆ Local storage capacity is limited by several factors, including the size of the SCSI enclosures, the number of SCSI connectors, and the number of datastores. Generally, only so many VMs can be run on a single host. As the number of hosts grows, the administrative overhead soon outweighs the cost savings.

- ◆ With shared storage, it's possible to have a common store for templates and ISOs. With local storage, each host needs to have a copy of each template.

- ◆ It's possible with shared storage to run ESX from diskless servers, and have them boot from SAN. This effectively makes the hosts stateless, further reducing deployment and administrative overheads.

- ◆ ESXi further reduces the need for sizable local storage.

With all that said, local storage has some advantages of its own. If you have situations where these features or benefits aren't a necessity, then you may find that these positives create an interesting new solution:

- ◆ Far and away the greatest advantage of local storage is the potential cost savings. Not only are local disks often cheaper, but an entire shared storage infrastructure is expensive to purchase and maintain. When a business is considering shared storage for a vSphere setup, this may be the first time it has ventured into the area. The company will have the initial outlay for all the pieces that make up a SAN or NAS solution, will probably have training expenses for staff, and may even need additional staff to maintain the equipment. This incipient cost can be prohibitive for many smaller companies.

- ◆ Local storage is usually already in place for the ESX or ESXi installable OS. This means there is often local space available for VMFS datastores, or it's relatively trivial to add extra disks to the purchase order for new servers.

- ◆ The technical bar for implementing local storage is very low in comparison to the challenges of configuring a new SAN fabric or a NAS device/server.

- ◆ Local storage can provide good levels of performance for certain applications. Although the controller cache is likely to be very limited in comparison to modern SANs, latency will be extremely low for obvious reasons.

- ◆ You can use local storage to provide VMFS space for templates and ISO files. Using local storage does have an impact. Localized templates and ISOs are available only to that host, which means all VMs need to be built on the designated host and then cold-migrated to the intended host.

◆ You can also use local storage for VM's swap files. This can save space on the more expensive shared storage for VMs. However, this approach can have an effect on DRS and HA if there isn't enough space on the destination hosts to receive migrated VMs.

◆ Many of the advanced features that make shared storage such an advantage, such as DRS and HA, aren't available on the more basic licensing terms. In a smaller environment, these licenses and hence the features may not be available anyway.

◆ Local storage can be ideal in test lab situations, or for running development and staging VMs, where redundancy isn't a key requirement. Many companies aren't willing to pay the additional costs for these VMs if they're considered non-essential or don't have SLAs around their availability.

What About Local Shared Storage?

Another storage possibility is becoming increasing popular in some environments. There are several different incarnations, but they're often referred to as *virtual SANs, virtual NAS,* or *virtual storage devices*. They use storage (normally local) and present it as a logical FC, iSCSI, or NFS storage device. Current marketplace solutions include HP's LeftHand, StarWind software, or DataCore's SANmelody.

These allow you to take advantage of many of the benefits of shared-storage devices with increased VMware functionality but without the cost overheads of a full shared-storage environment. To the cluster hosts, they appear as VMs on shared storage, which can be vMotioned and shared among multiple hosts. Templates can be seen by all the hosts, even if they're stored locally.

But remember that these solutions normally still suffer from the same single-point-of-failure downsides of local storage. There are products with increasing levels of sophistication that allow you to pool several local-storage sources together and even cluster local LUNs into replica failover copies across multiple locations.

Several storage vendors also produce cut-down versions of their SAN array software installed within virtual appliances, which allow you to use any storage to mimic their paid-for storage devices. These often have restrictions and are principally created so that customers can test and become familiar with their products. However, they can be very useful for small lab environments, allowing you to save on shared storage, but still letting you manage it the same way as your primary storage.

Additionally, it's feasible to use any server storage as shared resources. Most popular OSs can create NFS exports (perhaps excluding Microsoft, which prefers to promote its own Server Message Block [SMB] / Common Internet File System [CIFS] protocols), which can be used for vSphere VMs. In fact, several OSs are designed specifically for this purpose, such as the popular Openfiler project (`www.openfiler.com`) and the FreeNAS project (`http://freenas.org`). These sorts of home-grown shared-storage solutions certainly aren't what can be classed as enterprise-grade solutions, but they may give you an extra option for adding shared features when you have no budget. If your plan includes regular local storage, then some virtualized shared storage can enhance your capabilities, often for little or no extra cost.

Shared Storage

Shared storage provides the cornerstone of most vSphere deployments. Local storage is often still found in small setups, where companies are new to the technologies or lack the budget. To take full advantage of vSphere 4 and all it has to offer, a shared-storage solution is the obvious first choice. Shared storage underlines the primary goals:

Availability   Shared storage creates greater redundancy and reliability and reduces single points of failure.

Performance   Shared storage means better I/O performance and scalability.

Capacity   Shared storage aggregates storage and allows the use of advanced capacity-reduction technologies.

Choosing a Network Protocol

An increasingly discussed and debated storage topic is which protocol to use. VMware supports a few different protocols, and with that choice come decisions. With the advent of 10GbE, the network-based iSCSI and NFS have become far more competitive against FC-based SANs. Many of the midrange arrays available today come with multiple-protocol support included or easily added, so things are much less clear cut than before.

As you'll see, each protocol has its own ups and downs, but each is capable and should be considered carefully. Old assumptions can and should be questioned, and preconceptions are often being proven no longer true. It really is time to go back to the requirements and ask why.

In past VMware days, many advanced features or products only worked with certain types of storage. For the most part, this is no longer true: most products work with all supported protocols.

You need to compare the following protocols: FC, iSCSI (using both hardware and software initiators), and NFS exports. A newer addition to the list is Fibre Channel over Ethernet (FCoE); and you should also consider the increasing availability of 10GbE, which is making a big impact on the storage landscape with regard to protocol selection. Finally, note that InfiniBand is still theoretically a supported protocol for vSphere 4, although the lack of available driver support for InfiniBand adapter cards makes this a moot point. Table 6.3 summarizes the characteristics of each protocol:

TABLE 6.3:   Protocol characteristics

	LOCAL	**FC**	**FCOE**	**ISCSI**	**NFS**
Transfer	Block	Block	Block	Block	File
Transport	Direct SCSI	SCSI encapsulated in FC frames	SCSI encapsulated in FC frames over Ethernet	SCSI encapsulated in TCP/IP	File over TCP/IP

TABLE 6.3: Protocol characteristics *(CONTINUED)*

	LOCAL	FC	FCoE	iSCSI	NFS
Host interface	SCSI/SAS/ SATA/IDE controller	HBA	CNA	iSCSI HW – TOE iSCSI SW –NIC	NIC
Link speeds	Depends on bus speed of controller	Up to 8 Gbps	10GbE	Up to 10GbE	Up to 10GbE
Primary security controls	n/a		Zoning LUN masking	LUN masking CHAP IP security (such as ACLs)	Export permissions IP security (such as ACLs)
RDMs	No		Yes	Yes	No
Boot ESX from	Yes		Yes	4.0 HW only 4.1 SW added for ESXi *1	No
HA	No		Yes	Yes	Yes
vMotion	No		Yes	Yes	Yes
DRS	No		Yes	Yes	Yes
Storage vMotion	Yes		Yes	Yes	Yes
FT	No		Yes	Yes	Yes
MSCS clustering	Cluster in a box (CIB) only		Yes	Not supported	Not supported
Thin-provisioned VMDKs	Yes		Yes	Yes	Yes
Datastore file system	VMFS		VMFS	VMFS	NFS
Maximum datastores per host	Practically limited by size of local storage		256	256	64 (default is 8)

Continues

TABLE 6.3: Protocol characteristics *(CONTINUED)*

	LOCAL	FC	FCOE	ISCSI	NFS
Maximum datastore size (with extents)	≈ 64 TB (but practically limited by size of local storage)		≈ 64 TB	≈ 64 TB	Limited only by NAS file system *2
VMs per volume	256		256	256	Limited only by NAS file system

*1 Beginning in vSphere 4.1, a new feature called iSCSI Boot Firmware Table (iBFT) allows ESXi hosts to boot from the SAN. Only a limited number of network adapters are supported at this stage for this feature.

*2 16 TB is a common limit on NFS exports.

Fiber Channel

FC is the veritable stalwart shared-storage protocol and has been ever since it was first supported by ESX in version 2.0. It's a mature and well-trusted solution in datacenters, and traditionally it's the default solution of many Enterprise SANs. The FC protocol encapsulates all the SCSI commands into FC frames, a lossyless transport.

FC fabrics are specialized storage networks made up of server HBAs, FC switches, and SAN SPs. Each connector has a globally unique identifier known as a World Wide Name (WWN). A WWN is further split into a World Wide Port Name (WWPN), which is a port on a switch, and a World Wide Node Name (WWNN), which is a port on an endpoint.

Hosts can be attached directly to the SAN without the use of a fabric switch, but this restricts the number of hosts to the number of FC SP ports available. FC switches also allow for redundant links from each host to cross-connect to multiple SP controllers.

The FC protocol is a high-bandwidth transport layer with a very low latency. This low latency still sets it apart from other common storage protocols. The FC protocol technically has three different modes, but *switched* (FC-SW) is the only one you're likely to use in a vSphere environment (point-to-point and arbitrated loop are the two legacy modes). The interconnect speeds are set at 1, 2, 4, or the latest, 8 Gbps. FC fabrics ordinarily use OM2 cables with LC connectors (orange fibre optic cables) these days, although light-blue OM3 cables are becoming more popular with an increase in 8 Gbps use.

FC storage security is predominately handled via zoning. *Zoning* is an access control mechanism set at the FC switch level, restricting which endpoints can communicate. Anything outside the zone isn't visible to the endpoint. Zoning protects devices from other traffic such as registered state change notification (RSCN) broadcasts and is roughly analogous to VLANing in the Ethernet world. Zoning ensures that hosts that need to see the storage can do so, while those that don't need visibility don't interfere. You can set zones based on specific switch ports (*port zoning* or *hard zoning*) or define them via WWNs (*soft zoning*), which has the advantage of allowing recabling without needing to reconfigure the zoning information.

Several zoning topologies are available. The simplest method is to have one large zone with all devices in it. But for vSphere (and most other applications), the recommendation is to use what is called *single initiator zoning*. This means each HBA is in its own zone with the target device. This approach is considerably more secure and prevents initiators from trying to communicate with each other (which they shouldn't be doing in a vSphere setting). An even tighter convention is to create zones for a single HBA to a single SP. This takes longer to configure than one large zone; but if you use a sensible naming convention for the zones (for example, HOSTNAME_HBA1_SPA), they can be logical to follow and add to when required.

You can use LUN masking to grant permissions, allowing LUNs to be available to hosts. The LUN masks are set on the hosts themselves or on the SPs. LUN masking is also sometimes referred to as *iGroups, access control, storage presentation,* or *partitioning*. It effectively gives hosts the ability to disregard LUNs or lets SPs ignore hosts that shouldn't be accessing LUNs.

FC has many advantages when compared to other options:

- **High Speed:** Until 10GbE arrived, FC was always the high-speed option.

- **Lossyless with Dedicated Paths:** There is a low risk of oversubscription on the paths.

- **Low Latency:** If you have VMs that are sensitive to latency, FC will help prevent issues.

- **Existing FC Equipment:** There may already be some FC equipment in the datacenter.

- **Existing FC Skills:** Some staff may be familiar with FC.

- **Security:** With dedicated links of fibre optic cables, it's an inherently more secure solution.

- **Trust:** It's a long-trusted, mature storage protocol.

- **Dedicated Network:** Normally, the FC fabric is dedicated to storage traffic.

- **Efficiency:** FC frames don't have the TCP/IP overhead that iSCSI and NFS do.

But there are certain potential drawbacks to the FC protocol:

- **Cost:** FC switches, cables, and so on are normally more expensive than equivalent Ethernet equipment.

- **Initial Cost:** When you first use FC, a large CAPEX layout is required to get a working fabric.

- **Unfamiliarity of Technology:** If your team is new to FC, there is a relatively steep learning curve to implement it.

FIBRE CHANNEL OVER ETHERNET

FCoE is a relatively new addition to the protocol list available to vSphere architects. FCoE maps frame-based FC protocol over Ethernet alongside its IP traffic. Because Ethernet has no built-in flow control, FC needs special enhancements to prevent congestion and packet loss. These enhancements help to deal with the loss and retransmissions in IP-based transport, which is what makes FCoE special. FCoE is designed to run over 10GbE cables.

FCoE utilize converged network adapters (CNAs), which contain both FC HBAs and Ethernet NIC adapters. Some OSs offer software initiators that work with regular 10GbE NIC cards, although this isn't an option on vSphere yet. Because most CNAs are new to market, ESX hosts need extra drivers installed for them to be recognized. The drivers usually come in two parts, one for the HBA and another for the NIC. After the card is installed, it logically appears in the vSphere Client as both an HBA under the storage adapter configuration and as a NIC under the network adapter configuration.

FCoE can have a great deal of overlap with the existing FC deployments, so if you have an existing FC infrastructure, you should be able to introduce FCoE while avoiding a rip-and-replace style of migration. It's expected that FCoE will often be initially deployed as CNA cards and FCoE switches while the connections to the arrays and the arrays themselves remain FC fibre optic–based.

FCoE shares many of the advantages attributed to FC, along with the following:

◆ **Fewer Cables:** By combining storage and network with high-bandwidth cables, FCoE reduces clutter, increases airflow, and eases management.

◆ **Less Power:** Fewer cables means less power is needed.

◆ **CNAs Already Include 10GbE:** If you invest in CNAs but later decide to switch to iSCSI or NFS, then the hardware investment will still be valid.

◆ **FCoE Switches Can Interface with FC Equipment:** You should be able to use existing FC equipment while taking advantage of the converged cabling on the server side.

◆ **Low Overhead of FC:** FCoE still has a much lower latency than iSCSI or NFS.

But be mindful of these potential FCoE disadvantages:

◆ **Newness of the Protocol:** FCoE is barely ratified as a standard, and some questions still remain about whether it lacks the maturity of the other protocol standards available.

◆ **Expense:** FCoE is still relatively expensive. Core Ethernet switches that support FCoE are still at a premium.

◆ **Different Hardware Standards:** The protocol is still so young that de facto cables and connectors have yet to emerge. Some first-generation CNA cards can't upgrade to the latest standards.

◆ **Little Advantage if There Is No FC Already:** Datacenters without FC at the moment are likely to move toward 10GbE iSCSI or NFS, not FCoE.

◆ **Lack of Experience/Knowledge:** FCoE is a new, emerging standard, so there is less information relating to it.

iSCSI

iSCSI uses TCP to encapsulate SCSI traffic, allowing block-level storage LUN access across Ethernet cables. Used predominately over 1GbE links, iSCSI has recently been able to take advantage of 10GbE advances, letting it compete with the traditionally more performant FC protocol.

iSCSI became popular in datacenters predominantly through use by Microsoft servers (as opposed to FC, which was traditionally the focus of the Unix servers).

vSphere supports two types of iSCSI initiator:

HW (Hardware) Initiator   An iSCSI HBA that offloads iSCSI processing from the host's CPU. It's normally a 1GbE or 10GbE NIC card with TCP/IP Offload Engine (TOE) capabilities built in.

SW (Software) Initiator   Uses VMware's software implementation within the VMkernel, alongside a regular Ethernet NIC adapter. ESX hosts can't use SW initiators to boot from SAN or hold diagnostic vmkcore partitions, but vSphere 4.1 now supports ESXi hosts booting from SW initiators if the NIC supports iBFT.

The HW initiators have the advantage that they offload some of the CPU processing; but with recent advances in the vSphere SW initiator, this has become less of an issue. The current SW initiator uses very little CPU (around half a core); and with the increasing processing power of servers, it's generally thought that the additional cost of the HW cards is no longer worth the expense. SW initiators have become a much more popular method of connecting to iSCSI targets. They're easier to configure now that only a VMkernel port is required, so few choose to buy HW cards for new deployments. HW initiators are relatively rare and are used less and less these days.

Although it's possible to run an in-guest iSCSI software initiator to access raw block storage for a VM, it bypasses the ESX host's storage stack and so is treated like any other VM network traffic. It's unusual for VM traffic to be a bottleneck, but this is the sort of configuration that can saturate VMNICs. This isn't a recommended way to present storage to VMs: it doesn't have the flexibility of regular iSCSI storage, because it can't use Storage vMotion or vSphere snapshots.

NOTE   One side case for in-guest iSCSI software initiators is that they can allow you to present very large disks to VMs. VMDK files have a 2 TB limit, whether they're deployed on VMFS, on NFS, or as RDMs. However, with an in-guest iSCSI SW initiator, you can theoretically present as large a disk as your array will allow. Needless to say, this isn't a recommended setup.

vSphere has two methods to discover iSCSI targets:

Dynamic Discovery   Also known as SendTargets, the initiator polls the network for targets. Less configuration is required, although removed items can return after a rescan or reboot, or be lost if the target is temporarily unavailable.

Static Discovery   You must manually enter the IP addresses of the targets. The target survives rescans, but this method is available only when using HW initiators.

iSCSI has no FC fabric zoning, although because it's still block-level storage it can use LUN masking to ignore LUNs. Instead of zoning, iSCSI uses Challenge-Handshake Authentication Protocol (CHAP) as a way to provide rudimentary access control for the initiators and targets. CHAP is a three-way handshake algorithm based on a predefined private value, which verifies identity using a hashed transmission. Currently, HW initiators only allow for the use of one-way CHAP, as opposed to SW initiators, which can do mutual CHAP (bidirectional).

Most arrays also let you configure access control based on IP address or initiator name. Make sure your iSCSI traffic is only allowed onto an internal part of your trusted network, because the traffic isn't encrypted in any way. A nonroutable VLAN on a dedicated pair of redundant switches is ideal to segregate and secure iSCSI traffic.

Jumbo frames can be enabled on vSphere hosts and are supported by most iSCSI SANs. They help to increase performance, because the larger packet sizes reduce the overhead of processing the Ethernet packets. Typically, the frames are set to 9,000 maximum transmission units (MTUs). It's important that if you enable jumbo frames, all devices, end points (servers and storage), and network devices in between must support and be enabled for this. Enabling jumbo frames on some Cisco switches requires them to be reloaded (which causes a short network outage).

The Flow Control setting on switches, hosts, and arrays is another useful enhancement that should improve general throughput. Set it to *desired* or *receive* on switches and *transmit* or *send* on end points.

The Ethernet switch ports used for the storage network should have Rapid Spanning Tree Protocol (RSTP) or portfast enabled. This allows an immediate transition if an active link fails.

Chapter 5, "Designing Your Network," discussed various methods to providing suitable network redundancy for Ethernet-based storage. Later in this chapter the "Multipathing" section will discuss different multipathing techniques, including those covering the iSCSI protocol. But it's worth pointing out at this juncture that your iSCSI design should carefully consider redundancy. The fundamentals involve ensuring that at least two NICs (or HW initiators) are configured on each host for iSCSI traffic. These two NICs should be connected to two separate switches, which in turn are connected to two iSCSI controllers on the SAN.

Dedicated storage switches, which don't handle regular network traffic, make your storage transport more secure. They also help to prevent contention with other IP traffic, improving storage performance. If you don't have access to separate hardware, then you can use layer 2 VLANs to isolate the storage. You should avoid 100 Mbps equipment anywhere in the chain, because it doesn't provide the throughput required to run VMs effectively. Use 1 Gbps capable switches, NICs, and cables throughout as a minimum.

Ethernet isn't designed for storage, so it can suffer from congestion issues when numerous hosts are attached to a much smaller number of array controllers. This causes oversubscription, which means that packets get dropped and performance degrades. This can be the start of a vicious circle where TCP/IP needs time to see what was dropped and then more time to retransmit. A bad situation gets progressively worse. Using logical separation techniques such as VLANing doesn't help in these cases. If this becomes an issue, you should use dedicated storage switches; and if required, more capable switches with better backplane I/O capacity which will alleviate the oversubscription.

iSCSI has a number of advantages over the FC and FCoE protocols:

- **Inexpensive Equipment:** Compared to FC, the switches and cables are less expensive.

- **Simplicity:** Both the equipment and the protocol itself are well understood. Generally, companies don't need extra training to introduce this equipment. People are accustomed to cheap grey Ethernet cables.

- **NICs Are Cheaper than FC HBAs:** It's common to use regular Ethernet NICs with SW initiators for iSCSI, which are much cheaper than FC HBAs.

- **Reusable Equipment:** It may be possible to reuse some existing network equipment and cables.

- **Windows Administrator Approval:** iSCSI has long been used by Windows administrators, so it's well trusted and understood in most datacenters.

- **Longer Distances:** It's possible to connect servers to storage at much greater lengths than with FC.

However, you must also remember a number of disadvantages when considering iSCSI:

- **1GbE Inability to Compete with FC/FCoE:** Unless you're using 10GbE, then iSCSI won't perform as well as FC/FCoE.

- **Latency:** Even with 10GbE, iSCSI can't provide the low-latency efficiency available with FC.

- **10GbE Expense:** Although 1GbE may have felt like free infrastructure if you were reusing old or very cheap equipment, using 10GbE requires expensive switches and NICs and maybe even upgraded cabling.

- ◆ **Oversubscription:** Flooding network links is possible. This is a scaling issue.

- ◆ **TCP/IP Overhead:** The protocol isn't particularly suited to storage. The overhead of TCP/IP to provide for retries, acknowledgements, and flow control reduces efficiency.

- ◆ **Path Failovers That Can Cause Long I/O Delays Compared to FC:** To mitigate this risk, you may need to increase the SCSI timeout in every guest OS.

- ◆ **Lack of Support for Microsoft Clustering:** Again, due to potential long I/O delays during failover, Microsoft clustering isn't supported using iSCSI.

NFS

NFS is a very mature file-sharing protocol that allows several clients to connect at the same time. NFS file shares are known as *exports*. vSphere requires that NFS exports use version 3 of the protocol, even though version 4 has been available and ratified for many years.

NFS is fundamentally different from FC, FCoE, and iSCSI in that it isn't block-level storage, but file-level. It's common to refer to the block-level arrays as *SAN devices*, but refer to NFS as *NAS devices*, even though many SANs can now provide NFS exports. Block devices provision their disks as LUNs, which can be used as VMFS volumes or RDMs in vSphere. But NFS exports are used as a remote file system and VMs are placed directly on them. The NAS devices are responsible for the file locking, which allows them to host considerably more VMs per datastore than VMFS.

VMFS

VMware's Virtual Machine File System (VMFS) is the default file system to store VMs in vSphere 4. It's a highly optimized, clustered file system that can efficiently store very large disk files and present them across multiple hosts.

Traditionally, clustered file systems have been very complicated to set up and configure, but VMFS is simple to use. VMFS can enable advanced vSphere features, such as vMotion and HA, which rely on multiple hosts accessing the same VMs.

VMFS allows up to 32 hosts to connect to the same volume and is responsible for all the required file-locking operations. A VMFS volume on a single LUN can be dynamically grown up to its near 2 TB limit and can be expanded further with additional extents, allowing the total maximum size of approximately 64 TB.

VMFS can recognize SAN snapshot copies and mount them. A signature is written to each VMFS volume, and this can be resignatured to allow the snapshot copies to be used alongside the originals.

VMFS volumes use block LUNs from local, FC, or iSCSI arrays, as opposed to NFS file exports. RDMs are a special type of disk format that uses a mapping file on a VMFS volume to point to a separate raw LUN (RDMs are discussed in more depth in Chapter 7).

Traditionally, block storage (particularly FC) had better support for all the latest features. But these days, almost all premier features are available for NFS.

NFS has historically been criticized for its performance versus FC and iSCSI. This was due in large part to cheaper NAS devices not being able to stand up again enterprise-class SANs, rather than to a deficiency in the protocol itself. For the vast majority of workloads, NFS is more than capable; and coupled with 10GbE, performance can be comparable to FC 8 Gbps.

Bandwidth is closely related to the physical transport, and there isn't much between 8 Gbps FC and 10GbE NFS. IOPS tends to come down to cache and disk spindles/speed. The primary differences between FC and NFS are latency, failover times, and multipathing mechanisms.

NFS is easy to plan and configure, and it's normally far less costly than FC to set up and maintain. For this reason, it's very popular for small to medium companies and is often the default choice for VDI deployments.

By default, the number of NFS exports that any host can mount is only 8, but an advanced setting allows you to increase this to 64. Even if you think you'll never grow beyond the 8 datastore limit, it's a good idea to increase this number before provisioning the first storage, because an increase in the future requires host reboots.

NFS exports can be mounted on hosts via IP addresses or hostname, but IP address is the recommended choice. If local procedures require you to use hostnames, check to see whether the name servers are virtual. If so, it's advisable to either make an exception and use IP addresses when mounting them, or create entries in the /etc/hosts file of each host. Otherwise, it's possible to get stuck in a chicken-and-egg situation where the hosts can't resolve the NFS exports, because all the name servers are turned off (because they live on the NFS exports). Name resolution is so important to other vSphere services, particularly HA, that you should plan carefully if all DNS (or WINS) servers are virtual.

As with iSCSI, the network traffic isn't encrypted. And NFS doesn't use CHAP to authenticate initiators and targets, so it's even more important to only span a trusted network. Most NAS devices can isolate their traffic to specific IP hosts, but this is easy to spoof if the network isn't suitably isolated. Unfortunately, the vSphere hosts must mount the exports with root access, which is a security concern in itself. For this reason, dedicated isolated storage switches are highly recommended if security is an especially important design consideration.

You can adjust a number of advanced NFS settings to fine-tune the hosts to the particular NAS unit you're using. You should consult the storage vendor's documentation to ensure that you implement its best practices.

Much of the advice given in the previous section for iSCSI network configurations is just as applicable to NFS. If possible:

◆ Separate network devices to isolate the storage traffic.

◆ Use nonroutable VLANs.

◆ Use redundant network links.

◆ Optimize Ethernet flow control.

◆ Use jumbo frames.

◆ Enable RSTP or portfast on the switch ports.

◆ Use switches with sufficient port buffers.

NFS can offer the following advantages (again, many are common with iSCSI because they share the same physical transport layer):

- **Inexpensive Equipment:** In comparison to FC, the switches and cables are less expensive.

- **Simplicity:** Both the equipment and the protocol itself are well understood. Generally, companies don't need extra training to introduce this equipment.

- **Reusable Equipment:** It may be possible to reuse some existing network equipment and cables.

- **Longer Distances:** It's possible to connect servers to storage at much greater lengths than with FC.

And here are some NFS-specific advantages:

- **Trust:** NFS is a well-trusted, mature protocol, particularly among Unix administrators.

- **Inexpensive NAS Units:** NAS-only devices are often much more affordable than a SAN, although these are more suited to smaller environments.

- **Ease of Setup:** NFS is extremely easy to set up on vSphere hosts.

- **Scalability:** Datastores can be much larger and contain many more VMs than VMFS on block storage.

- **Thin Provisioning:** The disk format is set by the NFS server, and by default the VMDK files are thin-provisioned automatically.

- **Additional VM Options:** NFS arrays often have more integrated snapshot, backup, and replication options, because the array understands the file system and can touch the files directly.

- **No Block Size Limitations:** You don't have to worry about block sizes and VMDKs hitting 2 TB limits.

NFS has the following disadvantages in common with iSCSI:

- **1GbE Inability to Compete with FC/FCoE:** Unless you're using 10GbE, then NFS won't perform as well as FC/FCoE.

- **Latency:** Even with 10GbE, NFS can't provide the low-latency efficiency available with FC.

- **Expense of 10GbE :** Although 1GbE may have felt like free infrastructure if you were reusing old or very cheap equipment, using 10GbE requires expensive switches and NICs.

- **TCP/IP Overhead:** The protocol isn't suited to storage. The overhead of TCP/IP to provide for retries, acknowledgements, and flow control reduces efficiency.

- **Path Failovers Can Cause Long I/O Delays:** To mitigate this risk, you need to increase the SCSI timeout in every guest OS.

- **Lack of Support for Microsoft Clustering:** Again, due to potential long I/O delays during failover, Microsoft clustering isn't supported using NFS.

And these are NFS-specific limitations:

- Not ideally suited to very high I/O VMs that would normally get dedicated datastores/LUNs.

- Uses some additional CPU processing.

◆ Can't aggregate bandwidth across multiple Ethernet cables (see the "Multipathing" section).

◆ No boot from SAN; you can't boot from an NFS export.

◆ NFS is particularly susceptible to oversubscription because of the very high VM density possible on each datastore.

Protocol Choice at the End of the Day

After carefully looking at each protocol, their constraints, and their impacts, a number of key factors tend to decide which is best suited to a design.

Companies always favor sticking to an existing implementation, and for good reason. You're likely to already have several pieces, and you probably want to avoid a complete rip-and-replace strategy. The ability to carefully transition to a new protocol, especially regarding something as critical as primary storage, is an important consideration. If this is a trusted proven solution that you're merely hoping to upgrade, then existing skills and experience are tangible assets.

Performance is a factor that may influence your decision. In most general situations, FC or 10GbE with iSCSI or NFS is likely to be more than sufficient for 99 percent of your bandwidth needs. The IOPS come down to several things, but ultimately it's the SP cache, any SP "secret sauce," and the number and speed of the underlying disks. The protocol has very little impact in a properly designed environment. However, one key area where performance may influence the protocol choice is latency. If the design requires the potential for very-low-latency VMs (perhaps a real-time database), then FC is your friend (unless you can deal with the limitations of DAS).

Costs can influence the protocol used. Often, NAS devices are cheaper than SANs, and iSCSI SANs are cheaper than FC ones. But many of the latest midrange storage offerings give you the flexibility to pick and mix several of the protocols (if not all of them). FC has always been regarded as the more expensive option, because it uses its own dedicated switches and cables; but if you're trying to compare FC to protocols using 10GbE, and need new hardware, then both are comparatively priced.

10GbE has the added advantage of potential cable consolidation with your host's networking needs. FCoE CNAs is arguably the best of all worlds, because it gives you the greatest flexibility. They can connect to a FC fabric, can provide access to iSCSI or NFS, and act as the host's networking NICs. But the FCoE hardware is still in a state of flux. First-generation cards are now incompatible with the newer second-generation ones, and firmware upgrades don't help. Cisco is pushing forward with the Twinax cables with SPF+ connectors, so this is likely to become the de facto standard; but most companies are still reluctant to spend big, only to buy the Betamax of infrastructure cabling. It's possible to envision a day when VMware introduces a software FCoE initiator for 10GbE twisted-pair-based NICs.

An interesting design that's becoming increasingly popular is to not plump for a single protocol, but use several. Most arrays can handle FC and Ethernet connections, so some companies are using NFS for general VM usage, with their large datastores for more flexibility for growth and array-based utilities, and then presenting LUNs on the same storage via FC for the VMs more sensitive to I/O demands. It's the ultimate multipathing option.

Finally, remember that DAS can be a viable option in certain, albeit limited circumstances. If you're deploying a single host in a site, such as a branch office, then introducing an additional storage device only introduces another single point of failure. In that situation, shared storage would be more expensive, would probably be less performant, and offer no extra redundancy.

Multipathing

vSphere hosts use their HBAs/NICs, potentially through fabric switches, to connect to the storage array's SP ports. By using multiple devices for redundancy, more than one path is created to the LUNs. The hosts use a technique called *multipathing* to make the path-selection decisions.

Multipathing can use redundant paths to provide several features such as load balancing, path management (failover), and aggregated bandwidth. Unfortunately, vSphere 4 only allows a single datastore to use a single path for active I/O at any one time, so you can't aggregate bandwidth across links.

SAN Multipathing

VMware categorize SANs into two groups:

Active/Active   Active/active arrays are those that can accept I/O to all LUNs on all of their SPs simultaneously, without degrading performance (that is, across an SP inter-connect). Every path is active.

Active/Passive   Active/passive arrays allow only one SP to accept I/O for each LUN, using other SPs for failover. SPs can be active for some LUNs while being standbys for others — thus all SPs can be active simultaneously, but not for the same datastore. Effectively, a LUN is owned by a particular SP.

vSphere hosts by default can use only one path per I/O, regardless of available active paths. With active/active arrays, you pick the active path to use on a LUN-by-LUN basis (fixed). For active/passive arrays, the hosts discover the active path themselves (MRU).

Native Multipathing Plugin

vSphere 4 introduced a redesigned storage layer. VMware called this its Pluggable Storage Architecture (PSA); and along with a preponderance of Three Letter Acronyms, gave vSphere hosts the ability to use third-party multipathing software — Multipathing Plugins (MPPs).

Without any third-party solutions, hosts use what is called the Native Multipathing Plugin (NMP). The terminology isn't that important, but the NMP's capabilities are, because this is what dictates the multipathing functionality for the vSphere hosts. To further categorize what native multipathing can do, VMware split it into two separate modules:

- Storage Array Type Plugin (SATP) — Path failover
- Path Selection Plugin (PSP) — Load balancing and path selection

SATP

The host identifies the type of array and associates the SATP based on its make and model. The array's details are checked against the host's `/etc/vmware/esx.conf` file, which lists all the HCL-certified storage arrays. This dictates whether the array is classified as active/active or active/passive. It uses this information for each array and sets the pathing policy for each LUN.

PSP

The native PSP has three types of pathing policies. The policy is automatically selected on a per-LUN basis based on the SATP. However, as you can see in Figure 6.4, you can override this setting manually:

FIGURE 6.4
Path Selection
drop-down

Fixed   The default policy for active/active array LUNs. It allows you to set a preferred path, which the host uses unless the path has failed. If the preferred path fails and then become available again, the path automatically returns to the preferred one. With a fixed policy, you set the HBA to LUN mappings, providing basic load-balancing to maximize the bandwidth usage across the host's HBAs. Active/passive arrays can suffer from path thrashing if this policy is used.

Most Recently Used (MRU)   The default policy for active/passive array LUNs. The MRU policy takes the first working path it finds during bootup. If this path fails, the host moves to another working path and continues to use it. It doesn't fail back to the original path. No manual load-balancing can be performed because MRU doesn't have preferred paths. No configuration is required to use MRU.

Round Robin (RR)   RR rotates through all the available paths, providing automated load balancing. This policy can safely be used by all arrays, but active/active arrays with their all-active paths can queue I/O across every path. Microsoft-clustered VMs can't use RR-based LUNs.

MULTIPATHING PLUGIN

Array manufacturers can provide extra software plug-ins to install on ESX hosts to replace the NMP algorithms provided by VMware. This software can then optimize load-balancing and failover for that particular device. This should allow for greater performance because the paths are used more effectively, and potentially enable quicker failover times. Currently, EMC is the only vendor that has a MPP available, which is called PowerPath/VE.

ALUA

Asymmetric logical unit access (ALUA) enables an array to use the SP interconnects to service I/O. When the link is used, performance is degraded (asymmetric), and therefore vSphere ordinarily treats it as an active/passive array. When a host is connected to an ALUA-capable array, the array can take advantage of the host knowing it has multiple SPs and which paths are direct, and allows it to use fixed pathing without the risk of path thrashing. However, it's important to select the optimized path as the preferred one, or you may end up degrading performance. RR ignores the non-optimized paths of an ALUA array by default, but you can change this by modifying the plug-in with the `esxcli` command.

VMware licenses the ability to use both third-party MPPs and ALUA. To use either of these functions, you need to purchase vSphere Enterprise Plus licenses.

Additional iSCSI Considerations

iSCSI has some additional SAN multipathing requirements that differ depending on the type of initiator used.

Hardware iSCSI Initiators

When you're using hardware initiators for iSCSI arrays, vSphere 4 multipathing works effectively the same as it does for FC connections. The hosts recognize the HBAs as storage adapters and use the NMP with SATP selection and PSP pathing.

Some iSCSI arrays use only one target, which switches to an alternate portal during failover. Hosts detect only one path in these instances.

Software iSCSI Initiators

Software iSCSI initiators require additional configuration steps to use vSphere's storage MPIO stack. By default, SW iSCSI uses the multipathing capabilities of the IP network. The host can use NIC teaming to provide failover, but the initiator presents a single endpoint so no load-balancing is available.

To use the vSphere storage NMP and enable load-balancing across NICs, you must use a technique known as *port binding*. Don't use network link aggregation, because you want to define separate end-to-end paths. Follow these steps to enable port-binding for two NICs for iSCSI:

1. Create a vSwitch, add both NICs, and create 2 VMkernel ports, each with a separate IP address (each NIC needs a one-to-one mapping with a vmk port), as shown in Figure 6.5.

FIGURE 6.5
iSCSI multipathing vSwitch

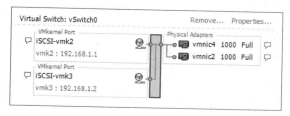

2. Bind the VMkernel ports to their own NICs. Each VMkernel port should have only one NIC set as Active, all other NICs on the vSwitch must be set to Unused.

3. Add the VMkernel ports to the SW initiator. You must do this on the command line. For example:

```
esxcli swiscsi nic add -n vmk2 -d vmhba33
esxcli swiscsi nic add -n vmk3 -d vmhba33
```

4. Enable the SW initiator.

NOTE   You must place the SW initiator in the same subnet as the iSCSI array's target, because port binding in vSphere can't route traffic.

NAS Multipathing

NAS multipathing is fundamentally different than SAN multipathing in vSphere because it relies entirely on the networking stack. MPIO storage tools such as SATPs and PSP aren't available, so IP-based redundancy and routing is used.

For each NFS export mounted by the host, only one physical NIC is used for traffic, despite any link-aggregation techniques used to connect multiple NICs together. NIC teaming provides failover redundancy but can't load-balance an export. But by creating multiple exports along with multiple connections, you can load-spread datastore traffic.

Chapter 5 looked at designs to provide network redundancy. As an outline, you can use two different methods to create NIC failover for an NFS mount:

◆ Create two (or more) vSwitches, each with a VMkernel interface. Each vSwitch connects to a separate redundant physical switch. The VMkernel interfaces and NFS interfaces are split across different subnets.

◆ With physical switches that can cross-stack, you need only one VMkernel interface (and so only one IP address). The NAS device still needs multiple IP address targets. The vSwitch needs at least two NICs, which are split across the two cross-stacked switches. The VMkernel's vSwitch has its load-balancing NIC teaming policy set to "Route based on IP hash." You need to aggregate the physical switch ports into an 802.3ad EtherChannel in static mode (dynamic LACP support isn't included with vSphere, but it's possible if you add Cisco Nexus 1000V switches to the configuration).

NFS datastores can hold many more VMs than VMFS datastores. Additionally, with the default being thinly provisioned VMs, NFS can more densely pack VMs onto a single connection point. Sharing the load across several NICs is particularly important when you're using 1GbE NICs.

Finally, give special consideration to the longer timeouts associated with NFS. FC and even iSCSI fail over much more quickly, but NFS can take long enough that you should adjust the VM's guest OSs to prepare them for the possibility that their disk may be unresponsive for a longer time.

Summary

Now that you understand the elements that make up the storage landscape, your design should consider all four primary factors (availability, performance, capacity, and cost) and reflect the importance of each.

Availability is likely to be very important to the solution unless you're designing storage for a noncritical element such as a test lab. Even what may be considered secondary nodes, like DR sites, need appropriate redundancy for high availability.

Performance is probably the key to any good storage design these days (high availability is almost taken as a given and doesn't need as much consideration — just do it). With advances in storage devices, it's easy to pack a lot of data onto a relatively small number of disks. You must decide how many IOPS your VMs need (and will need going forward) and use that number to design the solution. You can rely on spindles or consider some of the vendor's new technologies to ensure that performance will meet your requirements. Centralized company datacenters, headquarter buildings, and anywhere with large VDI implementations or intensive database servers will doubtlessly be avid consumers of these performance enhancements.

Capacity must always be considered, so the ability to assimilate your data requirements and understand future growth is very important. An appreciation of this will guide you; but unlike with performance, which can be difficult to upgrade, your design should include strategies to evolve capacity with the business's needs. Disks grow in size and drop in price constantly, so there is scope to take advantage of the improvements over time and not overestimate the growth. Capacity can be very important — for example, smaller offices and remote branch offices may consider capacity as a crucial element, even more important than performance, if they're only driving large file servers.

Cost will always dictate what you can do. Your budget may not be just for storage, in which case you need to balance it against the need for compute power, licensing, networking infrastructure, and so on. Most likely, the funds are nonnegotiable, and you must equate the factors and decide what the best choices are. You may have no budget at all and be looking to optimize an existing solution or to design something from hand-me-downs. Remember in-place upgrades and buy-back deals. There is always a chance to do more for less.

In addition to the fundamentals, other design aspects are worth considering. For example, before you purchase your next SAN, you may ask yourself these questions:

◆ How easy is this solution to roll out to a site? How easy is it to configure remotely? Is any of it scriptable?

◆ Physically, how large is it? Do you have the space, the HVAC, the power, the UPS, and so on?

◆ How is it managed? What are the command-line and GUI tools like? Can multiple arrays be managed together, and managed with policies? How granular is the security?

◆ What are the reporting features like?

◆ How easy is it to troubleshoot, upgrade firmware/OS, and add extra disk enclosures?

◆ Is there any vCenter integration? Are there any special plug-ins?

Extra array functionality may be required, but that's out of scope of this chapter. For example, things like SAN replication and LUN snapshots can play a part in other designs such as backups, DR, application tiering, and so on. Every situation is different.

Planning for the future is normally part of an overall design: you must prepare for how storage will grow with the business. Think about how modular the components are (controllers, cache, and so on), what the warranty covers, how long it lasts, and what support levels are available.

Finally, take as much time as possible to pilot gear from different vendors and all their wares. Use the equipment for a proof of concept, and test each part of your design: protocols, disks, RAID groups, tiering, and so forth. You may be able to clone all or at least some of your actual production VMs and drop them onto the arrays. What better way to validate your design?

Chapter 7

Virtual Machines

Virtual machines (VMs) are central to any vSphere design. After all, isn't that why we try so hard to optimize all the other pieces of the puzzle? Many organizations spend considerable time and resources ensuring that the network, servers, and storage are suitably redundant, efficient, and capacious. However, often the design of the VMs is paid lip service. You can gain tremendous benefits by giving a little thought to how the VMs are designed and configured.

This chapter will explore what makes up each VM, to help you understand how to take advantage of the different options and realize what impact these decisions will have on the rest of your vSphere design. The guest operating system (OS) within the VM can also affect overall performance, along with how each instance is deployed and managed. Interesting techniques exist to minimize the management required and improve standardization in an environment. Finally, we'll look at various strategies you can use to mitigate the effects of host failures on VMs.

It's important to realize that VM design is a balancing act between ensuring that each VM has the resources and performance characteristics it needs, and preventing waste. If a VM is over-provisioned in some way, it's unlikely to benefit and will eventually penalize the VMs around it.

Specifically, this chapter looks at:

♦ Hardware components, options, and resource allocation for each VM, with emphasis on the network and storage

♦ How the guest OS and applications affect VMs

♦ Using clones and templates to more efficiently deploy VMs

♦ How to protect the VM's availability

Components of a Virtual Machine

A VM is a construct of virtual hardware, presented to the guest OS. The guest sees the hardware as if it were a regular physical computer. Normally (excluding Virtual Machine Interface [VMI] options for now), the guest OS is unaware that it's potentially sharing the hardware with other VMs.

VMware presents very generic hardware to the guest, allowing the greatest compatibility for the widest range of OSs. Most modern OSs can detect and run on a vSphere VM without the installation of extra drivers. When you're creating a new VM, if the OS is listed in the wizard, then you can change the base hardware to be more appropriate. Different hardware options are available for some items, and VMware provides OS-specific drivers where appropriate. VMware also has additional optimized drivers that can improve on the more generic ones found in the OSs themselves.

Base Virtual Machine Hardware

As a base, all vSphere 4 VMs are created with the following hardware, regardless of the OS chosen, the underlying hardware, or any options you select in the *New Virtual Machine...* wizard:

- Phoenix BIOS
- Intel 440BX-based motherboard
- Intel PCI IDE controller
- IDE CD-ROM drive
- IDE floppy drive
- SVGA video adapter

In addition, CPUs and RAM are added. However, they're limited to the underlying hardware: you can't allocate more CPUs or memory than the physical host has installed. The number of CPUs and the amount of RAM are allocated by default based on the guest chosen, and you can manually adjust them later in the creation wizard. Other hardware options are available, either during the VM's initial creation or as additions later.

Hardware Versions

As VMware's hypervisors have evolved, so has the VM hardware shell that is presented to guests. The hardware versioning basically determines what functionality the hypervisor should expose to the VM. In vSphere 4, the latest hardware is version 7, as shown in Figure 7.1.

FIGURE 7.1
Virtual Machine
version 7

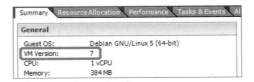

Although vSphere can happily run version 4 and version 7 VMs alongside each other, VMware Infrastructure 3 (VI3) hosts can't run version 7 VMs. It's relatively straightforward to upgrade VMs from version 4 to version 7. Unlike the upgrade procedure for VMs from ESX2 to ESX3, the VMware tools should be upgraded first. After you've upgraded the tools, you need to power off the VM; then, you can upgrade the hardware to version 7.

However, vSphere 4 can also create hardware version 4 VMs, which was the default for VI3 (ESX/ESXi 3.x). This aids backward compatibility when you have a mixed environment of VI3 and vSphere 4 hosts together, which is common during an upgrade. Also, VMs from third-party software vendors tend to come in version 4 packaging to maintain the greatest compatibility possible for their customers.

MISSING HARDWARE VERSIONS?

In case you were wondering where hardware versions 5 and 6 went, VMware shares the VM hardware versioning with its hosted hypervisor products (Workstation, Fusion, Server, and Player). As vSphere is considered an enterprise product, the releases aren't as frequent as they are for some of VMware's other products, and some versions have been skipped. If you're curious, this is where versions 5 and 6 fitted in:

Hardware version 5 Workstation 5.x, VMware Player 1.x, VMware Server 1.x, ESX Server 3.x

Hardware version 6 Workstation 6.0, VMware ACE 2.x, VMware Player 2.x, VMware Fusion 1.x

Although VMs can be upgraded to version 7, downgrading them is considerably trickier. One approach is to snapshot each VM before you upgrade it. Doing so provides a temporary rollback point; however, it isn't feasible to keep these snapshots long-term, and reverting changes to get back to a previous hardware version also destroys any changed data. Snapshots can only be used to guard against problems during the upgrade itself.

VMware Convertor is a tool primarily aimed at virtualizing physical machines in a process most commonly known as *P2Ving* (physical to virtual). However, Convertor can also be used to downgrade version 7 VMs to version 4 (or lower). It's a freely downloadable tool, and it works seamlessly with vCenter.

During a host upgrade project to vSphere 4, all the emphasis is placed on the hosts. Often the VMs are missed, because upgrading isn't a definitive requirement, and this is the one step that in a multihost, shared-storage environment actually needs VM downtime. Upgrading the VMs to version 7 not only brings proper host/VM compatibility but also introduces a number of improved features. These benefits include access to new storage devices and new network-card options, hot-plug support for CPUs and memory, passthrough to Peripheral Component Interconnect (PCI) devices, and larger hardware maximums. An upgrade project should not only feature upgrading the VMs to version 7 but also include taking advantage of the devices.

The best time to upgrade the VMs is when all the hosts in a cluster have been upgraded. If some VMs are upgraded before all the hosts are, then this can affect vMotion choices, distributed resource scheduling (DRS), high availability (HA) and distributed power management (DPM) effectiveness.

It's important to remember to convert the templates to a VM and upgrade them at this time as well, to ensure that all new VMs are deployed at version 7. Be careful if you maintain one set of templates for several clusters and sites, because you'll need to keep two versions until all the hosts are upgraded. Until the VMs are upgraded to version 7, you won't be able to configure certain hardware while the VM is running (even if you could do this hot on VI3 hosts). For example, if you can't add more disk space while the VM is running after a recent upgrade, you may want to check the version number.

Virtual Machine Maximums

Table 7.1 shows the maximum amount of each hardware component that you can add to a VM at hardware version 7 (if the host has sufficient resources).

TABLE 7.1:   Virtual machine hardware maximums

Hardware Component	Maximum Configurable
vCPU	8
RAM	255 GB
SCSI adapters	4
SCSI devices	60 (15 per adapter)
IDE devices (hard disks or CD-ROMs)	4
Floppy drives	2
Network cards	10
Parallel ports	3
Serial ports	4
VMDirectPath devices (PCI passthrough)	4 (2 for vSphere 4.0 hosts)
Remote consoles (vSphere Client MKS consoles) per VM	40

Hardware Choices

After you've created a VM, you can alter the default hardware. The following sections discuss each element and the options available to customize the VM.

CPU

A VM can have one to eight virtual CPUs (known as vCPUs). However, this depends on the number of logical cores the physical hardware has. This includes not only the number of filled CPU sockets, but also cores and HyperThreading (HT) cores enabled. Current vSphere licensing limits a VM's vCPUs to four, unless you have an Enterprise Plus license, which allows up to eight vCPUs to be allocated.

Converting a VM from a single vCPU to multiple vCPUs requires that the guest OS be able to handle more than one CPU — this is known as a symmetric multiprocessor (SMP). Some older OSs may not be ready for this; for example, an old P2Ved Linux VM may need its kernel recompiled for SMP. Some OSs can convert their kernels to SMP but have difficulty dropping back to uniprocessor hardware; for example, Windows 2000 would drop back to a single CPU without issue, but converting a Windows 2003 VM requires manual intervention. Adding a second vCPU to a VM therefore shouldn't be taken lightly.

Generally, it's considered prudent to start all VMs with one vCPU until you have a clearly identified reason to provide more. You should check that the applications on the VM can take advantage of additional vCPUs and can use multiple threads sufficiently before adding them. Too many vCPUs only penalizes the hosts, often without benefiting the applications on the VM. If a VM can't take advantage of the extra vCPUs, it can have a detrimental effect on other VMs' performance. Additionally, vSphere's fault tolerance (FT) feature only works with single-CPU VMs, so any design considering this should have only one vCPU for the VM to be protected.

Adding extra vCPUs to your VMs has an impact not just on the VMs themselves but also on other VMs on the same host, and even on other cluster members. More vCPUs change the reporting metrics, the HA slot size for all VMs in the cluster, and the ratio of vCPUs in a cluster. If there is any CPU pressure on the host, wasted non-used vCPUs will compromise the performance of all the host's VMs. vCPU allocation is a fine balance between an individual VM's requirement for performance versus the needs of the rest of the host/cluster.

In Chapter 4, "Server Hardware," we discussed non-uniform memory architecture (NUMA). However, it's worth considering how multiple vCPUs can impact NUMA hosts specifically. VMs with more vCPUs than there are cores on a host can see performance issues on NUMA-enabled systems. The VM is forced to use memory from a remote memory node, which in turn increases latency. vSphere 4.1 can recognize this and now has additional algorithms that improve the vCPU and memory allocation, known as Wide VM NUMA. If you're running VMs that fit this profile, then you may see benefit from ensuring that your hosts are running the newer version.

Several other CPU settings are available for each VM; you can find them on either the Options tab or the Resources tab. One of these worth mentioning briefly at this stage (because there is no obvious setting) is the ability in vSphere 4.1 to control the number of cores per vCPU. Actually, this feature worked in version 4.0, but it wasn't supported (and wasn't widely publicized). If OSs or applications have physical socket restrictions, this feature can present additional vCPUs as cores instead of sockets. To enable this, add the option cupid.coresPerSocket in the Configuration Parameters of the Advanced General section on the Options tab. Note, however, that multicore vCPUs can't use the hot-plug CPU feature, and the value must be an even number that must wholly divide into the vCPU setting.

Memory

You can apportion RAM to a VM in multiples of 4 MB, with a minimum of 4 MB and maximum of 255 GB (assuming the host has that much to give a single VM). Although 4 MB seems like a ridiculously small amount to give a VM, it's occasionally found when administrators want to prevent vSphere users from turning on their VMs. vSphere can now allocate such large amounts of memory that a VM's RAM tends to be limited only by the physical host.

Figure 7.2 shows four pointer levels for the VM. The Maximum, Default, and Minimum amounts are dictated by your guest OS choice. However, the Maximum Recommended For Best Performance pointer level changes depending on other VMs on the host. This pointer shows the level at which the host can't fulfill the full memory requirement without using the advanced memory techniques we explained in Chapter 4.

These advanced memory techniques mean the VM always sees the amount of memory you've allocated it, even though it may not physically have access to that much RAM. This can be because the host is reclaiming idle pages, sharing pages with other VMs (TPS), compressing them (since vSphere 4.1), or adhering to memory limits that have been set. In extreme cases, the VM's memory may not even be from physical RAM but being forcibly swapped to disk by the hypervisor. We covered this in much more depth in Chapter 4.

A VM's memory allocation has an effect if you don't assign it at the right level. Not enough memory, and the VM may be forced to swap with its own paging file, even if the host has ample amounts. Too much memory, and too much overhead is reserved, preventing other VMs from reserving it. Each VM should be allocated just a little more than the average memory usage, to allow for small spikes.

FIGURE 7.2
Memory hardware
options

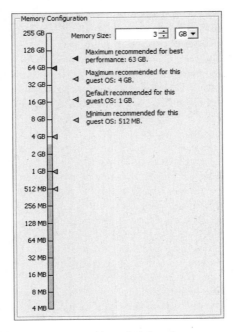

VMs running on NUMA-enabled hosts can be affected if they have more memory allocated to them than the lowest configured NUMA node. Memory is split across NUMA nodes depending on physical placement in the server. So, if you're running very large memory VMs on a NUMA host, you should check that the RAM is set properly in the DIMM slots, so VMs aren't forced to use nonlocal memory.

DISKS

Each hard disk allocated to a VM has a number of settings available to it, similar to Figure 7.3.

FIGURE 7.3
Disk hardware
options

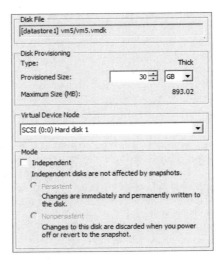

First, this dialogue box lists where the disk is located, on which datastore, and in which folder. It shows the disk's current allocation type and allows you to increase (but, it's important to note, not decrease) the size of the disk. Finally, when the VM is turned off, you can change the SCSI ID and set the VM's independent disk modes.

In the VM storage design section, we examine a VM's storage options in greater depth. It's worth noting at this stage, though, that each VM is limited to 4 IDE disks and potentially a total of 60 SCSI disks.

SCSI Controllers

When a SCSI hard disk is attached to a VM, a new SCSI controller is also added. Each SCSI adapter can have 15 disks connected to it, and you can add up to 4 SCSI controllers.

A VM can select from four different types of SCSI controller, which we'll discuss later in the VM storage design section. They're added automatically to best suit the guest OS; you have to manually change them if you have different needs.

In Figure 7.4, you can see that a SCSI bus-sharing policy is also set for each controller. By default, it's set to None, meaning that only that particular VM can lock the disk file. However, if guest clustering software running on multiple VMs needs concurrent access to the disk, you can set this to Virtual for cluster in a box (CIB) or Physical for cluster across boxes (CAB).

FIGURE 7.4
SCSI controller hardware options

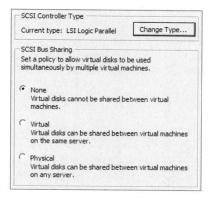

Network Adapter

The VM network adapter settings allow you to change several hardware options; but from a VM design perspective, they let you select different adapter types and manually set MAC addresses, as shown in Figure 7.5. Both of these options are discussed later, in this chapter's "VM Network Design" section. You can add up to 10 network cards to a VM, each with its own individual settings.

Video Card

You can't add a video card to or remove it from a VM; it comes as standard. Figure 7.6 shows how you can adjust the number of displays from one up to a maximum of four, allocate more video memory, and enable 3D support.

FIGURE 7.5
Network adapter
hardware options

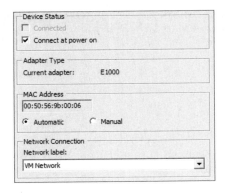

FIGURE 7.6
Video card
hardware options

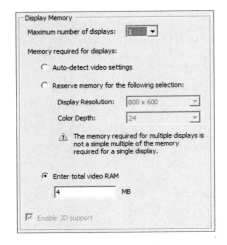

The default memory is 4 MB, which is enough for one screen with a resolution of 1176 × 885. Increase the memory if you need more screens or a higher resolution. This setting is most important for virtual desktop infrastructure (VDI) designs.

CD/DVD DRIVE

The CD/DVD drive allows you to connect to your client workstation's local drive, the host's optical drive, or an ISO image on a datastore. Figure 7.7 displays the typical options available.

FLOPPY DRIVE

The floppy drive is treated very similarly to an optical drive, although the settings also let you create new flp images. You can have a maximum of two floppy drives per VM.

FIGURE 7.7
CD/DVD drive
hardware options

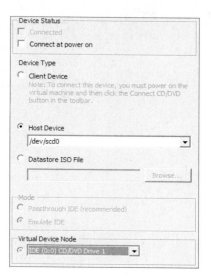

USB CONTROLLERS

With the release of vSphere 4.0, you could add a USB controller to VMs. However, although you could add the USB controller, it wouldn't attach any USB devices to the VM itself. This was considered by some to be a feature that VMware accidentally exposed before the company was ready to provide full device support.

This has been fixed as of vSphere 4.1, which allows devices to be hot-added to VMs. The controller must be in place first, which requires the VM to be turned off and at hardware version 7; but then you can pass USB devices though at any time. You can add only 1 controller per VM, and a total of 15 controllers per host server, but each VM can see up to 20 devices through the 1 controller. Only certain USB devices can be added, so there is a list of supported hardware. Hot-adding memory, CPUs, or PCI devices disconnects any USB device.

Improvements to vMotion and passthrough devices means that USB devices can remain connected to VMs, even when they're moved to other hosts (including DRS moves). But USB devices aren't compatible with either FT or DPM.

SERIAL PORT AND PARALLEL PORT

You can connect both serial ports (COM) and parallel ports (LPT) to a VM. They can be useful when an application requires either type of port for licensing purposes, like an old software dongle, or if there is a requirement to support old hardware, such as an old facsimile modem. As an alternative, you can attach these devices via a special Ethernet adapter, to avoid this hardware condition.

Figure 7.8 shows how a VM's serial/parallel port can pass through to the host's hardware, output the data to a file on a host's datastore, or present it as a named pipe to the guest OS.

vSphere 4.1 brought the ability to redirect the serial port over a network link via telnet or SSH, which enables the use of third-party serial concentrators.

FIGURE 7.8

Serial port hard-
ware options

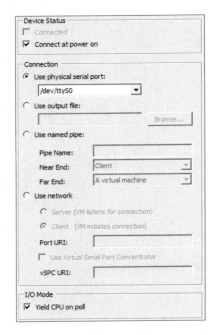

Each VM can have up to three parallel ports and four serial ports assigned.

PCI DEVICE

A VM can attach to a host's PCI or PCIe device directly. To enable passthrough, the host must first be enabled for VMDirectPath, which requires a reboot and is only supported with Intel VT-d (Nehalem) or AMD IOMMU (experimental) capable host CPUs, which must be enabled in the BIOS.

Currently, passthrough is only used for network adapters, but experimental support exists for some Fibre Channel host bus adapter (HBAs) and SAS adapters. Numerous limitations are imposed when you choose this as part of a design, because when a VM is configured with a passthrough PCI device, it's tied to the hardware: no FT, HA, hot-plugging, suspending, or record/replay operations are permitted. vSphere 4.0 VMs can't use vMotion (and by extension DRS) when a PCI device is passed through, so you should ensure that the hosts are running version 4.1 with VMDirectPath to remove this limitation.

Each host can have four VMDirectPath devices. However, a device that's configured for passthrough can't then be accessed by the VMkernel and subsequently used by other VMs.

PCI passthrough devices aren't often used, because users recall the poor I/O performance in previous ESX versions. But the paravirtual SCSI (PVSCSI) storage adapters and VMXNET 3 network adapters give VMs excellent near-native I/O results.

Considering the substantial feature restrictions when using this option, it's hard to recommend. Be cautious about including this in your design.

VMCI

VM Communication Interface (VMCI) is a new communication method that you can use between VMs on a single host or between a VM and the host itself. VMCI aims to minimize the overhead associated with traditional networking stacks. It doesn't use the guest or VMkernel networking stack, so it has relatively high performance compared to TCP/IP sockets.

However, applications need to be written specifically to use VMCI sockets. VMCI drivers are included in the Windows and Linux versions of VMware tools.

Removing or Disabling Unused Hardware

Each VM should be presented with only the hardware it requires. Like other vSphere resourcing, a VM should have what it needs but not waste host resources on what the VM doesn't require.

VM hardware that isn't needed can be removed, disconnected from the host hardware, disabled in the VM's BIOS, or even disabled in the guest OS. Typically, floppy and CD drives, USB controllers, LPT and COM ports, and unused NICs and storage controllers are likely candidates.

A guest floppy drive is rarely used in a VM. The only common use case is the presentation of driver FLP files during OS installations. You should be safe removing this device from your VMs.

Excess hardware unnecessarily uses interrupt resources. OSs poll devices on a regular basis, which requires CPU cycles to monitor. Other devices reserve memory that could be used by other VMs. Even excessive vCPUs use more interrupts than uniprocessor VMs. You can tweak the number of timer interrupts in Linux VMs; however, the most modern Linux kernels use a *tickless timer*, which varies the timer interrupt rate to reduce the number of wake-ups (introduced in the mainline 2.6.21 kernel). Older Linux VMs may benefit from a reduction in their timer interrupt settings.

You can disconnect optical drives and COM and LPT ports from the VM, or at least connect them to files instead of physical devices, when they aren't being used. Again, COM and LPT port are rarely used, so you should consider removing them from a VM altogether.

Some hardware can also restrict other features. For example, FT won't work while serial or parallel ports are connected or while CDs, floppies, USB passthrough devices, Fibre Channel N-Port ID virtualization (NPIV) ports, or any hot-plug features are enabled. If you don't need the hardware, disable or disconnect it. If you'll never need it, remove it.

Virtual Machine Options

In addition to the configurable hardware options, there are a number of additional options for each VM.

GENERAL OPTIONS

The general options displayed in Figure 7.9 provide basic information about the VM such as its name, the location of its configuration file, and which guest OS it's configured for. One important change you can make is the location of the VM's working directory. The default directory is alongside the configuration file, but this directory is where the VM's suspend and snapshot files are created. You may wish to change this for a VM's design, so you can dictate where these volatile files reside.

FIGURE 7.9
General options

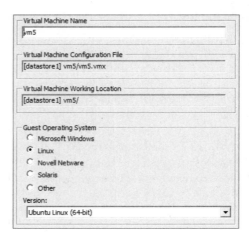

vApp Options

The vApp options let you set or change virtual appliance settings such as product descriptions. It's unlikely that you'll need to modify these unless you plan to distribute a VM as a virtual appliance.

VMware Tools

The various tools settings shown in Figure 7.10 determine how the power button should react, allowing scripts to run and time synchronization from outside the guest OS. One useful feature that isn't enabled by default, but that you may consider for your design, configures the tools to automatically upgrade themselves. If you're happy with this type of automatic software installation, then it can be a convenient way to keep your VMware tools up to date.

FIGURE 7.10
VMware tools
options

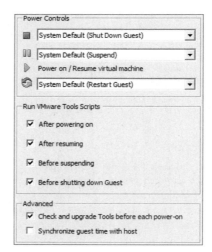

POWER MANAGEMENT

Power management corresponds to how the VM reacts when the guest OS is put in standby. You can leave the VM turned on (with the Wake-On-LAN option) or suspend the VM. This design decision is determined by balancing how long you're willing to wait for the VM to wake up, against saving host resources by suspending it.

ADVANCED

On the Options tab, you can change a number of advanced options.

General

The Advanced General section shown in Figure 7.11 includes a number of options; however, these are normally used only in remedial circumstances and under the advice of VMware's technical support staff. Clicking the Configuration Parameters button lets you add extra settings, which are inserted into the VM's configuration file. Nothing here is part of a standard VM design.

FIGURE 7.11
Advanced General
options

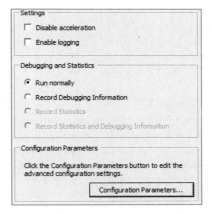

CPUID Mask

vMotion compatibility is discussed in Chapter 4 and is normally configured at a cluster level, but a VM can change its CPU mask on an individual basis as shown in Figure 7.12. This allows you to hide certain CPU features from the VM and let it vMotion across noncompatible hosts.

FIGURE 7.12
CPUID mask
options

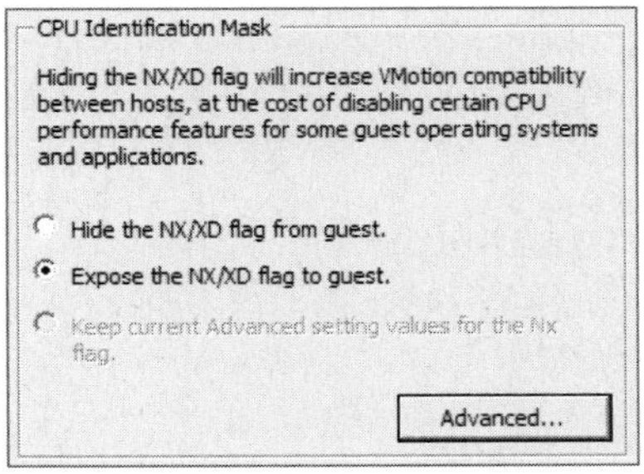

The only VMware-supported mask is the NX/XD execute bit, but clicking the Advanced button lets you to mask more flags. This can be useful in a test or lab environment where support is less important and where you may have an eclectic mix of old hardware.

Generally, it's easier to enable Enhanced vMotion Compatibility (EVC) across the entire cluster, as we'll discuss in the next chapter.

Memory/CPU Hotplug

This feature is visible only if the guest OS set in the general options is recognized as capable of supporting it. CPUs can be hot-plugged or removed, but memory can only be hot-added. VMware tools must be installed to use this feature; and despite the fact that you can hot-plug these devices, the VM must initially be turned off to enable this feature. So, you must plan ahead to have it dynamically available. If this is something you'll use, you must consider and test the guest OS, kernel SMP support, applications, and so on, because support depends on several guest factors.

Boot Options

Boot options give you control over the BIOS delay and let you access the boot order. These are normally changed only for a specific event; but for VM design, they can be important if you wish to disable options in the BIOS. vSphere 4.1 added the ability to automatically reboot the VM if no boot device is found.

Paravirtualization

Paravirtualization is a technique by which the guest OS is made aware that it's running atop a hypervisor and adjusts itself accordingly, potentially improving the guest's performance. VMware allows the VM to run as a paravirtualized VM under the moniker of VMI. Only certain guest OSs can benefit from this, primarily 32-bit Linux guests. VMI code has been included in mainline kernels since 2.6.22.

However, VMware has announced that vSphere 4 will be the last version to include VMI support; the company plans to retire it. With that in mind, it may be sensible to avoid this as part of any new design.

Fibre Channel NPIV

If a host server is Fibre Channel attached with an adapter that supports NPIV, this option can set the VM with its own World Wide Name (WWN) as shown in Figure 7.13. Using NPIV can arguably provide greater control over a storage area network (SAN) logical unit number's (LUN) usage. It can allow a SAN administrator to monitor a VM's traffic more closely, tie specific security zoning around it, and configure special quality of service (QoS) for it. To use this, the VM must have a raw device mapping disk (RDM) already added.

CPU/MMU Virtualization

Hardware virtualization offload support is automatically handled for VMs, but you can individually configure it for special use cases. Figure 7.14 lists the options available.

FIGURE 7.13
Fibre Channel NPIV
options

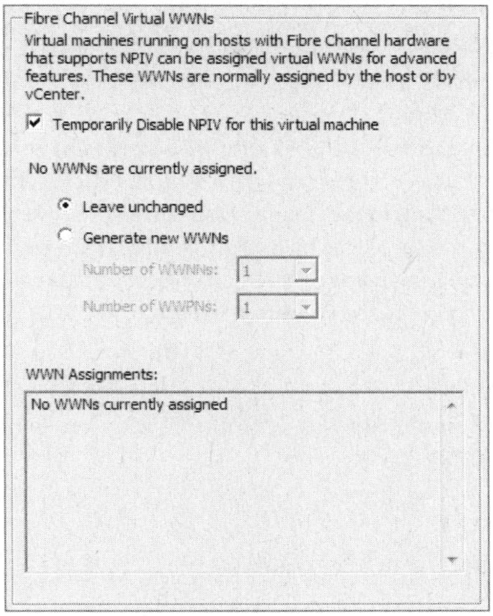

> **Fibre Channel Virtual WWNs**
>
> Virtual machines running on hosts with Fibre Channel hardware that supports NPIV can be assigned virtual WWNs for advanced features. These WWNs are normally assigned by the host or by vCenter.
>
> ☑ Temporarily Disable NPIV for this virtual machine
>
> No WWNs are currently assigned.
>
> ⦿ Leave unchanged
> ◯ Generate new WWNs
> Number of WWNNs: 1 ▾
> Number of WWPNs: 1 ▾
>
> WWN Assignments:
>
> No WWNs currently assigned

FIGURE 7.14
CPU/MMU virtual-
ization options

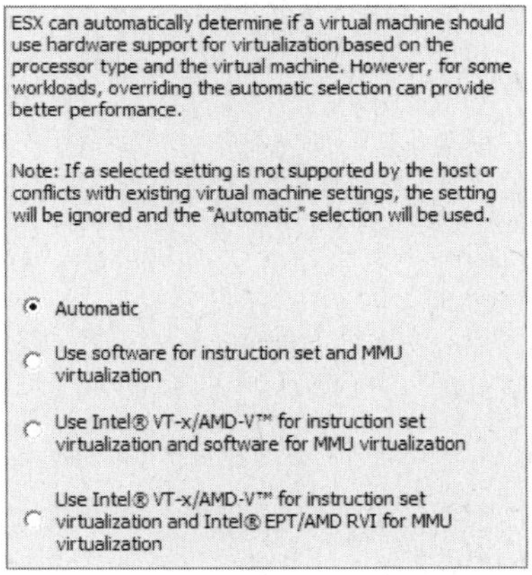

> ESX can automatically determine if a virtual machine should use hardware support for virtualization based on the processor type and the virtual machine. However, for some workloads, overriding the automatic selection can provide better performance.
>
> Note: If a selected setting is not supported by the host or conflicts with existing virtual machine settings, the setting will be ignored and the "Automatic" selection will be used.
>
> ⦿ Automatic
> ◯ Use software for instruction set and MMU virtualization
> ◯ Use Intel® VT-x/AMD-V™ for instruction set virtualization and software for MMU virtualization
> ◯ Use Intel® VT-x/AMD-V™ for instruction set virtualization and Intel® EPT/AMD RVI for MMU virtualization

Swapfile Location

Each VM has a swapfile (in addition to the guest's swap/pagefile settings) that the host can forcibly push memory pages to if it has to. The swapfile by default is stored in the same datastore folder as the VM's configuration file. However, this can be overridden by a host or cluster setting that determines the VM's default. You can override these host and cluster defaults in this VM option, setting to store along with the VM or to store on the host's chosen location.

Storing a swapfile on the host's datastore has the obvious advantage of saving valuable SAN input/output operations per second (IOPS) and avoiding SAN replication of transient data.

However, before you decide to move all VM swapfiles off shared storage, be aware that negative effects are associated with this choice. Enough local datastore space must exist to accommodate the swapfiles. A VM's swapfile is equal to its configured RAM minus any memory reservation. But when a host is a member of a DRS or an HA cluster, the total space required by a host is unpredictable while VMs move around. vMotions slow down significantly, because the swapfile must be copied from local disk to local disk before the transfer is complete. In most situations, it's undesirable to save swapfiles on local storage, due to the way this can affect DRS effectiveness and the fact that HA's ability to power-on the VMs may be compromised. If SAN performance or replication traffic is a concern, then a separate nonreplicated, lower-tier SAN LUN just for swapfiles is often a better solution.

Resources

Each VM has a number of resource attributes you can use to finely tune its resource allocation against other VMs.

CPU

The CPU resources panel allows you to set shares, a reservation, and a limit for the VM, as shown in Figure 7.15. You can set these resource-allocation options here for the VM, at the resource pool level in a DRS cluster, or both. If the resources are set at both, they're first carved up at the resource pool level; then, the individual VM settings apply within the resource pool.

FIGURE 7.15
CPU Resources
options

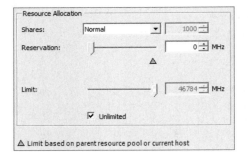

Generally, the vSphere hypervisor provides excellent scheduling. And normally, if hosts are sufficiently resourced, you can leave the default settings as they are. If you wish to control which VMs receive more priority or resources, it's fairer, more effective, and less prone to error to allocate these at a resource pool level.

The next chapter looks carefully at resource pool design, and we'll leave some of the discussion until then. However, because resources can be allocated here at the VM level, you need to understand the impact of doing so. A design should try implementing any scheduling at the resource pool level whenever possible.

CPU Shares

You can set CPU shares to a low (500 per vCPU), normal (1000), high (2000), or custom level. Shares only take effect during periods of contention, so as long as the host has enough resources to meet all the demand, the shares are never used. This allows all the resources to be used when a VM needs them, if they're available, and prevents the waste associated with Limits.

But shares depend entirely on what all the other VMs on the host are set to. CPU resources are not guaranteed with them, and their effective allocations will change as other VMs are added, change, or disappear.

The CPU shares set on a VM will impact the CPU allocation on all the other VMs on the host if there aren't enough CPU cycles to meet demand. Be careful of multi-vCPU VMs, because they receive shares in proportion to the number of vCPUs. Think of a VM that has two vCPUs. It's considered more important and so is given shares at the high level; this means it ends up with four times the shares of a normal, single-vCPU VM.

CPU Reservation

The CPU reservation is set to zero by default. If you increase this value, it guarantees that amount of CPU cycles regardless of any shares set. They're reserved as soon as you power on the VM, and can then affect the ability of other VMs to reserve CPU resources.

The VM can use more or less than the reservation set. If it isn't being used by the VM that's reserving it, other VMs can use the idle resources, at least until the reserving VM requires them. The reservation prevents other VMs from draining resources, to a certain point. However, the more you reserve for one VM, the less is available to be reserved by others. Excessive CPU reservations also negatively impact HA slot sizes. Although setting a reservation may prevent problems in one VM, it negatively affects the VMs around it.

CPU Limit

A CPU limit prevents a VM from using too many resources. The goal is to reduce VM performance! Think seriously before you set a limit anywhere, because doing so is rarely justified and is almost never a good idea.

A limit always restricts the VM, even when there is no contention. It's always applied. You can set a limit if a VM regularly runs out of control and impacts other VMs negatively. The textbook reason to impose limits is to prepare users for degraded performance as more VMs are added to a host. This creates a level of end-user consistency and cripples those VMs artificially. Frankly, that's a waste of resources. Generally, if you think you need limits, use shares and reservations instead.

MEMORY

Similar to CPU options, memory can be allocated at the VM and resource pool levels. Where possible, designs should aim to set these at the resource pool level. Memory shares, reservations, and limits operate like their CPU counterparts but differ in a few crucial ways. We'll look at how they differ next.

Memory Shares

Memory shares work just like CPU shares and are used only during memory contention. They entitle a VM to a certain slice of memory, in line with the other VMs' shares, subject to any reservations and limits set. To prevent wastage in VMs that have a high proportion of shares, but unused memory, an *idle tax* is factored in to the calculations. This reclaims more memory from

VMs that aren't using their allocated share. Memory shares shouldn't be changed unnecessarily, but they're preferable to reservations and limits.

Memory Reservations

A memory reservation is different from a CPU reservation because it's selfish and doesn't release idle resources back to other VMs the same way. Until a VM uses the memory, others can use the reserved memory; but as soon as it's used, it's not released until the VM is powered off. It's never reclaimed. Unfortunately, Windows addresses all of its memory when it boots up, so the entire memory reservation is held. Linux is nice and only touches the memory when it needs to, thus minimizing the impact.

Like a CPU reservation, a memory reservation may have a positive effect on the VM but can negatively affect its surroundings by reducing available memory and changing HA slot sizes.

Memory Limits

Just like CPU limits, memory limits are generally a bad idea. Memory limits are probably even worse, and are easily avoided, because you can set a VM's memory level far more effectively by reducing its RAM allocation.

When a VM boots up and applications start, they make memory-management decisions based on the amount of RAM they think they have. Setting a memory limit doesn't change this behavior: the VM still believes it has the full allocation, which it's likely to try to use. With a limit set, every request over the limit is forced into VM swap, seriously degrading performance. However, if you reduce the RAM setting, the guest is far less likely to swap as much, because it knows where the limit really is. Avoid memory limits if possible.

DISK

In vSphere 4.0, a VM can set shares on a per-disk basis. This VM disk share is only done across a host, not at a resource pool level, and it allows for a very rudimentary level of control. As a share, it applies only during I/O contention.

A feature known as Storage I/O Control (SIOC), introduced in vSphere 4.1, lets shares apply at the datastore level after certain latency thresholds are met. At the VM level, you can enforce IOPS levels on VMs, as shown in Figure 7.16, and prevent one VM from heavily affecting others.

ADVANCED CPU

The Advanced CPU resource option sets individual HT modes for a VM. Ordinarily, the vSphere hypervisor deals with HT very well with its optimized CPU scheduler. However, some software recommends that HT be disabled, because it can conflict with its own CPU multiprocessing techniques. This setting allows you to keep HT enabled on the hosts but change it for a particular VM if you wish.

Normally this option is set to Any, which allows the VM's vCPU to share cores with its other vCPUs or another VM's vCPUs. The second mode is None, which means the vCPU won't share the core with anything, and the hyperthread is stopped while the vCPU is using it. Finally, if you chose Internal and the VM has two vCPUs, the core will only be shared with itself; otherwise, any other number of vCPUs will revert to no sharing. You can set this option regardless of whether the VM is turned on or off.

FIGURE 7.16
Disk resources
options

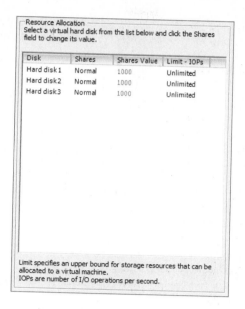

You can set the scheduling affinity to fix which cores are used. You should avoid this unless necessary, because it creates a limitation on vMotion; it's normally better to use other CPU resource settings.

The Advanced CPU panel shown in Figure 7.17 isn't visible if the VM is in a DRS cluster set to Fully Automatic or if the host doesn't have the hardware to support it.

FIGURE 7.17
Advanced CPU
options

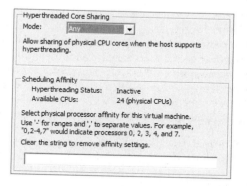

ADVANCED MEMORY

Like the Advanced CPU panel, the Advanced Memory panel is visible only under certain circumstances, such as when the host uses NUMA memory and isn't a member of a fully automatic DRS cluster. These settings, shown in Figure 7.18, allow you to select the NUMA node affinity. This forces the VM to use memory from certain nodes and not others. Because this is host-specific, the affinity settings are cleared when the VM moves to another host; and memory affinity only works effectively if you also specify the CPU affinity.

FIGURE 7.18
Advanced Memory
options

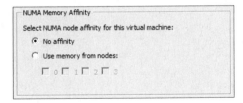

Applying specific NUMA CPU and memory settings can be useful if you have a very static environment with a smaller number of VMs. VMs with large, memory-intensive workloads can benefit from static NUMA mappings, but ordinarily such fine-grained adjustments aren't required.

Naming Virtual Machines

A VM's name is chosen during its creation or deployment from template, and sets the default moniker for its location folder and files. This name is transparent to the guest, but matching it to the VM's hostname avoids confusion. If the VM name is changed, the VM retains the original naming against its files on the datastore. However, migrating to another host via cold migration or Storage vMotion renames these files (although not during a regular vMotion). This helps ensure consistency; otherwise, troubleshooting issues can become more complicated if the names no longer match.

It's always advisable to avoid spaces and special characters in a VM's name. This is also beneficial because it makes working with the VM at the command line or with scripts much easier. Additionally, keeping all the letters lowercase makes for a more palatable keyboard experience.

VMware Tools

The VMware tools are a software package that you should install in each VM. The tools include optimized drivers, a tools service, a tools control panel applet, and a specialized memory driver. These tools improve the VM's performance and aid management. They facilitate the VM heartbeat, which hosts use to tell that the VM is responding. They can also enable time synchronization between the host and the VM, which we'll examine later in the chapter. You can use the tools to quiesce the file system, copy and paste operations to the console, and send shutdown commands.

Your VM design should include the installation of the VMware tools, because they provide important functionality. Every supported guest OS has a set of tools available.

Sizing Virtual Machines

Appropriate sizing is an important part of the overall VM design, because you need to give special consideration to each of the components we've just reviewed. As your vSphere environment grows, the initial sizing of VMs will become increasingly important. If you provide insufficient resources to users from the outset, this can leave a bad impression. Those first impressions of a virtualized alternative to the status quo can often be hard to overcome. However, wasteful allocation can grow to become a serious drain on your resources.

We already discussed disabling or removing unneeded hardware, but remember that there are real benefits to pruning your VMs. As a general rule, it's easier to add more hardware, capacity, or performance than it is to take it away. Often, resources can be hot-added to VMs, and OSs can normally cope with new hardware being presented. But removing hardware can be difficult — it nearly always requires at least a reboot, and often a complete rebuild is needed.

One of the difficulties with keeping VMs small is the attitude of software vendors and users. First, vendors regularly quote application requirements based on the minimum physical server available. Even though the application may be very small and have minimal CPU, memory, and disk requirements, the vendor will quote the latest quad-core CPU with 8 GB RAM and 146 GB mirrored disks. The other common error is that a physical server is always bought with the intention that initial scaling must provide all the performance and capacity the server will need for its entire lifetime. That's at least 3 years, and more normally 5 years. This doesn't take into account the dynamic growth that is possible with the abstracted vSphere layer that sits under each VM.

To best control VM sizing, you should start with sensible initial standards. A hardware tiering scheme is often helpful. For example, create a set size of VMs for small, medium, and large requirements, where each has a list of predefined hardware pieces. As each VM request comes through, fit the applications requirement to one of these standards. Always try to avoid pressure to unnecessarily bump up to the next level if you think it isn't warranted, but remain flexible enough to add extra resources as required.

Remember, one of the primary reasons for virtualization is to recoup the over-provisioning associated with nonvirtualized hardware. Don't just provide the same hardware in a VM that's present in the physical server you hope to replace. Design your vSphere servers and VMs to fit your purpose, so that all the workloads can function as required. Wasted resources in one VM will eventually hurt other VMs.

Virtual Machine Network Design

vNICs are the network adapters presented to VMs. Note that they're different from VMNICs, which is the name hosts give to physical network adapters.

Ordinarily, each VM has only one vNIC. Unlike with a physical server, you gain no benefit such as increased bandwidth or additional redundancy by adding a second vNIC.

There are a couple of reasons you might add a second vNIC. For example, you may wish to bridge two networks. Take care not to create the network loops that vSwitches help avoid. Firewall-appliance VMs need a second vNIC to bridge both sides of the DMZ. Also, you may want your VM to access more than one subnet, because in your environment different types of data are segregated onto separate VLANs — for example, if all backup agent traffic is forced onto its own subnet. Software-clustering solutions often require access to an extra heartbeat link, and a second vNIC makes it convenient to access this.

vNIC Drivers

Each VM can select from four different vNIC adapter types. Normally, a VM is deployed with one network adapter, and the type is automatically selected depending on the VM's hardware version, the host's version, and the guest OS. However, you can change this choice — for example, if the VM's hardware is upgraded after the VM has been built. It's often a great way to take advantage of new features or more optimized drivers.

FLEXIBLE

Flexible is the default vNIC type for 32-bit guests used for VMs deployed on 3.0 hosts. It will function as a vlance adapter if VMware tools aren't installed but as a VMXNET device if the VMware tools are detected:

Vlance A vlance adapter emulates an AMD PCnet32 LANCE network card, an old 10 Mbps NIC. It's used for maximum compatibility, because this driver is included in the default install of most modern OSs. Practically all Linux distributions include drivers for this adapter. But support is starting to be dropped — it's no longer included from Windows Vista onward.

VMXNET VMXNET was the first paravirtualized VMware driver, meaning that it was designed for the virtualized environment to minimize I/O overhead while passing traffic to the physical interfaces. There is no hardware equivalent, so the VMware tools must be installed.

E1000

An E1000 vNIC emulates an Intel E1000 network adapter. It's primarily the default for 64-bit guests.

VMXNET 2 (ENHANCED)

VMXNET 2 (Enhanced) is an upgrade to the first paravirtualized driver for ESX hosts. It includes support for performance features such as jumbo frames and certain hardware offloading.

Again, like the VMXNET vNIC, it requires the VMware tools to be installed, because there is no physical hardware equivalent. VMXNET 2 has been available since version 3.5, but the set of supported guest OSs is limited.

VMXNET 3

VMXNET 3 is the latest paravirtualized driver, introduced with vSphere 4.0. It was completely rewritten and didn't come from the VMXNET lineage. It supports lots of new performance features to improve network scalability and makes the most of IPv6 and newer 10GbE network cards.

This vNIC is supported only on VMs with hardware version 7, and guests must have the VMware tools installed. Check compatibility with your guest OS, because support for VMXNET 3 is the most limited. VMs upgraded to this driver can only run on vSphere 4 hosts.

GUESTS REPORTING INCORRECT NIC SPEEDS

The speed the drivers report within the guest OS aren't necessarily the actual speed of the network traffic. The drivers report what they believe they're capable of, but the actual speed depends on the underlying physical network adapter. Some drivers think they're capable of only 10 Mbps or 100 Mbps; but if the host is fitted with 1 Gbps NICs, then the VMs aren't limited by the drivers.

Table 7.2 describes the features available in each version of the vNICs in vSphere 4.

TABLE 7.2:   vNIC features

	FLEXIBLE	E1000	VMXNET 2 (ENHANCED)	VMXNET 3
VM hardware version	4 or 7	4 or 7	4 or 7	7 only
TSO IPv4	No	Yes	Yes	Yes
TSO IPv6	No	No	No	Yes
Jumbo frames	No	4.0 — No 4.1 — Yes	Yes	Yes
MSI/MSI-X	No	No	No	Yes
Large ring sizes	No	Yes	No	Yes
RSS	No	No	No	Yes
NAPI	No	No	No	Yes
LRO	No	No	No	Yes

TSO   TCP segmentation offload (TSO) reduces the CPU overhead associated with network traffic, to improve I/O performance. TSO-enabled NIC hardware can be used, but it isn't necessary to take advantage of TSO performance gains. It's supported only in certain OSs.

Jumbo Frames   Jumbo frames are any Ethernet frames larger than the standard 1500 bytes. This feature allows VMs to send frames up to 9000 bytes, which can reduces the I/O overhead incurred on each Ethernet frame. Each network device must be enabled for jumbo frames, end to end. To enable this for VMs, you must configure the vSwitch's maximum transmission unit (MTU), which changes this setting for all uplinks attached. Then, you must configure the NIC in the guest OS for jumbo frames.

MSI/MSI-X   Message signal interrupts (MSI) is supported by VMXNET 3 drivers with three levels of interrupt mode: MSI-X, MSI, and INTx. It allows the guest driver to optimize the interrupt method, depending on the guest's kernel support. MSI uses an in-band PCI memory-space message instead of an out-band PCI INTx pin. This can lower overall interrupt latency.

Ring Size   With each newer vNIC, the receive and transmit buffers have increased. A larger ring size creates more buffer, which can deal with sudden traffic bursts. There is a small impact on CPU overhead as the ring size increases, but this may be justified if your network traffic has bursty throughput. You can alter the buffer size in the VM's VMX configuration file.

RSS   Receive-side scaling (RSS) can be used by some new Windows guest VMs. It distributes traffic processing across multicore processors to aide scalability and reduces the impact of CPU bottlenecks with 10GbE network cards.

NAPI   New API (NAPI) is a feature for Linux-based guests to improve network performance by reducing the overhead of packet receiving. It defers incoming message handling to process messages in bundles. This allows for greater CPU efficiency and better load handling.

LRO   Large receive offload (LRO) is another Linux guest technology, which increases inbound throughput by aggregating packets into a larger buffer before processing. This reduces the number of packets and therefore reduces CPU overhead. With vSphere 4.0, the benefit is realized only if the traffic is between VMs on the same host.

vNIC DRIVER PERFORMANCE

The VMXNET 3 driver is the best performance choice if the VM is at hardware version 7 and the guest OS is able to support it. However, in a mixed environment with ESX 3.5 hosts, this driver limits your vMotion options.

If you can't use a VMXNET 3 driver, the next best performing driver is the Enhanced VMXNET, as long the VMware tools are installed. Again, be mindful that Enhanced VMXNET drivers require ESX 3.5 as a minimum, so be careful deploying them in a mixed environment with older 3.0 hosts.

From the remaining vNICs, VMXNET performs best. The E1000 then sits between the VMXNET driver and the lowest-performing vNIC, the aging vlance card.

MAC Addresses

vSphere automatically sets a VM's MAC address. Ordinarily, the MAC address that's created doesn't need to be altered. However, you may want to change it in the following circumstances:

- There are more than 256 vNICs on a physical host, because conflicts with the automatically generated MAC addresses can occur.

- vNICs on different hosts but the same subnet are allocated identical MAC addresses.

- You need to set a fixed VM MAC address to prevent the address from changing.

After a VM's MAC address is created, the MAC address will change only if the VM is turned off and then moved. However, some software installed in VMs tie its licensing to a MAC address, so in this case it's recommended that you set a static address.

You can see where the MAC address is set in the VM configuration settings shown in Figure 7.5. vSphere doesn't support arbitrary MAC addresses: the allowable range is 00:50:56:00:00:00 to 00:50:56:3F:FF:FF.

VLAN Tagging

Although vSphere's VLAN tagging options aren't strictly a consideration for a VM's networking design, they're worth mentioning briefly to help you understand how an 802.1q driver can be installed in a VM. Each VM's vNIC connects to one port group on a host. Each port group can use one of three types of VLAN tagging:

EST   External switch tagging (EST) is the default port group option, when no VLAN ID is entered (or a VLAN ID of 0 is stipulated). No tagging is performed on the vSwitch, so there is a one-to-one relationship with the VMNICs and the access ports on the physical switch.

VST   Virtual switch tagging (VST) is an extremely popular configuration in vSphere deployments to aggregate several VLANs onto a limited number of VMNICs. A VLAN ID number between 1 and 4094 is set on each port group, and any traffic passing out of the port group from a VM is tagged with the VLAN ID.

VGT   Virtual guest tagging (VGT) allows you to install 802.1q tagging software within the guest OS. This lets you run several VLANs through to your VM on a single vNIC. This can be particularly useful if you're P2Ving a physical server that used this configuration and you need to preserve the setup. To use VGT, set the port group's VLAN ID to 4095.

Virtual Machine Storage Design

One of the crucial design factors for VMs is its storage. vSphere provides a great deal of flexibility for storing VM data, and that gives rise to numerous decisions you must make.

Disks

Although this isn't necessarily vSphere specific, you should consider the number and size of disks to present to each VM. The disks that are presented to VMs have several layers of abstraction. A physical server or workstation with one or more disks inside, and perhaps hardware or software RAID, usually sees one large disk, which it splits into partitions to use. However, VMs are much freer to split their storage to exactly what is needed.

With this freedom, VMs are normally split into several smaller disks with a single partition on each. These disks are easily grown (assuming spare space exists in the datastores), but contiguous partitions make growing all but the last one on the disk more difficult. For that reason, it's advisable to create VMs with only one partition per disk.

The ease with which you can add disks of any size gives rise to more options when splitting up OS space. On Windows guests, it's common practice to split off the OS C drive and have separate disks for user data, program files, logs, swapfiles, and so on. For example, a Windows SQL VM may have a separate disk for the OS, the databases, the SQL logs, the swapfile, and a backup drive. A Linux VM can have separate disks for each slice of its file system, so a typical setup may have individual disks for /, /boot, /usr, /opt, /home, /etc, /tmp, /var, /var/log, and so on; the list can be endless to suit your requirements.

SPLITTING A VM'S PARTITIONS ONTO SEPARATE DISKS

If you're P2Ving an existing physical server with VMware Converter, and it has more than one partition on a disk, watch for the advanced disk options to select a customized target disk layout. This lets you split each partition out onto its own VMDK disk file during the P2V. And if you have a VM with multiple partitions on a single virtual disk, VMware Converter's V2V is an easy way to fix it.

Another advantage of splitting out each piece of file system is the granularity it gives you to select different performance profiles for different areas. The underlying storage from which the disks are carved can be on different RAID sets, with different disk speeds and different spindle counts, all providing different levels of performance. So, a database server can run its OS off an inexpensive RAID 6–based disk; its swap can sit on a fast but vulnerable RAID 0–based disk; and the transaction log and DB files can be on a high-performing, redundant but costly RAID 10–based disk.

This physical separation of logical components also allows you to split off areas of a VM that you want to treat differently. For example, you may want to avoid using SAN replication on certain transient data like swap space. Or you may wish to provide greater protection to some data on the underlying storage. Backups can be simplified by avoiding entire disks that don't ordinarily need to be backed up.

Each VM can have a total of 60 VMDK disks attached to it, each of which can be close to 2 TB, giving you the sort of scalability to quench even the most insatiable of capacity appetites. However, one of the advantages of virtual disks is the ability to make them smaller than usual. On a physical standalone server, you may as well use all of the disk capacity from the outset. With VMs, you should start the disks small and grow them as required. For each VM, you should consider the size of the OS, the applications, the user data in combination with the number of users, the swap, the logs and spooling data, and some room for growth.

Disk Modes

Regular VM disks are created as VMDK files. You can create these disk files on either block-based datastores or NFS exports. There are three disk modes to select from, as you saw earlier in Figure 7.3.

SNAPSHOT

The default disk mode, the one in which all disks are initially created as, is *snapshot* mode. It isn't named as such anywhere on the interface, but any VMDK disk that isn't independent is considered a snapshot mode disk (some older documentation refers to this as normal mode). Unsurprisingly, the discernible differentiator is that snapshot mode VMDK disks can use the snapshot feature.

vSphere VMDK snapshots aren't like SAN snapshots; they aren't copies, but change deltas. It's just a point in time, where the disk I/O is redirected to another disk file. You can then choose to either incorporate those changes back into the main disk (committing) or discard the changes to revert to the original snapshot (deleting). The most important thing to remember from a design point of view is that they're only intended for short-term use. If you want to keep whole copies of VMs at particular times, use vSphere cloning or a suitable backup solution.

Thick provisioned disks (the default on block based datastores) without snapshots are static-sized files. However, as soon as you take a snapshot, the static file remains, and new changes are written out to new space. This means that when a snapshot is taken, you can unexpectedly fill up your datastore without provisioning any new VMs. Interestingly, if your disks are spread across multiple datastores, the deltas from all disks are created in the VM's working directory, not within the disk's own directory. Creating snapshots also places restrictions on the VM, such as no longer being able to Storage vMotion the VM.

Finally, as each snapshot is taken, it creates a chain of deltas. As the number of delta files increase, the chaining becomes more complicated and more prone to issues. A break in the chain at any point can lead to data loss. The snapshots can also have an associated performance overhead, so if eking out every ounce of disk I/O is important, you should avoid leaving snapshots in place.

Don't plan to keep your snapshots too long. They're good for short-term use, such as when you're patching or testing changes. Thankfully, the snapshot algorithms keep getting better. vSphere 4.0 came with a much-improved way of dealing with snapshots, making them considerably more reliable. More patches have been released, which are included in 4.1, reducing the space required to commit snapshots. The best advice is to keep your hosts at the latest version.

INDEPENDENT PERSISTENT

Independent persistent disks operate like regular hard drives. All changes are immediate, and there is no potential performance degradation, as is associated with snapshot mode. However, with the lack of snapshot functionality, certain vSphere features are unavailable, such as Storage vMotion, VMware Data Recovery (vDR), and lots of third-party backup tools.

INDEPENDENT NONPERSISTENT

Independent nonpersistent disks differ in that all changes are lost when the VM is powered off (but not when it's rebooted). This returns the disk to its original state, losing all subsequent changes. This disk mode is useful for environments where you want to keep a consistent running image. A good example use case of nonpersistent disks is a kiosk-style terminal, or a teaching lab where you want to return to exactly the same configuration on a regular basis.

SCSI Controllers

vSphere 4 supports four types of SCSI controller:

Bus Logic Parallel   The BusLogic controller provides support for older OSs and is the default for Windows 2000 guests.

LSI Logic Parallel   The LSI Logic Parallel controller is supported for newer OSs with built-in support on Windows 2003 and later. VMware also recommends that you use the LSI-based controller for Red Hat installs.

Both default controllers should have identical I/O performance, and they only differ slightly in their hardware presentation. If the guest doesn't have either driver installed, pick whichever is easiest to install.

LSI Logic SAS   The LSI Logic SAS controller has built-in support for clusters on Windows 2008. It provides a small performance boost over the two legacy controllers. However, this controller is only available for VMs whose hardware is at version 7. Be careful using this controller if the environment still has ESX 3 hosts, because upgrading to version 7 hardware will lock the VM to the vSphere 4 hosts.

PVSCSI   The PVSCSI adapter is VMware's own paravirtualized controller for high-performance VMs. It can provide an increase in throughput while reducing CPU overhead. However, its use should be reserved for high-I/O VMs, because it can potentially have a higher latency than other controllers if I/O rates are lower. The PVSCSI driver coalesces interrupts to reduce the amount of CPU processing required. If the I/O is too low, then all it does is introduce delay.

You can use the PVSCSI driver on version 7 VMs, and it supports Windows 2003/2008 and Red Hat Enterprise Linux 5 (RHEL 5). With the initial introduction of PVSCSI controllers, there was no support for boot disks, but this was resolved for Windows guests in 4.0 Update 1. It's common to use a default controller for boot/OS disks for ease of install and then add a second controller for the higher-workload disks.

Depending on the guest you select, the default used is either the BusLogic or the LSI Logic controller, unless it's a Windows XP VM. Windows XP guests don't have the necessary drivers for these SCSI controllers and default to using IDE disks. Each VM can have up to 4 different controllers and up to 15 devices per controller.

Disk Types

vSphere VMDK disks come in three different types:

Zeroed Thick   All the space is allocated on the datastore at the time of creation. It isn't pre-zeroed, so it's quick to create. As the disk is written to, the space is zeroed as the I/O is committed. Zeroing the disk ensures that no old data from the underlying storage is found in the new disk.

Eager-Zeroed Thick   Again, all the space is preallocated to the disk on the datastore when the disk is first created. However, with eager zeroed thick disks, the entire space is zeroed out at this time. These disks can take a significant time to create, but when they're ready they exhibit a marked performance improvement over new zeroed thick disks. For this reason, ensure that any I/O-intensive disks are prepared this way or converted to this format if already provisioned.

Thin   Similar to thin provisioning on a storage array, VMDK thin disks are only allocated space as they grow from disk I/O. The disk starts small and is grown as the space is zeroed, ready for disk I/O. It won't grow beyond its allowed size. Despite speculation to the contrary, thin provisioning doesn't impact performance but performs extremely closely to that of zeroed thick disks. The main advantage of thin disks is the space you save by not allocating everything up front. However, some guest disk operations, such as defragmentation, cause thin disks to inflate. You must take care not to overcommit a VMFS volume with a thin disk in it. You can use appropriate vCenter alarms to mitigate the likelihood of this.

The different types are best seen when you add a new disk to a VM. You're given the option of which type of disk format you'd like, as shown in Figure 7.19.

When you create a new VM, the default format is zeroed thick. This is also the case when you add a new disk, because both the check boxes in Figure 7.19 are deselected by default. However, if the underlying storage isn't a VMFS volume but an NFS datastore, then the VMDK type is dictated by the NAS device, and the disks are thin-provisioned.

Fault tolerance requires eager zeroed thick disks, and Microsoft clustering needs it for its quorum and shared disks. The Support Clustering Features Such As Fault Tolerance option provisions disks in the eager zeroed thick format.

You can't simply switch between formats, but when you Storage vMotion a VM from one datastore to another, you're given the choice of what the destination format should be. This gives you a straightforward method to convert your disks to the format you need.

FIGURE 7.19
Disk provisioning
types

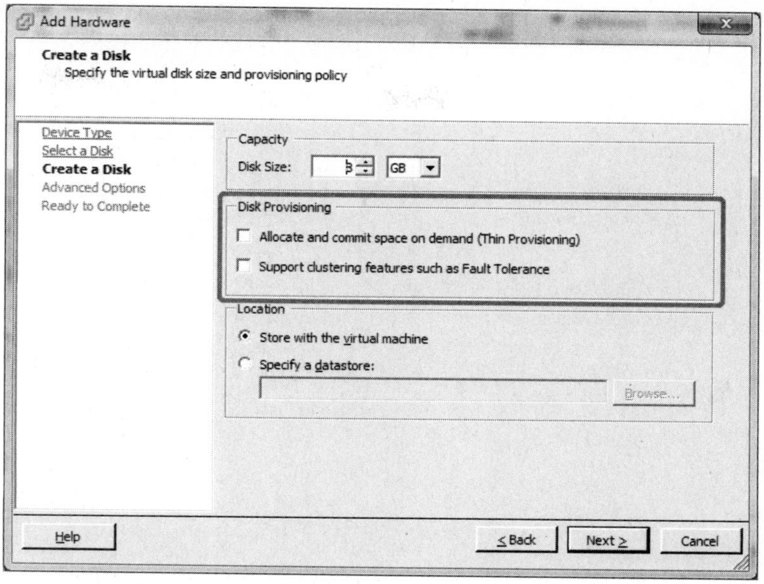

RDMs

RDM disks are an alternative to normal VMDK disks. RDMs are small mapping files to raw LUNs. They allow the ESX hosts to address the LUN as if it was a VMDK, but this means the VM can have direct access to the entire LUN.

The RDM file contains all the metadata required to manage and proxy the disk access, instructing the VMkernel where to send disk instructions. VMware recommends that you use RDMs only when justified, because the preferred disk format is regular VMDK virtual disks.

Two types of RDM exist — virtual and physical — and your use case will dictate which one is appropriate. Note that both types of RDM support vMotion, despite a common perception that this is available only on virtual RDMs.

VIRTUAL COMPATIBILITY MODE RDM

Virtual RDMs act just like regular VMDK files. They virtualize the mapped device so that they appear to the guest OS to be disks from a VMDK datastore. This allows the use of snapshots; and because the RDMs hide the underlying hardware, the LUN is potentially more portable when moving to new SAN equipment. Virtual RDMs are used for CAB-style Microsoft clustering. CIB can also use virtual RDMs, but VMware recommends using VMFS-based VMDKs unless you're likely to reconfigure them to a CAB cluster eventually.

PHYSICAL COMPATIBILITY MODE RDM

Physical RDMs have almost complete direct access to the SCSI device, which gives you control at much lower levels. However, this means you can't use the snapshot feature. Physical RDM mode is useful for SAN management agents that require access to hardware-specific commands. Physical RDMs are also used for physical to virtual (n+1) Microsoft clustering.

RDM Usage

RDMs are used for a variety of reasons:

Application Requirements   Some applications need to make direct calls to the block table. The common example of this, and one just discussed, is Microsoft clustering, which needs access to RDMs to cluster across vSphere hosts or from a vSphere host to a physical windows server.

SAN Technology   Some older SAN technologies like replication, deduplication, and snapshots may not work with VMFS volumes. SAN management and storage resource management (SRM) applications may need lower-level access.

NPIV   NPIV will only work with RDM disks. It allows a VM to claim a virtual port from the host's HBA, and it allows finer control of bandwidth priorities and QoS.

Migrating Data to Virtual   If a very large LUN is attached to a physical server, then it's possible to attach the LUN directly to the replacement VM. You should always try to move the data over to a VMFS volume, but sometimes an RDM can provide a good transitional platform.

Flexibility   If you think you may need to move an application from a VM back up to a physical server, perhaps to promote a staging server to a production physical server, then making it a physical RDM from the outset can make the migration much easier.

Misinformation   RDMs were considered by some the best solution for very high-performance I/O requirements. This belief isn't justified, and the performance differential is negligible, but the myth is still perpetuated in many quarters.

RDMs have several drawbacks. They're inherently less manageable, and they lack the portability that makes regular VMDK disk files the default choice. They also require the entire LUN to be dedicated to only one VM. This can cause serious scalability issues, because each host can have a maximum of only 256 LUNs. This may sound like a lot, but if they're being used by VMs with several disks, this ceiling can have an effect. Heavy RDM use also has other problems scaling, because the workload on the Storage team grows when they have to create and manage that many more LUNs.

RDMs shouldn't be anyone's first choice, but they're indispensible in certain circumstances. They're a useful tool that you can call on in your design if necessary, but try to avoid them if possible, because they're limiting.

Storage vMotion

Storage vMotion was initially introduced on ESX 3.5 hosts as a command-line option (it was in ESX 3.0 for upgrading purposes, but it was limited and known as DMotion in those days). However, it didn't make it into the GUI until vSphere 4.0, where it's now far more accessible to users.

From a design perspective, it's an interesting capability. It allows for zero-downtime datastore migrations. But you should note a couple of things while creating solutions around it.

First, Storage vMotion requires either Enterprise or Enterprise + licenses, which aren't available to a lot of users.

Second, you should be aware of the impact of Storage vMotion migrations. They're disk-intensive operations. The VM has to continue to read and write to the array while it's reading from the source and writing to the destination. Both source and destination are likely to have other VM traffic I/O, which can be affected by the Storage vMotion. So, if you're using Storage vMotion to migrate a large amount of data, although there may be no downtime, it can have a significant effect on the overall SAN performance.

Also, Storage vMotions use snapshotting to lock the data for the move. If the VMs being moved have very large disks or are very disk intensive, the Storage vMotion can eat up large chunks of space on the source datastore. Make sure you have sufficient room; otherwise, the datastore will quickly fill and cause issues to all the VMs sharing the datastore.

vSphere 4.1 introduced vStorage API for Array Integration (VAAI) offloading capabilities, which we discussed in the last chapter. It can reduce this impact significantly if used in conjunction with a compatible storage array.

Guest Software

vSphere can host a huge variety of guest OSs. Any x86-based OS will install in a VM, but only certain OSs are supported by VMware. Any supported guest OS has a VMware tools package that you can install. The list is always being updated, and you can find the latest version at www. vmware.com/pdf/GuestOS_guide.pdf.

Generally speaking, all modern versions of Microsoft Windows, Linux distributions from Red Hat, Novell SUSE, Debian, Ubuntu, and FreeBSD or Solaris are supported. Even some versions of older legacy OSs like Microsoft DOS, IBM OS/2 Warp, and Novell Netware are supported. Those not on the list should still work, albeit without support. However, without a compatible version of VMware tools, you may have to contend with driver issues.

Selecting an OS

vSphere demands 64-bit hardware to run on. But, it can can virtualize both 32-bit and 64-bit OSs very well. So, which version of the guest OS should you install in a VM? As a general rule, you can treat this decision in much the same way as if you were installing your OS on the bare metal. 64-bit OSs can address more memory and often perform better even with 32-bit applications.

Because VMs are so portable, it's easy to have OSs around much longer than they used to be. In most enterprises with physical server installs, the hardware is normally replaced at least every five years. If it hasn't been upgraded in that long, it's common to use this as an excuse to rebuild the server and update to the latest OS and application versions. However, infrastructure in vSphere is now abstracted from the hardware, so you may see OSs that are much older. Often, virtualization is used to remove old hardware, and very old OS installs aren't unheard of. It makes sense to install the latest version of any OS when you're deploying, and that should include the 64-bit choice.

Even though 64-bit hardware has been mainstream for many years, there are still some issues with driver support. This was always the one consideration against deploying 64-bit OSs. But with VMware's tight list of hardware and available drivers, this isn't an issue for vSphere VMs unless you need to pass through some legacy hardware. With OS vendors keen for users to migrate to 64-bit as soon as possible, there are no additional licensing costs, so little prevents you from using 64-bit from the outset.

There are some exceptions, however. One example is 16-bit Windows applications that need to be hosted but won't run on a 64-bit OS. Also, if you P2V an existing computer with a 32-bit OS, you're left with no choice.

One other OS option that can be worth considering, if you need a Linux-based guest, is JeOS. JeOS stands for *Just enough OS* and is the term for specially customized OSs that are fine-tuned for virtualized platforms. Without the need for extra drivers, these OSs can taper their kernels to make them smaller and more efficient. This is possible due to the modular Linux kernel; both Ubuntu and SUSE have launched their own JeOS-based offerings. These are used as the base of many virtual appliances. VMware has entered into a licensing agreement with Novell to use SUSE as base for some of their products which can benefit from a JeOS base.

Software Licensing

OS and application licensing varies between vendors for virtualization platforms. You should look carefully at your options with each vendor. Some vendors base licensing on the physical hardware the VM is running on at any one time. Confusion can reign, because this may be physical CPU sockets or physical cores, with or without HyperThreading.

Some vendors base their licensing on the VM's hardware, so it may be tied to the number of vCPUs or the VM's RAM. Ordinarily, vCPUs are presented as individual physical sockets, but an advanced VM setting allows them to appear as cores.

Some vendors license on the number of instances on site. Different rules may govern development/staging/test copies of software, and this is of particular interest because these tend to be more prevalent in virtualized environments. Applications can still use hardware dongles, either serial, parallel, or USB based, which have their own support challenges and can impact the VM's mobility within the cluster.

Just understanding Microsoft's licensing rules can be complicated, particularly because it changes so regularly. Of particular note is the server licensing, which is based on physical hardware and largely ignores the ability to migrate VMs between hosts. This may change soon, as Microsoft adapts its own hypervisor's capabilities and are able to migrate VMs as freely as VMware's hypervisor can. Currently, a standard 2008 edition license covers one VM while it's on one host. As soon as the VM migrates to another host, another license is required. An Enterprise edition licenses four VMs. In a large cluster of hosts, you can expect your licensing to become rather costly. For this reason, many opt to use the Datacenter license, which allows unlimited copies per host. You need one 2008 Datacenter license per host, and all the VMs are covered. With the downgrade rights, this license also covers your 2003 instances.

Another Microsoft-specific licensing issue is the activation scheme used in their nonvolume license agreement contracts. These VMs can trigger a need to reactivate the licensing if the hardware changes significantly. In these cases, it's always advisable to remove non-essential hardware, install the VMware tools, and upgrade the VM hardware if required, before activating.

One last special licensing issue worth discussing is that of physical hardware-based licenses. Some vendors, notoriously Oracle, base their licensing on the number of physical CPUs on the host, regardless of the number of vCPUs allocated to the VM. In highly dense hardware, which is commonplace in vSphere hosts, a license for a four-way server may be required even if the VM has access to only one vCPU. Add an eight-way host server to the DRS-enabled cluster, and your licensing costs double, even though the VM remains with one vCPU. These kind of draconian licensing terms create situations where some companies have to physically remove CPUs from servers and isolate VMs on standalone hosts, just to ensure licensing compliance.

vSphere 4.1 introduces the ability to create Host-Affinity rules, one of which is known as a "must" rule. This rule is designed specifically for strict licensing terms, and the following chapter explains how you can use it to lock VMs to a particular host. You will need to check whether this technique is regarded as sufficient by your vendor to satisfy their licensing terms.

Disk Alignment

As disk volumes are laid out on physical storage, it's important that the partitions line up with the RAID chunks. Unaligned partitions mean that write operations are more likely to span several chunks, increasing latency and reducing throughput. Disk alignment can be an issue for both VMFS datastores and guest partitions, as we mentioned in Chapter 6, "Storage," when discussing VMFS volumes. Having both unaligned only exacerbates the issue, affecting I/O performance even more. However, as long as VMFS volumes are created with the vSphere client, they will be aligned properly.

When you're designing VMs, it's important to understand the impact of unaligned guest partitions and how to create partitions to avoid this potential performance drain. Aligned disks save I/O by reducing the number of times a stripe is crossed and minimize the metadata operations required.

Two settings are fixed when the disks are first initialized by their OS:

Starting Offset   The first and most crucial is the starting offset. By default, on older OSs (Windows 2000 and 2003), this is set incorrectly, because these OSs reserve the first 63 sectors for the master boot record (MBR). When the disk is initialized and the first 63 sectors are reserved, they take up 31.5 KB of space, meaning every subsequent cluster will be slightly offset from the sectors. From Windows 7 and 2008, this has been fixed, and all disks have an offset of 1,024 KB (although disks initially sized below 4 GB are offset by 64 KB).

NEWER 1 MB SECTOR DRIVES

Until recently, hard drives were manufactured with 512-byte sectors, so eventually, all read and write operations were broken down into these sectors. SAN vendors vary in the stripe/chunk sizes they use, but commonly these are 32 KB, 64 KB, or 128 KB. With the introduction of GUID Partition Table (GPT), Windows (7 and 2008) and newer Linux partitioning tools have an offset of 1,024 KB. All arrays fitted with new 1 MB drives should work well with this new standard.

Cluster Size   The second setting is the cluster size (or file-allocation unit) after the initial offset is applied. Most file systems use 4 KB or larger clusters, so most I/O is a multiple of that. However, applications typically generate certain types of I/O sizes, so you can often customize the partitioning to work as well as possible with the application's needs. You should also check the storage array's advice, because choosing the same cluster size as the chunk/stripe that the array uses maximizes the storage efficiency. But as a rule, ensuring that the offset and the cluster size are cleanly divisible by 4 KB (4,096 Bytes) will give you the biggest benefit.

Linux users can use their disk-partitioning tool of choice, fdisk being the most popular, to correctly align the partitions. In Windows, use `diskpart.exe` (or `diskpar.exe` on Windows 2000) to create aligned partitions, and select the appropriate cluster size when formatting the partition.

The easiest way to handle this is to ensure that your template partitions are correctly aligned. That way, you don't need to worry about them in the future. Remember that if you create properly aligned small dummy disks in a Windows 7 or 2008 template, they will have 64 KB offsets even after you expand them beyond 4 GB. This isn't likely to be significant for performance per se, but it can cause inconsistencies across your environment.

If you already have a collection of existing VMs with misaligned disks, various third-party tools are available. However, they all involve some downtime, so the recommendation is to concentrate your efforts on the most I/O-intensive disks. Also, be aware that many P2V solutions, including VMware's own Converter product, don't correctly align the disks they create.

An ongoing debate exists about the usefulness of aligning system boot disks. VMware published a white paper several years ago stating that you shouldn't attempt to align boot disks. The company has subsequently withdrawn that advice, but many regard aligning boot disks as unnecessary. Properly aligning a boot disk does take extra effort, because you need to create the partition in a surrogate guest. System boot disks don't normally generate much disk I/O, as long as you split the data off onto its own disk. However, you should certainly try to generate aligned boot disks for your templates.

Defragmentation

File fragmentation within VMs is a hotly debated topic. VMware has produced papers to suggest that fragmentation on VMFS volumes isn't a concern due to the relatively small number of files; the small size of I/O requests compared to the large blocks, which keeps most requests within the same block; and a sub-block allocator technique that reduces disk wastage and encourages file coalescing.

However, many regard defragmentation as an essential performance tune-up for some guest OSs, most notably Windows. Power users have long advocated a regular cycle of defrag jobs to prevent a gradual slowdown. Research continues on the effectiveness of defragging VMs, although this is often sponsored and run by software vendors who sell products associated with its remediation.

Several issues stand against defragmentation of VM disks, particularly those on SAN storage. Storage arrays use several controller methods to optimize I/O to the disks, and the performance impact of fragmented I/O across disks often isn't clear. Most controllers have memory caches to collate I/O before writing it to the disks, and read-caching algorithms to grab the files in preparation for their being requested.

If guest OSs are defragged, thin-provisioned storage can lose its effectiveness as it writes blocks to new areas of the virtual disk. Some deduplication gains can also be lost every time a defragging job is run, and these gains are recovered until the deduplication is run again (deduping on primary storage is usually scheduled and not run in-line). Most storage vendors say that defragmenting file systems only increases disk I/O, works against their controllers' smarts, and does nothing to improve performance.

You may decide that you need to defragment some of your VMs. Generally speaking, third-party defraggers work better than the OS built-in ones, and some are starting to become more VMware aware. It's important that if you decide to run these jobs, they're offset and don't run simultaneously (which can put a large amount of I/O pressure on the storage). Defragmenting your templates before using them to deploy VMs may have the most potential benefit without causing an excessive strain. If you're contemplating guest defragmentation, you should run it on the most disk-performance-critical VMs.

Optimizing the Guest for the Hypervisor

Each guest has the opportunity to be optimized for running within a VM. This allows the guest OS and guest applications to run more efficiently and potentially faster, and it can reduce the load on the hosts, the network, and the storage.

CUTTING THE FAT

Basically, anything that's installed or running in a VM that isn't essential is a waste of host resources. When you multiply all those extraneous cycles by the number of VMs, even small inefficiencies can have an impact on overall performance.

CPU and Memory

You can do several things to reduce the CPU and memory load from VMs. First, optimize your antivirus software. Install the core virus-scanning engine in your VMs, and avoid the anti-spyware, firewall, and IDS extras that often come prebundled. You can switch to a host-based product that uses VMware's VMsafe APIs to protect the VMs without needing an agent installed in every guest. Also, follow the recommended exclusion lists for the OS and applications in the guest. This should reduce the overhead caused by files that unnecessarily burden a scanning engine.

Screensavers are waste of resources in a VM and should always be disabled, including pre-login screensavers. On Linux servers that don't need GUIs running, think about setting the default init level to not start an X windows session — normally, run level 3.

As we already discussed, consider paravirtualized network and storage adapter drivers, because they can reduce CPU overhead.

Filter through all the running services, and disable anything from starting that isn't required. Look carefully at the default installed software and strip out anything not required. Also, examine the running processes in top or Task Manager to find unnecessary items.

Disk

Optimizing the disk can mean two things in this context. First, and probably most important, you need to reduce storage I/O wherever possible. Avoid anything that's very disk I/O intensive if it isn't needed. It's also important to avoid too many I/O-intensive jobs happening at once. VDI deployments can suffer from *boot storms*, where all the desktops start up at the same time and the SAN load is overwhelming. These sorts of issues can also happen if scheduled tasks are set to run at the same time — for example, backups, antivirus scans, cron, and scheduled tasks scripts or defrag utilities. If these are all set via the same policy or deployed from the same image, then they may all try to run at once. You need to figure out a way to offset the regular tasks so they don't thrash the storage simultaneously.

Second, you can optimize the disk-capacity requirements. Any software you can uninstall will reduce the amount of disk space needed. Store install sets centrally, to avoid having copies on every VM. Enable circular logging and limit cache sizes, to avoid unnecessary build-up.

Clear temporary folders regularly, and use disk-analysis tools to determine where space is being used.

Network

Network load is rarely a bottleneck for VMs; however, for particularly network-demanding loads, it may be possible to save bandwidth. DRS clusters have a function known as *affinity rules.* We'll discuss these in more detail later, but affinity rules tell DRS to try to keep certain VMs together on one host. There are a few reasons why you may want to keep VMs together, but a primary one is that doing so avoids sending the inter-VM network traffic out onto the LAN if the VMs are on the same port group. Two or more VMs involved in a multi-server application will send most of their traffic between themselves. Having all the VMs on one host can make most of that traffic happen locally.

Time Settings

VMs can't match a physical machine's ability to keep time. VMs need to time-share a host's hardware and can be interrupted by being suspended and snapshotted, which wouldn't affect regular computers.

Two main options exist to keep a VM's time correctly synchronized. You can use the native guest tools, such as NTP in Linux guests or W32Time in Windows VMs; or you can use the VMware tools' time synchronization. The VMware tools have the advantage of knowing that VMs must catch up occasionally and be prepared for the clock to be off significantly. Also, the VMware tools don't need networking to be configured within the guest because they work directly on the host.

Native NTP and W32Time generally work well inside VMs and are usually turned on by default. VMware recommends that you use only one method of time sync; and because the native tools are normally running from the outset, this is how many VMs are configured. Additionally, some OSs and application software need to access the native time service, and sometimes they act as time sources themselves. Just be sure you don't set the VM to sync to its own hardware clock. For the most accurate timekeeping possible, VMware recommends using the guest OS's native tools.

Different versions of Linux and Windows have had different approaches to time synchronization. Two Knowledge Base (KB) articles cover the best practices for each, and you should consult them to ensure that your design incorporates this advice for the OSs you plan to deploy:

- Timekeeping best practices for Linux guests: `http://kb.vmware.com/kb/1006427`

- Timekeeping best practices for Windows: `http://kb.vmware.com/kb/1318`

Clones, Templates, and vApps

Throughout this chapter, we've offered a great deal of specific advice on how to customize and tweak each VM. However, it's likely that in your environment, many of the VMs you plan to build will have very similar requirements. To avoid spending hours poring over every component and every guest OS decision prior to deploying a new VM, you can use a standard build. Doing so enables you to roll out new VMs much more rapidly.

Along with creating VMs more expediently, standardized builds automate many of the steps involved. You can also allocate specific permissions to users to control new VM deployments.

Standardizing is an important design tool. It simplifies decisions regarding how a large deployment of VMs should be created and configured. Perhaps more important, you're likely to have tens of VMs for every host and maybe hundreds of VMs per vCenter. The payback from a well-designed VM standard build in ongoing management and administration can be very worthwhile. Shaving 5 GB of disk space, reducing the default RAM by 256 MB, or halving the standard vCPUs from two to one can have a massive impact on your overall hardware needs. But being too stingy can mean hundreds of servers or desktops that continually hit performance and capacity problems.

Clones

A straightforward method of deploying a new VM without building it from scratch is to *clone* an existing VM. VM clones are exact copies: the configuration and the disks are duplicated. The only difference is that cloning forces a new VM name for the copy.

Clones are useful for creating quick point-in-time copies as backups. Unlike snapshots, which should be kept only for the short term, can effect performance, and require babysitting, clones are wonderful tools to grab a quick backup of the entire machine.

Having an exact copy can be a great way to replicate a production setup, which you can isolate and test. By cloning several VMs in an application setup, you can test changes on exactly the same setup and be confident that upgrades will go smoothly.

Be careful when you make clones, because having exact duplicates on the same network usually creates problems. Being identical, a clone has the same guest hostname and IP address as the original. Bringing a clone up on the network at the same time as the original can therefore create IP and name conflicts. You should ensure that the primary is turned off or disconnected from the network, that the clone is isolated, or that the clone is reconfigured while offline to change its hostname and IP address. Be mindful of tiered applications, because clones can cause inconsistencies on other connected servers if copies are brought online at different times.

You can make clones while a VM is turned on or off. A *hot* clone produces a VM that is crash consistent, so it's always desirable to turn off the VM first. However, if the VM to be cloned is critical, and an outage isn't possible, hot-cloning can still grab an image. Just be sure to test that it hasn't corrupted the OS, applications, or important data. Certain OSs and applications are more robust than others — for example, a database server is more likely to have problems recovering from a hot clone than a fairly static application server.

Another useful cloning facility is vCenter's ability to create a scheduled task to make a clone. If a VM is changing regularly or is particularly critical, vCenter can automate the process of cloning on a regular basis. This shouldn't replace any normal backup procedures you follow but can be useful to augment them as an extra safety net.

Finally, your SAN vendor may have tools for cloning VMs quickly on the storage. This allows for faster cloning, which takes the load off the host and can automate the provisioning of large VM cloning that is often seen in virtual desktop cases. These tools may be useful to consider not just for desktops but also when you need to roll out several VMs at once, such as when you're deploying new branch offices with a standard set of server services.

Templates

A *template* is a master copy VM that is specifically set aside to produce new VMs. A template is a special type of VM that can't be turned on or changed and is only visible in the VMs and Templates view in vCenter. This protection helps to keep a clean and standard image from which other VMs can be created.

VM templates streamline the process of creating new VMs. They're easy for users to complete without having to customize hardware, VM options, and guest OSs. New VMs are available in minutes instead of after several hours; and often the burden of VM creation can be passed on to other members of the team, allowing greater flexibility and timely deployments.

Any VM can be converted or cloned into a template. However, because templates should be as immaculate as possible, it's advisable to build them from scratch so they're fit for their intended purpose.

Consider building a library of templates for your different OS and application needs. But don't expect to create a template for every scenario. Only include applications in templates if you expect to deploy a reasonable number of them and if their installation or customization is particularly onerous. Remember that it takes time to build up each template and that each one has a maintenance overhead associated with it. Even very large enterprises are likely to have only about a dozen templates, covering all the standard OSs and some of the larger applications.

Templates allow you to set permissions on how users can create new VMs, which again helps to control the types of VMs, the number of VMs, and what hardware can be allocated. For example, you may let only certain users deploy particular templates, limiting their OS or hardware choices. Template- and VM-creation permissions can also help curb the *VM sprawl* that is regularly seen when new vSphere servers appear.

You should consider how the use of templates will fit into your existing OS and application provisioning. If you have an automated process or set methodology for building physical servers and workstations, you can utilize those tools for building the base of your templates. This can lead to an even higher level of standardization and may reduce duplication between teams. However, be mindful that physical build tools often incorporate lots of drivers and specific details to deal with the abundance of hardware they may encounter. One of the advantages of vSphere VMs is its hardware abstraction, which means many of these features to deal with hardware and drivers aren't required.

Templates should be regularly updated. Applying OS and application patches and new antivirus definitions and policies minimizes the post-deployment steps and helps to reduce bandwidth. Rather than patch every new VM, why not patch one template? This means a regular cycle of patching should occur. To update or change a template, convert it into a VM, make the changes, and convert it back.

You should also think about how you'll push out new templates and template updates to multiple sites, if this is a requirement. Although hosts can use a common set of templates, those templates need to be stored on accessible storage. Normally, each site has its own shared storage; so if you're updating your templates regularly, you have two choices. You can either touch every template across every site with the same patches and updates, or you can keep one master set of templates that you update, and replicate these everywhere else. If you already possess some sort of SAN replication technology that only copies delta blocks, you can use it to minimize the bandwidth required to push out all templates again.

Guest Customization

A guest customization wizard automatically starts when you deploy a VM from a template. It asks all the questions required to customize the image and saves you from having to manually configure each piece in the guest. You can also use guest customization after cloning a VM, to make the clone safe to bring online alongside the original.

You can store a number of guest customizations, specific to each template or OS, which contain the majority of the answers needed in the wizard. Each of these guest customization specifications can be managed separately in the vSphere Client. Generally, one specification per OS is sufficient, because it is the license key that will separate them.

The source guest must have VMware tools already installed and must match the correct OS that is specified in the VM's resources settings. The customization searches for the OS on the first disk, which must be SCSI-based. It won't work if it can't find the OS files it expects. It basically mounts the virtual disk after deployment and makes the changes it needs directly on the guest's file system. Only certain Windows and Linux guest OSs are supported, so check the latest VMware documentation to ensure that your guests can be customized with this tool.

Sysprep

Sysprep is Microsoft's systems preparation tool, which you can use to make Windows images and generalize them. Doing so clears the settings that make each Windows installation unique and creates new hostnames, SIDs, and driver caches.

vCenter can take advantage of these tools during a guest customization if the tools are copied onto the vCenter server. Different versions of sysprep exist for different Windows OSs, so one must be uploaded for each version you expect to deploy. With Windows 2008 and beyond, you no longer need to install external sysprep tools. Normally, when you use sysprep with a disk-imaging system, you need to prepare images, seal them, create answer files, and so on. However, the guest customization process automates these steps and prompts the user during the template wizard.

Preparing a Template

When you're creating a VM to make into a template, start with a fresh image. Create the VM based on the correct OS, and then take the time to configure the hardware components and advanced options to suit the template. Follow the advice from throughout this chapter and think about the purpose of the VMs being deployed from this template. Try to pick what you consider the minimum hardware requirements.

You don't want to initially overprovision, or you'll waste valuable hardware resources for every VM that doesn't use them. But be realistic about the minimum OS and application requirements for the template, particularly memory and disk space. Under-provisioning will lead to extra work when every image has to be changed after you deploy it. Always try to use a single CPU, unless the template is specifically for an application that will always require more than one. Remember that newer OSs require different minimum levels: just because you could get away with 256 MB of memory and a 10 GB hard drive for a Windows XP VM, that doesn't mean a base Windows 2008 template should be the same.

For very large environments, consider a set of hardware tiered templates for the most common OSs. This not only saves you from having to change the hardware setup on each of these VMs after they're built but also helps to standardize the result.

Remember to go through each template and remove or at least disable the hardware that isn't required. Items such as floppy drives and serial and parallel ports are rarely needed and place a tax on the host hardware for every VM deployed. This is also a great opportunity to take advantage of newer hardware options such as VMXNET 3 and PVSCSI adapters.

When you're installing the OS and the applications, try to make the image as clean as possible. Make sure it's built from scratch, explicitly for its purpose. Follow the disk-alignment advice from earlier in the chapter to make sure all disks are aligned from the outset. Include all the tools that need to be installed on every VM, such as antivirus software, admin tools, and company templates. Apply OS or application customizations that are individual to your organization, such as specifying wallpaper, creating specific directories, changing drive letters, making registry settings, and modifying profiles.

Avoid including anything that won't be needed. For example, try to avoid the temptation to copy all the application-install files locally, because they will be duplicated every time. Keep one copy centrally. Disabling hibernation on Windows guests removes the very large `hiberfile.sys` file; this feature won't be used. Actively strip out software and stop services that the VMs don't need. Many of the basic premises that you follow when creating a standard workstation image for corporate desktops also apply here.

After the VM is built and the OS and applications are installed, be sure you patch the OS with all the latest updates and install VMware tools. Shut down the VM, and make any final hardware changes. You may want to think about setting the network adapter to a port group with no external access or to a clean subnet. Then, you can deploy each VM, patch it, and apply its antivirus definition update before attaching it to the corporate network.

OVF Standard

VMs can also be distributed in a standard format package known as Open VM Format (OVF). This is a template format created by the Distributed Management Task Force (DMTF) standards group to allow an interchangeable VM, which can be used by software companies to distribute VMs. The vSphere Client can import and export OVF files (or OVA files, which are tarball archives of OVF files encapsulated in one file).

OVF files tend to be used by software vendors to distribute hypervisor-agnostic VMs. These VM appliances normally include tuned OSs and applications that are easy for customers to deploy and easy for software companies to support.

One of the current limitations of the 1.0 standard is the lack of definition for virtual disks. OVF files can include disks in several formats, so non-VMware disk files need to be imported via VMware Converter first.

vApps

vApps are containers for one or more VMs that allow those VMs to be treated as a single entity. vApps can be powered on, powered off, and cloned in one action. You can import entire vApps, which collectively run an application or service, in much the same way that OVF files are distributed for single VM applications.

vApps are a potentially useful packaging technique, although they have been slow to amass large adoption.

Virtual Machine Availability

When you're designing VMs to provide greater uptime, remember the difference between VM-level clustering, OS-level clustering, and application-level clustering. They all provide alternative types of failover, but each is aimed at protecting different parts of the stack.

Host-level clustering ensures that the VM is turned on, and recovers it if it unexpectedly powers off for any reason (for example, if a host fails). Guest OS-level clustering checks that the OS is up and responding. Common techniques include checking network pings or the VMware tools' heartbeat. Application clustering monitors application services to ensure that certain software is responding to requests as it should.

vSphere 4 offers a multitude of high-availability options to protect your VMs from unexpected failures. In addition to the built-in solutions, several third-party VM failover and clustering methods exist. Table 7.3 shows how each option protects against the different types of failures:

TABLE 7.3:   VM availability options

PROTECTION MEASURES	HOST FAILURE	GUEST OS FAILURE	APPLICATION FAILURE
HA failover	✓		
Host VM startup	✓		
DRS Affinity rules	✓		
HA VM monitoring		✓	
HA Application monitoring			✓
Fault Tolerance	✓		
Microsoft clustering	(If CAB or n+1)	✓	✓
Microsoft NLB	(If VMs split with anti-affinity rules)	✓	

vSphere VM Availability

Most high-availability approaches included in vSphere are functions of DRS and HA clusters, and as such we'll discuss them in much greater length in Chapter 8, "Datacenter Design." Because they will affect your VM guest planning, we'll briefly explain each tool's use and how it can provide a more resilient base for your VMs:

HA Failover   HA enabled clusters protect VMs from host failures. If the cluster determines that a host failure has occurred, the VMs that were running on the failed host are automatically powered-up on alternate hosts.

VM Startup   On each host, you can set the VMs to start up (and shut down) automatically, controlling their startup order and a delay between each VM's startup. Figure 7.20 shows these settings. This automatic recovery for a host can be very useful in single-server, local storage sites or companies not licensed for HA. When a host is added to an HA-enabled cluster, this option is disabled.

FIGURE 7.20

VM startup/
shutdown

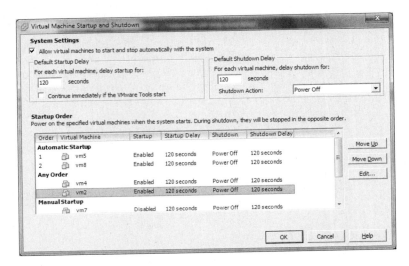

Affinity Rules   Affinity rules and anti-affinity rules are functions of DRS and aren't strictly for HA purposes. However, you can use anti-affinity rules to ensure that load-balancing VMs are spread across more than one host. This means that if a host fails, not all VM nodes will be lost at the same time.

Affinity rules can keep VMs together and can be used in availability planning. Keeping VMs together may seem like a contradictory way to provide better redundancy. But if you consider a situation in which multiple VM instances need to be up for an application to work properly, then splitting them apart won't help provide redundancy. Keeping them together on a single host lessens the chance that one of the VMs will be on a host that fails.

VM Monitoring   VM monitoring is a function of an HA cluster. It uses the VMware tools' heartbeat to check that the OS is still responding, and thus helps to protect against a Blue Screen of Death (BSOD) or kernel panics. The hostd daemon passes the heartbeat, which by default is sent out every second to the vCenter server. If a VM's heartbeat is lost, it checks for network and storage I/O to prevent false positives. If nothing is received for a set period, vCenter resets the VM. Different levels of sensitivity are available; you can configure them using the slider shown in Figure 7.21.

Application Monitoring   vSphere 4.1 has introduced a new application monitoring control that works in the same way, but for known applications. This functionality uses a VMware API, which software vendors must incorporate in their application to allow vCenter to provide monitoring.

FIGURE 7.21
VM monitoring

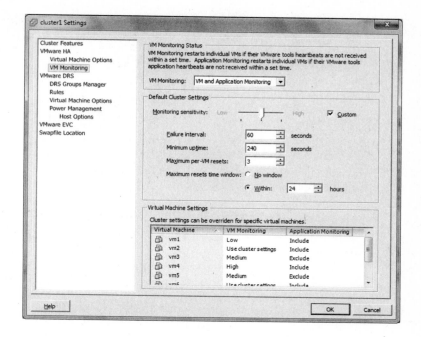

Fault Tolerance FT protects against failed hosts by keeping a second image of the VM running on a second host in the same HA cluster. FT impacts both DRS and HA designs; for this reason, a full examination is left to the next chapter.

However, for VM design, it's important to understand that FT places a number of restrictions on the VM being protected:

- It must be on shared storage that's visible to hosts in the HA cluster.
- Only single vCPUs can be protected.
- You can't use physical RDMs.
- No snapshots are allowed.
- You can't use Storage vMotion.
- You can't use NPIV.
- FT converts all disks to eager zeroed thick format.
- You can't use hot-plugging devices.
- No USB devices, sound devices, serial ports, or parallel ports are allowed.
- No physical or remote CD/floppy devices are allowed.
- The VMs must be hardware version 7.

- Only some guest OSs are supported (see http://kb.vmware.com/kb/1008027).

- You can't use VMI (paravirtualized) VMs.

- FT sets the VM's memory reservation equal to its RAM setting to prevent ballooning or swapping.

If you plan to protect a VM with FT, you should look carefully at how it will impact your VM design.

Third-Party VM Clustering

In addition to the host, DRS, and HA tools providing higher availability for VMs, you can use several in-guest clustering techniques. Guest OSs often have built-in clustering features, and many more third-party solutions are available. In this chapter we'll look at the two most common methods used, both for Microsoft OSs: clustering and NLB.

Microsoft Clustering

Microsoft Clustering Service (MSCS), or Failover Clustering as it's now known, is a widely used clustering technique for Microsoft servers. It's relatively complicated to configure, particularly in the VMware world. Many alternative options are now available to provide HA, but MSCS is so heavily ingrained as a solution that it's still a popular choice.

Microsoft clustering is available on Windows 2003 and 2008 in their Enterprise and Datacenter editions. It supports 8 nodes on 2003 and 16 nodes on 2008; but because vSphere emulates a SCSI connection as opposed to a FC switch fabric when presenting its disks, the clustering is limited to only 2 nodes. Windows 2000 MSCS VMs are supported in vSphere 4.0 but not in version 4.1, so before upgrading hosts to this version you must upgrade the guest OSs.

You can configure MSCS in vSphere three ways:

Cluster in a Box   CIB is the configuration when both MSCS servers are VMs running on the same vSphere host. Although it's marginally easier to set up, this configuration is somewhat pointless because it doesn't protect against a hardware failure of the single vSphere host. Even as a test setup, it's unlikely to mimic a production situation sufficiently. VMDK files are recommended for the shared disks, although virtual RDMs give you the option to move to a CAB solution in the future if a second host becomes available.

Cluster Across Boxes   CAB describes the situation when MSCS is deployed in two VMs, and the two VMs are split across two different hosts. This protects against a single host failure. If you're deploying this configuration, you should use vSphere 4.1, because version 4.0 doesn't support MSCS being part of a DRS/HA enabled cluster. Physical RDMs are now the recommended disk option with vSphere.

Physical to Virtual   Physical to virtual (n+1) clusters allow one MSCS cluster node to run natively on a physical server while the other runs in a VM. This configuration is popular when a physical server is still deemed a necessity, but failover can be handled by a VM. A physical RDM is required in this instance.

MSCS Limitations

MSCS has the following design limitations when run on vSphere:

- Windows 2000 VMs are no longer supported from vSphere 4.1; only 2003 SP2 and 2008 R2 are supported.

- DRS/HA cluster compatibility requires vSphere 4.1.

- Only two node clusters are possible.

- You must use VM hardware version 7.

- Shared disks need to be the eager zeroed thick type. See Figure 7.19 for the check box to enable this setting when creating disks in the client.

- Only Fibre Channel SANs are supported. iSCSI, Fibre Channel over Ethernet (FCoE), and Network File System (NFS) shared storage aren't supported.

- There is no support for vMotion, FT VMs, NPIV, and round-robin multipathing.

Disk Types

Table 7.4 shows the different disk types that are supported for each configuration:

TABLE 7.4:   MSCS disk options (items in bold show VMware's recommended option)

	VMDK	VIRTUAL RDM	PHYSICAL RDM
Cluster in a box (CIB)	**Yes**	Yes	No
Cluster across boxes (CAB)	No	Yes (not 2008)	**Yes**
Physical and virtual (n+1)	No	No	**Yes**

SCSI Controller Settings

SCSI controller settings create the most common design misunderstanding for MSCS VMs. There are two different settings, which sound very similar:

- Disk types (selected when you add a new disk): VMDK, virtual RDM (virtual compatibility mode) or physical RDM (physical compatibility mode)

- SCSI bus-sharing setting: virtual sharing policy or physical sharing policy (or none)

These settings are distinct. Just because you choose a virtual RDM doesn't mean the SCSI controller should necessarily be set to Virtual.

The SCSI bus-sharing setting is often missed, because you don't manually add the second controller (you can't). You need to go back to the settings after you've added the first shared disk. There are settings here:

- None: disks that aren't shared between VMs. This is used for disks that aren't shared in the cluster, such as the VM's boot disks. This is why shared disks must be on a second SCSI controller.

- Virtual: only for CIB shared disks.

- Physical: for CAB and n + 1 shared disks.

Design for an HA/DRS Cluster

Since vSphere 4.1, MSCS can be members of HA and DRS clusters. However, to make sure the HA or DRS clustering functions don't interfere with MSCS, you need to apply special settings:

DRS-Only Clusters   vMotioning MSCS VMs isn't recommended, so you need to set the VMs with an individual DRS setting of *Partially Automatic*. To ensure that all the cluster's affinity rules are considered must rules, you can set the advanced DRS setting ForceAffinityPoweron to equal 0 (zero).

For CIB VMs, create a VM-to-VM affinity rule to keep them together. For CAB VMs, create a VM-to-VM anti-affinity rule to keep them apart. These rules should be *must* rules. n+1 VMs don't need any special affinity rules.

HA-Enabled Clusters   To run MSCS VMs in an HA cluster, you need to use affinity rules. This means you must also enable DRS and implement the DRS VM-to-VM rules. HA also needs additional Host-to-VM rules, because HA doesn't consider the VM-to-VM rules when recovering VMs.

CIB VMs must be in the same VM DRS group, which must be linked to a host DRS group, containing just two hosts, using a *Must run on hosts in group* rule.CAB VMs must be in different VM DRS groups, which must be linked to the different host DRS groups using a *Must run on hosts in group* rule. Again, n+1 VMs don't need any special affinity rules. See figure 7.22 to see how these VMs should be configured in an HA cluster.

FIGURE 7.22
MSCS VMs using VM/Host DRS groups in an HA cluster

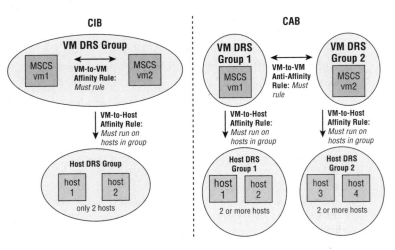

Microsoft **NLB**

Microsoft Network Load Balancing (NLB) is an IP-based clustering technique included in Windows 2000 Advanced Server, 2003, and 2008. All the hosts receive the requests, and a special network-driver algorithm decides which host should respond while all other hosts drop the request. An NLB cluster can support up to 32 nodes.

The NLB servers exchange a heartbeat to detect failures, and they redistribute requests to servers that continue to operate. NLB has two modes:

Multicast   Multicast mode adds a Layer 2 multicast address to the cluster adapter. However, some routers and Layer 2 switches don't support this, and you must add a static ARP entry to map the cluster IP address to the MAC address.

Unicast   Unicast has the advantage of working with all Layer 2 devices, but it causes all ports to be flooded with NLB traffic. Unicast NLB VMs need a second vNIC, and you must set the port group on the vSwitch to accept forged transmits.

VMware recommends that you use multicast mode whenever possible, because you don't need to make any changes on the hosts, and no broadcast port flooding will occur.

In a DRS cluster, be sure to set anti-affinity rules to try to protect NLB VMs against host failures.

Summary

VM design is a seminal topic, which all too frequently doesn't receive the sort of attention it should during a vSphere design. Its importance can't be stressed too heavily. A good VM design looks carefully at each VM component, analyzing what can benefit the environment and what is superfluous.

Good VM design makes use of the underlying hardware, identifying the needs of the VMs, and understands how to create a successful model. Undoubtedly the biggest common mistake is treating VMs like physical machines, undervaluing the gains you can make in customizing them and overprovisioning the hardware. Most physical hardware is more than sufficient for most purposes, so there is little benefit in stripping out hardware and software and changing the base system configurations that are offered. However, in vSphere, despite the defaults that give you workable VMs, when you hope to densely pack the host with tens of VMs, that extra 10 or 20 percent of performance can mean significantly more VMs.

VM storage is of particular note, because this is often where performance bottlenecks occur. CPU and memory are also critical because they lay claim to the server hardware and dictate how many VMs you can squeeze onto each, and how much additional capacity you have for growth and redundancy. Overprovisioning some VMs will only have a detrimental effect on the other VMs.

In addition to the VM's hardware, its guest OS, applications, and running processes are ripe for trimming. As we discussed regarding host hardware in Chapter 4, you may be able to scale VMs out instead of upward, avoiding very large VMs.

All these constituent parts can be melded into a small selection of templates. Templates give you the power to effectively enforce your discretionary work in a scalable fashion. It wouldn't be feasible to maintain this level of thoroughness for every VM, but templates provide the mechanism to create this initial consistency.

As you've seen, various options exist to protect your VMs. The next chapter looks at how vCenter design and cluster techniques can make the most of these VM designs, to effectively and efficiently spread resources across hosts, maintain high availability, and organize hosts and VMs.

Chapter 8

Datacenter Design

vCenter functionality gives rise to many design possibilities, particularly the combination of vCenter and the Advanced through Enterprise Plus licensing features. This chapter explores some of those options, such as the ability to design-in redundancy, and share resources efficiently between hosts to offer a fair proportion of hardware while enforcing VM protection. Unused servers can be shut down to reduce power costs, and VMs can automatically balance among hosts in concert with rules to apply control where required.

The chapter looks at the ways in which vSphere objects are flexible enough to create designs optimized for your particular environment. You can control security permissions, collectively manage objects, monitor and schedule tasks in your datacenters easily and effectively.

This chapter will cover the following topics:

◆ How objects in vCenter interact and create a hierarchy

◆ Why clusters are central to your vCenter design

◆ Resource pool settings

◆ Using distributed resource scheduling to load-balance, save power, and control VM placement

◆ How high availability recovers VMs quickly when host failures occur

◆ Using fault tolerance to provide maximum VM availability

vSphere Inventory Structure

Launching the vSphere client presents the Home dashboard, a collection of icons organized by function. The first functional area is Inventory, as shown in Figure 8.1.

FIGURE 8.1
vSphere Home dashboard

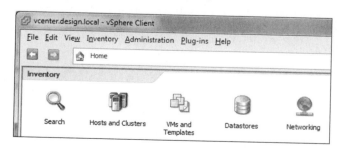

Inventory has four different views, along with a search option. The four views are:

◆ Hosts and Clusters

◆ VMs and Templates

◆ Datastores

◆ Networking

These views present items from the inventory, each following the same basic structure but still capable of including its own objects. Although the object types can differ, the hierarchical elements are common to all the views.

The relationship between the elements differs depending on how you use the client. The client can connect directly to hosts or vCenter servers. As discussed in Chapter 3, "Designing the Management Layer," you can also connect vCenter servers via linked mode, which aggregates multiple instances.

The inventory structure creates a delineation that serves a number of purposes. It helps you organize all the elements into more manageable chunks, making them easier to find and work with. Monitoring can be arranged around the levels with associated alarms; events will trigger different responses, depending on their place in the structure. You can set security permissions on hierarchical objects, meaning you can split up permissions as required for different areas and also nest and group permissions as needed. Perhaps most important, the inventory structure permits certain functionality in groups of objects, so they can work together. This chapter will discuss some of that functionality in much more depth.

Inventory Root

The inventory root object is a special type of folder. It's the starting point of all objects in the client and the top level for all permissions and alarms. Every object and function cascades from this one element, and their interrelationships can always be traced back to the root.

When connected directly to a host, the inventory root is the host itself. When the client is pointing to a vCenter server, the root object is effectively the vCenter server. If the vCenter server is part of a linked mode group, you'll see several root inventory objects, one for each vCenter. The vCenter root object can contain only folders and datacenter objects.

Folders

Folders are a purely organizational element, used to structure and group other elements. They let you manage objects collectively, such as applying permissions across a group of datacenters. Folders are a vCenter feature, so they're available only when the client is connected to a vCenter Server instance. Folders can also contain child folders, to allow for more complex organization.

Folders can only contain objects of the same type; you can use them at various levels and in different views to consolidate like items. Folders can contain subfolders, datacenters, clusters, hosts, VMs, templates, datastores, or networks. Each inventory view can have its own sets of folders, so the Hosts and Clusters view can have a folder structure that's different than that of the VMs and Templates view. But folders off the root object are common to all views.

They're a very flexible way to organize vCenter items without having to adhere to the normal rules that limit other objects.

Datacenters

Datacenters are the basic building blocks of a vCenter structural design. They make up all the objects needed for virtualization and are visible in all four Inventory views. Folders are useful for organizing elements, but datacenters are always required because they directly house the hosts, clusters, and VMs.

Datacenters are a vCenter-only construct; they aren't available to stand-alone hosts and aren't visible when the Client is directly connected to hosts. They're the boundary to vMotions, which means your datacenter design should consider the network and storage topology, as this is often what separates one datastore from another.

Remember that despite the moniker, a datacenter doesn't necessarily have to align with a physical datacenter or server-room location. However, network and storage connections do tend to be determined by geographical location, so it's common to see this parallel used.

Clusters

A cluster is a vCenter-only element that collects hosts together from a single datacenter to aggregate compute resources. A datacenter can contain multiple clusters. A cluster groups hosts to provide additional functionality, allowing the hosts and VMs to work together. Clusters can have hosts, resource pools, VMs, and vApps as child objects.

Cluster functionality is further described in later sections of this chapter.

Resource Pools

Resource pools can exist on vCenter instances in clusters or under hosts. They let you divide and apportion the available CPU and memory resources from a cluster or host. You can further subdivide resource pools by using subordinate resource pools. VMs draw their CPU and memory requirements from the resource pool in which they reside.

When you use resource pools on a vCenter cluster, the cluster must have distributed resource scheduling (DRS) enabled. You shouldn't use resource pools as a substitute for folders to organize VMs.

Resource pools are examined in more detail later in this chapter.

Hosts

A host represents a physical server running either vSphere ESX or ESXi hypervisor. Both types can coexist in a cluster, although the host's CPU will determine compatibility with other hosts in the same cluster.

Hosts can have resource pools and VMs under them in the structure. The host is the top-level root object when the vSphere client is logged in to a host directly.

Virtual Machines

VMs can be seen in all four Inventory views, but VM management tends to revolve around the Hosts and Clusters view and the VMs and Templates view. The former concentrates on a VM's physical hardware location: the host, cluster, and resource pool in which it resides. The latter shows the logical groupings you create in the datacenter to organize the VMs.

TIP If you have a sizable number of VMs, you'll find that whenever you expand a container that holds those VMs, the organizational left pane of the client is lost in a sea of VM objects. You can use a client option to maintain an overview. Choose Edit ➢ Client Settings ➢ Lists tab, and deselect the Show Virtual Machines In The Inventory check box. This setting only applies to the active view and unfortunately isn't persistent.

Templates

A template is a special type of VM that's only displayed in the VMs and Templates view. Because templates are a vCenter-only feature, they aren't visible when the client is connected directly to a host. Templates were discussed in Chapter 7, "Virtual Machines."

Datastores

The Datastores view shows all available storage for each datacenter. It collates all local host storage and shared SAN and NAS datastores, allowing common management for all types. You can organize this vCenter-only view using datastore folders to help pool all the sources into logical groupings.

Networks

In the Networking view, all the Port Groups and dvPort Groups are collected under each datacenter. As long as different hosts' port groups are named identically, this view treats them together, in the same way that vMotion understands them to be the same. This lets you manage them collectively so you can apply permissions and alarms. You can use folders in the Networking view to group and split port groups, although this view is available only through vCenter connections.

Why and How to Structure

From a design perspective, it's important to reiterate the advantages of using hierarchical structuring:

◆ Enables certain functionality via the grouping of similar elements

◆ Aids management

◆ Allows granular permissions

◆ Lets you monitor events and tasks at different levels

◆ Lets you set alarms and responses based on the structure

◆ Lets you align scheduled tasks to the same groupings

You can organize your vCenter pieces in several ways. The most successful hierarchical designs usually closely follow the business. This makes it easy for everyone to understand the structure, to apply the appropriate importance and focus to key elements, and to provide suitable resources.

Most designs follow one or more of the following approaches:

Geographical This structure is split according to the physical location of equipment.

Departmental This structure is appropriate if a business's IT equipment and staffing are delivered based on department.

Business Costing Structure   This hierarchy works if the OPEX and CAPEX are split into different areas and chargeback figures are subsequently applied.

Business Function   This structure is appropriate if a business is naturally split around the products and services it provides.

Projects   Certain projects may fund and resource separate parts of the infrastructure.

Priority   vCenter elements can enable redundancy and provide resource allocation. If some VMs require different service-level agreements (SLAs) or performance, then this can dictate structure.

Connectivity   The link speed and latency of both networks and storage may influence structure.

Equipment   Access to different server equipment (such as Intel or AMD), network switches, and shared storage can split infrastructure apart.

Licensing   In some cases, application software licensing may require segregated resources.

Usually, businesses use a hybrid solution consisting of several elements from this list. The hierarchy itself is normally scaled on the size of the business's VM deployment. A small company with one or two hosts may have a practically flat structure. However, a large organization can have many tiers. For example, an enterprise may have several linked vCenters to create a hard permissions division, each with a layer of folders to group several datacenters together; more folders under each datacenter to consolidate some hosts and clusters while segregating others; and an entire tree of resource pool levels to tightly control allocation. Figure 8.2 demonstrates some of the structural elements and options you may encounter.

FIGURE 8.2
vCenter structural
example

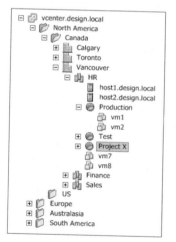

Clusters

vCenter clusters group hosts together for two main reasons. Clusters allow the hosts to work together, enabling the use of both high availability (HA) and DRS. These two cluster functions are examined more closely in their own sections later in the chapter. But it's worth considering the cluster itself as a vehicle to support hosts and VMs.

Although this isn't a strict requirement of a cluster, the cluster's power is realized when the hosts have access to the same shared storage and networking. This allows HA and DRS to work across the cluster, and prevents VM incompatibilities that would inhibit HA or DRS from functioning effectively.

It's often advisable to zone your shared storage to the clusters, because doing so simplifies I/O and capacity resourcing as well as storage management. vMotion is possible across clusters in the same datacenter; so, to provide more flexibility, you can zone at the datastore level.

To take full advantage of DRS, you should collocate servers with the same CPU manufacturer into the same cluster. As we'll explain in the next section, Enhanced vMotion Compatibility (EVC) can assist with compatibility between different versions from the same chip manufacturer. However, if you have a mixture of AMD and Intel, and you'll rely on any feature that uses vMotion, then you should split these two manufacturers' chips into separate clusters.

You should also keep the host versions consistent in a cluster. It's always advisable to keep all host patching at the same level. Mixing ESX and ESXi hosts in a cluster is a viable configuration and fully supported by VMware. But for several compatibility reasons, such as VM hardware versioning, it's common for older 3.5 hosts to be placed in a separate cluster.

There are several reasons why you may want to create a cluster to house hosts, even if you don't enable DRS or HA:

Future Planning Even though a cluster's benefits aren't realized until there are multiple hosts, when you initially deploy the first host, you may want to include it in a cluster. As your environment grows and hosts are added, the basic cluster will already be available.

Consistency If you have several other datacenter or cluster elements, you may find that even single-node clusters helps keep management decisions consistent. For example, you may want to apply all permissions at a cluster level across your organization. Even though you may not be using DRS or HA, the cluster can apply the same settings across all the hosts and to any future hosts you add.

Host Profiles Enterprise Plus licensing includes host profiles, which lets you apply a common host configuration to multiple servers. This profile can be deployed to a single host but can also be used across a cluster of hosts, which means greater host standardization for existing and future cluster hosts. Host profiles not only apply a set configuration during the initial deployment, in the way a scripted install might, but also allows compliancy checking throughout the lifetime of the host.

Monitoring When several hosts are members of a cluster, it's easy to compare their performance against each other. Alarms, tasks, and events for all the hosts can be viewed and managed together.

When you're considering clusters without DRS/HA enabled, note that although a stand-alone host can have resource pools, hosts in a cluster with DRS turned off can't. Adding a host to a cluster without DRS strips all the host's resource pool settings. A host without resource pools can still set shares, limits, and reservations, as discussed in Chapter 7, but they will be apportioned in relation to the host and can't be subdivided or spread across the cluster.

You can independently disable HA and DRS at any time at the cluster level. But doing so loses all the associated settings, including any advanced settings that were configured. If you need to temporarily stop a subcomponent of DRS or HA, you should disable the specific undesired function. This way, you can retain the configuration, so that when the feature is reenabled, the same settings are applied again. This is particularly important for DRS, because disabling DRS completely destroys all the resource pools.

There are two other separate cluster settings, which aren't directly related to DRS or HA functionality: EVC and default swapfile locations.

EVC

Enhanced vMotion Compatibility (EVC) is a feature that improves the ability to vMotion VMs between hosts that don't have CPUs from the same family. When you enable EVC, the cluster has to be set for either Intel or AMD chips and must have a minimum baseline level.

Chapter 7 discussed a compatibility feature that hides certain host CPU flags from the VM. Many of the CPU extensions presented by modern CPUs aren't used by VMs and can be safely hidden. EVC is a development of this, and works by applying CPU masks across all the hosts.

To enable EVC on a cluster, you must first turn off all the VMs. Therefore, it's important that when you create a new cluster, if you intend to house varying levels of CPU hardware in it, you enable this from the outset.

Each CPU type, whether Intel or AMD, has a list of compatibility levels. You should be sure you select the lowest level required to support the oldest CPUs that will be members of the cluster. Add the oldest host first: doing so ensures that the least feature-full host will be checked against the baseline before you start creating or transferring VMs to the cluster.

CAN I TURN ON EVC WITHOUT AN OUTAGE TO MY VMS?

If you have an existing cluster without EVC enabled, or a host that isn't at a compatible level, then it may be possible to enable EVC without an outage across the cluster's VMs. Carefully record all the cluster settings, including any advanced settings, resource pool configurations, VM options, and resource allocations. Create a new cluster, enable EVC at the lowest level required, and re-create the same cluster settings used in the old cluster. In the old cluster, clear the VMs from the least capable host (you can use DRS and maintenance mode to automate this step), and add that host to the new cluster. Start to vMotion the VMs across clusters, moving hosts when they have been freed up.

This technique works if you're using similarly compatible hosts or adding hosts that are newer. However, it may not work if you're adding older hosts. When you start to vMotion VMs, if the destination is an older-generation CPU or masked down to a lower level, this approach will fail.

Swapfile Policy

By default, a VM's swapfiles are stored along with its other files, in a location that's determined by the *working directory* setting. The swapfile in this case isn't the guest OS's pagefile or swap partition but the file used by the hypervisor to supplement physical RAM. You can find more details about host memory in Chapter 4, "Server Hardware."

The swapfile location is configurable on a VM-by-VM basis, but this cluster-level setting sets a default for all the VMs. You can choose to move all of these swapfiles to a location set on each host. This can be useful for a couple of reasons:

Moving Swap Off Expensive Storage If the VM is on expensive shared storage, then this approach gives you the option to move it onto less-expensive shared storage (for example, from a RAID 10 LUN to a RAID 6 LUN) or even local host storage.

Preventing Swap from Being on LUNs Using Certain SAN Technologies If the VM's LUNs are using SAN technologies such as replication, snapshots, and deduplication, then it may not be desirable to also store the swap in this area.

Moving swap onto another less-expensive or nonreplicated SAN LUN is practical, but moving it onto the local host disk does have implications. First, vMotions will take considerably longer, because the swapfile will need to be copied across the network every time. In addition, using local-host storage can have unexpected results for other cluster functions. You need to be sure there is sufficient space on all the hosts to hold any possible configuration needs. HA or DRS won't operate effectively if it can't rely on swap space being available on the hosts.

Cluster Sizing

There are several hard limits related to cluster sizing. First, you can have a maximum of 32 hosts per cluster, and 3000 VMs (although vSphere 4.0 allows only 1280). DRS and HA functions can impact the size of your clusters in their own way, as explained later in this chapter. Suffice it to say, just because you can have 32 hosts in a cluster doesn't mean you should plan it out that way.

Despite the fact that other aspects are likely to impose cluster-size constraints of their own, the following principles of cluster sizing are still relevant:

Larger but Fewer Clusters   Larger clusters generally mean they're more efficient. To provide n+1 or n+2 redundancy takes fewer hosts when you have fewer clusters. Fewer clusters also mean less management overhead; and because there is more scope for consolidation, the design should be less expensive.

Smaller but More Clusters   You may want to split your clusters more because they create hard resource divisions. Although resource pools can segregate resources, their shares are proportionate to the rest of the pool, which changes as you add and remove VMs. Splitting hosts into small clusters better guarantees resources.

Resource Pools

Resource pools group VMs to allow dynamic allocation of CPU and memory resources. They can contain VMs but also child resource pools, enabling very fine-grained resource allocation. Resource pools can be found either under stand-alone hosts or as members of a DRS-enabled cluster.

We looked at resource allocation in some depth in Chapter 7, examining the use of shares, reservations, and limits, and how they can impact other VMs. But setting these values on every VM is time-consuming, is error-prone, and doesn't scale effectively. Setting these values on a resource pool is much more efficient, and the values dynamically readjust as VMs and host resources are added and removed.

VM resource settings can also set shares and input/output operations per second (IOPS) as limits for storage; and network I/O controls can set shares and bandwidth limits for vNetwork distributed switches (vDSs). However, resource pools concentrate only on CPU and memory resources.

Resource pools can have sibling pools at the same level and child pools beneath them. Each stand-alone host or DRS cluster is effectively a root resource pool, and all resource pools subsequently derive from that point. Child pools own some of their parents' resources and in turn can relinquish resources to their children.

Resource pools are very useful tools, but you shouldn't think of them as a substitute for VM folders. In the Hosts and Clusters view, folders are available at the root of the vCenter instance above datacenters, and below datacenters but above hosts and cluster items. No folder items are allowed inside the clusters themselves. For this reason, resource pools are often misappropriated as a way of grouping VMs into logical silos. However, even with the default values and no adjustment of the unlimited reservations and limits, resource pools still apply normal pool-level shares. Because they're filled with VMs, all the pools will continue to have the same value despite some having more VMs than others. During periods of contention, some VMs will receive more attention than others. If you create pools purely to group and organize your VMs, then this unexpected resource allocation will be undesired and unexpected. A better method of grouping VMs is to use the VMs and Templates view, which provides for grouping VMs into folders.

Resource Pool Settings

For each resource pool, you set CPU and memory shares, reservations, expandable reservations, and limits, as shown in Figure 8.3.

FIGURE 8.3

Resource pool settings

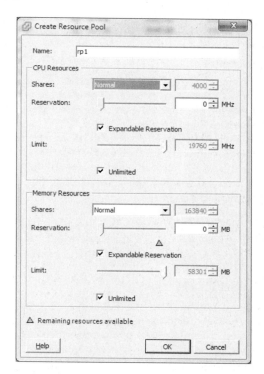

Most of these terms were discussed in Chapter 7, particularly the differences between how CPU and memory are handled. However, it's important to understand the concepts of allocation with regard to resource pools.

SHARES

The CPU or memory shares are relative to any sibling resource pools or VMs. Shares are used only during periods of contention and are always bound first by any reservations or limits. But if sufficient resources are available to all VMs in the resource pool, then shares are never invoked.

There are no guarantees with shares, and due to their dynamic nature, they can be unpredictable. A VM's resources are relative to the pool it resides in, so as the pool expands to accommodate new VMs, the pool's allocation is spread increasingly thin. Even if you give a particular resource pool a relatively high level of shares, if it has far more VMs than a sibling pool, you may find that its VMs actually receive fewer resources than those in a less densely populated pool.

Remember, VM shares are relative to the other VMs in the same pool, but resource pool shares are relative to sibling resource pools and sibling VMs. For this reason, it's recommended that you not make resource pools and VMs siblings at the same level in the hierarchy. VMs are unlikely to have share values comparable to the resource pools, so this would result in unbalanced clusters.

Resource pool shares are often the fairest way to allocated resources, but you must check them regularly to be sure you're getting the results you want. They're fickle if neglected for long and can eventually work against you. For example, it isn't uncommon to see a split of high, normal, and low resource pools. It's only human nature that everyone wants their VM in the high resource pool. You quickly end up with an overpopulated high resource pool that performs worse than the other two when resources become oversubscribed.

RESERVATIONS

A CPU or memory reservation guarantees resources to its resource pool occupants. Any reservation set is taken from its parent's unreserved amount, even if VMs don't use it. Reservations that are set too high can prevent other resource pools and sibling VMs from being able to operate properly or even from powering on.

Setting a resource pool reservation instantly prevents other siblings or the parent from reserving this amount themselves. Reservations should set the minimum amounts that are acceptable, because leftover resources are still apportioned over and above the reservation. If the resource pool reservations commit all of the cluster's memory, this can prevent VMs from vMotioning between hosts.

Resource pool reservations are a significantly better way to reserve memory than setting it on a per-VM basis. HA ignores the resource pool reservation, so these reservations don't have such a negative effect on HA slot sizes. They allow a guarantee for the VM's memory without the greed that is associated with VM-level memory reservations.

EXPANDABLE RESERVATIONS

The Expandable Reservation check box in the Create Resource Pool dialogue indicates whether a resource pool can steal resources from its parents to satisfy reservations defined at the VM's level. This is used during resource pool admission control, which is explained in the following section.

If powered-on VMs in a resource pool have reservations set that use the resource pool's entire reservation quota, then no more VMs are allowed to power-on — that is, unless the pool has an expandable reservation, which allows it to ask upward for more resources.

LIMITS

Just as with VM limits, resource pool limits artificially restrict the entire pool to certain amounts of CPU or memory. You can use this option to prevent a less important resource pool of VMs from impacting a more important pool. You should use this setting very sparingly; limits are hard and will take effect even if spare resources are available.

Admission Control

Admission control ensures that reservations are valid and can be met. The admission control depends on whether the resource pool's reservations are set as expandable.

Resource pool admission control is checked whenever:

◆ A VM in the resource pool is powered on

◆ A child resource pool is created

◆ The resource pool is reconfigured

If the reservations aren't expandable (the Expandable Reservation check box isn't selected), then admission control only checks to see whether the resource pool can guarantee the requirements. If it can't, then the VM doesn't power on, the child isn't created, or the pool isn't reconfigured.

If the reservations are expandable (the Expandable Reservation check box is selected, which is the default), then admission control can also consider the resource pool's parent. In turn, if that parent has its reservations set as expandable, then admission control can continue to look upward until the root is reached or it hits a pool without an expandable reservation.

Expandable reservations allow more VMs to be powered on but can lead to overcommitment. A child pool may reserve resources from a parent pool while some of the parent's VMs are powered off. Therefore, subordinates with expandable reservations must be trusted. This is particularly relevant if you use resource pools for permissions.

Distributed Resource Scheduling

Distributed resource scheduling (DRS) in vSphere clusters uses the power of vMotion to optimize cluster resources. Its primary function is to load-balance VMs across hosts to provide the best resource usage possible. DRS can use special rules to control VM placement, so that certain VMs can be kept together or apart depending on your requirements. A subfunction of DRS known as distributed power management (DPM) can use vMotion to selectively power down host servers while they aren't needed and power them back on automatically when they're required again.

Load Balancing

DRS monitors the CPU and memory load on the cluster's hosts and VMs, and tries to balance the requirements over the available resources. It can use vMotion to seamlessly move VMs when appropriate, effectively aggregating CPU and memory across the cluster.

DRS does this with two approaches. First, when VMs are powered on, it looks to see which host would be most suitable to run on. Second, while VMs are running, if DRS calculates that the resources have become unbalanced, it decides how to live-migrate VMs to minimize contention and improve performance.

When VMs in the cluster are powered on, DRS performs its own admission control to ensure that sufficient resources are present to support the VM. This is essentially recognition that the DRS cluster is itself a root resource pool and so follows the same resource checks.

DRS REQUIREMENTS

For DRS to load-balance effectively, you should adhere to a number of design requirements:

Shared Storage   In order for VMs to be vMotioned between hosts, they need to be stored on shared storage that all the hosts are configured to use.

vMotion-Compatible Hosts   The cluster's hosts should be vMotion-compatible with each other. This means their CPU must be of the same processor family. You can enable the EVC feature (discussed earlier) on the cluster to increase the likelihood that hosts will be compatible with each other. vMotion requires that the hosts be able to communicate with each other via TCP port 8000 in both directions.

vMotion-Compatible VMs   Chapter 7 explained the factors that prevent VMs from vMotioning across hosts in the cluster. Hardware version levels must be compatible with the hosts, and be sure you don't leave any host-attached hardware connected to the VMs.

No MSCS VMs   Microsoft clustering VMs can't vMotion between hosts.

VMkernel network   Each host needs to have a minimum 1 GbE connection to a shared VMkernel network.

DRS AUTOMATION LEVELS

A DRS cluster has an automation level that controls how autonomous the resource allocation is. Figure 8.4 shows the settings page for DRS levels.

FIGURE 8.4
DRS automation
levels

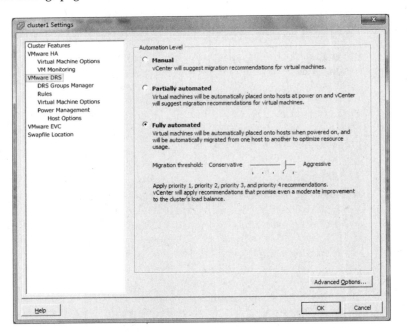

Manual   At the Manual level, DRS makes recommendations for the most suitable hosts during the VMs' initial placement and also makes ongoing migration suggestions. When the

VMs are powered on, DRS decides which is the best host and waits for the user to accept or override the recommendation. It continuously evaluates the cluster resources and proposes vMotions that would benefit the cluster and its VMs. At this level, DRS won't automatically evacuate VMs when the host is put into maintenance mode.

Partially Automated   The Partially Automated DRS level takes the initial placement recommendations and implements them without consulting the user. This ensures that from the outset, the VMs are on the best host, and notwithstanding the VMs' needs changing or hosts being added or removed, should mean a relatively balanced cluster. A partially automated cluster also makes ongoing migration suggestions but doesn't act on them independently.

Fully Automated   Fully automated DRS clusters not only place the VMs automatically on the best host when the VMs are powered on but also react to the resource levels on an ongoing basis, vMotioning VMs to different hosts as appropriate.

As you can see in Figure 8.4, the Fully Automated setting has a slider control that allows finer control over the cluster's propensity to vMotion VMs. The most conservative setting automatically moves VMs only when a top-priority migration is required — for example, if a host has been put into maintenance mode or standby mode. The most aggressive setting takes even the least advantageous recommendations, if it thinks they can benefit the clusters' resource-allocation spread.

VM OPTIONS (DRS)

DRS has the ability to override the cluster settings for individual VMs. Figure 8.5 displays all the possible options for a VM.

FIGURE 8.5
DRS VM options

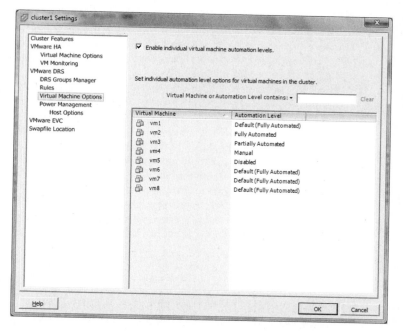

Each VM by default follows the cluster setting; but by being able to set a different level, you avoid the cluster being too prescriptive. Otherwise, the needs of single VM can force you to lower the cluster setting. With the per-VM option, if a particular VM needs to avoid being vMotioned, this doesn't have to affect the entire cluster. A common use of this override ability occurs if your vCenter server is itself a VM: you can pin that VM to a particular host. This makes it easy to find your vCenter VM in an emergency when it has been powered off.

BALANCING DECISIONS

The DRS threshold slider, shown in Figure 8.4, measures how much of an imbalance should be tolerated in the cluster. There are several reasons why the cluster should change after the initial placement of the VMs, such as changes to VM loads, affinity rules, reservations, or host availability.

Prior to vCenter 4.0, DRS used a star rating to show to show the varying levels of migration recommendations. A high star rating of 4 or 5 meant that a migration was highly recommended. However, with vSphere 4, this has changed to a priority rating, where a higher number indicates the opposite: the most-recommended migrations are given priority of 1 or 2. Although this makes sense, it can lead to confusion if you're used to looking for higher (not lower) numbers.

The DRS summary section, shown in Figure 8.6, displays the threshold settings.

FIGURE 8.6
DRS summary

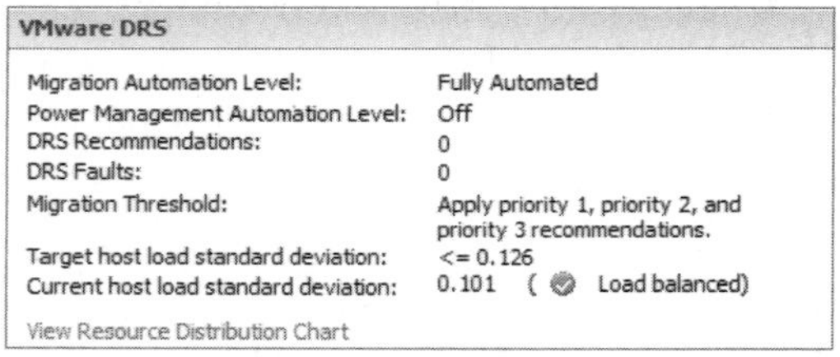

The threshold explains which priority level's recommendations are applied automatically. This threshold value, along with the amount of host resources available, determines the Target Host Load Standard Deviation. The Target is effectively a measure of how much the cluster is willing to accept a resource disparity.

Every five minutes, the DRS cluster calculates the corresponding Current Host Load Standard Deviation. The Current level is compared to the Target value; if it exceeds the Target, then a recommendation needs to be made. If the cluster is set to Fully Automated, then Current should always be below Target. But if the cluster is only Partially Automatic, then a Current value greater than Target shows that there are recommendations that haven't been followed.

If the cluster has decided that a migration needs to occur, it goes through a selection process to decide which is the next best candidate. It does this by evaluating each VM and seeing which one would make the largest improvement to the cluster. It also considers the vMotion history, and it drops VMs that have had problems migrating in the past. This is why DRS tends to move VMs that have the most vCPUs and biggest memory allocation: they're likely to have the greatest effect on the cluster's performance and reduce the amount of vMotions needed to balance the hosts.

DRS EFFICIENCY

Several factors determine how well DRS is able to perform. The hosts should be as similar as possible, to maintain vMotion compatibility and avoid different CPU and memory configurations. This allows the cluster to predict performance outcomes more accurately and consequently make better migration choices.

Try to minimize excessively loading VMs, because those with significantly more vCPUs or memory will ultimately reduce DRS opportunities. Where possible, shut down or suspend VMs that aren't being used, because they consume CPU and memory resources even when not being taxed. Disconnect any unused hardware, such as CD-ROMs, floppy drives, and serial and parallel ports, because they not only use CPU cycles but also reduce the vMotion possibilities. As stated earlier, reservations shouldn't be set too high and limits shouldn't be set too low, because this also affects the DRS calculations.

All DRS hosts should be able to access the same shared storage. If some hosts can only see portions of the storage, this separates the cluster and severely constrains the options for DRS migrations.

Temporarily disabling DRS causes all the resource pool and VM option settings to be lost. To preserve these for the future, you should set the cluster setting to Manual. That way, the resource pools will remain intact, and you just need to set the level back to what it was to restore the previous settings.

DRS Fully Automated mode ensures that the cluster is as balanced as it can be, without requiring intervention. When your hosts are as uniform as possible and your VMs maintain steady resource needs, you can set the cluster threshold more aggressively.

DRS doesn't solve underlying problems when there aren't enough resources to go around. It will however ensure that you're using the available resources in the best way possible.

Affinity Rules

Affinity rules are an additional feature of DRS that let you specify how to place VMs. The affinity rules that were present in vSphere 4.0 gave you control over keeping VMs together or apart. In vSphere 4.1, affinity rules took on a new set of functionality, known as VM-Host affinity rules. The original affinity rules for vSphere 4.0 are still available and now referred to as VM-VM affinity rules.

Both types of rules have the basic concept of *affinity* or *anti-affinity*. As you'd expect, affinity rules try to keep objects together, whereas anti-affinity rules aim to keep them apart.

VM-VM Affinity Rules

The VM-VM affinity rules have been around since pre-vSphere days and keep VMs together either on the same host (affinity) or on separate hosts (anti-**affinity**).

Figure 8.7 shows the DRS affinity rules screen. As you can see, the first rule is keeping VMs together, and the second is keeping them apart.

Rules can be created and not enabled. However, DRS disregards rules that aren't enabled. The vSphere client won't let you enable VM-VM rules that conflict with each other. For example, if a rule exists that keeps two VMs together, then although you can create a second rule to keep the same two VMs apart, you can't enable the second rule. The older rule will always take precedence, and the newer rule will be disabled if the older rule is ever enabled. If you have competing affinity and anti-affinity rules, DRS first tries to apply the anti-affinity rule, then the affinity rule.

Keep VMs Together

You may wish to keep VMs together on the same host to minimize the amount of inter-host network traffic. This is useful if two VMs work closely together — for example, an application that has a web server VM and a database VM. These two VMs may benefit from the reduced latency of the network traffic flowing between them, instead of between two hosts via a physical switch.

FIGURE 8.7
DRS affinity rules

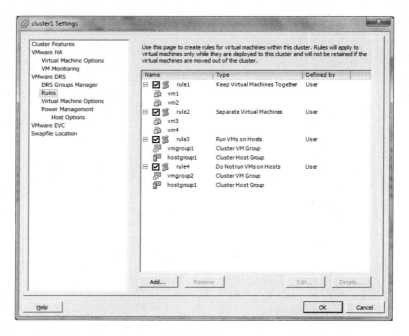

Also, if you have an application that needs multiple VMs to work, each of them being a potential single point of failure, then you may wish to keep them together. Allowing DRS to separate them only increases the chance that a host failure will affect the application.

Arguably, you can try to keep together VMs that are extremely similar, because you know this will benefit host transparent page sharing the most and reduce memory consumption. But DRS uses very sophisticated algorithms, so such rules are more likely to constrain potential optimizations and may make things worse.

Separate VMs

Rules to separate VMs tend to be used to guarantee that the VMs are always kept on different physical hardware. Applications that can provide redundancy between VMs can be protected against a single host failure. An example is a group of Network Load Balancing (NLB) web servers.

Another reason to keep VMs apart is if you know some VMs are very resource intensive, and for performance reasons you want them on separate hardware. This is particularly relevant if the VMs are inconsistently heavy and you find DRS doesn't do a good job of spreading their load.

With VM-VM anti-affinity rules, although you can state that you want VMs kept on separate hosts, you can't dictate which hosts. For that, you need a VM-Host rule.

VM-Host Affinity Rules

New with vSphere 4.1 are the VM-Host affinity rules that allow you to keep VMs on or off a group of hosts. To specify the groups of VMs and the groups of hosts for each rule, you use the new DRS Groups Manager pane (see Figure 8.8). Here you can create logical groupings of VMs and hosts that you want to use in your VM-Host rules.

FIGURE 8.8
DRS Groups
Manager

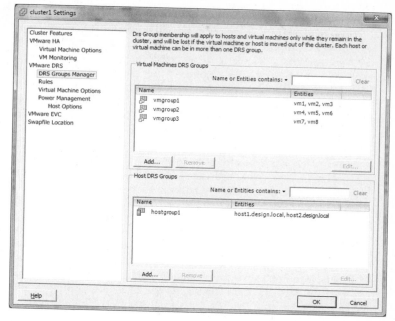

In Figure 8.7, the DRS Rules page, you can see that rules 3 and 4 use the VM groups and the hosts groups. The third rule specifies that a group of VMs should run on a group of hosts, whereas the last rule keeps the group of VMs away from the group of hosts.

In addition to the affinity and anti-affinity rules, VM-Host rules have the concept of *should* rules and *must* rules.

"Should" Rule

A "should" rule is one that DRS treats as a preference. DRS tries to adhere to the rules when it can but may violate them if other constraints are deemed more important. "Should" rules are always a best effort and allow DRS a certain amount of freedom. Similarly, DPM tries to conform to "should" rules but can break them if it needs to.

HA ignores "should" rules and powers on VMs in case of a failure regardless. But if DRS is set to Fully Automatic, it will then step in and rebalance the cluster according to the rules.

"Must" Rule

A "must" rule is a mandatory one that can't be broken by DRS, DPM, or HA. This level of strictness constrains cluster functionality and should be used only in exceptional circumstances. DRS won't power-on or load-balance VMs in a way that would violate a "must" rule, DPM won't power-off hosts if doing so would break a "must" rule, and HA will only recover VMs onto hosts that adhere to the "must" rule.

"Must" rules make certain hosts incompatible to VMs to enforce the rules for DRS, DPM, and HA. If DRS as a whole is disabled, these rules will continue to be enforced. DRS must be re-enabled if you need to disable a "must" rule.

Using VM-Host Rules

VM-Host affinity rules are useful in several ways. The classic "must" rule use case is to keep VMs tied to a group of hosts for licensing requirements. Some Independent Software Vendors' (ISVs) licensing depends on the physical hardware — often the CPU socket count. Prior to VM-Host rules, vSphere users created a separate cluster just for this purpose. Despite the fact that the separate cluster complied with the licensing terms, it often wasted spare resources, cost more in both OPEX and CAPEX terms, reduced redundancy possibilities, and gave the regular cluster fewer DRS/DPM/HA options. Such a situation is likely to use "must" rules.

Another good use of VM-Host rules is to keep VMs together or apart on a blade chassis or an entire rack. For the same reasons as VM-VM affinity and anti-affinity, you may consider blade systems one piece of hardware, even though as far as vSphere is concerned, they're all separate hosts. You can use VM-Host rules to keep network traffic together on one chassis or ensure that VMs are on blade hosts that are in different chassis to provide greater physical protection. These sorts of use cases are best set as "should" rules.

You can also use "should" VM-Host rules to provide soft partitioning for areas that previously you may have considered separate clusters in the same datacenters. You may have test and development environments that you want segregated from other VMs on their own hosts. You don't want the management overhead of complex resource pools and VM resource settings, but you want to keep all the VMs in the same cluster so you can take advantage of a pool of hosts that DRS and HA can optimize. Here you can use "should" rules to keep groups of VMs affined to hosts.

You should use mandatory "must" rules sparingly because they restrict the other cluster operations so much. They can divide the cluster, prevent HA from functioning properly, and go against DRS optimizations. If you're considering a "must" rule for a purpose other than licensing, consider a "should" rule with an associated alarm. You can create vCenter alarms to trigger an email whenever a "should" rule is violated. That way, you're aware of another cluster function breaking a rule without unnecessarily constraining the entire cluster.

Applying several overlapping affinity rules can complicate troubleshooting, because it can be difficult to comprehend the resulting effects. Use affinity rules only when you need to, and avoid creating more than one rule that applies to the same VM or the same host.

Distributed Power Management

Distributed power management (DPM) is an additional feature of DRS that looks to conserve power by temporarily shutting down hosts during periods of lesser activity. It monitors the total levels of CPU and memory across the cluster and determines whether sufficient resources can be maintained while some hosts are put into standby mode. If so, it uses DRS to migrate VMs off a host to clear it, preparing it for shutdown.

When the cluster deems that additional host resources are needed again, it brings them out of standby in preparation. The cluster either determines this by observing increased CPU or memory levels, or considers historical data to predict busier periods.

To bring the servers back online, it can use one of three different remote power-management protocols. In order, the cluster will attempt to use Intelligent Platform Management Interface (IPMI), then HP's Integrated Lights Out (iLO) and finally Wake On LAN (WOL) to send the power-on command.

DPM REQUIREMENTS

DPM has a number of requirements in order to function:

◆ DPM is a subfeature of DRS, which requires an Enterprise or Enterprise Plus license.

◆ The cluster must have DRS enabled.

◆ Hosts participating in the DPM set must be running vSphere 3.5 or later.

◆ Using the IPMI or iLO protocol requires a Baseboard management controller (BMC) IP address, a MAC address, and username/password credentials.

◆ WOL protocol use requires the following:

  ◆ Hosts' vMotion NICs must support WOL.

  ◆ Hosts' vMotion addresses should share a single subnet.

  ◆ The switch ports that the WOL cables connect to must be set to autonegotiate.

You should test each host thoroughly to ensure that it can wake properly when required. This is often forgotten when introducing new additional hosts to an existing DPM-enabled cluster.

DPM AUTOMATION LEVELS

The DPM Power Management page, shown in Figure 8.9, controls the level of automation across all the cluster's hosts:

FIGURE 8.9
DPM power
management

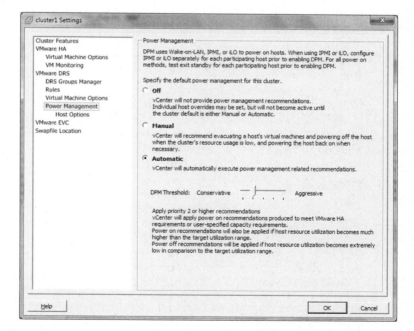

Off   This is the default setting on any enabled DRS cluster. DPM isn't used. Since vSphere 4.1, changing the setting to Off at any time will bring all hosts out of standby if DPM had shut them down.

Manual   This mode analyzes the cluster for hosts to shut down, and makes recommendations. It's particularly useful for initial testing to see what effect enabling the Automatic level may have.

It's probably less useful longer term, because the most likely times for DPM recommendations are during quiet periods (for example weekends and overnight), when administrative staff are less likely to be available to act on them. But you can use this mode for longer-term warm spares, which ordinarily can be shut down even during busier times based on these recommendations.

Automatic   The Automatic option reacts to DPM recommendations and acts to shut down hosts when it sees fit. This setting has a threshold level, which determines how conservative or aggressive the action is. The more aggressive the level, the more recommendations are acted on.

The DPM automation-level setting isn't the same as the DRS automation level. They act independently of each other.

DPM Host Options

When DPM is enabled on a DRS cluster, all the hosts inherit the cluster's settings. However, the Host Options settings allow you to manually override this on a per-host basis. Just as with the cluster itself, you can select Disabled, Manual, or Automatic for each host, or set Host Options to Default to use the cluster's setting.

This is particularly useful when you're introducing new hosts to the cluster and testing a host's ability to wake up when requested. Check a host's Last Time Exited Standby field to see if it was able to resume properly on the last occasion. This individual setting can also be useful if you want to maintain a minimum number of hosts left on despite any DPM recommendations, or if you want to prevent particular hosts from being shut down.

The cluster must be set to either Manual or Automatic for these options to be considered. You can't disable DPM for the entire cluster and enable it only for certain hosts in the Host Options section.

DPM Impacts

DPM takes advantage of spare cluster resources, so the more hosts that are available to it, the better. You should avoid the temptation to exclude too many hosts if they're capable of remotely waking, because the more choices the cluster has, the more potential power savings it can generate.

The cluster does consider historical patterns to try to predict when there will be an impending resource requirement. However, even when the hosts wake up, performance is always reduced for several minutes. It takes a while for DRS to spread the increasing load across to the newly powered-on hosts, and then some time for the benefits of transparent page sharing (TPS) and memory compression to take effect. If you need the fastest possible time to recover into a fully performant set of hosts, don't set the DRS slider too low.

With vSphere 4.1, a scheduled task associated with DPM lets you set a predefined time to disable DPM on a host and therefore wake up the host. This allows you to be sure the resources are ready when you know resource demands will increase, such as when lots of employees start work at the same time. You may know about certain busy periods, such as monthly billing cycles or scheduled work on a weekend, and want the hosts ready beforehand. Just remember, you'll need another scheduled task to re-enable DPM afterward, if you aren't planning to do it manually.

If any host is passing through USB devices, you should consider disabling DPM for that host. Although vSphere 4.1 can vMotion VMs with USB devices attached, if the host that has the physical connection is powered down, the VMs will obviously lose their connection.

DPM can be used with a mixed cluster and supports hosts from version 3.5 onwards. However, DPM can operate effectively only if the VMs are able to vMotion between all the hosts; think about VM hardware versions, EVC, attached hardware, and any other factors that will affect the VMs' ability to migrate seamlessly.

When DPM is looking to migrate VMs off hosts, it not only appraises the CPU and memory demands, but also adds the reservation levels set on the VMs and the cluster's resource pools. It does this to ensure that sufficient compute resource will remain available; it respects the reservation guarantees that are set. This demonstrates how you can use reservations to be sure a suitable number of hosts are left powered on, but also reinforces the advice that reservations have far-reaching impacts, shouldn't be set without reasonable justification, and shouldn't be set excessively.

Finally, remember that DPM also takes into consideration the cluster's HA settings. It doesn't power-off all the hosts it otherwise can, if it needs to keep hosts turned on to provide sufficient failover capacity. Again, this reiterates the fact that being overly cautious and setting very conservative values in some areas will have an impact on the efficiency of other features.

WHEN TO USE DPM

When designing vSphere clusters, many people question the usefulness of DPM. It can be advantageous in environments where demand varies a lot at different times. Shutting down hosts for extended times can save power and also reduce air-conditioning requirements in a busy server room. But if resource demand is fairly static, which is common in server workloads rather than desktops, the savings are minimal.

Many companies don't pay for their own power or air-conditioning, if they're co-located in third-party datacenters. Often, stringent change-control rules don't allow for automatic host shutdowns. And many power and cooling systems are designed to run at full load, so shutting down a handful of hosts that are potentially spread out through different racks won't provide any savings. Although DPM allows you to set whether specific hosts ignore the cluster's setting, it doesn't currently let you express a preference regarding the order in which hosts should be shut down (to target a certain rack space first). In addition, all the associated storage and networking equipment must remain powered on, even if some hosts are shut down.

DPM does have potential use cases. If a site has a heavy virtual desktop infrastructure (VDI) implementation, and the desktop users work predictable hours, then there is obviously scope to power down hosts overnight and on weekends. There may be longer holiday periods or designated shutdown periods when a site is mothballed.

Another possible scenario is disaster recovery (DR) sites that are predominately required for standby purposes. In the event of a failover, such sites need lots of spare hosts that can be resumed reasonably quickly. DPM allows them to fire up automatically, when more hosts are needed; this provides an excellent solution that requires little additional intervention.

Test and lab environments also tend to vary wildly in their requirements. These can be good candidates for DPM use because they often see much quieter periods, and generally it's acceptable if the time to recover to full capacity is several minutes.

DPM is just one more useful option in a business's toolkit. As hardware manufacturers incorporate more power-saving functionality into their equipment, it will become more useful. Larger cloud data providers with thousands of hosts undoubtedly will be interested in the potentially very large savings. The technology certainly has its place. However, you should remain mindful that in small environments, the savings may be minimal. Don't spend time and resources designing and testing a DPM solution if it's obvious from the outset that you won't recover enough energy savings to make it worthwhile. Or, you may want to apply DPM only in specifically targeted sites, rather than across all your hosts.

High Availability and Clustering

vSphere 4 encompasses several high-availability options. The primary technique is VMware's HA, but this is supplemented with both VM monitoring and fault tolerance (FT) capabilities.

High Availability

VMware HA is a clustering solution to detect failed physical hosts and recover VMs. It uses a software agent deployed on each host, along with a network heartbeat to identify when a host is offline. If it discovers that a host is down, it quickly restarts that host's VMs on other hosts in the cluster. This is a fast and automated recovery service, rather than what most consider a true high-availability clustering solution to be.

HA uses vCenter to license the feature and deploy the necessary agent software; but after hosts are enabled for the HA cluster, the heartbeat and failure detection are completely independent. An offline vCenter won't affect ongoing HA operations, only any reconfiguration that's required, such as adding or removing new hosts.

HA primarily protects against host failures, and as such no special consideration is required for the VM's guest OS or application. There are no requirements for VM-level agents to be installed, and any new VMs in the cluster automatically inherit the HA protection. HA can also protect VM OSs and applications via the VMware tools software, although it doesn't do this by default. It can detect when OSs aren't responding and allows applications to alert HA when critical services or processes aren't working as expected.

HA also monitors the capacity of the cluster and its ability to failover VMs from any host. It can enforce policies to ensure that sufficient resources are available.

One common misunderstanding about HA among newcomers to the technology is that HA doesn't use vMotion to recover VMs. The VMs crash hard when the host fails, but they're restarted promptly on alternate hosts. With vSphere version 4.1, HA can now take advantage of some of DRS's load-balancing to improve the restart decisions that HA makes, but it's still not a seamless transition. HA doesn't provide the same level of uptime as some other clustering solutions, but it is very easy to set up and maintain. Expect the VMs to be off for several minutes while they restart after a host failure.

HA REQUIREMENTS

To enable HA in a cluster, you should ensure that you meet the following requirements:

◆ The cluster's hosts must be licensed as Essential Plus or above.

◆ There must be at least two hosts in the cluster.

◆ All hosts must be able to communicate with each via their Service Console/Management Network VMkernel connections.

◆ Name resolution is critical for HA, so a properly configured DNS infrastructure is very important.

◆ The HA hosts must be able to see the same shared storage. VMs on local storage aren't protected.

◆ Hosts must also have access to the same VM networks. For this reason, it's important to use consistent port group naming across hosts.

◆ HA's VM and application monitoring functionality needs VMware tools to be installed in the guest OS.

◆ IPv4 must be used, because HA doesn't support IPv6.

CLUSTER SIZE

An HA cluster can hold a maximum of 32 hosts. Cluster sizing has been greatly simplified with the introduction of vSphere 4.1. vCenter 4.0 had a soft limit of 100 VMs per host (which rose to 160 with update 1), but this came down to only 40 VMs if the cluster had more than 8 hosts. With vSphere 4.0, there was a reluctance to tip over to the ninth host, because doing so reduced the total number of VMs. Eight hosts could hold 1280 VMs (8 × 160), whereas 9 hosts could hold only 360 VMs (9 × 40). In reality, this limitation rarely causes issues, because not many implementations have more than 40 VMs per host, except in desktop VDI solutions.

vSphere 4.1 increased those limits to 320 VMs per host, regardless of the number of hosts in the cluster, up to a limit of 3000. Note that with 3000 VMs per cluster, if you fully populate the cluster with 32 hosts, those hosts can have only an average of up to 93 VMs (3000/32). Still, these new limits mean the previous caution around clusters of nine or more hosts can now be ignored.

Remember that if you think you'll come close to any of these limits, you need to factor in the density of VMs after a failure. If you want to be prepared for 2 hosts failing in a 4-host cluster (n+2), then remember that although 4 hosts can hold 1280 VMs (4 × 320), during a failure of 2 hosts that maximum drops to only 640 VMs. You're unlikely to hit these limits; but if you're designing around them, you need to calculate based on the hosts available post-failure, for the designed level of cluster protection.

Creating very dense clusters has its ups and downs. The benefit of larger HA clusters is that you need less host hardware to provide redundancy, because splitting the cluster in two doubles the need for failover hosts. Also, DRS and DPM have more hosts to load-balance and can spread resources more efficiently. However, creating very large clusters has certain impacts; some companies like to segregate their clusters into smaller silos to create hard resource limitations. As you'll see, HA clusters can only guarantee to withstand four host failures at the same time. Some businesses are reluctant to use larger clusters, particularly with blade servers, where a blade-chassis failure can bring down a large number of VMs without HA working to recover them.

The actual cluster size depends on a number of other factors. It's likely to be designed in conjunction with DRS and possibly DPM. But the starting point usually depends on factors such as host resilience and VM criticality. For most businesses, n+1 is sufficient; but this is always a numbers game. The concept is similar to Chapters 6's discussion of the availability of storage, which explains how additional redundant pieces help to reduce the percentage of overall downtime — but do so with diminishing returns. Also, if you're contemplating an n+1 design, you may want to hold off on patching and hardware maintenance until quieter times: any time you purposefully remove a host from the cluster, you lose that failover capability. If individual VMs are considered very important, you may wish to consider the FT functionality discussed in the following section; but if you want to protect large proportions of your VMs more carefully, you should consider n+2. Additional hosts for pure redundancy are costly, and most businesses are likely to consider this only for their most crucial clusters.

PRIMARY AND SECONDARY HOSTS

The first five hosts joined to an HA cluster are marked as the *primary* HA hosts. All subsequent hosts are designated as *secondary* HA hosts. If HA is enabled on a preexisting cluster with six or more hosts, then five are randomly chosen to be the primaries.

The primary hosts maintain a replicated cluster state between themselves and coordinate VM failovers when required. HA can use this cluster state to tell the approximate state of the resources on each host, by tracking reservations. HA doesn't use vCenter or DRS to decide where to restart VMs. Instead, it uses these replicated state-resource calculations and additional checks to see whether the VM's network and datastores are available to the host. Secondary hosts send all their state information to the available primary hosts.

One of the primary hosts is always the active primary, and this primary host decides where to restart VMs, which order to start them in, and how to deal with VMs that fail to start. If the active primary host fails, one of the other primaries steps up and takes the role.

The primary hosts remain primary until they're put into maintenance mode, they become disconnected from the cluster, they're removed from the cluster, or the entire cluster is reconfigured for HA. At that point, a random secondary host is selected and promoted to primary status.

It's important to note that a secondary node isn't promoted when a primary fails. This means that if all the primary hosts fail before a secondary can be promoted, HA will stop functioning. No failovers will occur. If you have a host that you know will be offline for a while, it's important to put it into maintenance mode first if you can; or, if it goes offline unexpectedly, remove it from the cluster.

One of the current issues with this limit of five primary hosts is that there is no way for the vCenter client to tell which hosts are primary and which are secondary. You can get this information from the command line, but there is no supported way to specify which host is which. The only supported action is to reconfigure HA on the cluster, which runs another random re-election and (you hope) selects the physical servers you want. This process is tedious and not something you can plan your design around. The outcome is that for any design, you shouldn't group more than four hosts from the same HA cluster in the same blade chassis. If you're particularly risk-averse, you may want to avoid more than four hosts even being in the same rack.

FAILURE DETECTION

The HA hosts send heartbeats to each other every second by default. All the primary hosts send their heartbeats to all the hosts, whereas the secondary hosts only send theirs to the primary hosts.

If, after 15 seconds, a host doesn't send any heartbeats and doesn't respond to pings, it's deemed to have failed, and the active primary host starts to decide where to power-on the VMs from the failed host. You can change this 15-second interval via the advanced setting `das.failuredetectiontime`, if there are extenuating circumstances.

HOST MONITORING

After enabling HA in the cluster settings, you can begin protecting the hosts via their HA agents and heartbeats by switching on host monitoring. The check box to enable this feature is at the top in Figure 8.10.

FIGURE 8.10
HA settings

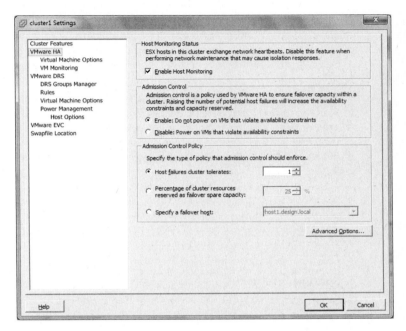

If you wish to disable HA host monitoring, you should do it with this setting rather than disable the entire cluster for HA. That way, you keep all your advanced settings, and VM and application monitoring can continue to function.

FT requires that HA host monitoring be enabled in order for it to protect its VMs properly. With vSphere 4.0, disabling HA host monitoring disabled all the FT VMs in the cluster; but vSphere 4.1 keeps them running with FT secondary copies (but they may not fail over as expected). This saves the FT clones from being re-created if HA host monitoring is disabled for a short time.

ADMISSION CONTROL

HA admission control is similar to the admission control used by hosts and resource pools. One notable difference is that HA admission control can be disabled. It's used to control oversubscribing the HA cluster. If enabled, it uses one of three methods to calculate how to reserve sufficient resources to ensure that there are enough hosts for recovery; the following subsections describe these policies. If it determines that the limit has been reached, it can prevent further VMs from being turned on in the cluster or VM reservations from being increased.

Without the protection of admission control, there is a greater chance that HA may not be able to power on all the VMs during a failover event. You may want to temporarily disable it if you plan to oversubscribe your cluster during testing or patching.

Host Failures Cluster Tolerates

The first admission control policy — and the default, which for that reason is used in most clusters — is the number of host failures the cluster will tolerate. In other words, it's the amount of capacity kept spare in terms of number of hosts.

HA calculates the amount of spare capacity in terms of number of hosts, via an arbitrary value called a *slot size*. This slot size determines how admission control is performed against the cluster:

Slot Sizes Slot size is the value of the largest VM requirement in the cluster, or the worst-case scenario. It finds the largest CPU reservation and largest memory reservation of every powered-on VM. If no reservations are set for these values, it assumes a value of 256 MHz for the CPU and 0 MB plus the VM's memory overhead. It then takes the largest resulting CPU figure of any VM and the largest memory figure of any VM, and uses this as the cluster's slot size.

Obviously, very large VMs with large reservations will skew this amount, highlighting the need to keep VM reservations to a minimum. Resource pool reservations don't affect HA slot sizes. You can use the advanced settings `das.slotCpuInMHz` and `das.slotMemInMB` to reduce a very high slot setting if you think something lower is appropriate, but doing so can fragment the reserved slots for the larger VMs and cause issue if resources are thinly spread across the cluster when a host fails. Although the spare resources will be available, they may not be enough on a single host to accommodate a large VM.

Runtime Information As shown in Figure 8.11, the vSphere client has an HA Advanced Runtime Info dialogue box. It's available only when you use this method of admission control. It highlights the slot size and host-capacity calculations.

FIGURE 8.11
HA Advanced
Runtime Info

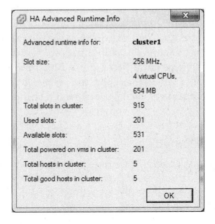

HA calculates how much CPU and memory are available for VMs on each host, after the virtualization overhead is taken into account. It does this for all connected hosts that aren't in maintenance mode and works out how many slots each host can hold. Both CPU and memory slot sizes are compared, and the smaller (more conservative) of the two is used. Starting with the smallest host, HA determines how many hosts will accommodate all the slots. Any hosts left over, which will be the larger ones to ensure that worst-case failures are considered, are totaled to give the failover capacity.

Despite any slot size calculations, the maximum number of host failures allowed is always four. As discussed previously, a cluster can only guarantee to recover from four failures, because any more may remove all the primary hosts at once and prevent any VMs from being failed over.

This method of admission control is useful primarily because it requires no user intervention after it's initially configured. New hosts are added to the slot size calculations automatically, to ensure that larger hosts are guaranteed protection. As long as you don't use advanced slot size settings, this method doesn't suffer from the resource fragmentation that is possible with the percentages method discussed next.

But this type of admission control is inflexible and can be overly conservative. It works well if all the VMs have the same CPU and memory requirements; but a small number of large VMs will significantly bias the slot sizes, and you'll need extra hosts to maintain the failover capacity.

Percentage of Cluster Resources Reserved

The Percentage of Cluster Resources Reserved admission control policy uses cluster totals compared to VM totals to calculate a percentage value of spare capacity.

This policy adds up all the powered-on VMs' CPU and memory requirements, considering their reservations. If the reservations are set to 0 (zero), then it takes 0 MB plus any overhead for memory, and adds 256 MHz for CPU. It then adds together all of the hosts' available CPU and memory resources. It creates a percentage difference for both CPU and memory, and if either is less than the admission control policy states, it enforces admission control.

Using percentages for admission control is very useful because it adjusts as hosts are added or removed from the cluster, while continuing to respect any set reservations. Unlike the very conservative policy regarding the default number of host failures, the percentage policy is more adaptable. If all the hosts have similar CPU and memory, then calculating the percentages to give a one- or two-host failover capacity is simple. Be aware that although you can set high percentages in clusters with many hosts, you should keep the maximum to the equivalent of four hosts; otherwise, you won't be guaranteed that all primaries will remain available.

Hosts with very different capacities can lead to problems, if the percentage set is lower than the resources of the largest host. Every time a host is added or removed, you may need to recalculate the percentage each host gives to the cluster, to ensure that each is sufficiently protected. Very large VMs may have problems restarting if the spare capacity is spread thinly over the remaining hosts; so, set large VMs to have an earlier restart priority, and always watch to make sure any large VMs can still fit on each host.

Specify a Failover Host

This policy designates a particular host as the one to fail over to, reserving an entire host as a spare. When this policy is selected, no VMs can power on or migrate to the designated host.

This means an entire host is unavailable for use, and it needs to be the most powerful host in the cluster to ensure that it can recover from any host failure. If you have unbalanced hosts in the cluster, with one host having a very large number of CPUs and another having much more RAM than the rest, then you may find that no particular host is suitable to specify as the failover host.

VM Options (HA)

HA's Virtual Machine Options settings let you control the order in which VMs are restarted in the cluster if there is a host-failure event, and what the cluster's hosts should do if a host becomes isolated from the rest of the network. Figure 8.12 shows these settings. There is also a section below the cluster settings where you can override these two settings on a per-VM basis.

FIGURE 8.12
HA Virtual Machine
Options

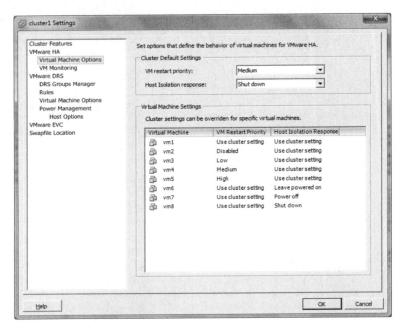

Restart Priority

The VM Restart Priority setting allows you to specify the order in which VMs are restarted if a host fails. If resources are constrained and you didn't implement proper admission control, it's particularly important to have the more critical VMs start first. Otherwise, when it's time to restart the lower-priority VMs, there may not be enough resources to start them.

You can choose to start certain VMs first if they provide essential services, such as Domain Controllers and DNS servers. In addition, the order in which some VMs start is important for certain multiserver applications. For example, you may need a database server to start before its application server (as you would for a split virtual vCenter instance).

You can also disable restarting some VMs in the case of a host failure. For example, you may choose not to restart some development and test VMs if you think the extra load on fewer hosts will adversely affect your production VMs. VMs disabled here will react to the VM-monitoring feature on a host that is still up, unless it's disabled in that section as well.

If two hosts fail simultaneously or in quick succession, then the active primary host begins starting the VMs from whichever it determines was the first host to fail. It restarts all of that host's VMs in their restart priority and doesn't begin to restart the second host's VMs until all the VMs from the first are finished. This is the case even if there are higher-priority VMs on the second host.

Host Isolation

When a host stops receiving heartbeats from the other cluster members, it attempts to ping an isolation address, which by default is the host's management VMkernel default gateway. If it can't reach the isolation address, it assumes that it has become isolated and takes the appropriate action, which by default in vSphere 4 is to shut down the VMs gracefully (be careful, because this default has changed several times during HA's lifetime). By shutting down the VMs, it's anticipating other cluster hosts attempting to power them on.

If it can successfully ping the isolation address, the host concludes that the other hosts in the cluster have failed. In this case, if it's a primary host, it tries to initiate restarts from the other hosts. If it's a secondary host, it waits until it can reach a primary and receive instructions.

The host isolation response determines how the VMs react if a host becomes isolated from the heartbeat network but remains turned on. There are three options: Shut Down, which is the vSphere 4 default; Power Off; and Leave Powered On. Shut Down attempts to use the VMware tools to cleanly shut down the VM, thus preventing crashing the guest OS. If after five minutes the VM hasn't shut down, the host powers it off hard. You can change this timing with the advanced setting das.isolationshutdowntimeout if there are VMs you know take longer to shut down cleanly.

When a host becomes isolated, the remaining hosts think the isolated host has failed and attempt to restart its VMs. However, because the isolated host is still running, it has a file lock on the VMs' disks that prevents the other hosts from seizing control of them. The other hosts continue to retry restarting the VMs, because they expect the isolated host to shut them down, or eventually the requests time out.

If you're concerned about these false positives, you may want to change the cluster setting to Leave Powered On. If your network is less reliable than it should be, you don't want your VMs powering down regularly. However, the alternative is to keep VMs running on hosts that aren't functioning correctly. This is one instance where you may want separate rules for some VMs, because you know that for some VMs a quick restart isn't terrible invasive — for example, a DHCP server. You can also increase the das.failuredetectiontime setting, which is normally set to 15 seconds and which specifies the amount of time to wait without a heartbeat before a host is deemed to have failed and the restart process begins. This can be increased to 30 or 60 seconds to prevent false positives along with redundant Service Console connections. But increasing the timeout too much means waiting longer for VMs to restart if a host does fail.

With vSphere 4.0, you can end up with a situation called *split brain* for VMs stored on iSCSI or NFS datastores. Basically, if a host becomes isolated and loses its connection to the storage as well because of the same network issue, other HA hosts can seize control of the VMs' disks and restart them. However, because the isolated host hasn't failed, it continues to run the VMs as processes; so, when it's reintroduced to the network, it fights the recovery hosts for control of its VMs. vSphere 4.0 Update 2 has resolved this issue: the isolated host checks the file lock and drops the VMs upon reconnection when the host realizes it has lost control of those VMs. For this reason, if you still have pre–4.0 Update 2 hosts in the cluster, you may want to set any iSCSI/NFS-based VMs to an isolation response of Power Off.

HA IMPACTS

vSphere 4.0 HA is run independently from other cluster functionality. Its primary interaction is with the calculation of slot sizes depending on VM reservations. It ignores affinity rules and can't work with DRS or DPM during failovers.

vSphere 4.1 has much tighter integration and is affected by DRS, DPM, and affinity rules. During failover, if resources are spread thinly over the cluster and HA needs to restart one very large VM, it can ask DRS to make room for it by vMotioning existing VMs around. It can also ask DPM to power-on hosts if it's shut some down, to provide additional resources.

The new VM-Host affinity rules can limit the choices HA has to restart VMs after a host failure. If there is a VM-Host mandatory "must" rule, then HA honors it and doesn't restart a VM if it would violate the rule. If it's a soft "should" rule, then HA restarts the VM, thus breaking the rule, but creating an event that you can monitor with an appropriate alarm. Multiple VM-Host rules can also fragment the resources in a cluster, enough to prevent HA power-ons. HA asks DRS to vMotion VMs to a point where every VM can be recovered but may not be able to achieve it within the rules. As per the recommendations for VM-Host affinity rules, only use "must" rules if you have to, and be aware that doing so can limit HA so much that VMs may not be recovered.

In vSphere 4.0, resource pools can adversely impact VMs during an HA situation. HA initially recovers VMs into the root of the cluster, even if they had been deep in a resource pool with a share value that was appropriate only to that pool. This can cause a temporary but massive imbalance, with a few failed-over VMs running at the same level as the root resource pools, potentially starving those resource pools. The VM's shares were created relative to the resource pool they were in, not the root they're recovered to. Remember from earlier in the chapter that running VMs and resource pools at the same level can create unexpected resource allocation, and this failover activity often creates such a situation without realizing it. vSphere 4.1 accounts for this and recovers VMs to the root of the cluster but with adjusted shares relative to their allocation before the failover. With either version, this is usually temporary, because when DRS is also enabled on the cluster, it can move the VMs back into the correct pools automatically.

HA Recommendations

The most crucial factor for HA to work successfully is the communication of the heartbeat. The two most important design aspects related to this in HA are network redundancy and name resolution.

The most common risk to an HA cluster is an isolated host, which by default causes the host's VMs to shut down. You must ensure that there is complete redundancy for the management VMkernel (Service Console for ESX hosts) connection at all points through the network to every host. You can either:

◆ Configure more than one VMNIC on the management VMkernel's vSwitch

◆ Add a second management VMkernel connection to a separate vSwitch on a separate subnet

The management VMkernel connection must have a default gateway that all the hosts can reach. Hosts use it to decide whether they have become isolated; so, if your management VMkernel subnet doesn't have a gateway, you should change the `das.isolationaddress` parameter to an IP address that can be pinged. If you use a second management VMkernel connection on a separate subnet, then specify a second isolation address for the alternate subnet with `das.isolationaddress2`. If you're conducting maintenance tasks on your network devices or the host's networking configuration, you should temporarily disable host monitoring to prevent any false failovers.

If the network suffers from intermittent connectivity problems, then you can raise the default 15-second failure reaction time by increasing `das.failuredetectiontime`. The downside of extending this value is that when a host does fail, you'll have to wait that much longer for the hosts to recover the VMs. Additionally, VMware recommends 60 seconds for a single management VMkernel connection on two VMNICs, and at least 20 seconds if you use two separate management VMkernel connections. Enabling PortFast on the physical switches should reduce spanning-tree isolation problems.

Try to minimize the number of network devices between hosts, because each hop causes small delays to heartbeat traffic. If you use active/passive policies for the management VMkernel connections, configure all the active VMkernel links from each host to the same physical switch. Doing so helps to reduce the number of hops.

HA relies heavily on name resolution, so every host must have access to correctly configured DNS servers, where all hosts have resolvable host records. Avoid using local host files for name resolution, because they're inevitably error-prone, and managing them as the cluster grows becomes increasingly laborious.

The following firewall ports must be open between all hosts in the same cluster. When HA is enabled on the cluster, these ports are automatically opened on the host's own firewalls. However, if there are any physical firewalls between the hosts, then these need to be configured:

◆ Incoming TCP/UDP: 8042-8045

◆ Outgoing TCP/UDP 2050-2250

If the cluster is configured for DRS, then you should already have common port group names across all the hosts; otherwise, the vMotions will fail. But if you only enable HA, it's possible to misconfigure your hosts with different port group names between the hosts. Use the Networking view in vCenter of the cluster to confirm consistent naming standards.

Customize the VMs' restart policy to suit your environment. Doing so improves the chances that the more critical servers will be restarted successfully if you don't have admission control enabled or if the failover levels are insufficient. Also, the restart policy will ensure that the servers that need to start first, which subsequent servers rely on, will be ready.

Create an alarm with an associated email action to warn you if an HA failover has occurred. You'll want to check that all the necessary VMs come back online and that services are restored. Then, investigate the state of the failed host, to see if it's ready to rejoin the cluster. You can also use alarms to warn you when a cluster becomes overcommitted or invalid.

VM and Application Monitoring

VM monitoring is an additional feature of HA, which watches the VMware tools' heartbeat, looking for unresponsive guest OSs. If HA determines that the guest has stopped responding — for example, due to a Windows BSOD or a Linux kernel panic — then it will reboot the VM.

With vSphere version 4.1, application monitoring was added. For an application to share heartbeat information with HA's monitoring, it relies on either the application's developers adding support via a special API available to select VMware partners, or setting them up yourself using the available SDK. If the application or specific service stops, VMware tools can be alerted, and vSphere can restart the VM.

Figure 8.13 shows the available VM Monitoring settings. At the top, in the drop-down box, you can select VM, Application, or VM and Application Monitoring. The next section allows you to select the monitoring sensitivity, with an option to customize each setting individually. The last section is the VM override area, where you can choose settings for particular VMs.

FIGURE 8.13
VM Monitoring

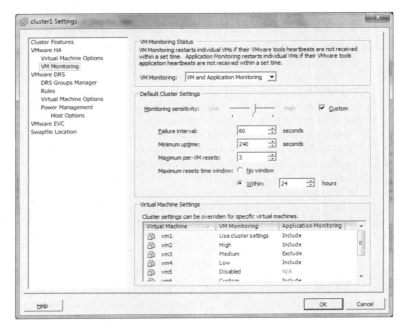

If heartbeats from the guest OS or application are lost from a VM in the Failure Interval period, disk and network I/O are checked to prevent any false results. The I/O activity interval is an advanced cluster setting, which by default is 120 seconds, but you can customize it with the das.iostatsinterval setting. HA VM monitoring has a minimum uptime value that waits a period of time after the VM is started or restarted before making monitoring failovers; this allows the VMware tools to start. If you have a guest OS or application that is known to start very slowly, you should extend this value to be sure everything has started and the initial CPU demands have tapered off. This feature also limits the number of times a VM is reset in a certain period. This prevents a VM from being repeatedly restarted, if the same error continuously reoccurs and causes OS or application failures.

If HA decides a failure has happened after checking heartbeats and I/O, it takes a screenshot of the VM's console and stores it in the VM's working directory. The VM is then immediately restarted. This console screenshot can be very useful in troubleshooting the initial error, because it often contains kernel error messages from the guest OS.

Adjusting the monitor's sensitivity, especially with custom values, affects the monitoring responsiveness and success rate. If you set the sensitivity too high, then you may suffer unnecessary reboots, particularly if the VM is under a heavy workload or the host's resources are constrained. On the other hand, if you set the sensitivity too low, then it will take longer to respond, and critical services may be down longer than you want.

A successful implementation of VM monitoring depends on testing each OS and application. Every instance may have different sensitivity requirements. For this reason, the VM overrides section is very useful; it lets you test each VM with its own settings before introducing it to the cluster's settings. It's advisable to have as few VMs with their own individual settings as possible, after you've determined the most appropriate cluster-wide sensitivity settings.

Fault Tolerance

VMware fault tolerance (FT) is a new clustering technology that was introduced with vSphere 4. It creates an identical running copy of a VM on another host, which can step in seamlessly should the first VM's host fail.

FT records all the inputs and events that happens on the primary VM and sends them to replay on the secondary VM, in a process known as vLockstep. Both primary and secondary VMs have access to the same VM disks via shared storage, so either can access the disks for I/O.

Both VMs are kept synchronized and can initiate the same inputs and events identically on their respective hosts. Only the primary VM advertises itself on the network, so it can capture all the incoming network I/O, disk I/O, and keyboard and mouse input. These inputs and events are passed to the secondary VM via a dedicated VMkernel connection known as the FT *logging link*. They can then be injected into the running secondary VM at the same execution points. All the outputs from the secondary VM are suppressed by its host before being committed, so only the primary actually transmits network responses to clients and writes to disk. The outside world is oblivious to the secondary VM's existence.

The mechanism to create and maintain the secondary VM is similar to vMotion; but instead of fully transferring control to the second host, it keeps the secondary VM in a permanently asynchronous mirrored state. The initial creation of the FT VM happens over the vMotion connection; then, the remaining lockstep occurs over the FT logging network. The clustering is only for host failures and won't protect VMs against OS or application failures, because those are replicated to the second VM. But FT does protect VMs against host failures more effectively than HA, because there is no downtime or loss of data, whereas HA needs to restart the VMs, creating a short outage and crash-consistent VMs.

The VMs need to be members of an HA cluster, to detect and restart hosts should a failure occur. Like HA itself, FT uses vCenter purely for the initial creation of the FT pair but isn't dependent on vCenter and isn't disrupted if it becomes unavailable. The cluster is also responsible for keeping the VMs on different hosts, so when FT is enabled on a VM, the secondary VM is created and never coexists on the same hardware as the primary.

The primary VM is continuously monitored for failures so the secondary can be promoted, be brought onto the network, and spawn a new secondary copy. Failures are detected by checking the VMs for UDP heartbeats between the servers. FT also watches the logging connection to prevent false positives, because regular guest OS timing interrupts should always create a steady stream of logging traffic. FT uses a special file-locking technique on the shared datastore to tell if there is a split-brain networking issue, instead of a host down. This prevents an isolated host from incorrectly trying to promote the secondary VM and advertise itself.

FT by itself only protects a VM from host failure, not OS or application failures. However, you can combine this with HA's VM monitoring and new application monitoring. The VM monitoring detects OS problems such as kernel panics/BSODs and restarts the primary VM. This in turn causes the primary to create a new secondary copy. Remember that because the primary and secondary VMs always share the same storage, FT won't protect you against a SAN failure.

FT Versions

With the introduction of vSphere 4.1, FT versioning was bumped from version 1 to version 2. Not only has the label changed, but there are also a number of interesting developments that can alter your design.

With FT version 1 on vSphere 4.0 hosts, the build number (effectively, the patching level) is compared: VMs can only run on hosts with exactly the same version. For that reason, it's important to differentiate the FT versions, because this build number checking restricts any FT version 1 VMs to those vSphere 4.0 hosts.

Version 2 FT VMs have a more sophisticated version-control technique that allows the hosts to be slightly different if it can tell FT would be unaffected. This make patching the hosts considerably simpler, because with version 1 you need a minimum four-host cluster to successfully patch them without having to disable FT for an extended period.

Figure 8.14 shows the FT details section from a 4.1 host's summary page, where it details the FT version. On 4.0 hosts, this would show the host's build number instead.

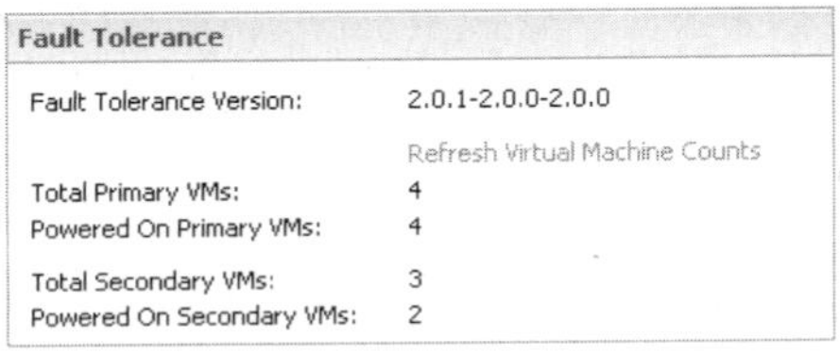

FIGURE 8.14
FT details

Fault Tolerance	
Fault Tolerance Version:	2.0.1-2.0.0-2.0.0
	Refresh Virtual Machine Counts
Total Primary VMs:	4
Powered On Primary VMs:	4
Total Secondary VMs:	3
Powered On Secondary VMs:	2

With FT version 1, the VMs can be part of a DRS-enabled cluster; but as soon as FT is enabled, the primary and secondary VMs' DRS is disabled via the VM options. The primary stays where it was when FT was enabled, and the secondary is automatically placed.

FT version 2 can now use DRS for both initial placement and load-balancing, but the cluster must be EVC enabled. EVC improves the cluster's ability to place VMs on hosts. The secondary VM assumes the same DRS settings as its primary. If EVC is disabled in the cluster, the FT VMs are DRS disabled as they were with version 1. This load-balancing is also useful for patching and maintenance, because version 1 VMs can be vMotioned around (but this is still a manual process).

Whenever a FT VM is powered on, it uses anti-affinity rules to ensure that the secondary copy is running on a different host. With vSphere 4.1 also come additional affinity rules that were discussed earlier in the chapter. You can use VM-Host affinity rules to specify the hosts on which you want the FT VMs to run. When you set particular hosts, both the primary and secondary VMs adhere to the rule and only run on those hosts. But with a VM-VM affinity rule, this only applies to the primary, because that is the VM other VMs interact with. If the primary fails, the secondary will be promoted, and DRS will step in and move VMs as the rule requires.

vLockstep Interval

The primary VM always runs slightly ahead of the secondary VM with regard to actual physical time. However, as far as the VMs are concerned, they're both running at the same virtual time, with inputs and events occurring on the secondary at the same execution points. The lag between the two VMs in real time is affected by the amount of input being received by the primary, the bandwidth and latency of the logging link between the two, and the ability of the host running the secondary VM to keep up with the primary VM.

If a secondary VM starts to significantly lag the primary, then FT slows the primary by descheduling its CPU allocation. When the secondary has caught up, the primary's CPU share is slowly increased.

The lag between the two VMs is known as the *vLockstep interval* and appears in the FT summary shown in Figure 8.15.

FIGURE 8.15

FT summary

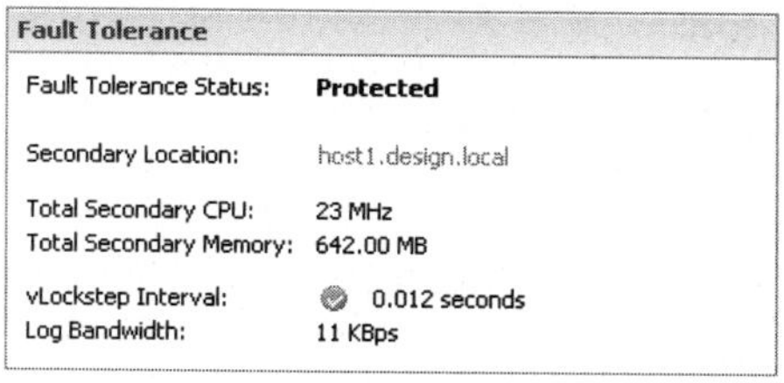

Fault Tolerance	
Fault Tolerance Status:	**Protected**
Secondary Location:	host1.design.local
Total Secondary CPU:	23 MHz
Total Secondary Memory:	642.00 MB
vLockstep Interval:	0.012 seconds
Log Bandwidth:	11 KBps

All network transmits and disk writes are held at the primary VM until the secondary acknowledges that it received all the preceding events to cause the output. Therefore, sufficiently large latency on the logging link can delay the primary, although normal LAN-style response times shouldn't cause a problem.

REQUIREMENTS AND RESTRICTIONS

The process of recording and replaying VMs is very complex; hence a number of strict requirements and restrictions apply to the environment.

This is a relatively new feature from VMware, and it's still evolving; as such, it has a tendency to change frequently. You should check the latest VMware documentation to make sure these restrictions still apply, because each new version works to remove the existing constraints and improve functionality.

The following lists are aimed at version 2, but additional version 1 limitations or differences are highlighted:

Clusters

◆ At least two hosts that can access the same networks and storage that the FT-protected VMs will use. Hosts must be running a compatible FT version. If they're using version 1, then the hosts must have the same build number.

◆ Host certificate checking must be enabled on the cluster. This is the default on vCenter 4.0 and 4.1, but upgraded installations may not have it enabled.

◆ The cluster must have HA enabled with host monitoring.

◆ Primary and secondary VMs can't span across multiple clusters.

◆ If cluster hosts are separated from each other by firewalls, FT requires ports 8100 and 8200 to be open for TCP and UDP between all hosts.

Hosts

◆ Advanced, Enterprise, or Enterprise Plus licensing

◆ FT-compatible hardware (see the FT HCL for updated listings)

◆ FT-compatible CPUs (`http://kb.vmware.com/kb/1008027`)

◆ Hardware virtualization enabled in the BIOS (Intel VT or AMD-V)

◆ Access to the vMotion network via a VMkernel connection

◆ Access to the FT logging network via a VMkernel connection

VMs

◆ Must be hardware version 7.

◆ Must be on shared storage.

◆ A few guest OSs aren't supported, and some that are supported need to be powered off to enable FT (`http://kb.vmware.com/kb/1008027`).

◆ Only a single vCPU.

◆ Can't use IPv6.

◆ Can't use Storage vMotion.

◆ Can't use or have snapshots (which rules out VMware Consolidated Backup (VCB) and many backup utilities that rely on snapshots).

◆ Can't use or have linked clones.

◆ No physical raw device mapping disks (RDMs); virtual RDMs are allowed.

◆ No paravirtualized guests (VMI).

◆ No N-Port ID virtualization (NPIV).

◆ No NIC or HBA passthrough (VMDirectPath).

◆ VMs can't have any of the following devices attached:

  ◆ Vlance vNICs

  ◆ VMXNET3 vNICs with FT version 1

  ◆ PVSCI devices

  ◆ VMCI connections

  ◆ Serial ports

  ◆ Parallel ports

  ◆ CD drives

  ◆ Floppy drives

  ◆ USB passthrough devices

  ◆ Sound devices

VMware has created a freely downloadable tool called SiteSurvey (www.vmware.com/support/sitesurvey) that can connect to your vCenter instance and analyze clusters, hosts, and VMs to check whether they're suitable for FT. It highlights any deficiencies and makes recommendations.

ENABLING FT

When FT is turned on for a VM, it disables the following features:

- Nested page tables (Extended Page Tables/Rapid Virtualization Indexing [EPT/RVI]). If this has been enabled, then the VM must be turned off to disable it. FT only does this per VM, so the host remains enabled, and other VMs on the host can still take advantage of this hardware optimization.

- Device hot-plugging.

- FT version 1 also disables DRS on the primary and secondary. But version 2 leaves them enabled as long as EVC is enabled on the cluster.

Turning on FT also converts all of the VM's disks to the eager-zeroed thick format, removes any memory limits, and sets the VM's memory reservation to the full allocation of RAM.

Enabling FT then creates the secondary VM. If the VM is already powered on when you turn on FT, it's automatically enabled at the same time.

WHEN TO USE FT

FT provides excellent protection against host failures, despite not protecting VMs from OS or application faults. But some of the restrictions listed here make FT less useful for some designs.

In particular, two requirements severally limit how it's used. First, the licensing needed to enable FT on VMs is Advanced or above, meaning that many companies can't take advantage of this feature. Second, the fact that only single-vCPU VMs can be protected really restricts its use. The sort of Enterprise customers who pay for additional licensing features are also the entities most likely to run their more critical VMs with multiple vCPUs.

With the long list of restrictions and the additional demands to run the secondary VMs, most businesses only protect their most crucial VMs with FT. Not only does the cluster need to provide the extra resources for the secondary, but enabling FT also sets the full memory reservation for the primary, and in turn the secondary, to prevent any chance of ballooning or swapping. Enabling FT on the VM prevents you from changing any CPU or memory shares, limits, or reservations.

Enabling FT can also reduce the performance of VMs by up to 10% just with the additional overhead. If the secondary VMs CPUs can't keep up with the primary, then this can reduce its performance even more.

DRS also restricts the number of primary and secondary VMs per host to a default of four. You can change this value with the advanced setting das.maxftvmsperhost; if you set it to 0 (zero), the limit is ignored.

However the higher protection afforded by FT makes it extremely useful. Most popular guest OSs are supported; and FT is unaware of the application stack running, so the best use cases tend to rely on the services that are most important to the business. Because this feature is in addition to HA, it makes sense to use it only when a quick HA failover is unacceptable. You may want to consider using FT in your design:

◆ For the most business-critical applications

◆ During periods when a particular application is more crucial to the business

◆ When there are no other appropriate clustering techniques for the application

There are scheduled tasks available to turn FT on and off, so VMs can be protected on demand. You can automate when FT is used, so the additional resources are consumed only during those periods when you need the protection.

FT IMPACTS

FT works very closely with HA and also interacts with DRS functions (even more so with vSphere 4.1). You should note some of these impacts while considering your design.

As we stated earlier, the VM-VM affinity rules that are available in 4.0 and 4.1 apply only to the primary VM, because that is where all the I/O traffic is directed. FT keeps both VMs apart through its own hidden anti-affinity rule, so you can't force them together on the same host.

There is a difference between the versions though, if the primary has an additional VM-VM affinity rule. With version 1, if there is an affinity or anti-affinity between the primary and another VM, then when a failover happens a violation can occur. DRS can't move the newly promoted secondary, and its original position may be in conflict with the rule. With version 2, as long as the cluster is EVC enabled, DRS can move the promoted secondary VM to avoid any rule violation. Without EVC enabled, you lose the DRS enhancements in vSphere 4.1.

If you're using FT version 2 with vSphere 4.1, the VM-Host affinity rules apply to both primary and secondary, so both are effectively kept in the same VM group and have an affinity or anti-affinity with a group of hosts. This means that even if the FT fails over to the secondary VM, it will also be in the correct group of hosts for licensing or hardware association as required.

FT reserves the full allocation of memory on the primary VM and removes any previously set limits. To assist the secondary VM with keeping pace with the primary's host, you have the option of setting a CPU reservation as well. Both these reservations can have a significant impact on HA. The likely candidates for FT protection will probably have a reasonable amount of RAM allocated to them, and setting several FT VMs in the same cluster will change the HA slot sizes and so HA's efficiency. With larger VM reservations set in the cluster, DRS finds it harder to turn on more and more VMs if strict admission control is set.

With FT version 1, you can't use DRS for active load-balancing, which means DPM may not be able to evacuate a selected host to shut it down. In this case, you can exclude the hosts that are running your primary and secondary FT VMs until you're able to upgrade the hosts to vSphere 4.1.

DPM won't recommend powering off any hosts running an FT VM if it can't vMotion it. FT version 2 VMs must be in an EVC cluster with fully automated DRS, for DPM to vMotion them and consider shutting down the host.

HA is able to protect FT VMs when a host fails. If the host running the primary VM fails, then the secondary takes over and spawns a new secondary. If the host running the secondary VM fails, then the primary creates a new secondary. If multiple hosts fail, which effects both primary and secondary, then HA restarts the primary on an alternate host, which in turn automatically creates a new secondary. The improvements in vSphere 4.1 mean that during an HA failover, HA can more intelligently place the new primary, and FT should create the new secondary on the most suitable host.

FT RECOMMENDATIONS

Along with the long list of requirements and restrictions that FT places on the hosts and VMs, a number of design recommendations will improve the efficiency of FT:

Clusters

◆ All cluster hosts should have access to same networks and shared storage. Otherwise, the hosts selected for the secondary VMs will be limited.

◆ It's important that all the hosts have similar performance characteristics so primary and secondary VMs can run at similar speeds. VMware recommends that host CPUs shouldn't vary more than 400 MHz.

◆ All cluster hosts should have the same power-management, CPU instruction sets, and HyperThreading BIOS settings.

◆ The strict build-level dependency on 4.0 hosts makes running FT VMs in a mixed ESX and ESXi cluster inadvisable because it's difficult to keep both sets of hosts at the same patch level. You should use 4.1 if you have a mixed cluster.

◆ You can create a resource pool for all your FT VMs with excess memory, to ensure that VM overhead is accounted for. Because FT is turned on, the VM's memory reservation is set to the full amount of allocated RAM. But this doesn't account for any memory overhead.

Hosts

◆ You should have fully redundant network and storage connections. FT will fail over a VM if the host loses all paths to its Fiber Channel (FC) connected datastore, but this shouldn't replace redundant FC links.

◆ The use of active/passive links with other VMkernel traffic provides a simple way of providing logging-traffic redundancy.

◆ You should split the vMotion and FT logging subnets and use separate active links for each.

◆ You should use at least 1 GbE links for the logging network. Using jumbo frames can improve the efficiency of the logging network even further. The FT logging connection is likely to be the limiting factor on the number of FT VMs you can have on each host. If you're consolidating host traffic via 10 GbE links, you need to implement some sort of QoS for the FT logging link to prevent any bursty traffic from saturating the link. With vSphere 4.1, vMotions can use up to 8 Gbps of bandwidth, and each host can vMotion eight VMs at once. Without control, this can flood the connections shared with FT logging.

◆ Adding more uplinks on the logging connection's vSwitch doesn't necessarily increase distribution of the traffic across multiple links. You can use IP-hash load-balancing with EtherChannel to provide some load-balancing across multiple links. Source port ID or source MAC address load balancing policies won't balance logging traffic.

◆ Host time should be synchronized to an available Network Time Protocol (NTP) server.

◆ VMware advises that you run at most four primary VMs and four secondary VMs on each host. Because the logging traffic is largely asymmetric from primary to secondary, spreading them between hosts improves the use of the logging connection. Also, because all the network I/O and disk I/O is being directed to and from the primary, the primary's host has more load that can be balanced by splitting primary and secondary VMs.

VMs

◆ If the secondary VM is struggling for CPU resources on its host, causing the primary to slow down, you can add a CPU reservation to the primary that will be duplicated to the secondary. This should help with CPU contention on the secondary host.

◆ When you initially turn on FT for a VM, the disks are converted to eager-zeroed thick, which can take time to process. You can convert the disks ahead of time, during quieter periods, to ensure that FT can be turned on more quickly.

◆ Turning on FT disables some performance features, such as nested page tables. Don't turn on FT unless you're going to use it.

◆ If you're enabling FT on VMs with more than 64 GB of memory, you can encounter issues because there may be insufficient bandwidth to transfer all the changes in the default vMotion timeout of 8 seconds. You can increase the timeout in the VM's configuration file, but doing so may lead to the VM being unresponsive longer when you enable FT or during failovers or vMotions.

◆ VMs enabled for FT should have a maximum of 16 virtual disks.

◆ Enabling FT causes spikes in CPU and saturates the vMotion network while the secondary VM is created. Try to avoid enabling and disabling FT frequently.

◆ The secondary VM uses up additional resources on its host, equivalent CPU and memory levels to that of the primary. So, don't enable VMs unnecessarily.

◆ High guest OS timer interrupts cause increased logging traffic. Some Linux OSs allow you to reduce this setting, and you may wish to consider doing so if the logging bandwidth is constrained.

◆ Each FT VM's guest OS should have its time synchronized to an external time source.

Summary

This chapter has looked carefully at vCenter's datacenter structures and the functionality available to protect and optimize your clusters.

A clever datacenter design allows you to manage the hosts and VMs more efficiently and more intuitively. Fortunately, many of the structural pieces can be changed and honed easily, often with little or no downtime, so retrospective design changes are often relatively painless. It's worth considering your entire vSphere environment, because the power of vCenter's permissions, events/tasks, alarms, scheduled tasks, and views can make a big difference; this central infrastructure tool is simple to manage and effective, which enables staff instead of burdening them.

There are several cluster tools to make the most of your physical resources. First, you can use resources pools to divide and allocate CPU and memory as required, ensuring that the VMs that need resources receive them fairly and as you want them apportioned. DRS is critical to resource management; it places VMs appropriately on hosts and keeps the cluster suitably balanced with vMotion. You can achieve more granular control over VM placement with affinity rules, particularly with the advances in vSphere 4.1 and VM-Host rules. Finally, DPM makes power savings possible by shutting down hosts that aren't required.

In addition to all the resource optimizations, you can design clusters to provide differing levels of protection for your VMs. HA can restart VMs on alternate hosts, VM monitoring watches for unresponsive guest OSs and applications, and FT maintains online stand-in copy VMs.

Datacenter design is very important to the overall efficiency of your vSphere environment. It can enhance the working ability of your hosts and their VMs, making the most of your CAPEX layout and reducing the accompanying OPEX overhead. It's one part of the design worth regularly reevaluating, because nothing remains static and there are usually areas that can benefit from further optimizations. When you're looking at the datacenter design, it's important to examine it as a whole, because so many of the elements interact, work together, and even constrain each other. Think of all the elements in this chapter, and apply each part to best effect.

Chapter 9

Designing with Security in Mind

In this chapter, we'll change our point of view and look at a design from the perspective of a malicious user. We won't say *hacker*, because usually your virtual infrastructure won't be exposed to the outside world. Because this book isn't about how to protect your perimeter network from the outside world, but about vSphere design, we'll assume that the security risks that need to be mitigated come from the inside. We'll discuss these topics:

◆ The importance of security in every aspect of your environment

◆ Potential security risks and their mitigating factors

Why Is Security Important?

We're sure that you don't need someone to explain the answer to this question. Your personal information is important to you. Your company's information is no less important to your company. In some lines of business, the thought of having information leak out into the public is devastating. Consider the following theoretical example. Your company is developing a product and has a number of direct competitors on the market. Due to a security slip, the schematics for a new prototype of your product have found their way out of the company. Having the schematics out in the open can and will cause huge damage to the company's reputation and revenue.

At VMworld 2010, the slide in Figure 9.1 was presented, showing that the number of virtual OSs is larger than the number deployed on physical hardware—and that number is only expected to rise.

Your corporate databases will run as VMs, your application servers will be virtual, and your messaging servers will also run as VMs (or perhaps all of these are already true). There is also a good chance that in the not too distant future, your desktop and perhaps even your mobile phone will be VMs.

You need to ensure that the data stored on all these entities is as safe and as secure as it can possibly be.

Separation of Duties

A centralized model of administration can be a good thing but can also be a major security risk.

Risk Scenario

John, your VI Admin, has *all* the keys to your kingdom. John has Domain Admin credentials. He also has access to all the network components in your enterprise. He has access to the physical datacenter where all the ESX hosts are located. He has access to the backend storage where all your VMs are located and all of the organization's Common Internet File System (CIFS) and Network File System (NFS) shares that store the company data.

FIGURE 9.1

Increase in the number of VMs deployed

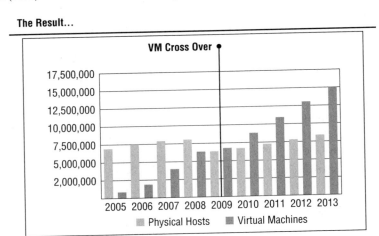

And now John finds out that he will be replaced/retired. You can imagine what a huge security risk this may turn out to be. John could tamper with network settings on the physical switches. He could remove all access control lists on the network components and cause damage by compromising the corporate firewall, exposing information to the outside, or perhaps even opening a hole to allow access into the network at a later date.

John could also tamper with domain permissions. He could change passwords on privileged accounts and delete or tamper with critical resources in the domain.

John could access confidential information stored on the storage array, copy it to an external device, and sell it to the competitors.

John could then access the vCenter Server, power off several VMs (including the corporate mail server and domain controllers), and delete them. Before virtualization, John would have had to go into the datacenter and start a fire to destroy multiple servers and OSs. In the virtual infrastructure, it's as simple as marking all your VMs and then pressing Delete: there go 200 servers. Just like that.

Risk Mitigation

The reason not to give the keys to the kingdom to one person or group is nightmare scenarios like the one we just described.

Ironically, the larger the environment, the easier it becomes to separate duties across different functions. You reach a stage where one person can't manage storage, the domain, the network, and the virtual infrastructure on their own. The sheer volume of time needed for all the different roles isn't possible.

Setting up dedicated teams for each function has certain benefits, but also certain drawbacks:

Benefits Each member's expertise is concentrated on one field and not spread out over a number of duties. This allows them to focus on their specific duties and become experts in their field.

Each team manages its own realm and can access other realms but doesn't have super-user rights in areas not under its control. Active Directory admins don't have full storage rights, network admins don't have Domain Admin privileges, and so on.

Drawbacks   There will be only one (maybe more) expert in any certain field. If that expert is sick, away on vacation, or leaves the company, the rest of your team has to do a crash course in solving complex issues in a time of need. You'll find it difficult to have complete coverage on your team.

Having only one person dealing with the infrastructure doesn't allow for out-of-the-box thinking. The same person could be the one who designed and implemented the entire infrastructure and has been supporting it since its inception. Therefore, this person could be deep in a certain trail of thought, making it extremely difficult to think in new ways.

Shell Access to the ESX Host

If only everything could be done from the vSphere client (some administrators cringe at the thought) … but it can't. Certain things need to be done from a command line—either from a remote management station or on the ESX host. This can have certain security risks, as you'll see.

Risk Scenario

Mary, your VI Admin, was with the company for many years. But her relationship with the company went downhill, and her contract was ended—and not on a good note.

One morning, you come into the office, and several critical servers are blue-screening. After investigation, you find that several ESX host and VM settings have been altered by the root user through an SSH session to the ESX server.

Who changed the settings? Several people know root credentials and could have made the changes. Going through the logs, you can see that the system was accessed at a certain time by the root user, but that's where the trail ends.

Risk Mitigation

By default, and rightfully so, root SSH access to the server isn't allowed on an ESX server. Up to version 4.1, it was unsupported on ESXi; and as of 4.1, it can be activated (but issues an alert about this configuration change). Denying root access is also part of VMware's security best practices.

But as we all know, in certain cases it's necessary or just plain easier to perform actions on the host from the command line. How can you provide shell access properly, allowing for auditing and security?

LOCAL USERS ON THE HOST

The answer is to create a local user on each ESX host for each user who needs shell access. This is easy:

```
useradd -u 5001 -G esxadmin user -m
passwd user
```

You now have a local user to log in to the ESX host, and with this command you've added the user to a group called esxadmin. But this user and members of the group don't have any rights on the server. To rectify this, you allow these users to perform the appropriate management roles using sudo.

Sudo is a security mechanism in Linux that allows users with lower permissions to perform operations that require elevated privileges on a system. If you were to compare this to something in the Microsoft world, the closest you could get would be the Runas command. Allowing someone to run a command as another user is usually done to run something with elevated permissions. Sudo and Runas aren't quite the same, however: with Runas, you have to provide credentials for the elevated account. Using sudo, you can perform elevated operations without knowing the elevated account's credentials.

To grant users the correct rights to perform the appropriate command you have to add them to the sudoers. You do this with the visudo command, the proper way to provide permissions with sudo. There is a large amount of text in the file; you would add the text below into the file.

```
%esxadmin        ALL=NOPASSWD:        ALL
```

Here you add the esxadmin permission to perform all commands without requesting a password for each action. This makes management less disturbing for your user. But if you want to force the use of a password with the command, you configure the line like this:

```
%esxadmin        ALL=(ALL)        ALL
```

Now you have a local user for remote management. But this setup is lacking because it requires two sets of credentials. The VI Admin has domain credentials they use for vCenter management purposes and another set of credentials they have to manage (and update) that isn't connected to the domain. Wouldn't it be better to have one set of credentials for both purposes? Let's see how.

LOCAL USERS WITH ACTIVE DIRECTORY INTEGRATION

The process of creating the users on the hosts is almost the same, but in this case you don't assign a password to the user:

```
useradd -u 5001 -G esxadmin user -m
```

Next, you configure the ESX host to authenticate to Active Directory:

```
esxcfg-auth --enablekrb5 --krb5realm=design.local --krb5kdc=dc1.design.local
--krb5adminserver=il.nds.com
```

Of course, you can get the command's full help from the host, but let's go through the syntax:

◆ --enablekrb5 enables Kerberos authentication.

◆ --krb5realm is the Active directory domain.

◆ --krb5kdc defines the key distribution center (KDC) for the Kerberos realm.

◆ --krb5adminserver defines the administrative server for the Kerberos 5 realm against which the user should be checked.

This command doesn't add your ESX host into the domain; it just directs the authentication traffic to your domain controllers.

You'd think this would be enough—and it was, until ESX version 4.1. But you now have to complete an additional step (there's also one more recommended setting). You must do this with the remote vCLI:

```
C:\Program Files (x86)\VMware\VMware vSphere CLI\bin>vicfg-user.pl
--server esx1.design.local --username root  --protocol HTTPS
--entity group --group esxadmin --operation modify  --role admin
```

What does this command do? In essence, it makes a persistent change to the configuration, adding all the members of the esxadmin group to the admin role, which allows them access to the server through the remote shell. If you don't perform this step, you'll get "Access denied" messages when you try to log in through SSH.

You also need to update the /etc/security/access.conf file with an extra line:

```
+:esxadmin:ALL
```

The last recommended setting is to force authentication of the root user to be local and not through the domain. You should do this because if you have for some reason incorporated an Active Directory user in your domain with the name *root*, that user can log in to any ESX host. Creating a user named root in your domain isn't a good idea, but to take precaution you should disable Active Directory authentication for the root user with the following command:

```
esxcfg-auth --enforce-local-auth=root
```

Returning to the risk scenario outlined earlier, we mentioned that after the user logged in as root, the audit trail ended. That is why you use sudo. Activities performed with sudo are written to a log with a clear indication of what was done when and by whom. This should make you feel more secure and your auditors a lot happier as well.

ESX and Active Directory Integration

ESX 4.1 was the first version that allowed you to fully integrate your ESX host into your Active Directory domain. This can simplify things quite a bit but doesn't cover the full scope of host permissions.

The limitations are the following (as of ESX 4.1):

◆ There's a limit on the number of groups a user can be a member of.

◆ The ESX Admins is hard coded.

◆ You can assign only three roles: Admin, read-only, and no-access.

The level of control you have over what a user can do on the host is definitely not the same as what you can accomplish with sudo. With sudo, you can define that a specific user can perform one command but not another: for example, that a user can run esxcfg-nas commands but not esxcfg-vswitch commands. Sudo lets you achieve the granularity you want for your environment.

ESXi vs. ESX

But what about ESXi? Much of this book deals with both versions of the hypervisor. But VMware has publicly announced (more than once) that ESX 4.x will be the last version of ESX with a Service Console; from here on out, it will be ESXi only.

As we all know, there is no Service Console in ESXi; and the BusyBox console has no sudo option or ability to limit different users to different subsets of commands. Therefore, permissions should move to the vSphere Management Assistant (vMA).

vMA Remote Administration

VMware usually releases a version of its management appliance with the relevant releases of ESX. In the future, the segregation of permissions will move to your remote appliance. The vMA is a Linux box where you can apply the same rulesets you can apply on your full ESX hosts. If this is the case, you'll apply the same process you used for the ESX console. You'll assign certain users to a group, and apply the rights to that group of users.

In the earlier example, you shouldn't have enabled root console access to the host, and you should have required each user to log in with their unique username. You should have integrated these users with Active Directory authentication, thereby adding options for an audit trail with additional event logging of successful/failed logins to Active Directory. But could you have stopped the malicious changes? Taking these measures may prevent users from attempting such malicious activity and will help you hold them accountable if they do.

vCenter Permissions

vCenter gives you extensive control over the actions you can perform on almost every part of your infrastructure. This presents some challenges.

Risk Scenario

Bill is a power user. He has a decent amount of technical knowledge, knows what VMware is, and knows what benefits can be reaped with virtualization. But unfortunately, with knowledge can come pitfalls. Bill was allocated a VM with one vCPU and 2 GB RAM. The VM was allocated a 50 GB disk on Tier-2 storage. You also allocated the Administrator role to Bill on the VM because he asked to be able to restart the machine if needed.

Everything runs fine until one day, you notice that your ESX host performance has degraded drastically. After investigating, you find that one VM has been allocated four vCPUs, 16 GB RAM, and three additional disks on Tier-1 storage. The storage allocated for this VM has tripled in size due to snapshots taken on the VM. As a result, you're low on space on your Tier-1 storage. This VM has been assigned higher shares than all others (even though it's a test machine). Because of this degradation in performance, your other production VMs suffered a hit in performance and weren't available for a period of time.

Risk Mitigation

This example isn't too bad of an outage—it could have been a lot worse. But the obvious reason this happened was bad planning.

Let's make an analogy to a physical datacenter packed with hundreds of servers. Walking around the room, you can do the following in front of a server:

◆ Open a CD drive and put in a malicious CD.

◆ Plug in a USB device.

◆ Pull out a hard disk (or two or three).

◆ Connect to the VGA port, and see what's happening on the screen.

◆ Switch the hard disk order.

◆ Reset the server.

◆ Power off the server.

Going around to the back of the server, you can do the following:

- Connect or disconnect a power cable.

- Connect or disconnect a network port.

- Attach a serial device.

- Attach a USB device.

- Connect to the VGA port, and see what's happening on the screen.

As you can see from this list, a lot of bad things could happen. Just as you wouldn't allow users to walk into your datacenter, open your kernel-based virtual machine (KVM), and log in to your servers, you shouldn't allow users access to your vSphere environment unless they absolutely need that privilege. And when they do get access, they should only have the rights to do what they need, and no more.

Thankfully, vSphere has a large number of privileges (226 by default) that you can assign at almost any level of the infrastructure: storage, VM, network cluster, and so on. Control can be extremely granular for any part of your infrastructure.

Let's get back to our analogy of the physical server room. In theory, you could create a server rack that was completely secure. The only thing a specific user with access would be able to do is reset a physical server. Granted, to create such a server rack would be complicated; but with vSphere, you can create a role that allows the user to do only this task. Figure 9.2 show such a role.

FIGURE 9.2
Creating a reset-server-only role

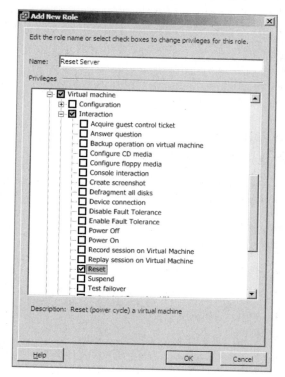

And with vSphere, you can assign practically any role you'd like. For example, you can allow a user to only create a screenshot of the VM, install VMware tools on a VM, or deploy a VM from a template—but not create their own new VM. You should identify the minimum tasks that your user needs to fulfill their jobs and allocate only the necessary privileges. This is commonly known as the *principle of least privilege*. Give your users only those powers that are absolutely essential to do their work. For example, a helpdesk user doesn't need administrative permissions to add hosts to the cluster but may need permission to deploy or restart VMs.

To sum up the risk example, if Bill had been allocated the privileges shown in Figure 9.3, you wouldn't have suffered an outage.

FIGURE 9.3

Example of a limited user role

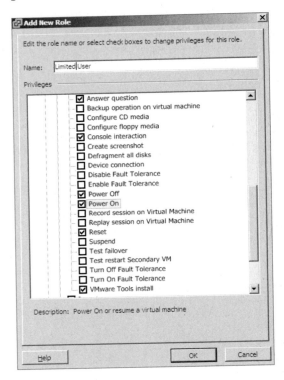

If Bill only had the options shown, he wouldn't be able to:

◆ Create a snapshot

◆ Add more hard disks

◆ Change his CPU/RAM allocation

◆ Increase his VM shares

With the proper design strategy, you can accommodate your users' needs and delegate permissions and roles to your staff that let them do their tasks, but also make sure their environment is stable and limited to only what they should use.

Managing Network Access

We touched on this topic in Chapter 5, "Designing Your Network," when we discussed planning your management layer. Let's go into a bit more detail here.

Risk Scenario

Rachel, a hacker from the outside world, has somehow hacked into your network. Now that Rachel has control of the machine, she starts to fish around for information of value. Using a network sniffer, she discovers that there is a vCenter Server on the same subnet as the machine she controls. Rachel manages to access the vCenter Server, creates a local administrative user on the server, and then logs in to the vCenter with full Admin privileges.

She sees where all the ESX hosts are and where all the storage is, and she performs a vMotion of a confidential Finance server from one host another. She captures the traffic of the VM while in transit and is able to extract sensitive financial information. The potential damage here is catastrophic.

Risk Mitigation

We won't get into how Rachel managed to gain control of a computer inside your corporate network, but we'll deal with the fact that all the machines were on the same network.

MANAGEMENT NETWORK

Your servers shouldn't be on the same subnets as your users' computers. These are two completely different security zones. They probably have different security measures installed on them to protect them from the outside world.

You can provide extra security by separating your server farm onto separate subnets from your user computers. These could even be on separate physical switches if you want to provide an additional layer of segregation. The question you may ask is, "How will this help me?"

You can deploy a security device (an intrusion protection system, for example) that will protect your server farm from a malicious attack from somewhere else on the network. Such appliances (they're usually physical appliances) examine the traffic going into the device and out to the server. With the assistance of advanced heuristics and technologies, the appliance detects suspicious activity and, if necessary, blocks the traffic from reaching the destination address.

But let's go a level deeper. In essence, the only traffic that should be exposed to your outside network is usually your VM traffic. Your end users shouldn't have any interaction with management ports, the VMkernel interfaces that you use for IP storage, or out-of-band management ports such as Integrated Lights-Out (iLO), Integrated Management Module (IMM), *Dell* Remote Assistance Cards (DRAC), or Remote Supervisor Adapter (RSA). From a security point of view, your users shouldn't even be able to reach IP addresses.

But what *does* need to interact with these interfaces? All the virtual infrastructure components need to talk to each other:

◆ ESX management interfaces need to be available for high availability (HA) heartbeats between the hosts in the cluster.

◆ The vCenter Server needs to communicate with your ESX hosts.

◆ ESX hosts need to communicate with IP storage.

- Users with vSphere permissions need to communicate with the vCenter Server.

- Monitoring systems need to poll the infrastructure for statistics and also receive alerts when necessary.

- Scripting with PowerCLI and using the remote CLI to perform remote management tasks on your hosts.

Depending on your corporate policy and security requirements, you may decide to put your entire virtual infrastructure behind a firewall. In this case, only traffic defined in the appropriate rules will pass through the firewall; otherwise, it will be dropped (and should be logged as well). This way, you can define a very specific number of machines that are allowed to interact with your infrastructure.

MANAGEMENT STATIONS

What kind of remote management do you need?

- vSphere Client

- vCLI

- PowerShell

- Shell access

From this list, you can see that you'll need at least one management station, and perhaps two. The vSphere client and PowerShell need a Windows machine. At the present time, there is no vSphere client for Linux/MAC. VMware will probably release one in the future, given the demand for such a client from the virtualization community. Not everyone wants to be dependent on Microsoft forever, VMware included. Granted, you could probably also run the other two interfaces on the same Windows machine, but it could be more beneficial to have them running on a vMA.

We've mentioned in this book more than once that the future is ESXi, and remote management will have to be performed not on the host but from an external location. VMware provides the vMA and PowerCLI, which lets you perform these tasks—and much more. We discussed the vMA in Chapter 3, "Designing the Management Layer," and we examined some security points earlier in this chapter.

With these management stations, you can provide a central point of access to your infrastructure, and you don't have to define a large number of firewall rules for multiple users who need to perform their daily duties.

You'll of course have to provide the correct security for these management stations as well.

NETWORK PORT-BASED ACCESS

The Cisco term for this is *port security*. You define at the physical switch level which MAC addresses are allowed to interact with a particular port in the switch. Utilizing this approach, you can define a very specific list of hosts that interact with your infrastructure and which ports they're allowed to access. You can define settings that allow certain users to access the management IP but not the VMkernel address. Other users can access your storage management IPs but not the ESX hosts. You can achieve significant granularity with this method.

vMotion Traffic

Traffic between hosts during a vMotion operation isn't encrypted *at all*. This means the only interfaces that should be able to access this information are the vMotion interfaces themselves, and nothing else.

One way you can achieve this is to put this traffic on a nonroutable network/VLAN. By doing so, you ensure that nothing outside of this subnet can access the traffic. This does create certain serious challenges related to long-distance vMotion.

Long-distance vMotion isn't a reality for most organizations, because it requires considerable additional resources (storage and/or network connectivity between sites). Latency between different sites and, of course, stretching the network or the VLANs between the sites, can be quite a challenge. Comprehensive network design is beyond the scope of this book.

Going back to the earlier example, if you had segregated the infrastructure network from the corporate traffic, your dear hacker friend Rachel wouldn't have discovered that there was a vCenter server. She wouldn't have been able to access the vCenter Server because her IP wouldn't have been authorized for access, and she wouldn't have been able to sniff the vMotion traffic. Even though she could still have compromised some users' computers, this wouldn't have led to the compromise of the entire virtual infrastructure.

The DMZ

Your infrastructure will sooner or later contain machines that have external-facing interfaces. It's best to plan that design properly to avoid mistakes like the one we'll describe next.

Risk Scenario

Harry, the sysadmin in your organization, wanted to use your virtualization infrastructure for a few extra VMs that were needed (yesterday, as always) in the DMZ. So, he connected an additional management port to the DMZ and exposed it to the outside world. Little did he know that doing so was a big mistake.

The ESX host was compromised. Not only that, because the host was using IP storage (NFS in this case), the intruder managed to extract information from the central storage and the network as well.

Risk Mitigation

In the previous section, we mentioned that the end user shouldn't have any interaction with the management interfaces of your ESX hosts. The only thing that should be exposed are the VM networks.

A traditional DMZ environment is similar to the diagram in Figure 9.4

A virtual DMZ will look similar to Figure 9.5.

Notice that the Service Console (or management ports) isn't exposed to the DMZ, but the VM network cards are exposed—just like their physical counterparts from Figure 9.4.

DMZ configurations can be divided into three categories:

◆ Partially collapsed with separate physical zones

◆ Partially collapsed with separate virtual zones

◆ Fully collapsed

FIGURE 9.4
Traditional DMZ
environment

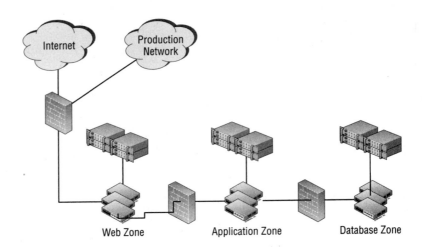

FIGURE 9.5
Virtual DMZ
environment

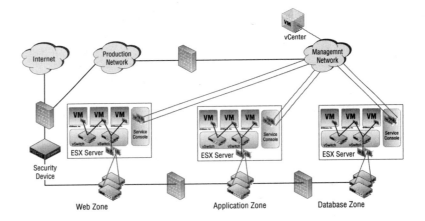

PARTIALLY COLLAPSED DMZ WITH SEPARATE PHYSICAL ZONES

Let's start with Figure 9.6 to describe this configuration.

In this configuration, you need an ESX cluster for each and every one of your zones. You have complete separation of the different application types and security risks. This of course isn't an optimal configuration, because you can end up putting in a huge number of hosts for each separate zone—which is the opposite of the whole idea of virtualization.

PARTIALLY COLLAPSED DMZ WITH SEPARATE VIRTUAL ZONES

In this configuration, you use different zones in your cluster for all your zones. The separation is done only on the network connections of each zone, with a firewall separating the different network zones on the network level. You have to plan accordingly to allow for a sufficient number of network cards for your hosts to provide connectivity to every zone.

FIGURE 9.6
Partially collapsed
DMZ with separate
physical zones

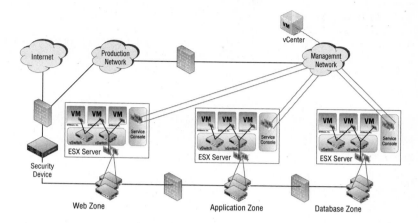

This configuration makes much better use of your virtualization resources, but it's more complex and error prone. Therefore, you should apply the same change-control and change-management procedures to the virtual DMZ as those you have in place for your physical DMZ.

FULLY COLLAPSED DMZ

This is by far the most complex configuration of the three, as you can see in Figure 9.7.

FIGURE 9.7
Fully collapsed
DMZ

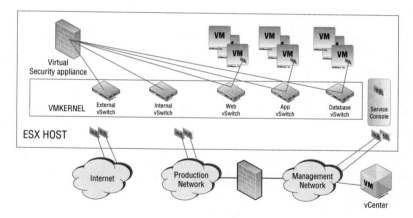

In this configuration, there are no physical firewalls between the different security zones: the firewall is a virtual appliance (running as a VM on the ESX cluster) that handles network segregation. As noted in the previous configuration, you should make sure your processes are in effect and audited regularly for compliance.

SEPARATION OF STORAGE

How possible it for someone to break out of a compromised ESX host onto a shared network resource? That depends who you ask. Has it been done? Will it be done? These are questions that have yet to be answered. But you can minimize this risk even further by using Fibre Channel (FC) host bus adapters (HBAs) or Fibre Channel over Ethernet (FCoE) HBAs.

The theory is that there is as little network connectivity as possible between the corporate network (the storage array) and the DMZ, thus reducing the network exposure. But if an attack can be crafted from within the SCSI stack to escape onto the network, this would still be a difficult task to accomplish. Then again, purchasing a new storage array and changing your entire storage infrastructure just for your DMZ servers isn't always a viable solution.

Going back to the example, the situation with Harry and the exposed management port on the external facing network should never have happened. Keeping these ports on a dedicated segment that isn't exposed to the outside world minimizes the chance of compromising the server. In addition, using the FC infrastructure that is currently in place minimizes the possible attack surface into your network from the DMZ.

You should take into consideration two more important things regarding the DMZ. First, it's absolutely possible to set up a secure DMZ solution based completely on your vSphere infrastructure. Doing so depends on proper planning and adhering to the same principles you would apply to your physical DMZ; the components are just in a slightly different location in your design. Second, a breach is more likely to occur due to misconfiguration of your DMZ than because the technology can't provide the proper level of security.

Protecting the VMs

You can secure the infrastructure to your heart's content, but without taking certain measures to secure the VMs in this infrastructure, you'll be exposed to risk.

Risk Scenario

Larry just installed a new VM—Windows 7, from an ISO he got from the helpdesk. What Larry did *not* do was install an antivirus client in the VM; he also didn't update the OS with the latest service pack and security patches. This left a vulnerable OS sitting in your infrastructure.

Then, someone exploited the OS to perform malicious activity. They installed a rootkit on the machine, which stole information and finally caused a Denial of Service attack against your corporate web server.

Risk Mitigation

A VM should always be treated like any other OS on your network. And you shouldn't allow vulnerable machines on your physical network (or your virtual infrastructure, for that matter).

In order to control what OSs are deployed in your environment, you should have a sound base of standardized templates from which you deploy your OSs. Doing so provides standardization in your company and also ensures that you have a secure baseline for all VMs deployed in the infrastructure, whatever flavor of OS they may be.

Regarding the patching of VMs, you should also treat them like any other machine on the network. VMware Update Manager can provide patching for certain guest OSs, but this functionality will be discontinued in future versions of vSphere. VMware has decided that it should patch only the vSphere environment and leave the guest OSs to the third-party vendors. This is actually a good thing, because you should have only one system that manages the security patches of your OSs, virtual or physical. The additional overhead of having to manage two different systems for your environment isn't worthwhile.

Don't forget about providing endpoint protection for your VMs as well. Looking at the current situation in the industry, very few products can provide a solution that lets you protect your VMs by using a layer in the hypervisor to protect all the VMs on the host.

VMware announced the release of vShield Endpoint at VMworld 2010, which will do just this. But as of Q4 2010, none of the Endpoint security vendors have a product ready for market. This will be the correct way to go in the future, but not yet.

What is vShield Endpoint? The technology adds a layer to the hypervisor that allows you to offload antivirus and anti-malware functions to a hardened, tamper-proof security VM, thereby eliminating the need for an agent in every VM. vShield Endpoint plugs directly into vSphere and consists of a hardened security VM (delivered by VMware partners), a driver for VMs to offload file events, and the VMware Endpoint security (EPSEC) loadable kernel module (LKM) to link the first two components at the hypervisor layer.

There are multiple benefits to handling this method of protection:

◆ You deploy an antivirus engine and signature files to a single security VM instead of every individual VM on your host.

◆ You free up resources on each of your VMs. Instead of having the additional CPU and RAM resources used on the VM for protecting the OS, the resource usage is offloaded to the host. This means you can raise the consolidation ratios on your hosts.

◆ You eliminate the occurrence of antivirus storms and bottlenecks that occur when all the VMs on the host (and the network) start their malware and antivirus scan or updates at the same time.

◆ You obscure the antivirus and anti-malware client software from the guest OS, thus making it harder for malware to enter the system and attack the antivirus software.

Until this technology is widely available, you'll have to protect your VMs the old way. And you have to plan accordingly for certain possibilities.

ANTIVIRUS STORMS

As we mentioned before, antivirus storms happen all the time in the physical infrastructure, but they're much more of an issue when the infrastructure is virtual. When each OS is running on its own computer, each computer endures higher CPU/RAM usage and increased disk I/O during the scan/update. But when all the OSs on a host scan/update at the same time, it can cripple a host or a storage array.

You'll have to plan how to stagger these scans over the day or week in order to spread out the load on the hosts. You can do so by creating several groups of VMs and spreading them out over a schedule or assigning them to different management servers that schedule scans/updates at different times. We won't go into the details of how to configure these settings, because they vary with each vendor's products.

ENSURING THAT MACHINES ARE UP TO DATE

Each organization has its own corporate policies in place to make sure that machines have the correct software and patches installed. There are several methods of achieving this.

One option is checking the OSs with a script at user login for antivirus software and up-to-date patches. If the computer isn't compliant, then the script logs the user off and alerts the helpdesk.

A more robust solution is Microsoft's Network Access Protection (NAP). Here, only computers that comply with a certain set of rules are allowed to access the appropriate resources. Think of it as a DMZ inside your corporate network. You connect to the network, and your computer is scanned for compliance. If it isn't compliant, you're kept in the DMZ until your computer is updated; then you're allowed full access to the network. If for some reason the computer can't be made compliant, you aren't allowed out of the DMZ. This of course is only one of the solutions available today; there are other, similar ones.

Looking back at the risk example from the beginning of the section, if you had only allowed the deployment of VMs from predefined templates, Larry wouldn't have been able to create a system that was vulnerable in the first place:

◆ The VM would have been installed with the latest patch level.

◆ Antivirus software would have been deployed (automatically) to the VM.

◆ No rootkit could have been installed, and there would have been no loss of information.

◆ Your corporate web server would never have been attacked, and there would have been no outage.

And you would sleep better at night.

Change Management

This isn't really a security feature, but it's still something that should be implemented in every organization.

Risk Scenario

Barry is your junior virtualization administrator. He downloaded a new vApp from the Internet: an evaluation version of a firewall appliance. He deployed the appliance, started the software setup, answered a few simple questions, and filled in a few fields (including his administrative credentials to the virtual infrastructure)—and all of a sudden, a new vSwitch was created on all ESX hosts, and all traffic was routed through the appliance.

You start to get calls that some of your applications aren't working correctly. Web traffic isn't getting to where it should go. You begin to troubleshoot the problem from the OS side. After a long analysis (far too long), you're enlightened about the change that Barry made.

The result is far too much downtime for the applications, and far too much time spent looking in the wrong direction.

Risk Mitigation

You don't want changes made to your infrastructure without them being documented and tested before the fact. Bad things are sure to happen otherwise.

There is a mantra about how to implement proper change control and change management in IT. The following is from Wikipedia:

> The **Information Technology Infrastructure Library (ITIL)** *is a set of concepts and practices for Information Technology Services Management (ITSM), Information Technology (IT) development and IT operations.*
>
> —*Wikipedia*

There are those who hate ITIL with a passion, and those who swear by it. To explain this in more depth would take a full book on its own, so let's see if we can simplify a bit.

TEST ENVIRONMENT

Prepare a test environment that is as close as possible to your production environment. We say "as close as possible" because you can't always have another SAN, an entire network stack, a blade chassis, and so on. You need a vCenter Server, central storage, and some ESX hosts. The beauty of this is that today, all of these components can be VMs. Numerous sessions from VMworld and a large number of blogs explain how to set up such a home lab for testing purposes. And to lower the cost of the licensing for this lab, you can purchase low-end bundles (Essentials and Essentials Plus) for a minimal cost.

Play around in your test environment before you implement anything on your production systems. Document the changes so they can be reproduced when needed when you implement for real.

Before you make the changes, answer these questions:

◆ What are the implications of this change?

◆ Who or what will be affected?

◆ How much of a risk is this change?

◆ Can the change be reversed?

◆ How long will it take to roll back?

CHANGE PROCESS

All the points in the previous list should be evaluated and approved by all the relevant parties involved. This way, you can identify all the angles—and not only from the point of view in your position.

We aren't always aware of the full picture, because in most cases it isn't possible to be. In most organizations, the storage team, the network person, the helpdesk team, and the hardware person aren't the same person. They aren't even on the same team. You can benefit from the different perspectives of other teams and learn how changes will impact your users. Having a process in place for involving all stakeholders in change decisions will also ensure that *you're* involved in changes initiated by other groups.

In the risk example, Larry should never have installed this appliance on the production system. He should have deployed it in the test environment, and you would have seen that changes were made in the virtual network switches that could cause issues. Larry also should have brought this change through a proper change-management process.

Not every organization implements ITIL, not every organization wants to, and not every organization needs to. You should find the process that works for you: one that will make your job easier and keep your environment stable and functioning in the best fashion.

Protecting Your Data

What would you do if someone stole a server or a desktop in your organization? How much of a security breach would it be? How would you restore the data that was lost?

Risk Scenario

Gary is a member of the IT department. He was presented with an offer he couldn't refuse, albeit an illegal one: he was approached by a competitor of yours to "retrieve" certain information from your company.

Gary knew the information was stored on a particular VM in your infrastructure. So, Gary cloned this VM—not through vCenter, but through the storage (from a snapshot), and he tried to cover his tracks. He then copied the VM off of the storage to an external device and sneaked it out of the company.

Three months down the road, you find out that your competitor has somehow managed to release a product amazingly similar to the one you're planning to release this month.

Investigations, audit trails, and many, many hours and dollars later, you find the culprit and begin damage control and clean up.

Risk Mitigation

This example may be apocryphal, and you can say that you trust your employees and team members, but things like this happen in the real world. There are people who will pay a lot of money for corporate espionage, and they have a lot to gain from it.

In this case, put on your paranoid security person hat, and think about the entry points where you could lose data.

A Complete VM

Walking out past the security guard with a 2U server and a shelf of storage under your coat or in your pocket is pretty much impossible. You'd be noticed immediately. But with virtualization, you can take a full server with up to 2 TB of data on one 3.5" hard disk, put it in your bag or in your coat pocket, and walk out the door, and no one will be any the wiser.

One of the great benefits of virtualization is the encapsulation of the server into a group of files that can be moved from one storage device to another. VMs can be taken from one platform and moved to another. This can also be a major security risk.

How do you go about protecting the data? First and foremost, trust. You have to trust the staff that has access to your sensitive data. Trust can be established via procedures and guidelines inside your company. Who is allowed to access what? Where? And how?

At the beginning of the chapter, we talked about separation of duties. Giving one person too much power or too much access can leave you vulnerable. So, separation of duties here has clear benefits.

In the risk example, the clone was performed on the storage itself, not from the vCenter Server. vCenter provides a certain level of security and an audit trail of who did what and when, which you can use to your advantage.

You should limit access to the VM on the backend storage. The most vulnerable piece here is NFS, because the only mechanism that protects the data is the export file that defines who has what kind of access to the data. With iSCSI, the information is still accessible over the wire, but it's slightly more secure. In order to expose a logical unit number (LUN) to a host, you define the explicit LUN mask allowing the iSCSI initiator access to the LUN. And last but not least, don't forget FC. Everything we mentioned for iSCSI is the same, but you'll need a dedicated HBA to connect to a port in the fabric switch as well. This requires physical access to the datacenter, which is more difficult than connecting to a network port on a LAN and accessing the IP storage.

How can the data be exported out of your datacenter? Possibly over the network. If that is the case, you should have measures in place alerting you to abnormal activity on the physical switches. You can use the corporate firewall to block external uploads of data.

If this data has to be copied to physical media, you can limit which devices are able to connect to USB ports on which computers and with which credentials. A multitude of security companies thrive on security paranoia (which is a good thing).

Backup Sets

What about the backup set of your data? Most organizations have more than one backup set. What good does it do, if your backups are located in the same location as your production environment—and the building explodes? To be safe, you need a business continuity planning/disaster recovery (BCP/DR) site.

And here comes the security concern: how is data transported to this site? Trucking the data may be an option, but you'll have to ensure the safety and integrity of the transport each time the backups are moved offsite, whether you use sealed envelopes, armed guards, a member of your staff, or the network. When sending data over the network, you should ensure that your traffic is secured and encrypted. You should choose which solution is suited for you and take the measures to protect the transport.

Virtual Machine Data

In this case there are no significant differences between a VM that is accessible from the network and its counterpart, the physical server. You should limit network access to your servers to those who need and have the correct authority to access these files. The ways of exporting the files from the VM are the same as with a full VM, as we discussed earlier.

Back to your "faithful" employee, Gary. Gary shouldn't have been granted the same level of access to all the components, the virtual infrastructure, and the storage backend. Your security measures should have detected the large amount of traffic that was being migrated out of the storage array to a non-authorized host. In addition, Gary shouldn't have been working in your organization in the first place. Some organizations periodically conduct compulsory polygraph tests for IT personnel who have access to confidential information.

And last but not least, you should protect your information. If data is sensitive and potentially damaging if it falls to the wrong hands, then you should take every measure possible to secure it. Be alert to every abnormal (or even normal) attempt to access the data in any way or form.

Cloud

Any virtualization book published in this day and age that doesn't mention cloud computing is pretty bizarre, so let's not deviate from this norm.

Risk Scenario

Carrie set up the internal cloud in your organization. She also contracted the services of a provider to supply virtual computing infrastructure somewhere in the cloud.

Due to a security issue at the cloud provider, there was a security breach, and your VMs were compromised. In addition, because the VMs were connected to your organization, an attack was launched from these hosts into your corporate network, which caused additional damage.

Risk Mitigation

VMware announced its private/public cloud solution at VMworld 2010. Since then, several large providers have begun to supply cloud computing services to the public using VMware vCloud.

Again, put on your paranoid thinking cap. What information do you have in your organization? HR records, intellectual property, financial information—the list can get very long. For each type of information, you'll have restrictions.

But how safe is it to have your data up in the cloud? That depends on your answers to a few questions.

CONTROL

Do you have control over what is happening on the infrastructure that isn't in your location? What level of control? Who else can access these VMs? These are questions you should ask yourself; then, think very carefully about the answers. Would you like someone to access the data you have stored at a provider? What measures can be taken to be sure this won't happen? How can you ensure that no one will be able to access the VMs from the ESX hosts on which these VMs are stored?

These are all possible scenarios and security vulnerabilities that exist in your organization as well—but in this case, the machines are located outside your network, outside your company, outside your city, and possibly in a different country.

Using the cloud may also present several different legal issues. Here's an example. You have a customer-facing application on a server somewhere in the cloud. The provider also gave services to a client that turned out to be performing illegal activities. The authorities dispatched a court order to allow law-enforcement agencies to seize the data of the offender—but instead they took a full rack of servers from the datacenter. What if you had a VM on one of the servers in that rack? This is a true story that happened in Dallas in 2009. It may be pessimistic, but it's better to be safe than sorry.

Here's something else to consider: will you ever have the same level of control over a server in the cloud that you have in your local datacenter, and what do you need to do to reach that same level? If you'll never have the same level of control, what amount of exposure are you willing to risk by using an external provider?

DATA TRANSFER

Suppose you've succeeded in acquiring the correct amount of control over your server in the cloud. Now you have to think about how to transfer the data back and forth between your corporate network and the cloud.

You'll have to ensure the integrity and security of the transfer, which means a secure tunnel between your network and the cloud. This isn't a task to be taken lightly; it will require proper and thorough planning. Do you want a set of rules for your data flow from your organization out to the cloud to be the same as that of the flow of information from the cloud into your corporate network?

Back to the risk example. Carrie should have found a sound and secure provider, one with a sound reputation and good security. In addition, she should have set up the correct firewall rules to allow only certain kinds of traffic back into your corporate network, and made sure that only the relevant information that absolutely needed to be located in the cloud was there.

The future will bring many different solutions to provide these kinds of services and to secure them as well. Because this technology is only starting to become a reality, the dangers we're aware of are only the ones we know about today. Who knows what the future will hold?

Security in vCenter Linked Mode

Linked Mode allows you to connect different vCenter Servers in your organization. We discussed the design considerations in Chapter 3, but let's go deeper into security.

Risk Scenario

XYZ.com is a multinational company. It has a forest divided into child domains per country: US, UK, FR, HK, and AU. At each site, the IT staff's level of expertise differs—some are more experienced than others.

Gertrude the VI Admin joined the vCenter Servers together in Linked Mode. But suddenly, things are happening in her vCenter environment that shouldn't be. Machine settings are being changed, VMs are being powered off, and datastores are being added and removed.

After investigating, Gertrude finds that this is being done by a user in one of the child domains. The user is part of the Administrators group at one of the smaller sites and isn't supposed to have these permissions.

Risk Mitigation

Proper planning is the main risk mitigator here. When you connect multiple vCenter Servers, they become one entity. If a user/group has Administrator privileges on the top level, and these permissions are propagated down the tree, then that person will have full administrator permissions on every single item in the infrastructure!

There are two basic ways to divide the permissions after you go to a multidomain structure with vCenter Servers in different child and parent domains: per-site permissions and global permissions.

PER-SITE PERMISSIONS

In this case, each site maintains its administrative roles but isn't given full administrative rights to the other sites. Figure 9.8 shows such a structure.

FIGURE 9.8
Per-site permission structure

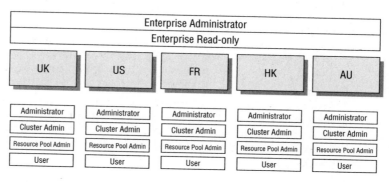

You can see that each site has its own permissions. But on the top level are two groups: Enterprise Administrators and Enterprise Read-only.

The need for the first group is pretty obvious: you'll have a group that has permissions on the entire structure. But what is the need for the second group?

To allow the insight from the other sites into one another you'll need to allow a certain level of permissions. For most organizations, this isn't a security risk, because the permission is read-only; but in some cases, it's unacceptable to allow the view into certain parts of the infrastructure (financial servers, domain controllers, and so on). In that case, you can block propagation at that level. Figure 9.9 depicts such a configuration.

FIGURE 9.9
Blocking access to a specific location

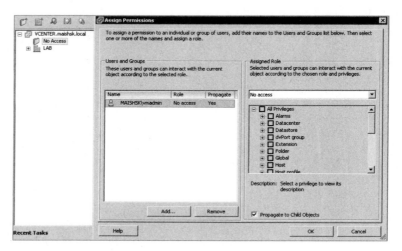

GLOBAL PERMISSIONS

In this model, roles are created for different tasks, but these roles are global. They must be applied at every vCenter tree, but this only needs to be done once. Figure 9.10 shows such a structure.

FIGURE 9.10
Global permission structure for Linked Mode

Which is the preferred structure? That will depend on your specific environment and needs.

In the risk example, Gertrude should have completed her homework before allowing people she didn't trust to access the vCenter environment. And if there were places she didn't want people to have access to, she should have denied access to those parts of the infrastructure.

Firewalls in Your Virtual Infrastructure

VMs are replacing physical machines everywhere, and certain use cases call for providing security even inside your virtual environment. We won't be talking about risk and risk mitigation, because you can provide a secure firewall in your environment by continuing to use your current corporate firewall. But doing so presents certain challenges, as you'll see.

The Problem

Herbert has a development environment in which he has to secure a certain section behind a firewall. All the machines are sitting on the same vSwitch on the same host. Herbert can't pass the traffic through his corporate firewall because all traffic that travels on the same vSwitch never leaves the host.

He deploys a Linux machine with iptables as a firewall, which provides a certain solution, but the management overhead makes this too much of a headache. In addition, in order for this to work, he has to keep all the machines on the same host, which brings the risk of losing the entire environment if the host goes down.

The Solution

There are two ways to get around this problem. One is to use the physical firewall, and the second is to use virtual firewalls that have built-in management tools to allow for central management and control.

PHYSICAL FIREWALL

The main point to take into consideration is that in order to pass traffic through the physical firewall, the traffic must go out of the VM, out through the VM port group and vSwitch, out through the physical NIC, and from there onto the firewall, as shown in Figure 9.11.

FIGURE 9.11
Traffic flow with a physical firewall

Certain use cases make this configuration not viable, mainly because all traffic has to travel onto the wire. This adds extra overhead to the traffic.

VIRTUAL FIREWALL

A virtual firewall is a VM with one or more vNICs. It sits as a buffer between the physical layer and the VMs. After the VMs are connected to a virtual firewall, they're no longer connected to the external network; all traffic flows through the firewall, as you can see in Figure 9.12.

FIGURE 9.12
Traffic flow through a virtual firewall

VMware provides a vast suite of applications called VMware vShield that will protect your virtual environment at different levels. Table 9.1 describes the differences between the products.

TABLE 9.1: VMware vShield product comparisons

FEATURE	vShield Edge 1.0	vShield Zones 4.1	vShield App 1.0	vShield Endpoint 1.0
Deployment method	Per port group	Per host	Per host	Per host
Enforcement	Between virtual datacenter and untrusted networks	Between VMs	Between VMs	Within the guest VM
Antivirus, anti-malware	No	No	No	Yes
Site-to-site VPN	Yes	No	No	No
NAT, DHCP services	Yes	No	No	No
Load balancing	Yes	No	No	No
Port group Isolation	Yes	No	No	No
Stateful firewall	Yes	Yes	Yes	No
Change-aware	Yes	Yes	Yes	No
Hypervisor-based firewall	No	Yes	Yes	No
Application firewall	Yes	Yes	Yes	No
Flow monitoring	No	No	Yes	No
Groupings for policy enforcement	Only 5-tuple* based policies	Only 5-tuple based policies	1) 5-tuple 2) Security groups: resource pools, folders, containers, and other vSphere groupings	Any available vCenter groupings for VMs

VMware
A 5-tuple is defined as the combination of source IP address, destination IP address, source port, destination port, and protocol.

Other third-party vApps provide similar functionality. And because this is an emerging market, you should perform a full evaluation of which product will fit best into your organization's current infrastructure.

Auditing and Compliance

Many companies have to comply with certain standards and regulatory requirements, such as HIPAA, the Sarbanes-Oxley Act, the Data Privacy and Protection Act, ISO 17799, the PCI Data Security Standard, and so on. As in the previous section, this isn't so much a question of risk but more of a problem and solution.

The Problem

You have put your virtual infrastructure in place and continue to use it and deploy it further. You add hosts, import some VMs, add new storage, deploy a new cluster—things change, and things grow. And with a virtual infrastructure, the setup is more dynamic than before. How do you make sure everything is the way it should be? Are all your settings correct? How do you track all of these changes?

The Solution

There are several ways you can ease your way into creating a compliant and standardized environment, including using host profiles, collecting centralized logs, and performing security audits.

HOST PROFILES

VMware has incorporated a feature called Host Profiles that does exactly what its name says. You can define a profile for a host and then apply the profile to a host, to a cluster, and even to all the hosts in your environment.

A *profile* is a collection of settings that you configure on a host. For example:

- vSwitch creation
- VMkernel creation
- Virtual machine port group creation
- NTP settings
- Local users and groups

This is just a short list of what you can do with host profiles. To enhance this, Host Profiles not only configure the hosts with the attached profile, but it also alerts you when a change is made to a host that causes it to no longer be compliant.

For example, someone may add a new datastore to the ESX host or change the name of a port group. Why are these changes important? Because in both cases, the changes weren't made across all the hosts in the cluster—vMotion may fail or may succeed, but the destination host won't have the port group, and the VM will be disconnected from the network after the migration.

Using Host Profiles can ease your deployment of hosts and keep them in compliance with a standard configuration.

NOTE Host Profiles is an Enterprise Plus feature only, which means you'll need to have all servers in your cluster at the license level in order to use this feature.

CENTRALIZED LOG COLLECTION

Each ESX server is capable of sending its logs to a syslog server. The benefit of doing so is to have a central location with the logs of all the hosts in your environment. It's easier to archive these logs from one location, easier to analyze them, and easier to perform root-cause analysis, instead of having to go to every host in the environment.

An additional benefit of deploying a remote syslog server becomes apparent when you deploy ESXi in the environment. ESXi can't preserve logs over system reboots/failures. This can be particularly problematic if an outage was unexpected and you have no logs previous to the outage. A syslog server will be a critical element in your design, now that ESXi will be the default hypervisor.

SECURITY AUDITS

You should conduct regular audits of your environment. They should include all components your environment uses: storage, network, vCenter, ESX, and VMs. You shouldn't rely on the external audit that you undergo once a year, because there is a significant chance that if something has changed (and this is a security risk), you don't want to wait until it's discovered in the external audit (if you're lucky) or is exploited (in which case you aren't so lucky any more).

As we said earlier, environments aren't static: they evolve, and at a faster pace than you may think. The more hands that delve into the environment, the more changes are made, and the bigger the chance of something falling out of compliance with your company policy.

Create a checklist of things to check. For example:

◆ Are all the hosts using the correct credentials?

◆ Are the network settings on each host the same?

◆ Are the LUN masks/NFS export permissions correct?

◆ Which users have permissions to the vCenter Server, and what permissions do they have?

◆ Are any dormant machines no longer in use?

Your list should be composed of the important issues in your environment. It shouldn't be used in place of other monitoring tools or compliance tools that you already have in place but as an additional measure to secure your environment.

Summary

Throughout this chapter, you've seen different aspects of security and why it's important to keep your environment up to date and secure. You must protect your environment at every level: guest, host, storage, network, vCenter, and even outside your organization up in the cloud.

Identifying your weakest link or softest spot and closing that hole is your way to provide the proper security for your virtual infrastructure.

In the next chapter, we will go into monitoring and capacity management.

Chapter 10

Monitoring and Capacity Planning

Monitoring the VMware vSphere environment and anticipating future growth via capacity planning are integral parts of a good vSphere design. Although related, monitoring and capacity planning aren't the same. Monitoring is more about the present or the recent past, whereas capacity planning is about the future.

This chapter will cover the following topics:

◆ The importance of monitoring and capacity planning

◆ Selecting monitoring and capacity-planning tools

◆ Incorporating monitoring into your design

◆ Different aspects of monitoring and capacity planning

◆ Building capacity planning into your design

Nothing Is Static

The best VMware vSphere designs are capable of changing, growing, and evolving. Just as the needs of the business that is implementing VMware vSphere in its environment will change, grow, and evolve over time, the vSphere design must be able to do the same thing. As the organization increases in size, the vSphere environment must also be able to increase in size. As the organization brings on new types of workloads, the environment must be able to handle, or adapt to handling, these new types of workloads. The design can't remain static.

The challenge for a vSphere architect, then (and we use the term *architect* here to mean anyone who designs vSphere environments), is to build environments that can grow and adapt. What does this mean, exactly? Specifically, a design that is capable of growing and adapting has the following qualities:

◆ The design should be *flexible* — it should accommodate both the addition as well as the removal of resources. There must be a framework present in the design whereby administrators can add servers, storage, or networking to or remove them from the design without having to redo the entire design.

◆ The design should be *instrumented* — it should incorporate monitoring as an integral component, providing the organization implementing the design with a means to know about the current utilization and behavior of the components within the design. Without instrumentation, it's impossible to know if resources must be added to or removed from the design.

Throughout this book so far, we've attempted to show you how to accomplish the first item in this list: how to build frameworks into your design so that you can add or remove resources in a way that doesn't compromise the overall design.

This chapter is primarily focused on the second item: instrumentation. Specifically, this chapter discusses how and why architects should incorporate monitoring and capacity planning into VMware vSphere designs. Monitoring and capacity planning are the two sides of the instrumentation coin: one side tells you what's happening in your environment right now, and the other side tells you what will happen in your environment in the future.

Let's start by looking at how and why you should incorporate monitoring into your designs.

Building Monitoring into the Design

Designing a VMware vSphere environment that lacks sufficient monitoring is like designing a car without an instrument panel — there is no information available to operate it! Hence our use of the term *instrumentation*. It enables operators of the vSphere environment you've designed to run it, to know what it's doing, and to be aware of the behaviors and limitations of the components that make up the design. Just as the various instruments in a car notify the operator of what's happening in the various systems that form an automobile, the monitoring that you incorporate into your vSphere design will notify the operator of how the various systems that form your design — compute, memory, storage, networking, security — are behaving and operating. This information makes it possible for the operator to use the flexibility you designed into the environment to add resources, remove resources, or reassign resources as needed.

Like so many other aspects of design, incorporating monitoring into a VMware vSphere design means answering a number of questions:

◆ What monitoring tools will the design use?

◆ What items are monitored?

◆ What values, or thresholds, will represent abnormal operation? What thresholds will represent normal operation? In other words, how do the operators determine if something is wrong with the design?

◆ What will the environment do, if anything, when an abnormal threshold is detected?

◆ Will the monitoring tools alert the operators? If so, how? Using what mechanisms?

The following sections address each of these questions.

Determining the Tools to Use

Like so many other areas of vSphere design, the first two questions are somewhat interrelated: the choice of tools can affect what items can be monitored, and the items that must or should be monitored can sometimes determine what tools need to be used.

For the purposes of this chapter, we'll group monitoring tools into three categories:

◆ Built-in tools that are supplied with VMware vSphere as part of the typical installation

◆ VMware-supplied tools that are supplied by VMware outside of the VMware vSphere product suite

◆ Third-party tools written by independent software vendors (ISVs)

Among these three categories, your job as a VMware architect or lead designer is to select the right tools or combination of tools that will meet the organization's functional requirements with regard to monitoring. You may end up using only built-in tools, if those meet the requirements. Alternately, you may end up with a mix of tools from all three categories in order to satisfy the requirements for the design.

Let's take a closer look at some of the tools that fall into these categories.

USING BUILT-IN TOOLS

VMware vSphere offers a number of tools that are built into, or provided as part of, the standard product suite. Depending on the size of the intended VMware vSphere environment and the monitoring needs of the organization, it's entirely possible that the built-in tools will be sufficient.

What are some of these built-in monitoring tools? A few of them are described next:

vCenter Server's Alarms   vCenter Server offers a fairly extensive set of alarms to monitor and alert on things like loss of network uplink redundancy, cluster high availability (HA), host memory usage, and VM CPU utilization. Figure 10.1 shows a screenshot taken from the vSphere Client when connecting to vCenter Server; this figure shows some of the alarms that are predefined in vCenter Server.

FIGURE 10.1
vCenter Server's alarms functionality can alert on many different conditions in the virtualized environment.

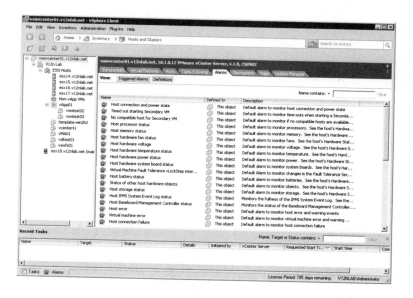

vCenter Server's Performance Charts   In addition to alarms, vCenter Server offers an extensive set of performance charts, which can help administrators get a better view of the behavior of the environment. Administrators also have the option of building custom performance charts, to see the specific data in which they're interested. This may be specific performance counters or all counters for a specific time window. Figure 10.2 shows some of the standard performance charts in vCenter Server.

FIGURE 10.2
vCenter Server offers both standard and custom performance charts to provide the specific information administrators need to see.

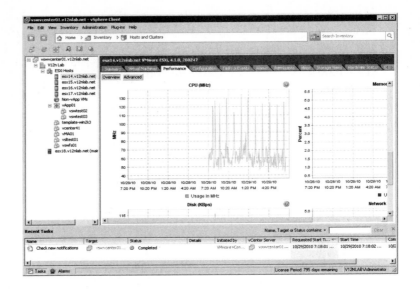

Performance Monitor Counters (Windows Guests Only) When the VMware Tools are installed into VMs running a Windows guest OS, new VMware-specific Performance Monitor counters are installed. Two VMware-specific objects, VM Memory and VM Processor, contain a number of different performance counters that are specific to virtualized instances of the Windows OS. Using these tools, administrators can capture more detailed information about the behavior of Windows instances running in a VMware vSphere environment. Figure 10.3 is a screenshot taken from a virtualized instance of Windows Server 2008 R2, showing the new performance objects and counters.

VMware provides other tools that can provide insight into the operation of a VMware vSphere environment, but we wouldn't necessarily classify them as monitoring tools. They include tools like esxtop and resxtop, both of which provide useful and detailed information about the operation and behavior of specific VMware ESX/ESXi hosts. But neither of these utilities was designed as a long-term monitoring solution. vCenter's alarms and performance charts can not only present near real-time information, but also operate in a longer-term arrangement to provide current as well as past information.

The decision whether to use the built-in tools boils down to whether they meet the functional requirements of your organization. Further, because these tools are supplied in the standard environment, the question is most often not whether the tools will be used, but whether the tools will be used alone.

The answer to this question lies in the organization's functional requirements. The vCenter Server alarms, for example, only work within the framework of vCenter Server and are therefore bound to the same integration mechanisms as the rest of vCenter Server. Does your organization need more than the ability to send an email message, throw an SNMP trap, or run a script or an application if an alarm occurs? If so, then using vCenter's alarms alone may not meet your functional requirements. Does your organization need more detailed performance information than the vCenter Server or Windows Performance Monitor can provide? If so, then you may need to employ other tools in addition to or even instead of the built-in tools.

FIGURE 10.3

VMware Tools adds new VMware-specific performance objects and counters to virtualized Windows Server instances.

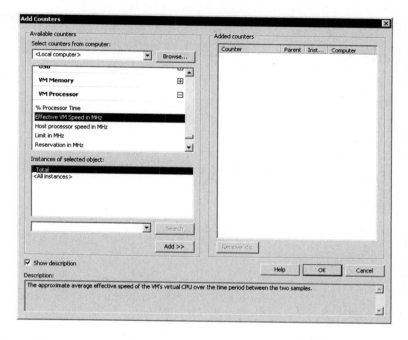

In cases like this — where the built-in tools don't meet the functional requirements for monitoring — VMware offers some additional tools that may help.

USING ADDITIONAL VMWARE TOOLS

As the VMware product line has matured, VMware has also added more products, especially management products. Some of these management products may find a way into your VMware vSphere design where warranted by your organization's monitoring needs. Several of these management products provide monitoring functionality in some form or fashion; one example is VMware AppSpeed (see Figure 10.4).

VMware AppSpeed uses probes that monitor network traffic; then, it parses the network traffic to provide insight into application-level protocols and metrics such as latency, through-put, and usage. Because AppSpeed works with information moving across the wire, it's useful in monitoring multitier applications, such as an application consisting of multiple VMs. For example, you can use AppSpeed to monitor the behavior and performance of traffic between a front-end web server and the back-end database server. AppSpeed is aware of some application protocols and is capable of decoding common types of traffic like database traffic for Oracle, MySQL, and Microsoft SQL.

If your environment or organization needs greater application-level awareness than can be provided using the built-in tools, you may want to consider incorporating AppSpeed into the design. This will affect overall utilization and capacity and network design, because AppSpeed affects both in some way.

FIGURE 10.4
AppSpeed provides application-level awareness and monitoring for multitier applications.

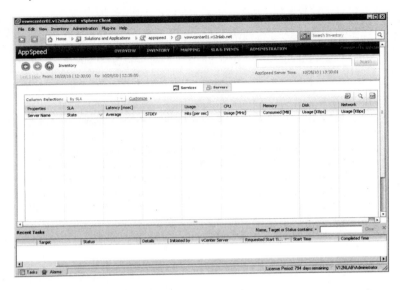

VMware offers a couple of other applications that you may also need to incorporate into your design, based on the monitoring requirements that have been specified:

◆ VMware vFabric Hyperic for application management of web and custom applications

◆ VMware vCenter Application Discovery Manager for application-level discovery and dependency mapping

NOTE VMware's public web site at www.vmware.com/products has more detailed information about the features and functions found in the products mentioned in this section.

In continuing to evaluate which tools to use in monitoring your VMware vSphere environment, if neither the built-in tools nor additional tools from VMware provided the necessary functionality to meet the organization's requirements, you must incorporate third-party tools into the design.

Using Third-Party Tools

In addition to the tools supplied with the VMware vSphere suite and the other VMware products, a number of third-party tools have been created by a variety of ISVs. These products vary widely in functionality, complexity, and cost, and architects designing VMware vSphere environments should carefully evaluate these products to find the one that most closely matches the needs of the environment.

A few third-party monitoring tools include the following:

◆ Zenoss (www.zenoss.com) is an open source monitoring solution that claims to offer agentless visibility into both physical and virtual environments.

- ◆ Quest (`www.quest.com`) is well known for a number of management and monitoring solutions. In the virtualization space, Quest vFoglight claims to offer virtual infrastructure monitoring and VMware ESX(i) management in a single product.

- ◆ Veeam (`www.veeam.com`) offers several virtualization-focused products, including Veeam Monitor. Veeam Monitor provides monitoring functionality and uses vCenter Server's alerting framework.

- ◆ VKernel (`www.vkernel.com`) provides monitoring functionality as part of its Capacity Management Suite.

- ◆ eG Innovations (`www.eginnovations.com`) provides an agent-based monitoring solution that supports multiple virtualization platforms as well as a number of specific applications.

NOTE   There are many, many more third-party tools than the few that we've listed; inclusion in our list doesn't constitute an endorsement. A quick Google search will reveal a wide variety of third-party monitoring solutions that you can evaluate for inclusion in your VMware vSphere design.

Incorporate tools such as these into your designs on an as-needed basis to meet the functional requirements of your organization. The features and functions of these products vary widely from product to product, as do the system requirements to run the product. Be sure to perform the necessary testing to ensure that the products work in your environment and that you have a solid understanding of the resource requirements before folding a third-party solution into your design.

Your testing should include more than functional testing, though. When you're testing third-party tools for inclusion in your environment, we recommend that you include scaling and integration testing. You'll want to be sure the tool you're considering scales properly with your environment. As the environment grows, will the tool continue to perform consistently and acceptably? Does the tool hit a performance ceiling before the environment scales to its anticipated limits? Integration is another important point. Will you be able to extract data from the tool for use elsewhere? That may be necessary in some environments, and the use of proprietary database engines can limit integration into existing environments.

Licensing is another area to evaluate carefully. Some tools are licensed on a per-socket basis, and other tools are licensed on a per-VM basis. Will the costs of the tool fall within acceptable limits as your environment grows? Or will spiraling licensing costs make you unable to keep the tool as your environment scales?

When you've determined what tools to use, you're ready to proceed with selecting what items those tools will monitor.

Selecting the Items to Monitor

As we mentioned earlier, sometimes the choice of what items to monitor will affect the tools that should be used to monitor those items. Because of this fact, you'll need to have a reasonably solid idea of what items you want to monitor in your design as you evaluate tools and products to incorporate into the design.

Just as the list of third-party tools is far too long to try to include each and every product, providing a list of things you should monitor in your VMware vSphere environment probably isn't possible. There are simply too many things, and the list of items you need to monitor is heavily influenced by your organization, functional requirements, business needs, and other factors.

Common things that you may want to monitor include the following:

◆ Storage capacity, as in the number of terabytes (TB) available on the storage platform(s)

◆ Storage performance, typically monitored by watching the latency in milliseconds (ms) of transactions or storage operations

◆ Storage overallocation, if you're using thin provisioning at either the vSphere layer or in the storage array itself

◆ Storage utilization, defined as a comparison of the total storage available and the amount of storage actually being used

◆ CPU utilization on both VMware ESX/ESXi hosts as well as within virtualized guest OS instances

◆ RAM utilization on both the VMware ESX/ESXi hosts as well as in the virtualized guest OS instances

◆ Memory overcommitment, to ensure that excess memory pressure doesn't significantly impact performance in a negative fashion

◆ Network utilization, which lets you see how much network bandwidth is actually being used

◆ VM availability, which monitors for the availability of individual VMs

◆ Host availability, checking to ensure that VMware ESX/ESXi hosts are up and running and accessible across the network

◆ Storage availability, monitoring whether the storage is accessible and responsive to I/O requests from hosts and guests

◆ Application availability, to ensure that applications in guest OS instances are running and responding to requests in an appropriate manner

This is just a sample list; your final design should specify a much more comprehensive list of the items you'll monitor. One way to approach this may be creating a list of questions about the environment and then ensuring that the correct items are being monitored to answer those questions. For example, consider the question "How many terabytes of storage are available for use?" By monitoring storage capacity, either at the array level or the hypervisor level or both, you can be sure that the information to answer that question is available to the operators of the virtualization environment.

Earlier in this section and in this chapter, we've mentioned the close relationship between the items to be monitored and selecting the tools you use to monitor. These two items often influence one another. Consider this example: your design requires application-level awareness, such as the ability to verify the availability of specific services in a guest OS instance. What tools are most appropriate?

In this case, the built-in tools are insufficient. They lack application-level awareness and the ability to monitor individual processes within VMs. For this reason, you probably need to select an agent-based third-party tool. With an agent installed in the guest OS instance, the monitoring solution gains more application-level awareness and knowledge, and can monitor for specific service availability.

Selecting the items to monitor must also extend beyond the virtualization environment. As a core technology in your data center, virtualization will touch many other areas, as you've seen throughout this book so far. Your VMware vSphere design should also specify the items that need to be monitored in other areas of the infrastructure. Some examples may include the following:

◆ Storage capacity and storage performance monitoring, taken from the array using tools provided by the storage vendor (these metrics may provide additional insight at a deeper level than would be available from the virtualization layer)

◆ Network utilization or network errors, taken from the networking equipment that sits upstream of the virtualization environment

◆ Hardware-related errors reported via hardware agents or via CIM to a centralized server management console (these may also be reported up through vCenter Server, but with less detail)

◆ Application-level errors or reports that are specific to the particular applications running in the guest OS instances on the VMware vSphere environment (for example, performance reports taken from a database)

Failure to properly define how all these metrics will be monitored means you've potentially omitted a source of data that could provide ongoing feedback about the health and performance of your VMware vSphere environment. This is why it's important to be as thorough and detailed as possible when defining the items and metrics that are included in the design for monitoring.

After you've selected the items to monitor, you'll need to determine the thresholds for those items.

Selecting Thresholds

A monitoring threshold determines a behavior or operation that is considered normal or abnormal. Because every design and every implementation is slightly different, it's not practical for us to provide a comprehensive list of thresholds and items. These need to be determined on a per-project basis.

Let's look at an example. In the early phases of virtualization adoption, customers were virtualizing low-level workloads that had very low CPU utilization. These included things like Active Directory domain controllers, web servers, DHCP or DNS servers, and similar workloads. It was easy to stack lots of these workloads together and achieve high consolidation ratios while still seeing host CPU utilization less than 50–60%. As a result, many organizations tuned their thresholds so that high host CPU utilization, in excess of 80%, would result in an alarm. Why? Simple: because these CPU values were uncommon given the workloads running on the virtualized infrastructure.

As virtualization has matured, however, customers are now virtualizing more substantial workloads, and these more substantial workloads — which include applications like Microsoft SQL Server, Microsoft Exchange, SAP, and others — naturally generate higher CPU loads. Consolidation ratios are lower with these types of workloads, and overall host CPU utilization is higher. As a result, organizations have to retune their thresholds to accommodate the fact that host CPU utilization is now generally higher.

We present this example to reinforce the statement made at the start of this section: thresholds are intended to identify abnormal behavior and generally need to be defined on a per-customer, per-project, or per-implementation basis. Although VMware can and does present general guidelines for thresholds, both in the form of predefined alarms as well as in performance white papers and similar documents, in the end the thresholds you use should be defined based on the specific workloads you are or will be running. For this reason, we don't provide any recommendations for thresholds in this book.

What if you don't know what workloads you'll be running on the virtualized infrastructure? There will always be an amount of uncertainty with regard to the workloads that will run on your environment. After all, who can tell the future? Who can know what sorts of workload the organization will need to deploy six months from now or a year from now? The answer lies in capacity planning, which we'll discuss later in this chapter in the section "Incorporating Capacity Planning in the Design."

With the items to monitor, the tools with which to do the monitoring, and thresholds defined, it's now time for you decide what action to take when a threshold is reached.

Taking Action on Thresholds

For most, if not all, monitoring solutions, an action is taken when a threshold is reached. When host CPU utilization exceeds the threshold you've defined as acceptable and normal, "something" happens. That "something" may be sending an SNMP trap to your SNMP management system, or it may be running a script. The "something" may be different based on which threshold was reached. Whatever the "something" is, you'll need to define this action in your design.

As you'll see with many different areas of virtualization design, this area both is heavily influenced by and heavily influences the selection of the monitoring tools. If you aren't considering the influence that this has on your selection of monitoring tools, you're missing a key component. For example, if you decide to use vCenter Server's alarms as the sole monitoring tool for your virtualized environment based only on the types of items it monitors and the granularity it provides, but you haven't considered the types of actions vCenter Server can take, you've missed half the picture. It's important to consider both aspects when selecting a monitoring solution.

If the monitoring solution offers the ability to execute a script or an application, then you have tremendous flexibility in generating actions. Essentially, the actions you can take are limited only by the limitations of your chosen scripting language. Given that VMware has enthusiastically embraced PowerShell and offers extensive PowerShell integration, having the ability to execute a PowerShell script in response to a threshold having been reached or exceeded is a useful feature.

Here's an example of how you can use scripting (with potentially any scripting language, but especially with PowerShell) with alarms. Let's say you create an alarm in vCenter Server that monitors datastore free space. When that threshold of available free space in the datastore triggers the alarm, you can have the action set to execute a PowerShell script that initiates a storage vMotion operation to migrate a VM to another datastore.

We hope this gives you some ideas about how you can use scripting and automation to broaden the reach of the actions taken by your alarms when thresholds are reached. However you use actions, though, you should be sure to thoroughly document the actions (and any accompanying scripts, if they exist) in your design documentation.

NOTE   If you'd like to learn more about PowerShell and how you may be able to use it to help create custom actions for your monitoring thresholds, one good resource is *VMware vSphere PowerCLI Reference: Automating vSphere Administration* (Sybex, 2011), by Alan Renouf and Luc Dekens.

One final area remains to be addressed: alerting the operators when abnormal values are detected. In some instances, you may include alerting the operators in the actions you've defined when a threshold is reached. If alerting is handled separately, you'll need to define it. We'll cover this in the next section.

Alerting the Operators

In the event that alerting the operators of the virtualization environment is handled separately by the monitoring solution, you also need to decide how and when operators are alerted by the monitoring solution. In many cases, alerting is integrated with the actions that are taken when a threshold is met or exceeded. This is the case, for example, with vCenter Server alarms, where one of the possible actions is sending an email message via SMTP.

For those solutions that don't offer integrated alerting, or for those situations where alerting may be handled via an existing alerting mechanism such as an enterprise systems management tool, you'll need to define, in the design, the alerting structure that will apply to the monitoring system. Will administrators be alerted every time a threshold is met or exceeded, or only after a threshold is exceeded a certain number of times within a specified time window? Will the same type of alert be used in all cases, or will a different type of alert be used for more urgent situations? For example, excessive CPU utilization or high memory utilization within a virtualized instance of a guest OS may not need the same type of alert as a problem with storage availability or host availability. Your design needs to include a description of the types of alerts that will be provided and which thresholds will generate alerts. Some thresholds may generate alerts, but some thresholds may not. This all has to be included in your design.

Building an appropriately configured monitoring solution and strategy into your VMware vSphere designs is a key task. Without the instrumentation that a monitoring solution provides, it would be difficult, if not impossible, to truly understand the behavior of various workloads in the environment.

Capacity planning involves shifting the focus on monitoring from problem resolution to problem prevention. A solid monitoring solution tells you when a bottleneck is present; capacity planning attempts to prevent things from become a bottleneck. Monitoring is reactive; capacity planning is proactive. We'll dive into capacity planning in the next section.

Incorporating Capacity Planning in the Design

We've already said this, but it's a useful distinction between monitoring and capacity planning: monitoring tells you what *has happened* or *is happening*, and capacity planning tells you what *will happen*.

Capacity planning comes in two varieties, both of which are important to the architect of a VMware vSphere design:

- Capacity planning before virtualization occurs, such as that done by VMware Capacity Planner

- Capacity planning after virtualization, such as that done by VMware CapacityIQ or similar products

In this section, we'll look at both types of capacity planning and why they're important to a solid VMware vSphere design.

Planning Before Virtualization

Previrtualization capacity planning invariably involves the assessment of nonvirtualized systems by gathering information such as physical hardware; utilization of resources like CPU, memory, disk, and network; inventorying installed software on the systems; interaction with other systems on the network to understand dependencies; and analyzing all the data to provide estimates or suggestions of what a virtualized environment would look like. This process can be done manually using built-in tools supplied by OS vendors with their OSs, but we recommend the use of an automated tool to help with this task. If you prefer to manually assess your environment before virtualization, we discuss that process in more detail near the end of this section.

USING TOOLS FOR PREVIRTUALIZATION CAPACITY PLANNING

Should you choose to use a tool, a few tools provide the necessary functionality for previrtualization capacity planning:

◆ VMware Capacity Planner (www.vmware.com/products/capacity-planner)

◆ Novell PlateSpin Recon (www.novell.com/products/recon)

◆ CiRBA (www.cirba.com)

Although the tools differ in feature sets, functionality, implementation, and operation, they share the same end result: providing sufficient information for a virtualization architect to properly design an environment that can support the workloads that are proposed to be migrated into this environment.

These tools enable a proper virtualization design by providing critical information necessary for a good design. This information includes the following:

◆ Resource usage in each of the major resource categories (CPU, memory, storage, and networking)

◆ Resource usage patterns, such as when workloads are their busiest or when certain types of resources are most heavily used

◆ Hardware inventory information that you can use to determine whether existing hardware can be repurposed into a virtualized environment

◆ Software inventory information

Although these technical details are important, sometimes nontechnical details are also important. Facts like business unit ownership, compliance, and regulatory requirements can also have a significant impact on the design of a VMware vSphere environment.

For example, consider the idea of business unit ownership. In some organizations, IT assets are owned by individual business units rather than by a central IT group. In these instances, consolidation can typically only occur within a business unit's IT assets rather than across the IT assets of multiple business units. If the previrtualization capacity-planning tool can't account for this additional dimension, then the consolidation recommendations will be skewed because workloads will be stacked without consideration of IT asset ownership, thus potentially placing one group's workload on another group's physical assets. The results won't properly reflect the reality of how consolidation or virtualization will actually occur.

Some of the more advanced tools account for this functionality by incorporating additional business rules. You can use these business rules to model how the virtualized environment would be affected by including other criteria into the planning process. For example, if PCI-compliant and non-PCI-compliant systems must be kept separate, how does that affect the design? If DMZ and internal systems must not share common storage, how does that affect the design?

In many cases, VMware vSphere architects aren't given the opportunity to choose the previrtualization planning tool; they're called in after the initial analysis is performed and the results prepared. Although this situation isn't ideal, it's fairly common. In the cases where you're allowed to select the previrtualization capacity-planning tool, carefully compare the features of the tools to ensure that you select the tool that incorporates and analyzes the information necessary for your organization. If your organization is one in which individual business units own IT assets, then you may need a tool that incorporates business ownership as a factor for helping to determine consolidation ratios and how to stack applications onto a virtualized environment.

The importance of previrtualization capacity planning and the information it provides should be pretty obvious. Without a clear understanding and knowledge of the types of work-loads that will be placed into the virtualized environment, it's almost impossible to craft an effective design. How will you size the storage if you don't know how much storage capacity (in gigabytes or terabytes) is required, or if you don't know how many input/output operations per second (IOPS) are required? How many hosts will you need? Without some sort of assessment of current CPU utilization, you'll be guessing.

Manually Performing Previrtualization Capacity Planning

So far, our discussion of previrtualization capacity planning has focused on the use of capacity-planning tools. As we mentioned earlier, it's possible to do previrtualization capacity planning without the use of additional tools. In these situations, you'll need to manually perform the tasks that are automated by tools. These tasks are summarized at a high level next:

1. Gather performance-utilization information for the physical servers that are included in your list of potential virtualization candidates. Applications and utilities provided by the OS vendors are key here, so use things like Performance Monitor on Windows Server–based systems or tools such as vmstat and top on Linux-based systems.

    Gather information about processor utilization, memory utilization, memory-paging activity, disk utilization for both local disks and storage area network (SAN) attached disks, and network utilization. You need to decide whether you'll gather average utilization only, peak utilization only, or some combination of the two.

    This utilization data also helps you establish a performance baseline, a reference point against which you can compare later. Performance baselines are helpful in a couple of ways: they help protect against skewed perceptions after virtualization ("It's slower now that it's virtualized") and can provide assistance when you're troubleshooting by making it easier to identify abnormalities in the environment.

GATHER BOTH PEAK AND AVERAGE UTILIZATION DATA

Gathering only peak utilization data or only average utilization data will leave you exposed in your analysis. If you gather only peak utilization data, then your consolidation estimates will be much lower than they probably need to be. However, you'll be guaranteed that resources will exist to meet the peak requirements.

If, on the other hand, you gather only average utilization, then you're likely to come up with consolidation estimates that are much closer to what is actually required. However, in this case you run the risk of stacking workloads whose peaks will cause a resource shortage to occur when they all ask for resources at the same time. This may cause the virtualized infrastructure to be unable to satisfy the resource requirements during these periods of peak demand.

What is the best approach? You should gather both peak utilization data and average utilization data, and do your best to incorporate both aspects into your consolidation assessment.

---

2. Gather inventory information for your virtualization candidates. Inventory information is necessary because utilization and performance data are typically reported as percentages. 90% CPU utilization may be a concern for a workload running on the latest and greatest 3.0 GHz processors, but 90% CPU utilization on a 400 MHz CPU is an entirely different story. The same goes for memory usage, disk usage, and network usage.

3. Standardize the data you've gathered across different OSs. Virtualization makes it possible to run Windows Server–based systems and Linux- or Unix-based systems on the same physical hardware. However, the utilization/performance data provided by these OSs is in different formats and measurements. If you don't standardize the data across different OSs, then you'll only be able to estimate consolidation within groups of systems running the same OS instead of across all systems and all OS instances. This will generally result in lower consolidation ratios. Depending on the organization, this may be acceptable; but in many cases, organizations want to achieve the highest possible consolidation ratio.

   The process for standardizing the data depends on the tools being used and the OSs involved, but typically it involves converting the values into standard values that apply across OSs. For example, you can convert CPU utilization to gigahertz or megahertz and convert memory utilization into gigabytes or megabytes. Converting the percentage-based utilization data to solid numbers is also a byproduct of this step and a necessary part, as you'll see in the next step.

4. After you've standardized the data, you're finally ready to begin the process of stacking workloads. What do we mean by *stacking workloads*? For a group of workloads, you take the standardized resource-usage numbers created from the previous step and add them together. The result represents a rough analysis of what those workloads would look like if they were all running on the same hardware. You then compare the combined values against a reference point. The reference point is typically a set of limits on an anticipated hardware platform. This boils down to a trial-and-error process in which you compare various combinations of workloads against the reference point until you find the optimal combination for your environment.

   For example, let's say you're planning to use servers that have two quad-core 2.53 GHz CPUs. That is a total of just over 20 GHz of CPU capacity. If you say you only want your hosts to be 80% utilized for CPU capacity, then you can stack workloads until you reach 16 GHz of utilization. You must repeat this process for each of the four major resource areas: CPU, memory, disk, and network. As you stack workloads, you also need to account for other sorts of limits, such as limiting the number of VMs per logical unit number (LUN) due to IOPS or limiting the number of VMs per host in order to minimize the size of the fault domain. Finally, if you can, you should also factor in nontechnical rules such as business-unit ownership or regulatory compliance when performing your analysis, because these rules will also affect the consolidation ratio as well as the placement of workloads on physical hosts.

As you can see, this can quickly become a complex multidimensional analysis. You'll probably need to perform this process multiple times against multiple reference points (for example, different hardware platforms or hardware configurations) in order to find the optimal combination of workloads, hardware platform, and hardware configuration. Keep in mind that this process isn't about the raw consolidation ratio — it's about finding the right balance of workloads on physical servers for maximum efficiency.

A MANUAL ANALYSIS WILL PROVIDE A ROUGH GUESS AT BEST

Performing a manual capacity-planning exercise before virtualization will provide a rough estimate, at best, of what the consolidation results will look like. Why? A manual analysis probably won't take into account VMware vSphere's memory-management functions, such as transparent page sharing, memory ballooning, and memory compression. A manual analysis also isn't likely to be able to take into account the effect of combining I/O workloads and the effect this will have on I/O performance, for example. Still, it will suffice to provide a rough estimate of what will be required.

---

5. Your final product provides at least three pieces of information. First, it gives you a rough idea of how many servers are required to virtualize the selected candidates. Second, it provides a list of which workloads are stacked with which other workloads after consolidation. Third, it identifies workloads relying on hardware that can't be virtualized (fax servers relying on a fax board, for example) and workloads whose resource utilization exceeds limits you've defined.

As you can see by this high-level description, manually performing previrtualization capacity planning is time consuming and difficult, especially in larger environments and environments that have nontechnical business rules affecting the results. For this reason, we recommend that you use one of the tools mentioned earlier for the majority of instances.

Capacity planning before virtualization is important, as we've already discussed, but capacity planning during virtualization is also important. The next section examines capacity planning during virtualization.

Planning During Virtualization

Capacity planning after virtualization (or during virtualization, if you prefer) typically involves the use of historical performance and monitoring data to perform trending analyses. The results of these trending analyses are used to create projections of virtualization usage that help administrators understand how quickly resources are being consumed and when additional resources will need to be added to the virtualization infrastructure.

USING TOOLS FOR CAPACITY PLANNING DURING VIRTUALIZATION

As with previrtualization capacity planning, a number of products on the market provide this functionality:

- ◆ VMware CapacityIQ (www.vmware.com/products/vcenter-capacityiq)

- ◆ VKernel Capacity Management Suite (www.vkernel.com/products/capacity-management-suite)

- ◆ Hyper9 (www.hyper9.com/product_overview.aspx)

- ◆ Quest vFoglight (www.quest.com/vfoglight)

Although capacity planning during virtualization is, in large part, about forecasting trends in resource usage, a number of other features have come to be included in this category as well. These features include the following:

- ◆ Identifying inactive or idle VMs that may be consuming capacity. This is targeted at encouraging more effective VM lifecycle management. By decommissioning inactive VMs that may no longer be in use, organizations gain more efficient use of virtualization resources.

- ◆ Identifying VMs that aren't right-sized — that have been configured with more resources than they typically use based on historical performance data. Again, by right-sizing VMs, organizations can use virtualization resources more efficiently.

- ◆ Identifying orphaned VMs and VM resources, such as virtual disks that are still on the storage platform but are no longer referenced by an active VM.

Through the addition of these features and their association with tools that also perform capacity planning, many of the products and solutions are now referred to as *capacity management* or *capacity optimization* solutions. The fundamental purpose is the same, though: providing insight into resource usage in the virtualized environment and helping virtualization administrators know when more resources need to be added.

When it comes to selecting a tool to help with capacity planning (or capacity management, if you prefer), you'll want to answer some questions. The answers will help you determine which tool is right for your environment:

What Is the Resource Impact of This Tool? One of the basic principles of quantum physics is that you can't observe something without changing it. This principle holds true in virtualized environments as well — you can't observe the virtual environment without changing it. Usually, this change comes in the form of resource usage by the tools that are intended to watch resource usage. What you need to know, then, is how many resources this tool consumes. How much additional memory will it require? Will it require additional memory on every VMware ESX/ESXi host in my environment, or just on one? Does it require an agent installed in your guest OS instances? If so, what is the resource impact of that guest OS agent? How CPU intensive is the tool, or how CPU intensive are certain features of the tool?

Does It Meet Your Functional Requirements? At the risk of sounding like a broken record, we can't stress enough the importance of solid functional requirements. What specific features do you or your business require from this solution? Do you need the ability to do trending analysis of resource usage? Most solutions offer this functionality. Do you need the ability to identify orphaned VM resources, such as snapshots or virtual disks, which are no longer in use? Not all tools offer this functionality. Without a clear understanding of the basic functional requirements, you'll be unable to select the tool that best meets your needs.

What Impact Does This Tool Have on Your Design?   Even if the capacity-planning tool is very lightweight and doesn't consume a great deal of resources, it will still have an impact on your design. Will it require specific configurations, such as probe VMs, to be installed on every VMware ESX/ESXi host? Does it require a certain type of networking configuration to be used, or does it only support a particular storage protocol? What is the financial impact on the design? In other words, how much does the tool cost? What is the operational impact on the design? Put another way, who will operate this software, and how does that fit into the design's existing or proposed operational model?

Based on the answers to these questions, you can begin to go about incorporating a capacity-planning tool into your overall design. After the selection of the capacity-planning tool is complete, you can amend your design, where necessary, to account for increased resource usage by the tool or to adjust for any changes to the operational procedures required in the design. You should also amend your design to account for the new functionality this tool adds; for example, you may want to add operational procedures that discuss creating regular reports about inactive VMs, orphaned VM resources, or resource-usage trends. You may also consider building a design that is a bit leaner with regard to extra resources, knowing that the capacity-planning tool can provide recommendations about when additional resources will need to be added. This may help reduce initial acquisition costs and make the design more palatable for your organization.

MANUALLY PERFORMING CAPACITY PLANNING DURING VIRTUALIZATION

As with previrtualization capacity planning, it's possible to perform capacity planning after virtualization without the use of additional tools. There will almost certainly be a feature gap between the use of third-party tools and a manual capacity-planning process, but this is nevertheless a viable approach for any VMware vSphere design.

What's involved in manually performing capacity planning? As with previrtualization planning, several steps are involved.

1. Determine the specific aspects of the design for which you'll perform capacity planning. At the very least, we recommend that you include processor utilization, memory utilization, storage utilization from both a capacity and a performance perspective, and network utilization. As you add more utilization information, the analysis will become more complicated and more in-depth, so balance depth of information against your own skill in analyzing and correlating the data.

2. Begin gathering utilization data for the selected resource types. For example, begin periodically logging utilization data. You may be able to gather this utilization data directly from your VMware ESX/ESXi hosts, or you may need to extract it from vCenter Server.

   For example, if you want to gather data about guest OS storage latency as reported by Storage I/O Control in vSphere 4.1, you need to get that information from vCenter Server. If you want information about CPU usage, you can get it directly from a host or from vCenter Server. It's possible that you can use vCenter Server's existing performance data, as long as vCenter Server's polling frequency and data-rollup schedule are acceptable for your purposes. (Many third-party tools rely on vCenter Server's database.) The same tip regarding peak and average utilization mentioned earlier in our discussion about manually performing previrtualization capacity planning also applies here.

3. When you have the utilization data, you need to analyze it in some fashion to get an idea of any trends that are hidden in the data. For example, you can use an Excel spreadsheet and chart to show you trends in average CPU usage over time.

4. Extrapolate those trends to see where things will stand one month, two months, or three months into the future. It's up to you how far out you want to look. Extrapolating data will tell you that you'll run out of memory in two months based on the current growth data, for example.

A simpler, but potentially less accurate, means of managing capacity centers on planning around VM growth. For example, if you know that the number of VMs in your environment will increase by 25% per year, you can use the following formula to calculate how many additional hosts will be required in the next year:

(Growth rate × VM count × Length of time) ÷ Consolidation ratio

An environment with 200 VMs and an expected consolidation ratio of 15:1 results in the following calculation of additional hosts needed in one year:

(25% × 200 × 1) ÷ 15 = 4 additional hosts (rounded up)

Or consider an environment with 300 VMs, an expected (or measured) consolidation ratio of 12:1, and an expected growth of 20% over the next year:

(20% × 300 × 1) ÷ 12 = 5 additional hosts

Although this formula gives you an idea of how many hosts will be needed over the course of the next year, it doesn't tell you when those hosts will be needed. For that, you need to go back to monitoring resource usage and extrapolating data. Between these two methods, though, you should be able to get a fairly good handle on managing the growth of your VMware vSphere environment.

Other aspects of capacity management, such as identifying inactive VMs or orphaned VM resources, can be addressed through the definition of operational procedures that specify routine and regular audits of the environment and the VM configurations. This can be time consuming, but the cost savings resulting from more efficient use of virtualization resources may offset the expense of the additional operational overhead. Further, using automation tools such as vCenter Orchestrator and/or PowerCLI can reduce operational overhead and streamline tasks.

Capacity planning, like monitoring, can be an extremely useful and important part of your vSphere design. In some ways, it's every bit as important as the storage, networking, and cluster designs. In the next chapter, we'll put your design skills to the test in a review of a sample design intended to help you pull it all together.

Summary

In this chapter, we've discussed the importance of incorporating monitoring and capacity planning into your VMware vSphere design. A design can't be static; it must be flexible enough to grow or shrink as the company adopting the design also grows or shrinks. Monitoring provides the instrumentation necessary to determine the need to grow or shrink. When combined with capacity planning, operators not only know the immediate needs but can also attempt to forecast future needs. In many ways, monitoring and capacity planning are two sides of the same coin: one is reactive and targeted for the here and now (monitoring), and the other is proactive and targeted for the future (capacity planning).

When you're selecting a monitoring solution, ask yourself questions that help you determine the company's specific organizational and functional requirements. These requirements will often play a significant role in selecting the appropriate monitoring solution.

Capacity planning isn't quite as well developed as monitoring; there are still a limited number of products and vendors supplying capacity-planning products. Nevertheless, building capacity planning into the design allows future operators or IT directors to get a better idea of the growth trends and forecasted rate of acquisition for VMware ESX/ESXi hosts, network capacity, memory, and storage. Using this trending and forecasting data, administrators can add capacity to their environments before running out of resources.

Chapter 11

Bringing It All Together

In this final chapter, we'll pull together all the various topics that we've covered throughout this book and put them to use in a high-level walkthrough of a VMware vSphere design. Along the way, we hope you'll get a better understanding of VMware vSphere design and the intricacies that are involved in creating a design.

This chapter will cover the following topics:

- ◆ Examining the decisions made in a design
- ◆ Considering the reasons behind design decisions
- ◆ Exploring the impact on the design of changes to a decision
- ◆ Mitigating the impact of design changes

Sample Design

For the next few pages, we'll walk you, at a high level, through a simple VMware vSphere design for a fictional company called XYZ Widgets. We'll first provide a business overview, followed by an overview of the major areas of the design, organized in the same fashion as the chapters in the book. Because VMware vSphere design documentation can be rather lengthy, we'll include only relevant details and explanations. A real-world design will almost certainly need to be more complete, more detailed, and more in-depth than what is presented in this chapter. Our purpose here is to give you a framework in which to think about how the various vSphere design points fit together and interact with each other and to help promote a holistic view of the design.

We'll start with a quick business overview and a review of the virtualization goals for XYZ Widgets.

Business Overview for XYZ Widgets

XYZ Widgets is a small manufacturing company. XYZ currently has about 60 physical servers, many of which are older and soon to be out of warranty and no longer under support. To help both reduce the cost of refreshing the hardware and gain increased flexibility with IT resources, XYZ has decided to deploy VMware vSphere in its environment. As is the case with many smaller organizations, XYZ has a very limited IT staff, and the staff is responsible for all aspects of IT — there are no dedicated networking staff and no dedicated storage administrators.

XYZ has the following goals in mind:

◆ XYZ would like to convert 60 existing workloads into VMs via a physical-to-virtual (P2V) process.

◆ XYZ would like the environment to be able to hold up to 100 VMs in the first couple of years. This works out to be about 33% growth in the anticipated number of VMs over the next year.

◆ XYZ wants to streamline its day-to-day IT operations, so the design should incorporate that theme. XYZ management feels the IT staff should be able to "do more with less."

These other requirements and constraints also affected XYZ's vSphere design:

◆ XYZ has an existing Fibre Channel (FC) storage area network (SAN) and an existing storage array that it wants to reuse. Because this design decision is already made, it can be considered a design constraint.

◆ There are a variety of workloads on XYZ's existing physical servers, including Microsoft Exchange 2007, DHCP, Active Directory domain controllers, web servers, file servers, print servers, some database servers, and a collection of application servers. Most of these workloads are running on Microsoft Windows Server 2003, but some are Windows Server 2008 and some are running on Linux.

◆ A separate network infrastructure refresh project determined that Cisco Catalyst 3750 switches would be the new standard access-layer switch moving forward (replacing older 100 Mbps access-layer switches), so this is what XYZ must use in its design. This is another design constraint.

◆ XYZ would like to use Active Directory as its single authentication point, as it currently does today.

◆ XYZ doesn't have an existing monitoring or management framework in place today.

◆ XYZ has sufficient power and cooling in its data center to accommodate new hardware (especially as older hardware is removed due to the virtualization initiative), but it could have problems supporting high-density power or cooling requirements. The new hardware must take this into consideration.

YOUR REQUIREMENTS AND CONSTRAINTS WILL LIKELY BE MUCH MORE DETAILED

The requirements and constraints listed for XYZ Widgets are intentionally limited to major design vectors to keep this example simple while still allowing us to examine the impact of various design decisions. In real life, of course, your requirements and constraints will almost certainly be much more detailed and in-depth. In fact, you should ensure that your design constraints and requirements don't leave any loose ends that may later cause a surprise. Don't be afraid of being too detailed here!

Now that you have a rough idea of the goals behind XYZ's virtualization initiative, let's review its design, organized topically according to the chapters in this book.

Hypervisor Selection (VMware ESX vs. VMware ESXi)

XYZ's vSphere design calls for the use of VMware ESX 4.1. XYZ's design team selected VMware ESX because some of the company's staff had prior experience with the VMware vSphere product family and because some of the staff has experience managing Linux-based systems. Although technically only the Service Console of VMware ESX is based on Linux (and not the hypervisor itself), the IT team felt that this experience was relevant. VMware ESX will be installed locally on the physical servers.

vSphere Management Layer

XYZ purchased licensing for VMware vSphere Enterprise Plus and will deploy VMware vCenter Server 4.1 to manage its virtualization environment. To help reduce the overall footprint of physical servers, XYZ has opted to run vCenter Server as a VM. The vCenter Server VM will run both vCenter Server 4.1 as well as an instance of Microsoft SQL Server 2008 on an installed instance of Windows Server 2008 R2 64-bit. This server will also run vCenter Update Manager to manage updates for the VMware ESX hosts. XYZ won't use vCenter Update Manager to manage updates to guest OS instances. No other VMware management products are planned for deployment in XYZ's environment at this time.

Server Hardware

XYZ Widgets has historically deployed HP ProLiant rack-mount servers in its data center. In order to avoid retraining the staff on a new hardware platform or new operational procedures, XYZ opted to continue to use HP ProLiant rack-mount servers for its new VMware vSphere environment. It selected the HP DL380 G6, an Intel Xeon 5500-based server, configured with two quad-core CPUs and 48 GB of RAM. The servers will have a pair of 72 GB hot-plug hard drives configured as a RAID 1 mirror for protection against drive failure.

Network connectivity is provided by a total of six Gigabit Ethernet (GbE) network ports, and SAN connectivity is provided by a dual-port 4 Gbps FC host bus adapter (HBA). (More information about the specific networking and shared storage configurations is provided in an upcoming section.) Previrtualization capacity planning indicates that XYZ will need 10 servers in order to virtualize the 100 workloads it would like to virtualize (a 10:1 consolidation ratio).

Networking Configuration

As we mentioned, each of the proposed VMware vSphere hosts has a total of six GbE network ports. XYZ Widgets proposes to configure these GbE ports as uplinks for a vNetwork distributed switch (vDS, or dvSwitch). The vDS will contain port groups for the following traffic types:

♦ Service Console

♦ vMotion

♦ NFS

♦ Fault tolerance (FT)

♦ VM traffic spanning three different VLANs

A group of Cisco Catalyst 3750 switches provides upstream network connectivity, and every server will be connected to multiple switches for redundancy. Because the Catalyst 3750 switches support multichassis link aggregation, the vDS will be configured with the "Route based on IP hash" load-balancing policy, and the physical switches will be configured accordingly. Each Catalyst 3750 switch has redundant connections to XYZ's network core. XYZ believes that the use of NFS for templates and ISOs won't generate unsustainable network traffic that can't be handled by the network infrastructure.

Shared Storage Configuration

XYZ Widgets already owned a FC-based SAN that was installed for a previous project. The determination was made, based on previrtualization capacity planning, that the SAN needed to be able to support an additional 7,000 I/O operations per second (IOPS) in order to virtualize XYZ's workloads. To support this workload, XYZ has added a pair of 200 GB enterprise flash drives (EFDs) and thirty 600 GB 15K FC drives. These additional drives support an additional 18 TB of raw storage capacity and approximately 10,000 IOPS (without considering RAID overhead).

The EFDs will be placed into a RAID 1 (mirrored) group and presented as a single 200 GB LUN. This 200 GB LUN can be used for limited workloads that require the absolute highest levels of performance. The 15K FC drives will be placed into a RAID 5 storage pool. Approximately 2 TB of the storage capacity from the FC drives will be presented via NFS for templates, ISOs, and other software; the remainder will be carved into 1 TB LUNs and presented to the VMware ESX hosts.

As described earlier, the VMware ESX hosts are attached via FC HBAs to redundant SAN fabrics, and the storage controllers of XYZ's storage array — an active/passive array according to VMware's definitions — have multiple ports that are also attached to the redundant SAN fabrics. The storage array is Asymmetric Logical Unit Access (ALUA) compliant.

VM Design

XYZ has a number of physical workloads that will be migrated into its VMware vSphere environment via a P2V migration. These workloads consist of various applications running on Windows Server 2003 and Windows Server 2008. During the P2V process, XYZ will right-size the resulting VM to ensure that it isn't oversized. The right-sizing will be based on information gathered during the previrtualization capacity planning process.

For all new VMs moving forward, the guest OS will be Windows Server 2008. XYZ will use a standard of 4 GB RAM per VM and a single vCPU. The single vCPU can be increased later if performance needs warrant doing so. A thick-provisioned 40 GB Virtual Machine Disk Format (VMDK) will be used for the system disk, using the LSI Logic SAS adapter (the default adapter for Windows Server 2008). XYZ chose the LSI Logic SAS adapter for the system disk because it's the default adapter for this guest OS and because support for the adapter is provided out of the box with Windows Server 2008. XYZ felt that using the paravirtual SCSI adapter for the system disk added unnecessary complexity. Additional VMDKs will be added on a per-VM basis as needed and will use the paravirtualized SCSI adapter. Because these data drives are added after the installation of Windows into the VM, XYZ felt that the use of the paravirtualized SCSI driver was acceptable for these virtual disks.

VMware Datacenter Design

XYZ will configure vCenter Server to support only a single datacenter and a single cluster containing all 10 of its VMware ESX hosts. The cluster will be enabled for VMware High

Availability (HA) and VMware Distributed Resource Scheduling (DRS). Because the cluster is homogenous with regard to CPU type and family, XYZ has elected not to enable VMware Enhanced vMotion Compatibility (EVC) at this time. VMware HA will be configured to perform host monitoring but not VM monitoring, and VMware DRS will be configured as Fully Automated and set to act on recommendations of three stars or greater.

Security Architecture

XYZ will ensure that the Service Console firewall on the VMware ESX hosts is configured and enabled, and only essential services will be allowed through the firewall. Generally accepted best practices for VMware ESX, such as disallowing root login via SSH, enforcing strong passwords, requiring the use of sudo, and limiting knowledge of the root password to only critical staff, will be followed. Logins to VMware ESX hosts will be integrated into XYZ's existing Active Directory infrastructure.

vCenter Server will be a member of XYZ's Active Directory domain and will use default permissions. XYZ's VMware administrative staff is fairly small and doesn't see a need for a wide number of highly differentiated roles within vCenter Server.

Monitoring and Capacity Planning

XYZ performed previrtualization capacity planning. The results indicated that 10 physical hosts would provide enough resources to virtualize the existing workloads and provide sufficient room for initial anticipated growth. XYZ's VMware vSphere administrators plan to use vCenter Server's performance graphs to do both real-time monitoring and basic historical analysis and trending.

vCenter Server's default alerts will be used initially and then customized as needed after the environment has been populated and a better idea exists of what normal utilization will look like. vCenter Server will send emails via XYZ's existing email system in the event a staff member needs to be alerted regarding a threshold or other alarm.

Examining the Design

Now that you've seen an overview of XYZ's VMware vSphere design, we'd like to explore the design in a bit more detail through a series of questions. The purpose of these questions is to get you thinking about how the various aspects of a design integrate with each other and are interdependent on each other. You may find it helpful to grab a blank sheet of paper and start writing down your thoughts as you work through these questions.

These questions have no right answers, and the responses that we provide here are simply to guide your thoughts — they don't necessarily reflect any concrete or specific recommendations. There are multiple ways to fulfill the functional requirements of any given design, so keep that in mind! Once again, we'll organize the questions topically according to the chapters in this book; this will also make it easier for you to refer back to the appropriate chapter where applicable.

Hypervisor Selection (VMware ESX vs. VMware ESXi)

As you saw in Chapter 2, "VMware ESX vs. VMware ESXi," the choice to use VMware ESX or VMware ESXi is a key decision point in vSphere designs and will affect other design decisions.

XYZ has chosen to use VMware ESX instead of VMware ESXi. What impact will this choice have in the future? This is a pretty open-ended question, but we know for certain that XYZ is now a position that will require a migration at some point in the future. VMware has publicly stated that vSphere 4.1 is the last version of vSphere that will include VMware ESX; all future releases will include only VMware ESXi. By selecting VMware ESX as its hypervisor platform, XYZ Widgets now finds itself in the position of having to migrate from VMware ESX to VMware ESXi at some point in the future.

What impact would it have on XYZ's design to switch to VMware ESXi now? From a functionality perspective, this change would have very little impact. XYZ licensed vSphere Enterprise Plus, and VMware ESX and VMware ESXi share the same core functionality when applied with a vSphere Enterprise Plus license. Both of them would be managed through vCenter Server.

The real impacts come elsewhere. What about hardware agent support? The information we've provided doesn't specifically call out XYZ's use of hardware agents, but this would be one potential area of concern.

Are there other potential areas of concern? Some things for you to think about include VMware ESXi software updates (how are these handled compared to VMware ESX?), hardware troubleshooting (is there a way to run vendor-recommended diagnostic or troubleshooting tools on the hosts?), and management in the event of a loss of vCenter Server (how will the hosts be managed if vCenter Server is unavailable?).

vSphere Management Layer

We discussed design decisions concerning the vSphere management layer in Chapter 3, "Designing the Management Layer." In this section, we'll examine some of the design decisions XYZ made regarding its vSphere management layer.

XYZ is planning to run vCenter Server as a VM. What are the benefits of this arrangement? What are the disadvantages? As we discussed in Chapter 3, running vCenter Server as a VM can offer some benefits. For example, XYZ can protect vCenter Server from hardware failure using VMware HA, which may help reduce overall downtime. Depending on XYZ's backup solution and strategy (not described here), it's possible that backups of vCenter Server may be easier to make and easier to restore. However, there is one key potential concern with XYZ's proposed configuration: the interaction between the vDS and its control plane (which resides in vCenter Server). In this case, the vDS control plane depends on the vDS it's managing in order to manage it. In the event that network connectivity to vCenter Server is lost, XYZ may run into a problem getting that network connectivity restored (depending on the cause of the outage).

Are there other disadvantages that you see? What about other advantages to this configuration?

Is there an alternate configuration that might mitigate some of the concerns with running vCenter Server as a VM? There are at least two different ways to address this potential concern. First, XYZ could opt to deploy the Nexus 1000V distributed virtual switch from

Cisco. This takes the control plane out of vCenter Server and places it into a pair of VMs (or a physical appliance). The downside of this approach is its additional cost.

XYZ could also choose to utilize a hybrid networking approach that uses a vNetwork standard switch for management traffic and a vDS for all other traffic. This removes the dependency on vCenter Server for management traffic but reduces the number of uplinks available for other types of traffic. Figure 11.1 shows what this hybrid configuration might look like.

FIGURE 11.1
A hybrid network configuration for XYZ's vSphere environment

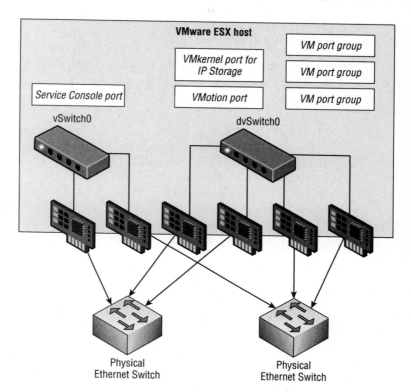

What is the impact of running vCenter Server, SQL Server, and vCenter Update Manager in the same guest OS instance? The resource needs of the vCenter Server VM will clearly be much greater than they would have been without combining these applications. VMware's recommendation of 4 GB RAM for vCenter Server will handle up to 50 hosts; XYZ will only have 10 hosts. By allocating 6 GB or 8 GB RAM to this VM to account for the additional overhead of SQL Server, XYZ should see acceptable performance.

Overall, the configuration complexity is slightly reduced because there is no need for a dedicated service account for authentication to SQL Server and because there are fewer VMs to manage (only one VM running all three applications instead of three VMs each running one application). On the downside, a fault in this VM affects multiple services.

Server Hardware

Server hardware and the design decisions around server hardware were the focus of our discussion in Chapter 4, "Server Hardware." In this section we ask you a few questions about XYZ's hardware decisions and the impact on the company's design.

What changes might need to be made to XYZ's design if it opted to use blade servers instead of rack-mount servers? The answers to this question depend partially on the specific blade-server solution selected. Because XYZ was described as using primarily HP servers, if the blade-server solution selected was HP's c7000 blade chassis, a number of potential changes would arise:

◆ The design description indicates that XYZ will use 10 physical servers. They will fit into a single physical chassis but may be better spread across two physical chassis to protect against the failure of a chassis. This increases the cost of the solution.

◆ XYZ plans to use a cluster size of 10 VMware ESX hosts. If it's spread across two blade chassis, that leaves five blades in each chassis. XYZ is therefore exposed to a potential situation where VMware HA won't function correctly if one of the blade chassis goes offline. This is the case because all five VMware HA primary nodes could potentially end up in a single chassis. Protecting against this situation requires the addition of third chassis, which further drives up the cost. It would be up to XYZ to determine whether the risk of chassis failure warranted the need to protect against the possibility.

◆ Depending on the specific type of blade selected, the number of NICs might change. If the number of NICs was reduced too far, this would have an impact on the networking configuration. Changes to the network configuration (for example, having to cut out NFS traffic due to limited NICs) could then affect the storage configuration.

What if XYZ decided to use 1U rack-mount servers instead of 2U rack-mount servers like the HP DL380 specified in the design description? Without knowing the specific details of the 1U server selected, it would be difficult to determine the exact impact on the design. If you assume that XYZ has switched to an HP DL360 or equivalent 1U rack server, you should ensure that they can maintain enough network and storage connectivity due to a reduced number of PCI Express expansion slots. There might also be concerns over the RAM density, which would impact the projected consolidation ratio and increase the number of servers required. This, in turn, could push the cost of the project higher. You should also ensure that the selected server model is fully supported by VMware and is on the Hardware Compatibility List (HCL).

Would a move to a quad-socket server platform increase the consolidation ratio for XYZ? We haven't given you the details to determine the answer to this question. You'd need an idea of the aggregate CPU and memory utilization of the expected workloads. Based on that information, you could determine whether CPU utilization might be a bottleneck.

In all likelihood, CPU utilization wouldn't be a bottleneck; memory usually runs out before CPU capacity, but it depends on the workload characteristics. Without additional details, it's almost impossible to say for certain if an increase in CPU capacity would help improve the consolidation ratio. However, based on our experience, XYZ is probably better served by increasing the amount of memory in its servers instead of increasing CPU capacity.

Networking Configuration

The networking configuration of any vSphere design is a critical piece, and we discussed networking design in detail in Chapter 5, "Designing Your Network." XYZ's networking design is examined in greater detail in this section.

What are some potential concerns with XYZ's proposed virtual networking configuration? How might you address those potential concerns?   As described earlier, the interaction between running vCenter Server as a VM and running a vDS could pose a problem; the loss of vCenter Server means that XYZ loses the ability to perform any network configuration. If network configuration is necessary to restore vCenter Server to proper operation, then XYZ is caught in an interdependency that it can't easily resolve. However, there are also other potential concerns here.

XYZ is using six uplinks and has specified that it will use link aggregation with those six uplinks. But most networking vendors recommend the use of one, two, four, or eight uplinks due to the algorithms used to place traffic on the individual members of the link-aggregation group. Using six uplinks will most likely result in an unequal distribution of traffic across those uplinks. The link-aggregation configuration is also more complex than a configuration that doesn't use link aggregation.

TIP   For more information about how the load-balancing algorithms on Cisco's switches work, refer to www.cisco.com/en/US/tech/tk389/tk213/technologies_tech_note09186a0080094714.shtml.

What changes would need to be made, if any, to XYZ's design if it decided to use standard vSwitches instead of a vDS? What are the advantages and disadvantages to this approach?   Switching to vNetwork Standard Switches would remove the potential concern about running vCenter Server as a VM with a vDS. Depending on how XYZ chose to allocate the uplinks to the vSwitches — one configuration is illustrated in Figure 11.2 — it might also address the concerns over unequal load distribution in the link-aggregation groups. The example configuration in Figure 11.2 uses two uplinks, so this would work well with the load-balancing algorithms that many physical switches use.

Of course, this configuration has drawbacks as well. Administrative overhead is potentially increased because changes to the network configuration of the VMware ESX hosts must be performed on each individual VMware ESX host, instead of being centrally managed like the vDS. The fact that vSwitches are managed per host introduces the possibility of a configuration mismatch between hosts, and configuration mismatches could result in VMs being inaccessible from the network after a vMotion (either a manual vMotion or an automated move initiated by VMware DRS).

On the flip side, given that XYZ is using Enterprise Plus licensing, it could opt to use host profiles to help automate the management of the vNetwork standard switches and help reduce the likelihood of configuration mismatches between servers. Host profiles won't help in the physical world, though; if XYZ wants to continue to use link aggregation, there will now be separate link aggregation groups on each physical switch that must be created and managed for each vSwitch. This also adds administrative overhead.

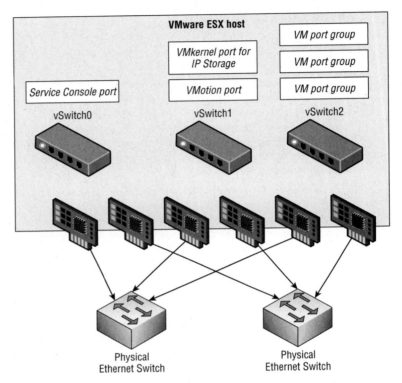

FIGURE 11.2
A potential configuration for XYZ using vNetwork Standard Switches instead of a vDS

What impact would switching to 10GbE have on XYZ's design? A change to 10GbE would have an impact in a number of areas of the design. Some potential changes might include the following:

◆ A significant reduction in the number of network ports, most likely down to two 10GbE ports instead of six 1GbE ports. This would mean that the network configuration would have to be revised to accommodate that change.

◆ A dramatic increase in throughput available on the network links. This speed boost would make the use of NFS or iSCSI more attractive because it would offset the complexity involved in trying to improve bandwidth of IP-based storage protocols over 1GbE links (a potential reduction in VMkernel ports, simplified NFS export or iSCSI target configuration, and a reduced need for link aggregation).

In this particular example, keep in mind that XYZ wants to reuse its FC SAN and storage array, so a full switch to IP-based storage protocols might not be applicable. However, the use of 10GbE might open the door for FC over Ethernet (FCoE), which would allow XYZ to use its existing SAN and still take advantage of 10GbE links.

◆ Networking equipment would have to be swapped out; the Catalyst 3750 doesn't support enough 10GbE ports to be cost effective. A different network switch would need to be included in the design.

Shared Storage Configuration

The requirement of shared storage to use so many of vSphere's most useful features, like vMotion, makes shared-storage design correspondingly more important in your design. Refer back to Chapter 6, "Shared Storage," if you need more information as we take a closer look at XYZ's shared-storage design.

How would XYZ's design need to change if it decided to use NFS exclusively for all its storage? Are there any considerations to this design decision? Some changes are immediately apparent. First, XYZ would no longer need FC HBAs in its servers and would probably want to add more network connectivity in place of the HBAs. Second, the way in which the storage is presented to the hosts would likely change; XYZ might opt to go with larger NFS exports. The size of the NFS exports would need to be gated by a few different factors:

◆ The amount of I/O being generated by the VMs placed on that NFS datastore, because network throughput would likely be the bottleneck in this instance.

◆ The amount of time it took to back up or restore an entire datastore. XYZ would need to ensure that these times fell within its agreed recovery time objective (RTO) for the business.

With regard to network throughput, although XYZ's design calls for the use of link aggregation, it's important to understand that even with link aggregation, the bandwidth between any two single endpoints — in this case, a VMkernel port being used for NFS traffic and the IP address of the NFS export — is still limited to the bandwidth of a single member of the link-aggregation group. In this case, that's 1 Gb of network throughput. The only way to address this would be for XYZ to move to 10GbE. As mentioned earlier, a move to 10GbE would also have impacts in other areas.

Finally, a move to only NFS would prevent the use of raw device mappings (RDMs) for any applications in the environment, because RDMs aren't possible on NFS.

How would XYZ's design need to change if it decided to use FC exclusively for all its storage? If XYZ were to eliminate NFS from its design, it would eliminate some of the networking traffic. However, because XYZ's target servers use a quad-port NIC, it's unlikely that it could or even should reduce the number of network ports available in its servers. The shared-storage configuration would need to change slightly, but the change wouldn't be significant. This is a relatively low-impact change, but it's also a change that doesn't, in our opinion, offer much real benefit.

Would a switch to FCoE have a significant impact on XYZ's design? First, a switch to FCoE could potentially block XYZ from taking advantage of other server form factors, depending on the company's server vendor. Not all server vendors support FCoE with its blade servers. FCoE also implies 10GbE, which entails all the impacts we described earlier. The networking equipment would need to be swapped out, because the Catalyst 3750 switches specified in the design don't support 10GbE and don't support FCoE.

A switch to FCoE does allow XYZ to continue to use its existing FC-based SAN and FC attached storage array, because FCoE and FC are interoperable. This might be a good interim step for XYZ if it planned to eventually phase out its FC equipment.

How would XYZ's design need to change if it decided to use iSCSI (via the VMware ESX software iSCSI initiator) instead of FC? As with replacing FC with NFS, the hardware configuration would need to change. XYZ would want to replace the FC HBA with an expansion card offering additional network ports. The company might also want to change the network configuration to account for the additional storage traffic and to help ensure that iSCSI traffic wasn't negatively affected by other traffic patterns. This could involve moving iSCSI traffic off to a dedicated vNetwork Standard Switch or using traffic shaping to provide priority for iSCSI traffic.

The storage configuration might also need to change, depending on the I/O patterns and amount of I/O generated by the VMs. XYZ might also want to procure dedicated network switches for the iSCSI traffic in order to provide maximum performance and maximum redundancy. Doing so would have an impact on the project budget.

Finally, using the software iSCSI initiator would affect CPU utilization by requiring additional CPU cycles to process storage traffic. This could have a negative impact on the consolidation ratio and require XYZ to purchase more servers than originally planned.

The default multipathing policy for an active/passive array is usually most recently used (MRU). Does XYZ's array support any other policies? What would be the impact of changing to a different multipathing policy if one was available? We noted that XYZ's storage array is an active/passive array, so the multipathing policy would typically be MRU. However, we also indicated that XYZ's array supports ALUA, which means the Round Robin multipathing policy is, in all likelihood, also supported. Assuming that typical storage best practices were followed (redundant connections from each storage processor to each SAN fabric), this means the VMware ESX hosts will see four optimal paths for each LUN (and four non-optimal paths) and can put traffic on all four of those active paths instead of only one. This would certainly result in a better distribution of traffic across storage paths and could potentially result in better performance.

VM Design

As we described in Chapter 7, "Virtual Machines," VM design also needs to be considered with your vSphere design. Here are some questions and thoughts on XYZ's VM design.

Does the use of Windows Server 2003 present any considerations in a VMware vSphere environment? In general, the only real consideration with regard to Windows Server 2003 comes in the form of file-system alignment within the virtual disks. Windows Server 2003 is a fully supported guest OS, and VMware vSphere offers VMware Tools for Windows Server 2003. However, by default, NTFS partitions created in Windows Server 2003 aren't aligned on a 4K boundary, and this misalignment can potentially have a significant impact on storage performance as the environment scales. XYZ should take the necessary steps to ensure that file-system partitions are properly aligned, both for systems that are converted via P2V and for systems that are built fresh in the virtual environment.

Many variations of Linux are also affected, so XYZ should ensure that it corrects the file-system alignment on any Linux-based VMs as well.

Note that Windows Server 2008 does properly align partitions by default.

What impact would using thin-provisioned VMDKs have on the design?   The performance difference between thick-provisioned VMDKs and thin-provisioned VMDKs is minimal and not an area of concern. Potential concerns over SCSI reservations due to frequent metadata changes aren't an issue in an environment of this size and would be eliminated entirely if XYZ used vSphere 4.1 and an array that supported the vStorage APIs for Array Integration (VAAI). Operationally, XYZ would need to update its monitoring configuration to monitor for datastore oversubscription to ensure that it didn't find itself in a situation where a datastore ran out of available space.

VMware Datacenter Design

The logical design of the VMware vSphere datacenter and clusters was discussed at length in Chapter 8, "Datacenter Design." Here, we'll apply the considerations mentioned in that chapter to XYZ's design.

What impact would it have on the design to use 2 clusters of 5 nodes each instead of a single cluster of 10 nodes?   Cluster sizing affects a number of other areas. First, a reduced cluster size might give XYZ more flexibility in the definition of cluster-wide configuration settings. For example, does XYZ need an area where DRS is set to Partially Automated instead of Fully Automated? Do regulatory factors prevent XYZ from taking advantage of automated migrations that might drive this requirement? It's possible to set DRS values on a per-VM basis, but this practice grows unwieldy as the environment scales in size. To reduce operational overhead, XYZ might need to create a separate cluster with this configuration.

Reducing cluster size means you reduce the ability of DRS to balance workloads across the entire environment, and you limit the ability of VMware HA to sustain host failures. A cluster of 10 nodes might be able to support the failure of 2 nodes, but can a cluster of 5 nodes support the loss of 2 nodes? Or is the overhead to support that ability too great with a smaller cluster?

Does the use of vCenter Server as a VM impact XYZ's ability to use VMware Enhanced vMotion Compatibility?   Enhanced vMotion Compatibility (EVC) will be very helpful to XYZ over time. As XYZ adds servers to its environment, EVC can help smooth over differences in CPU families to ensure that vMotion can continue to migrate workloads between old and new servers.

However, the use of vCenter Server as a VM introduces some potential operational complexity around the use of EVC. VMware has a Knowledge Base article that outlines the process required to enable EVC when vCenter Server is running as a VM; see kb.vmware.com/kb/1013111. To avoid this procedure, XYZ might want to consider enabling EVC in the first phase of its virtualization project.

Security Architecture

We focused on the security of vSphere designs in Chapter 9, "Designing with Security in Mind." As we review XYZ's design in the light of security, feel free to refer back to our security discussions from Chapter 9 for more information.

Does the default configuration of vCenter Server as a domain member present any security issues? If so, how could those issues be addressed? Recall that, by default, the Administrators local group on the computer where vCenter Server is installed is given the Administrator role in vCenter Server. When vCenter Server is in a domain, the Domain Admins group is a member of the local Administrators group. This confers the Administrator vCenter role on the Domain Admins group, which may not be the intended effect. To protect against this overly broad assignment of rights, you should create a separate local group on the vCenter Server computer and assign that group the Administrator role within vCenter Server. Then, remove the local Administrators group from the Administrator role, which will limit access to vCenter Server to only members of the newly created group.

What impact on security would switching to VMware ESXi have? From a security perspective, there are advantages and disadvantages in switching to VMware ESXi. One advantage is that VMware ESXi no longer has a user-accessible Linux-based Service Console; in the past, this Linux-based Service Console generated most of the security vulnerabilities and patches that were released. However, one disadvantage is that you lose access to some of the security fine-tuning that is possible with VMware ESX.

Conceptually, VMware ESXi is more secure due to the removal of the Linux-based Service Console (which was based on Red Hat Enterprise Linux), but it hasn't yet been formally proven one way or another that VMware ESXi is more or less secure than VMware ESX. Following a strict process of mitigation and remediation of security vulnerabilities can help eliminate most of the security concerns with both VMware ESX and ESXi.

Monitoring and Capacity Planning

Chapter 10, "Monitoring and Capacity Planning," centered on the use and incorporation of monitoring and capacity planning in your vSphere design. Here, we examine XYZ's design in this specific area.

If XYZ needs application-level awareness for some of the application servers in its environment, does the design meet that requirement? As currently described, no. The built-in tools provided by vCenter Server, which are what XYZ currently plans to use, don't provide application awareness. They can't tell if Microsoft Exchange, for example, is responding. The built-in tools can only tell if the guest OS instance is responding, and then only if VM Failure Monitoring is enabled at the cluster level.

If XYZ needed application-level awareness, it would need to deploy an additional solution to provide that functionality. That additional solution would increase the cost of the project, would potentially consume resources on the virtualization layer and affect the overall consolidation ratio, and could require additional training for the XYZ staff.

Summary

In this chapter, we've used a sample design for a fictional company to illustrate the information presented throughout the previous chapters. You've seen how functional requirements drive design decisions, and how different decisions affect various parts of the design. We've also shown examples of both intended and unintended impacts of design decisions, and we've discussed how you might mitigate some of these unintended impacts. We hope the information we've shared in this chapter has helped provide a better understanding of what's involved in crafting a VMware vSphere design.

Index

Note to the Reader: Throughout this index **boldfaced** page numbers indicate primary discussions of a topic. *Italicized* page numbers indicate illustrations.